# MAN OF TOMORROW

ALSO BY JIM NEWTON

*Justice for All: Earl Warren and the Nation He Made*
*Eisenhower: The White House Years*
*Worthy Fights,* with Leon Panetta

# Man of Tomorrow

*The Relentless Life of Jerry Brown*

# Jim Newton

Little, Brown and Company

New York Boston London

Little, Brown and Company
Hachette Book Group
1290 Avenue of the Americas, New York, NY 10104
littlebrown.com

First Edition May 2020

Little, Brown and Company is a division of Hachette Book Group, Inc. The Little, Brown name and logo are trademarks of Hachette Book Group, Inc.

The publisher is not responsible for websites (or their content) that are not owned by the publisher.

The Hachette Speakers Bureau provides a wide range of authors for speaking events. To find out more, go to hachettespeakersbureau.com or call (866) 376-6591.

ISBN 978-0-316-39246-4
Library of Congress Control Number: 2020932872

10 9 8 7 6 5 4 3 2 1

LSC-C

Printed in the United States of America

*For Karlene, with love*

# Contents

# Prologue

P lay ball!"
 Umpire Jocko Conlan, known for his cheerful command of the game and the bow tie behind his chest protector, inaugurated the 1960 baseball season in a brand-new park by a sparkling San Francisco Bay.[1] The sky was open and blue, the seats gray and framed with orange, the bay choppy and bright. Sailboats skittered across the horizon.

The crowds made their way to Coyote Point, south of San Francisco, drawn to the city's proud new edifice, the $15 million stadium known as Candlestick Park. Fans poured across the landscape, arriving by "land, sea and air," the *San Francisco Examiner* reported. Cable cars were enlisted— this was San Francisco, after all. Special buses departed from one of the city's juiciest landmarks, Trader Vic's, at 10:00 a.m.; cocktails were served aboard. Bay Aviation Services, brainchild of a local entrepreneur, charged passengers $10 to hop on a helicopter at the Ferry Building, whirl around the Bay Bridge, and land at Hunters Point, where a station wagon covered the rest of the trip to the ballpark. And as for arriving by sea? Hilary A. Belloc, a "socialite, lecturer, real estate investor and erstwhile crab fisherman," piloted his thirty-six-foot ketch, the *Signe,* to the waters off the point. Dropping anchor, Belloc caught his ring finger in the anchor cable: the finger was cut clean off, but he made it to the park anyway, sealing his place in history as Candlestick's "first casualty." Meanwhile, well-dressed fans—men in coats and ties, women in furs—loaded up at the St. Francis Yacht Club, thirty or forty to a craft. And still more groups were delivered by ferry; high heels clacked over the gangplank.

"Normandy," grumbled Sidney Keil, secretary of the Great Golden Fleet, "was never like this."[2]

It was a busy week in California. Authorities in Petaluma arraigned a woman and her handyman in connection with a string of arson fires; the handyman ratted out his boss. A swimmer discovered the skeleton of a skin diver in the waters off Catalina Island in Southern California; authorities puzzled over it, the latest diver disappearance in the area.[3] The House Un-American Activities Committee laid plans for a meeting the next month in San Francisco; critics took note. And in cultural news, a young actress named Jane Fonda opened in her first movie, *Tall Story,* with Anthony Perkins. He played a basketball player, she a freshman cheerleader "eager to snare a tall husband." The *Examiner* described Fonda as "reserved" and remarked on her "shapely legs."[4]

In Los Angeles, the state's flagship paper made news of its own. A day before the San Francisco Giants debuted their new diamond, Norman Chandler took the stage at the Biltmore Hotel. At his invitation, 725 of the region's luminaries gathered for a luncheon, where the senior Chandler promised a "special announcement." The *Los Angeles Times* publisher kept his remarks and reminders of his family history brief. "A newspaper," he said, "must be the image of one man, whether you agree with him or not." For fifteen years, that man had been Norman Chandler—and his father before him and his grandfather before him. They had forged their family enterprise as an engine of growth, a bulwark against organized labor and a stalwart of the Republican Party. But those men were gone or going. Now the *Times* was to receive its fourth leader. Said Chandler: "I hereby appoint, effective as of this moment, Otis Chandler as publisher of the *Times*."[5]

Otis Chandler, Norman's thirty-two-year-old son, had learned of his father's intention just an hour earlier and still was recovering from the shock. When Norman made his announcement, Otis was sitting at his father's elbow. Broad-shouldered and barrel-chested, Otis, a former shot-putter, rose to his feet, smiled, and said: "Wow!"[6] It was a childish remark, one he would always regret. In the ensuing decades, however, he went on to greatness, converting a woebegone excuse for a paper into a publication of national note, one worthy of the state where it was headquartered.

Back at the ballpark, San Francisco took its turn. Completing their journey to the stadium, fans filled the stands and took their seats, voices raised with the excitement of a moment, of participating in more than a game. It was a happening, a tick in history. All told, 42,269 fans made it to the park that afternoon.[7]

Candlestick hummed with promise and hinted at conflict. Women donned scarves to fend off the breeze and bundled against the possibility of a Bay Area chill—"The coldest winter I ever spent was a summer in San Francisco," as Mark Twain did not say but as generations grew up believing he did. A heralded new heating system to counter foggy evenings at Candlestick was supposed to supply relief. Sadly, it never worked. Candlestick was cold at night, but it could put on a show in the afternoon.

In the audience that sparkling day were California's present and future. Governor Pat Brown, "burly and ebullient,"[8] builder of aqueducts and monuments, strode onto the field just before the game and winced at the response. There were some cheers for the governor, but there were boos, too. Brown had just postponed the execution of Caryl Chessman, the notorious red-light bandit and rapist whose case had become an international cause célèbre and a dividing point for Californians. The crowd let Brown hear its displeasure. The boos would haunt Pat Brown for the rest of his life.[9]

It was Brown's second comedown in two days: the night before, at the city's "civic send-off" for its new team, Brown had remarked that he hoped to be in the stands when "the Giants and the Los Angeles Dodgers meet in the World Series next fall."[10] Teams in the same league can't meet in the series, so Brown was forced to explain his mistake. As they say in politics, when you're explaining, you're losing.

And, in politics, for everyone who's losing, another is winning. Sitting near Brown at the ballpark was Richard Nixon, vice president of the United States and a candidate for president. He had been a California congressman and, briefly, senator before joining the presidential campaign of Dwight Eisenhower in 1952. Ike never knew quite what to make of Nixon—appreciating his work ethic and devotion, suspicious of his partisanship and edginess, wary in a way that tore at Nixon's insecurities. In their eight years together in Washington, Ike and Nixon never played a round of golf. Nixon nursed hurt feelings along with powerful ambition.

On that sunny afternoon in 1960, Brown was an embattled governor, Nixon a potential president. Nixon mugged in the locker room with Willie Mays, the greatest of all the Giants, perhaps the greatest player of all time. The crowd that booed Brown welcomed Nixon with a "tremendous cheer."[11]

Joining Nixon and Brown among the dignitaries was another Brown, Pat's only son, Edmund G. Brown Jr. They did not, at least then, have much in common beyond their disdain for their given names. Edmund senior was Pat; Edmund junior was Jerry. Jerry was twenty-two years old, just emerged from three and a half years in seminary and charting a new course for himself at the University of California, Berkeley. His mother and father had picked him up at Berkeley en route to the ballpark, so together they endured the crowd's displeasure.

For Jerry Brown, the boos that greeted his father had special personal meaning. Pat Brown had been prepared to allow the Chessman execution to go forward until his son, in an appeal to politics and faith that would become a trademark, caught his father at home alone one evening and convinced him that their Catholicism did not permit this act. The jeers at Candlestick were aimed at the father, but they struck the son, too. Reflecting back on that moment decades later, Brown wondered if it might have been the first inkling that Nixon could challenge his father for dominance of California.[12]

The crowd cheered Nixon as he threw out one of the ceremonial first pitches. The vice president shook the hand of the governor's son. He did so limply. Nixon had a hot dog in one hand and mustard on his chin.

Young Jerry Brown had grown up with royalty, particularly of a political stripe, but on that day, in the new park, he got a full dose.[13]

At 2:21 p.m. on April 12, 1960, Sam "Toothpick" Jones—nicknamed for the twig he rolled around his mouth while on the mound and sealed in the history books as the first black pitcher to throw a no-hitter—took a short look at St. Louis Cardinals right fielder Joe Cunningham and brought his first pitch to the plate. No one was cooler than Jones. His other nickname was Sad Sam. He rarely grinned.

Cunningham fouled out to third base.

The Giants batted in the bottom half of the first inning, the debut appearance of their offense in the new park. They did not waste time. Leadoff hitter Don Blasingame, the Giants' second baseman, reached first on an error and was bunted over. Mays, batting third, drew a walk. The powerful, lanky Willie McCovey fouled out, then Orlando Cepeda, a whirlwind of an outfielder, tripled to center, scoring two. The home team won the first game in its new park by a score of 3 to 1. Mays, McCovey, and Cepeda would all find their way to the Hall of Fame.

Sad Sam smiled. San Francisco basked.

Play ball.

# Part One

# Growing Up

# 1

# Two Californias

The San Francisco of Jerry Brown's childhood was normal. Sort of. Few cities have defined themselves more enthusiastically around change—migration, disaster, boom and bust, sleaze and glamour—and the war years were typical in a city where tumult was the norm. On the day of Edmund G. Brown Jr.'s birth, April 7, 1938, the local papers carried news of strikers commandeering a sugar plant, Hitler gaining influence in Germany and strengthening his hold on Austria, and a local nurse stabbing a woman—a crime blamed on the nurse's use of "mad weed."[1]

Brown was born in a city that had been turned into a battlefield in a country on the cusp of war. In 1934, a general strike, the largest in American history, brought labor and law enforcement into fierce San Francisco combat after a confrontation that left two dead and scores wounded.[2] The state called in troops to force open docks; labor mounted barricades and tossed bombs to shut them down. Struggling to recover and with an eye toward the grand, city leaders set out to hold an international exposition and plunged into the task of building a man-made island in the middle of San Francisco Bay. Its name: Treasure Island. The Golden Gate International Exposition opened on that whimsical piece of landfill in February of 1939, but sputtered, closed, then reopened in 1940, when exhibits such as *Sally Rand's Nude Ranch*, featuring half-naked women playing sports, did the trick.[3]

It was a city of grand gestures and discreet enclaves. Lofty homes in Pacific Heights peered down through the fog into the military base at the Presidio—and the Golden Gate beyond. The Tenderloin teemed with vagrants, their desperation leaking into the nearby Financial District, still reeling from the collapse of the stock market and its slow recovery. San Francisco attracted the early glimmerings of the beatniks, soon to take root in North Beach beneath the city's tribute to its firefighters, Coit Tower, and later to congregate at City Lights bookstore. Newly constructed bridges linked San Francisco to Marin County (via the Golden Gate Bridge) and to Oakland (via the Bay Bridge). As the 1940s opened, the Bay Area was bustling and busy, worried about war but removed from the troubles of Europe and Asia.

That changed on December 7, 1941. Bombs fell on Hawaii, and Americans recoiled at the duplicity of Japan's surprise attack. Franklin Delano Roosevelt declared war against Japan the following day. Germany followed by declaring war on the United States. The America First Committee, the leading isolationist group of the period, folded its opposition and retreated into what would prove a protracted state of remission. States of emergency were declared in most American cities. Schools closed along the West Coast. Military recruiting limits were lifted, and recruitment centers stayed open twenty-four hours a day to keep pace with enlistments. The Customs Service blocked departures of all vessels attempting to leave the United States. Authorities called for the distribution of one million gas masks, then asked for more.[4]

Racial tensions moved up the dial. "Jap town is under strict surveillance," San Francisco police announced.[5] In Washington, the Justice Department announced that it had "seized" 2,303 "enemy aliens," including 1,291 Japanese.[6] In Tokyo, Japan's Home Ministry announced that it had taken 1,270 American and British nationals into custody.[7] In defiance of those actions, some sounded a call for unity. "We are fighting," the Oakland Tribune declared in a front-page editorial. "We must now put to one side all of the petty differences among us. We must mobilize every last resource."[8] Pleas for unity and common sense would soon become vanishingly rare.

As America plunged into war—two wars, really, on opposite sides of the planet—San Francisco became the operations center of the Pacific theater and, along with San Diego, emerged as one of two major disembarkation points for sailors, soldiers, marines, and airmen headed into combat against Japan. The Bay Area was anchored by the army's Presidio but also included major air corps installations in Marin County and San Francisco. Fort Mason bordered the Presidio, and the East Bay included major facilities in Oakland and to the north, where Mare Island trained sailors and pumped out vessels. One million soldiers were processed through Camp Stoneman, a little-known base northeast of San Francisco, where as many as thirty thousand men lived at any given time.[9]

The navy ruled Southern California, though it had a major presence in the north as well. Treasure Island, in fact, served as the navy's western command. To the south, the hastily built Camp Pendleton, with its main entrance at Oceanside, straddled an enormous stretch of the Pacific coast between Orange and San Diego Counties.[10] A few miles north, Marine Corps Air Station El Toro shuttled troops and equipment, while to the south, the San Diego harbor hummed with America's growing fleet of carriers, battleships, destroyers and submarines.

California would never be known for its calm, and war only exacerbated the state's tendency to flail and blame. More than 110,000 Japanese and Japanese American men and women lived along the West Coast of the United States, and though two-thirds were American citizens—many having never even seen Japan—their loyalty came into question. No less a champion of fairness than California attorney general Earl Warren surveyed Japanese landholdings and imagined suspicious patterns—farms near rail yards and airports and other sensitive installations. Maps prepared by Warren's office became some of the most convincing, and absurdist, evidence of sinister intent. "Such a distribution of the Japanese population appears to manifest something more than a coincidence," Warren testified before the US House of Representatives' Tolan Committee on February 21, 1942.[11] Never mind that Japanese people owned those parcels because they were cheap and because the owners were prevented by racial discrimination from acquiring more desirable property: in the dim light of fear, Warren saw subversion. It was not his best moment.

Nor was he alone. The removal of the Japanese from the West Coast was ordered by FDR in February of 1942 and upheld by the United States Supreme Court twice. Their absence left a hole in the life of the region, a vacuum temporarily filled by the arrival of thousands of young men, most of them volunteers, clamoring to fight the Japanese forces in the Pacific while dreading it as well. Those men swarmed into San Francisco, swelling the city's bars and brothels, both of which it boasted in abundance: indeed, this migration was in some ways reminiscent of California's first, when gold miners, almost all of them men, stopped over in San Francisco for a last taste of women and booze before heading to the Sierras. Then it was for fortune, later for country, but 1940s San Francisco would have been familiar to a forty-niner.

It was there that a young family was setting out on a life that would shape California as abruptly as any earthquake, as profoundly as any migration. Pat and Bernice Brown were compatible but different—he a gregarious, Catholic, ambitious, and outgoing young man, she a more intellectual, Protestant, and retiring young woman. They met in high school and, once their quite different educations were complete, were together the rest of their lives.

Born in San Francisco in 1905, Pat hawked Liberty Bonds in World War I and was so spirited that his friends took to calling him Pat, short for Patrick Henry. The name stuck, and when he took to politics, he recognized the political value of it in San Francisco, where it didn't hurt to be thought of as Irish. In fact, his ancestors were half-German, too. The family patriarch, August Schuckman, first arrived in California in 1852. A few years later, he returned to Germany, where he married his wife, Augusta, and the couple immigrated yet again to California in 1863. They settled northwest of Sacramento, buying a stagecoach stop in Colusa County, tucked into unnamed foothills at a modest crossroads. August established himself as an innkeeper.

Bernice Layne was the daughter of an honest cop and a quietly Episcopalian mom. She was born in San Francisco in 1908, when the city was still recovering from the ruin of its 1906 earthquake and fire, and she was raised there with her four brothers and sisters. Bernice was a solid student, accomplished in math and intoxicated by reading.

She plowed through her young studies and entered Lowell High School early, before age twelve. The following year, Pat, a few years older but still at Lowell as well, asked her out. Her parents would not allow her to go. Pat persisted.[12]

Thus began the pattern of their lives—Pat dogged, eager, and open-faced; Bernice angular, incisive, and quietly determined.

After high school, Pat went to work—first at his father's photo studio, with a dice game in the back, and later as an apprentice to a local lawyer. He skipped college and moved directly to San Francisco Law School. Bernice, true to her form, crossed the bay and attended the University of California, Berkeley. Pat and Bernice courted across the bay, no small feat in the days before the Bay Bridge. Still running ahead of her age, Bernice graduated in 1928, not yet twenty, and took a job as a school-teacher. One condition of her employment was that she remain single. She defied it.

Bernice and Pat eloped to Reno, Nevada, and were married there on October 30, 1930. She was twenty-one. He was twenty-five.[13] They complemented each other. He loved people and crowds and parties; she preferred family and travel and quiet. But he appreciated her calm, and she learned to love more garrulous company. Bernice even came to enjoy politics. Still, they retained their essentials: when the two took up golf, Pat began playing immediately with friends. Bernice took lessons for eighteen months before playing with anyone else. Once she did, she regularly beat her husband.[14]

Pat and Bernice eventually would live in Sacramento and Los Angeles, but their early years were set in San Francisco. They rented an apartment on Fillmore Street, then moved to Chestnut Street, both in the Marina, then to the Twin Peaks neighborhood, and then to the corner of 17th Street and Shrader Street—on the edge of Haight-Ashbury, which was then far different from what it would become. They settled there with their two daughters, Barbara, born in 1931, and Cynthia, born two years later. Bernice was pregnant with their third child, and the Shrader Street home had an extra bedroom.[15] Jerry was born in April of 1938, and a few years later, the family moved one more time, to 460 Magellan Avenue, where the youngest, Kathleen, was born. That neighborhood, known as Forest Hill, would be the Browns' home for the rest of Jerry's youth.

Pat Brown was excited by politics early and for good reason. His combination of intelligence, engagement, and genuine compassion made him a natural for public service—and, specifically, for elected office. Many politicians resent campaigning—the showmanship, the grubbing for money, the pleading for attention. Indeed, although those aspects of politics would later irritate Jerry, once he sidestepped into his father's business, the demands of vote getting did not bother him. Pat loved the rub and hustle.

Pat Brown started his political life as a Republican and made his first stab at elected office at the age of twenty-three, when he ran for the California state assembly. He got walloped, but defeat did not deter him. After switching his party affiliation in 1935, he supported Democrat Culbert Olson for governor only to be disappointed by not landing a job in the administration. He then took aim at San Francisco's district attorney, Matthew Brady, a veteran with a reputation for losing cases and prosecuting union activists. Brown lost again, but this time he made an impression on the electorate. In 1943, Pat Brown was elected district attorney for San Francisco. His son, Jerry, was five years old.

Given their common careers, Jerry would most often be compared to his father, but he was more his mother's son. They looked alike, for one thing. Jerry inherited his mother's profile and her incisive eyes. She read for pleasure, unlike her husband, who devoured newspapers and reports but was never much drawn to books. There, too, Jerry followed after his mom. Pat was so extravagantly extroverted that it would be difficult for anyone to resemble him there: Jerry was less shy than some assumed, but he found greater succor in close company, again resembling his mother.

Finally, and perhaps most relevant to Jerry's career, Bernice Brown was studiously frugal, a coupon clipper from the earliest days of her marriage into her husband's governorship and beyond. Pat never got the hang of counting pennies, but Jerry did. Once grown, he would elevate government parsimony to a near-moral command, and his devotion to balanced budgets and limited government would set him apart from his Democratic colleagues and rivals for most of the rest of his life. He had his mother's example, reinforced by later vows of poverty and a general inclination toward cheapness, to thank for that.

At West Portal Elementary School, the kindergarten class assignment one day in November was to draw. Jerry, not destined for a career in art, sketched a colorful but uninspired clown. To his surprise, the teacher gathered all her students' work into a book and presented it to Pat Brown, the newly elected district attorney, to congratulate him on his victory. Naturally, the teacher put Jerry Brown's work on the cover: Jerry sensed the favoritism—he knew his picture was not the best and did not deserve the special attention it received—and he was mortified, the first of many instances when he drew extra, sometimes unwanted, praise for being his father's son.

Bernice Brown ran the family home. She cooked, often with assistance from her daughters. When things broke—a hinge twisted or a light burned out—her brother, who lived down the street, came to lend a hand. Pat Brown, at least in the memory of his children, did not change a lightbulb or boil a pail of water. He responded with a flash to the problems of his constituents, but he did not help around the house.[16]

The family often skipped breakfast—Bernice liked to sleep in—but gathered for dinner.[17] They would wait for Pat to return home from work and then would sit down together. There were "big, volatile conversations," Kathleen Brown recalled. "You were expected to have a position and defend it." Not everyone enjoyed it. The oldest, Barbara, was entering high school and was enchanted by literature and learning; the dinner table conversation didn't have much place for Chaucer. Her aversion to politics started early.[18]

As young Jerry grew older, he and his father often clashed, as fathers and sons will, especially when both are as strong-willed as Edmund Brown senior and junior. The two would remember these conversations differently over time. To Pat, they were exciting and provocative. Jerry sometimes regarded them as oppressive, forcing him under rather propelling him upward.

Jerry veered from his father's approach to debate. Pat stirred the pot, urging his children to join in boisterous disputes. Jerry staked out more cerebral ground. Pat was in the world; Jerry somehow beyond it. Even their Catholicism was different. Pat was culturally Catholic but hardly devout. It was not until Barbara was seven years old that her mother and father were married in the church. Until then, they were bound by the civil ceremony of their elopement, without any religious blessing.[19] But Jerry, whose study with the Jesuits began in high school, absorbed both the order's intellectual and spiritual commands, energized by its love of learning and drawn to the exploration of the infinite and the mysterious.

If Pat and Jerry had their differences, they had their bonds as well. One was Pat's enthusiasm for the outdoors, particularly California's vast and varied landscape. Family vacations were almost always in California and usually outdoors—the valleys and peaks of Yosemite National Park, the gurgling waters of the Russian River, beaches and deserts, arroyos and redwood groves. Some of Jerry's earliest memories are of camping in Yosemite, of sloshing through streams and gathering in campgrounds, of cold baths and bracing morning air. Many years later, he would discover an intellectual and spiritual kinship with the environment, and he would connect with it on that level. It is worth noting, though, that his earliest appreciations of it were more primal and offered a rare opportunity for him to connect with his father entirely outside the distracting business of politics.

Meanwhile, there was a war to win. California did its part, and the Brown family adjusted its patterns, meals, and travels to suit an all-consuming conflict. Little Jerry followed the war in the newspapers and was left with images and fleeting memories. MacArthur evacuated Manila, and that stuck because it sounded like *vanilla*. Ration stamps doled out meat and butter and gasoline. When the family traveled to Palm Springs for a vacation, the train passed through orchards draped in camouflage.[20]

California's other major center, Los Angeles, enjoyed a far different history and midcentury status. Conservative cousin to San Francisco's counterculture, Los Angeles was unlike its northern "relative" in other ways as well. San Francisco was compact, stuffed onto the tip of a peninsula, its city and county consolidated into a single government. Los Angeles was vast, "seventy-two suburbs in search of a city,"[21] more than four hundred square miles, straddling a small mountain range and stretching from barrio to beach.

Los Angeles created itself as anti–San Francisco. The city to the north was home to dockworkers and labor, strikes and, later, beatniks, and, even later, hippies. Los Angeles was an "open" city—open to business-men, that is. Los Angeles cultivated its reputation for hostility to labor and did so under the enthusiastic leadership of its puckish and parochial newspaper, the *Los Angeles Times*. Under a succession of owners— the founder, General Harrison Gray Otis, followed by his son-in-law Harry Chandler and grandson Norman Chandler—the *Times* of the mid-1900s dedicated itself to two things: the expansion of Los Angeles and the cabining of organized labor. It was largely successful at both, though not without cost.

Culturally and physically, Los Angeles was anti–San Francisco as well. San Francisco came to life in the gold rush, which affected every aspect of its existence. Its immigrants were needed to build rails, to make and maintain camps. So it attracted miners and campers—Chinese, especially, and a large number of Chileans. As the gold petered out, many of those migrants went home, but others stayed, settling into familiar fields. Chinese ran laundries and restaurants and eventually built the transcontinental railroad. Japanese entered landscaping and truck farming. Chileans scattered in search of other ores. All centered in San Francisco, they gave northern California its early experience of multiculturalism.

Southern California, meanwhile, grew up in farming, ranching, harvesting—and, later, munitions and defense. At first, that meant seasonal work—harvesting crops, driving cattle—and those who came to do it largely arrived from Mexico, often returning at the end of a season, though sometimes settling down. Despite state laws prohibiting Japanese from owning land, Japanese immigrants and their children managed to acquire parcels, often as leases. As California historian Kevin Starr notes in his seminal history of the period, by 1940, Japanese farmers "maintained a 50 to 90 percent position in such crops as celery, peppers, strawberries, cucumbers, artichokes, cauliflower, spinach, and tomatoes." The total value of Japanese agricultural land in California in 1940 was approximately $65.8 million.[22]

Finally, there was the look and feel of the two cities. San Francisco was tall, compact, and grand. The Golden Gate Bridge, its signature monument, was built more for aesthetics than transportation (there weren't many people living in Marin County or other areas north of the city when it was complete). Los Angeles, meanwhile, was sprawling and residential. Its great works of architecture were homes, while its center was spongy and uninviting. Sprawl suited a city whose leaders were landowners and developers, so Los Angeles reached over the Hollywood Hills into the San Fernando Valley. It was a land of suburbs and all that flowed from that.

Those were the poles of California politics in Jerry Brown's youth—the politics of the state he would come to master and that would coalesce again during the years of his governorships and the long gap between them. Successful politicians found a way to unify the state's disparate instincts—liberal San Franciscans could exist under the same tent as urban Angelenos, mustering enough votes to overcome conservative Orange County, moderate San Diego, and the state's Republican interior. Or sometimes that Center-Right coalition would dominate: San Diego, Orange County, and suburban Los Angeles would band together to block Northern California liberals and Los Angeles minorities, with the Central Coast splitting its vote. Through the early twentieth century, as California grew, its politics oscillated as those coalitions formed and reformed.

For the most part, however, until 1934, California's center of gravity resided largely within the Republican Party. Individual districts and regions moved back and forth between columns, but the state as a whole hewed to the right or center-right. That was aided by the way California, and most of the rest of the country, parceled out voting power. In California, the state assembly and governorship were seized by one faction or another, but the districting system of the day—one state senator per county—ensured that rural areas had influence in excess of their populations (much the same way as small states have outsize authority in the US Senate and Electoral College). In California, rural, mostly Republican legislators controlled the state senate, a system that allowed Butte County or Imperial County, for example, to have the same number of votes as Los Angeles or San Francisco. That system would persevere until the United States Supreme Court, with *Reynolds v. Sims* in 1964, struck it down as a violation of the principle of one man, one vote. "Legislators are elected by voters, not farms or cities or economic interests," the chief justice, writing for the majority, memorably asserted. The chief justice who wrote that decision was Earl Warren.[23]

In statewide elections, San Francisco offered up liberals, but the *Los Angeles Times* hewed a strict line in Southern California, and its free-market conservatism helped elect a series of moderate to conservative Republican governors, in varying degrees controlled by the state's business elites.

The Depression rattled that. Dispossessed and disheartened, California's poor rallied in 1934 around a campaign so unlikely and a candidate so outlandish that it is difficult to comprehend in retrospect. Upton Sinclair—novelist, vegetarian, Socialist, anti-Semite, oddball—had run unsuccessfully for governor before on the Socialist Party ticket. Now he reemerged as a Democrat and tapped the anxieties of a careening state. "End poverty in California" was his slogan—EPIC, as it became known. Sinclair presented himself as a man for his time.

Gaunt, devoted, and driven, Sinclair campaigned for governor but set out to change the world—a dual sense of purpose that some of his successors, including Jerry Brown, would emulate. "We plan a new cooperative system for the unemployed. Whether it will be permanent depends upon whether I am right in my belief about the permanent nature of the depression," he wrote, full of vigor.[24] At first dismissed, Sinclair grabbed the cognoscenti by their throats when he secured the Democratic gubernatorial nomination, in August of 1934. He polled 436,220 votes, 51.6 percent of the Democratic ballots cast in the primary, and faced off against a colorless incumbent, Frank Merriam, who had only recently ascended to the office upon the death of his predecessor.[25] For the guardians of order, certainly Republican order, the devil was at the door.

The *Los Angeles Times* framed the debate in terms its readers expected. Merriam, it said as its editors sifted through the devastating election results, "represents sound, liberal, broad and thoroughly proven leadership." Sinclair, by contrast, "is a visionary, a consorter with radicals, a theorist. Whether deluded by his own doctrines and schemes, he has succeeded in deluding thousands of persons into giving him their support and confidence."[26] In the view of the *Times,* the recently converted Socialist was "a political opportunist" to boot.

The powers of California gathered against Sinclair that fall. Hollywood, the *Times,* the *San Francisco Chronicle,* the state Republican Party, big business, big agriculture, and even a young Earl Warren mounted a campaign to defeat Sinclair and wipe his influence from politics. Daily newsreels included one infamous spot featuring fake vagrants flocking to California to sign up for Sinclair's promised benefits. "They keep coming," the narrator intoned, a theme that would return to California under another guise some sixty years later, proof that demonizing immigrants was neither new nor novel but rather time-tested and effective. By the fall of 1934, voters may not have been persuaded to think much of Merriam, but they were at least terrified of Sinclair. That was enough. A third-party candidate, Raymond L. Haight, ran on the Progressive Party ticket and carried nearly 13 percent of the vote, enough to deny Merriam a majority but not the governorship and enough to keep Sinclair far away from the levers of power. Merriam's 1.1 million votes handily topped Sinclair's 879,537. The establishment held.

But not for long. Four years later, Merriam had lived down to his potential, and the Depression remained in control of California. Sinclair himself was no longer viable as a candidate, but one of those drawn to the EPIC campaign picked up where his mentor had left off. Culbert Olson, born and raised as a Mormon in Utah before migrating to California, was a dedicated pacifist and devoted atheist. Upon winning the November election, the distinguished, nattily dressed Democrat became the first representative of his party in forty-four years to seize the California governorship, which he assumed even as Pasadena's annual

Rose Parade opened under gray skies four hundred miles to the south. When Olson took the oath of office as California's governor, in 1939, he raised his right hand and put his left hand in his pocket rather than atop a Bible, refusing to swear to God. Warned that the oath might not be valid without a Bible, Olson took a second oath a few days later, this time smiling impishly and crossing the fingers of his right hand.[27]

For Olson, the joys of governing were short-lived. In his first week on the job, he presided over the pardon and release of Tom Mooney, a labor activist and political prisoner, an icon of California's Left. Just hours later, at the state fairgrounds to attend a barbecue in celebration of Mooney's release, Olson began to speak, faltered, and fell into the arms of his son. A statement by the governor's office explained that he was rushed to Sutter Hospital, where he was recovering from "nervous exhaustion." Olson would be bedridden for weeks, recovering just in time for his wife to fall ill and die. His administration never again found its footing, and, with the outbreak of war on December 7, 1941, his pacifism would seem naively out of place.

Four years after Olson's triumphant swearing-in and dramatic pardon, he would turn the office back to the Republicans. This time, however, it would take on a different cast.

Earl Warren began the study of law in awe of the man who would become California's first great governor. Then a young prosecutor, Hiram Johnson took over a corruption case against mob boss Abe Ruef when a dismissed juror, furious at what he perceived as the insult of not being seated, arrived in court with a loaded pistol and shot Johnson's senior colleague. The lawyer, amazingly, survived, but Johnson was elevated to first chair and took on the senior prosecutor's duties. The electrifying case launched Johnson on his political career—he would be elected the first progressive Republican governor of California, in 1910. Warren, elected in 1942, could be said to be the second.

As it was with Johnson, Warren's progressivism was both reformist and sometimes blindered. Warren joined with the vast majority of Californians in enthusiastically—and tragically—supporting the internment of Japanese and Japanese Americans during World War II, a position for which he never entirely or adequately apologized. It was, he often reflected, a sad but understandable expression of wartime necessity. Indeed, *necessity* was a watchword for Warren and the progressives, whose pragmatism could be limiting—confining adherents to problem solving rather than indulging grand imagination—but also liberating from partisan bonds. Warren did not accept the view of many of his fellow Republicans that government was suspect and required containment. On the contrary, Warren believed that government should ease the burdens of the governed but that it should do so practically, within sensible limits.

Warren assumed the governorship in 1943 and held it longer than any other person until Jerry Brown surpassed him during his return to the governorship in the twenty-first century. Warren's tenure was significant in many respects: he expanded the state's highway system (with a model that Dwight Eisenhower copied for his interstate highway act), added to its university system, and presided over extraordinary growth, including the reintegration of Japanese Americans after the war. He quietly advanced the desegregation of its schools and pursued, though unsuccessfully, universal health insurance for Californians. Perhaps his most lasting contribution, however, was to reorient the politics of what soon became the nation's largest state. Gone, at least for a time, were the teeth-gnashing gyrations between voracious conservatives such as Merriam and ethereal liberals such as Olson. In their place arrived Warren's particular brand of progressive Republicanism, an alternative to partisanship that countered ideology with common sense and a fusion of activist government and fiscal restraint that would skip a generation with the Browns—Pat was a more conventional Democrat and loved to spend, but Jerry would come to embrace much of Warren's worldview.

In practice, that helped to create a Center-Left consensus in California, open to taxes so long as they produced discernible public benefits and averse to deficits and government handouts. After his disastrous support of the internment, Warren—and, with him, the state—would quietly overcome progressivism's racist history and appeal to a grander sense of inclusion and equity (in Warren's case, some of his growth would only become visible during his consequential tenure as chief justice of the United States). In the meantime, California's parties bent around the force of his popularity. In 1950, seeking his third term—something no predecessor had ever achieved—Warren defeated FDR's son Jimmy Roosevelt by more than one million votes. Big as the victory was, it surprised no one, given the results from his reelection in 1946. In that campaign, Warren took advantage of his stature and the state's Progressive-era election rules, filing for both the Republican and Democratic nominations. He won both. No governor before or since has ever registered such a triumph.

Warren unsuccessfully sought the presidency in 1952 but left the campaign on good terms with Eisenhower, who promised Warren the "first vacancy" on the Supreme Court.[28] Following the sudden death of chief justice Fred Vinson, in 1953, Eisenhower produced, after a brief hesitation, the promised nomination, and Warren accepted. He delivered his farewell address to California on October 2, 1953. A recess appointment, Warren donned the robes as chief justice three days later, on October 5. The transition was so abrupt—he would not be confirmed by the Senate until March 1, 1954—that Warren had to borrow a robe for the occasion. As he strode to the bench to take the oath of office, he tripped and nearly fell.

As the 1950s closed, California rested comfortably in the grasp of its leading Republicans—Governor Goodwin "Goody" Knight, Senator William Knowland, and Senator Thomas Kuchel—all of whom owed their jobs to Warren, whose politics they reflected. California was hardly tranquil. Any place as big and diverse as California would always have crises. But the state's politics seemed to have settled into equilibrium. Modeled on Warren's leadership and populated by his appointees and allies, Republicans held sway but did so by cooling partisanship and emphasizing progress. True, for many that was an act, but it worked. The 1958 elections seemed an opportunity to solidify and extend that reign.

# 2

# Faith, Politics, and Death

If it's possible to be a precociously devout Catholic adolescent, that was Jerry Brown. Serious, meditative, and religious to an uncommon degree, he recalled that "my grandmother Ida used to read me Bible stories." They were illustrated, and Brown's attention was riveted on the images—Joseph and his multicolored coat, Moses surrounded by bulrushes. "That world interested me. I was drawn to it." Something struck deep within the little Brown. He saw the pictures as more than entertainment. "It was important," he realized.[1]

As a boy, Brown challenged the nuns at his Catholic schools. If stealing a penny was a venial sin, was stealing two? How about three? "When does a venial sin become a mortal sin?" Jerry Brown asked one nun after another. The nuns, with a patience and befuddlement that California's future leadership would someday come to appreciate, wondered at what they had. One, responding to Jerry's inquiries, asked a question of her own: "Do you stay up nights thinking about these things?"[2]

Like his older sisters, Jerry Brown began his schooling in San Francisco public schools. As he grew older, he asked to attend Riordan High School. His father urged Lowell. They settled on St. Ignatius, one of San Francisco's premier Catholic high schools, whose curriculum was built on Jesuit practice. There, he excelled as a debater—no one who knew him as an adult was surprised to learn that—and enthusiastically marshaled arguments for and against the Electoral College, free trade, and capital punishment.[3] And, in a decision against type, he tried out for and secured a spot as a cheerleader. To Brown's relief, his parents never attended any of his games.[4]

Young Jerry Brown devotedly attended Mass. His friends arranged a surprise birthday party for him one year, but he missed most of it—the party fell on the same night as Holy Thursday, marking the Last Supper, and Brown followed his religious curiosity to St. Brendan's to observe its services (Brown arrived at the party two hours late, insisting he could hardly be blamed for failing to realize a surprise had been planned for him).[5]

Upon graduating from St. Ignatius, he was determined to become a priest, but his parents, simultaneously supportive and slightly mystified, urged him to try a year of college first. Still seventeen, he heeded their pleadings and enrolled at Santa Clara University, then an all-men's school considered "quiet and conservative," with a lights-out rule at 10:30 p.m.[6] Brown's year at Santa Clara was uneventful save for his incessant questioning and tendency to absorb classical music and plunge into deep thought, often at the same time. At the end of that year, Brown, then eighteen and able to decide his future for himself, transferred to the Sacred Heart Novitiate in Los Gatos, south of San Francisco.

On August 14, 1956, the day before the Feast of the Assumption, Brown and two friends said goodbye to loved ones and drove from San Francisco to Los Gatos, tossing loose change out the windows in order to arrive penniless. Pat Brown was away when his son left—a parting he later regretted missing.[7] Jerry Brown felt his father's quiet disapproval, compounded by his lack of understanding. The senior Brown could not comprehend why anyone, much less his son, would choose to live quietly in isolation when so much action beckoned outside.

For Jerry Brown, the decision was deep but also obvious. "If eternity is the goal and Catholicism is the path, why not go first class? Go with the Jesuits," he said in 2015, a reflection that is both true and glib, deflective in the way Brown could be in matters of spirituality and religion.[8] It is important to note that Brown devoted himself to his faith in an era that preceded Vatican II and its liberalizing influences. Jerry Brown entered a liturgical tradition of Latin and mystery, of regalia and powerful vows of poverty, chastity, and obedience. Though he would come to embrace Catholic social doctrine, that is not what drew him to the seminary. It was the search for God and the spiritual, not social justice, that first motivated young Jerry Brown.

There were elements of rebellion in Brown's decision. He was, to begin with, rejecting the ephemeral world of politics. The seminary, he noted later, was "the exact opposite" of the life his father had chosen.[9] Growing up the son of a politician meant interruptions, following and reacting to news, reaching out, bearing witness to the raising of money and trading of favors. It meant being singled out in kindergarten for a drawing that didn't deserve it. "It kind of embarrassed me," Brown recalled. "I rejected this backslapping world."[10] At the Sacred Heart Novitiate, he was ushered into a period of prayer and contemplation. He shared a cubicle with three others, without running water, his mattress on a wire frame. He rose at sunrise and meditated for much of the morning. He practiced mortification. The goal, he recalled, was "to try to overcome the self-indulgent, weak part of human nature."[11] Novices were not sworn to silence, but idle conversation was not permitted. Work consisted of chores—sweeping and tidying the grounds, cleaning toilets and washing dishes. In the fall, Brown and his fellows picked grapes in the seminary's forty-acre vineyard, laying the foundation for Sacred Heart's award-winning wines, most notably an acclaimed black Muscat. Some of the work was routine; some was invigorating. It was all to be undertaken with resolve and purpose.

Reading was restricted to the New Testament and the lives of Jesuit saints. "If you wanted to read about a Franciscan, you had to get permission," Brown said later. "Even reading the Old Testament required permission."[12] The son of one of California's leading politicians had no newspapers, radio, or television and thus almost no sense of the world outside.

Brown was moved by the order's rules and its enforced contemplation. The Jesuits, according to the eleventh rule of Saint Ignatius, as taught to Brown and contained in the "Summary of the Constitutions" consulted at Sacred Heart, "abhor completely and without exception all that the world loves and embraces" and "accept and desire with all their strength whatever Christ and our Lord loved and embraced."[13] That meant the rejection of conventional honors and prestige in favor of the modest garments Jesus wore and the simple joys he experienced. Rule 12 was no less demanding. The "first and foremost" duty of the Jesuit in pursuit of spiritual perfection was "abnegation and continuous mortification." As governor, Jerry Brown would point to those two rules and suggest that critics understand them in order to understand him. They would explain his rejection of opulence and ceremony—underscoring his refusal to occupy the governor's mansion or travel in a limousine, his rejection of gifts and skepticism of campaign contributors. And they would place Brown's power and achievements in a certain context—subservient to God and mindful of nature and its immutable commands. Brown learned as a Jesuit that he was subject to truths that were beyond his capacity to alter. It was a lesson that he would draw upon for the rest of his life.

As was discipline. "It was called the life of perfection," he remembered. "We were living the life of perfection that included vows of poverty, chastity, and obedience…We examined our conscience at 11:45 and nine o'clock in the evening every day, seven days a week." Searching their consciences, the novices would identify a flaw and resolve to correct it, a process that could take months or years but that was pursued with relentless determination.[14]

Against such resolve, movements to perfect mankind—whether through civil rights or the Great Society or the New Soviet Man—would seem both inspiring and small, a vantage point few politicians of the era would share with Brown. From those days hence, he would regard human impatience, even his own, with a cocked eyebrow.

He thrived in the seminary. "I liked the intensity…the focus on religious, ascetical practices…the lives of the saints, the doctrines, the practices, the solidarity of the community, this clarity of being on the same path," Brown said. "It had meaning to it; it had purpose. We were there to prepare to be a Jesuit priest, to do the work, the important work of a Jesuit priest."[15]

It was work that contained none of the relativism of politics: "If you feel you're called by God to do something, that's different from saying, 'Should I go to UCLA?'…That kind of random, trivial choice is different from [the one you make] to save your immortal soul [for] all eternity. Those are much bigger stakes."[16]

As he grew older, Brown's incorporation of his Catholicism into his politics would deepen. He would, beginning with his years away from politics and his reentry in the early 1990s, speak with concern about the tendency of Americans to reduce all values to those of the marketplace, to raise the accumulation of capital above all other ambitions. "We're seeing in the disruption of families, the rise of crime, the growth of inequality, that we need an offsetting idea to the market," he said in 1992 and often thereafter. "And that's the moral idea of social and economic justice. I come out of a Catholic social tradition that in encyclicals and in bishops' letters says there is a moral imperative of justice…there has to be a living family wage and a way for every family to prosper."[17]

On a more basic level, Brown infused his politics with a Jesuitical appreciation for structure and limits, ideas that he would expound on when he later discovered Zen Buddhism. *"Age quod agis,"* the Jesuits say. "Do what you are doing." The earth and worldly pursuits have their place, and man must find his within it. That suggests modesty in the face of truth or God. Doing what one does rejects doing for show or attention; it is not the catchphrase of many who enter politics. It does not, for example, suggest unbounded optimism—a political disease in modern life—much less false hope or grandiosity. It does, however, capture an essential aspect of Brown's approach to the world and its organization.

As did the notion of "discernment." An essential component of Ignatius's teachings, discernment asks that believers consider God in evaluating choices in daily life. Predicated on the notion that God speaks to each person individually, discernment involves evaluating choices based on what is best, what "better leads to God's deepening life in me." That suggests the application of reason, though founded within a moral structure. Once Brown entered politics, applying that principle would be both profound and commonplace.

At the seminary, Jerry Brown was mostly beyond his parents' reach. He inhabited a world unfamiliar to either and particularly mysterious to Bernice. They exchanged letters—Jerry supplied updates on readings and routines, and his father replied with caring, sometimes impatient responses, interested in his son's progress but eager for him to move beyond the seminary's initial detachment and to engage with more conventionally intellectual pursuits. "Two years of virtual silence," Jerry Brown said later. "That didn't grab him."[18] Still, despite Jerry's isolation and their uncertainty about it, the Brown parents often visited on Sundays, going for walks with Jerry in the hills of Los Gatos, returning with admiration and bafflement. Bernice would sometimes cry on the way home.

But Jerry was still his father's son. Neither the seminary's distance from home nor its isolation was enough to break him entirely from worldly things, and when his father turned to the next step in his political career, Jerry was ready with advice. The questions for Pat Brown in 1957 were twofold: whether to run for reelection as attorney general, a job he enjoyed and was in no hurry to leave, or seek another office. If the latter, the next question was which office, as two tempting possibilities would be open the following year: the United States Senate seat held by William Knowland and the governorship of Goody Knight.

That calculation was complicated by a strange wrinkle in that year's campaign season. Initially, Knight had planned to run for reelection and assumed Knowland would do the same. Then, at the end of an interview with CBS Radio on January 7, 1957, Knowland startled his interviewer, Griffing Bancroft, in response to what he thought was a routine question: "Do you plan to seek reelection to the Senate in 1958?" Knowland answered, "I do not plan to be a candidate for reelection to the United States Senate," adding that he did not know what he planned to do instead.[19]

SHOCK WAVES REVERBERATING FROM KNOWLAND'S DECISION, the *Daily Independent Journal* of San Rafael, California, declared the following day.[20] Knowland disingenuously suggested he wanted to spend more time with his family or devote himself to the family newspaper in Oakland. No one bought that. Some speculated that Knowland was aiming to challenge Nixon for the Republican presidential nomination. Among those whose fortunes were potentially affected, the report noted, was "Atty. Gen. Edmund G. Brown, the state's No. 1 Democrat." Brown incorrectly read Knowland's announcement as a retirement and predicted it would clear the way for electing a Democrat to the Senate. Others—correctly, as it turned out—wondered whether Knowland might instead be eyeballing a challenge to Knight for the governorship.[21]

With those calculations in play six months later, on July 3, 1957, Jerry Brown sat at a typewriter and composed a long letter to his father—a notable departure from their routine correspondence. "I'll start by first saying that I think you have already made your choice," Jerry began, "Governor."

Having said that, Jerry Brown then presumed to try to talk his father out of it. He began with a smart appraisal of the tactical situation. Republicans coveted the governorship only partly for the office itself, Brown observed. The real appeal was as a launching pad to the presidency or at least to control of the Republican delegation at the 1960 national convention. That would make them fight harder, and dirtier, to win it, Jerry Brown predicted, especially since Knowland would run with the backing of his father, *Oakland Tribune* scion Joe Knowland: the Knowlands, Jerry noted, were "pretty powerful boys."

The Senate seat, by contrast, was the more "stable position." Moreover, with Knowland's announcement, it was now vacant and there for the taking. As he said, "If you run for Senator, you will not have to meet so much opposition." And if Pat Brown won the Senate seat and Knowland won the governorship, Brown would still be the state's top Democrat and thus in position to control its delegation at the Democrats' 1960 national convention.

Jerry Brown's arguments were tactically sound and bravely presented, given his youth and singular remove from the state's complicated and fast-moving politics. What is most striking about his letter, however, is its dual reliance on the grittiness of politics and the loftiness of faith. "God has endowed you with certain talents and abilities and has given you opportunities to make use of them," Jerry, now the Jesuit, remarked. "He has put you where you are for certain definite reasons."

Concluding, Jerry noted: "When you come right down to it I can't say much about your political future except that you have a duty to God and your religion, upon which your decisions ought to be much in accordance." Not even twenty and isolated from news, Jerry Brown already was demonstrating some of what would later make him a unique figure in American politics: a pragmatic liberal deeply committed to faith. It also says something about Pat Brown that he ignored his son's advice.

Given the seminary's remove from worldly intrusion, Brown was surprised on a November evening in 1958 when he was invited to the fathers' recreation room to watch television. What external event could possibly warrant the distraction of ephemeral life? That night, the priests yielded to the temptations of politics, bringing out the television set in time to watch a profound change in the leadership and direction of California. Two "right-to-work" bills that had antagonized the state's labor movement were defeated, voters gave Democrats majorities in both houses of the state legislature, and "a genial, 53-year-old Irish Catholic,"[22] as one newspaper described him, ended more than a decade of Republican occupation of the governor's mansion. Pat Brown defeated William Knowland in a landslide. "This election is a mandate for progressivism in our public life," Pat Brown said triumphantly.[23] Jerry quietly registered his father's achievement and joined him for a family photograph when Pat moved into the governor's mansion, in Sacramento, soon after the inauguration—Pat and Bernice smiling, Jerry more serious in his cassock.

While Jerry Brown removed himself from the world, Pat Brown leaped to change it. His election opened a new era—though one with some echoes of the not-so-distant past—in the politics of California.[24] Brown was the first Democrat to hold the office since Culbert Olson's under-whelming service ended in 1942, throttled by the rise of Republican Earl Warren. Brown, himself a former Republican, brought the zeal of the converted to his tenure, championing New Deal democracy in the form of civil rights, public works, and unbounded faith in growth. And yet he brought some of Earl Warren, too, relying on bipartisanship and expan-sion. Warren and Brown, not coincidentally, were close friends, so close that Warren lent subtle political support to Brown even during Warren's time as chief justice, when he was expected to abjure politics.

Brown took the oath of office on January 7, 1959, and unambiguously asserted his intention "to bring to California the forward force of responsible liberalism."[25] To Brown, that meant "a reasonable, rational, realistic" program to protect the dignity of individual conscience, to uphold "justice and fair play," and to establish bulwarks against "economic abuse and selfish threats." Brown's twelve-part plan to achieve that ranged from the establishment of a minimum wage to a new approach to crime to a gigantic investment in education ("5,000 new classrooms a year, when we now build 2,500"). He harked back to national and state progressive heroes, including former governors Hiram Johnson and Earl Warren, both Republicans but of that peculiarly California stripe. Overarching Brown's politics was his personality: he bragged that California's leadership was "one of the ablest legislative bodies in the United States." He thanked the outgoing governor, Goody Knight, and offered to work with any and all, "together in harmony."

What followed was not an unmitigated success, but it was significant and lasting. Pat Brown set out to lead and to build. And he did. Within weeks of his inauguration, he had proposed a state budget and a host of taxes to support it. By summer, his program had been enacted.

In his diary, Brown recorded his triumph with telling calm: "Budget passed," he wrote simply. "All tax bills passed."[26]

Brown's tenure would be marked by the strains of growth and then by the challenges of maturity. He was overjoyed by California's ascendance: when, in 1962, census numbers suggested that California had at last passed New York as the nation's most populous state, Brown exuberantly laid plans for a statewide celebration. They were mostly a bust.

More concrete signs of progress were warmly received. An essential aspect of California's appeal was its fairness—its escape from the racist history of the East and South. Brown, less than a year into his governorship, lent his support to the Fair Employment and Practices Act, whose mission was to combat racial and other discrimination in employment and housing, prohibitions that were later updated to protect against discrimination by "gender, gender identity," and "gender expression."[27] The proposal also limited the use of a person's criminal history in making judgments about housing and employment. It passed on September 18, 1959, nine months after Brown became governor, even as Soviet premier

Nikita Khrushchev stormily threatened to call off his visit to America after being insulted by the mayor of Los Angeles. (The mayor, Norris Poulson, had the temerity to suggest that the Soviets would not, contrary to Khrushchev's boasts, succeed in "burying" the United States.) The act provided for the creation of a commission to enforce its edicts, and the five-member board was seated in October, with Brown proclaiming that it would become a "real instrument for obtaining voluntary compliance with the law." For those who were less enthusiastic, the governor warned that the commission would enforce the law "without restraint and without fear."[28] The commission was chaired by John Anson Ford, a respected member of the Los Angeles County Board of Supervisors, who said that Brown urged him not to "exact reprisals" for past discrimination but rather to "administer a law so that all men, regardless of race, color, religion, national background, would have an equal chance with employers."[29] Joining Ford on the original commission were four other members, identified in the *Los Angeles Times* as a "Roman Catholic," a "Jew," a "Negro," and a representative of business.[30]

Despite wily and determined efforts by the commission, discrimination was a stubborn foe, and the coming years would be marked by setbacks as well as progress. In the meantime, Brown would press "the forward force of responsible liberalism" across issues as varied as school construction and the death penalty, sometimes stepping nimbly through California's divided politics, other times vacillating in ways that disappointed his admirers. Brown was open-minded and good-natured, hard qualities to dislike in any man but ones that left him with a tendency to be agreeable and easily swayed. His son would learn those lessons and would never, once he reached power, be accused of glad-handing—deal making, yes, but out of pragmatism, not uncertainty.

As 1959 ended, Jerry Brown was coming to the end of a long, slow, and difficult-to-describe loss of enthusiasm for the life he had boldly chosen as an eighteen-year-old. In one sense, his changing heart was consistent—he remained driven by a search for meaning and stimulation and a frustration with the question of how best to pursue those.

Pat Brown tried his best to visit his son every month, and when he arrived in early December, he found Jerry wrestling with doubt, deep in reflection and consideration of how best to fulfill his purpose. Pat Brown was impressed. "He is a fine, wonderful boy," he noted in his diary.

The governor and the seminarian walked together, as they often did, comparing notes on their vastly different lives. "He told me that he would probably leave his studies for the priesthood," Pat Brown wrote. "He felt it had been a wonderful 3½ years, that his Catholicism was stronger than ever," but that he had come to the conclusion that he no longer benefited from its "rules of obedience" and rather believed he could put its teachings to better use outside the priesthood. Pat Brown was not a perfect father, but he knew his son's instinctive resistance to parental direction. Realizing that to push his son would be to risk Jerry pushing back, Pat remained quiet: "I didn't advise him one way or the other."[31] Jerry Brown interpreted his father's silence as disapproval: "Disapproval on the way in, disapproval on the way out," he said years later.[32]

But Jerry Brown's mind was made up. He was celebrating Christmas with a few of his fellow novices—third-year students—and was reading Sigrid Undset's *Kristin Lavransdatter* at the time. "It's so vital and intense," he recalled decades later, remembering themes of tension and the Church and the life of a medieval woman. "And then the seminary seemed so denuded of—there was not romance, money, sex, success, failure. You know, it's all proscribed. And every hour they ring the bell and you go from one thing to the next. It's very regimented."

Brown's decisions to join the priesthood and then to leave it preoccupied him for decades thereafter. One afternoon in 2015, fifty-five years after he left the seminary and embarked on his worldly path of law and politics, he sat in his Oakland office. Aides ambled about, and shelves heaved with a wildly eclectic collection of books—campaign biographies, works of history, and a recent papal encyclical that he was then reading in preparation for a trip to Rome. Old campaign bumper stickers were haphazardly posted on the walls, along with a sign from an earlier campaign for president. His two corgis, Colusa and Sutter, playfully misbehaved. Brown was in light spirits, animated and talkative. And yet when the conversation turned to the question of why the priesthood had not held him, he paused and thought hard. "At some point," he said, softly, "it wears off."[33]

When it came time to leave, a friend picked him up from the seminary, and they headed straight to San Francisco. They drove to a gallery in North Beach and caught a poetry reading, then dropped in at the Co-Existence Bagel Shop, headquarters of the underappreciated poet Bob Kaufman (cofounder of the journal *Beatitude*), smoky and full of coffee and sawdust, wine and talk (but no bagels: the shop did not serve bagels, just beatniks).[34]

Brown returned to the temporal and turbulent life of California beyond the walls that had, for three years, contained him in Los Gatos: "I tried that," he said later. "Now I want to try this." For Brown, the priesthood was no longer his future, but the question that had impelled his study remained. He was, he said, "still looking for beatitude."[35]

Jerry Brown enrolled at UC Berkeley, joining an educational institution that his father oversaw though keeping himself at a distance from him physically and emotionally. He found a place to live at the university's International House, where he met Rose Bird, later to secure important positions in Brown's universe, and, among others, Kenneth Reich, a future *Los Angeles Times* reporter who would dog Brown in office. Jerry majored in classics, a natural after his time at the seminary, but found satisfying courses in history and political philosophy as well. Decades later, he could still quote professors—notably, Sheldon Wolin—from those days and could recite from memory his answers to questions on Berkeley exams.[36]

Jerry no longer wore a cassock, but as a Berkeley student he carried his principles and devotion close to heart, and he remained more of a counterpart to than a chip off the block of Pat Brown. Though just twenty-one, Jerry was unafraid to voice his views and draw on his time of reflection—even, perhaps especially, in conversation with his father.

That was most apparent on February 18, 1960. California's attention was divided that day: at Squaw Valley, near Lake Tahoe, the 1960 Winter Olympics were opening, a triumphant and joyful recognition of California's place at the center of the sports universe. Pat Brown was scheduled to preside over the opening ceremony that night, but he elected to pass, feeling instead the obligation to tend to California's other riveting event: the pending execution of Caryl Chessman. Bernice Brown took their youngest daughter, Kathleen; they, along with Richard Nixon, opened the games.

Chessman was a violent thug who was arrested in 1948, at the age of twenty-six, already having done more than his share of damage. But the crimes for which he was convicted—and the death sentence imposed—created political and legal complications for Chessman and those involved in his case as well as genuine cause for moral reflection. These were amplified after Chessman's initial date with the gas chamber, in 1952, was delayed, and at the urging of San Quentin's warden he wrote a memoir that displayed surprising intelligence and drew international demand for his clemency. The same warden who encouraged Chessman to write forbade him from penning a sequel. He wrote one anyway.

Chessman used his fame to plead his innocence and demand justice for himself. He was not contrite. On the contrary, he taunted those who confined him and judged him, including Brown. By the time Pat Brown became governor, he already had signaled his lack of compassion for Chessman, upholding the warden's ban on Chessman's writing after the first book was such a success.

Now that Brown was governor, he held Chessman's fate in his hands. Rather than plead for mercy, Chessman derided Brown's authority over him. "I wonder if Mr. Brown has not brought his politically advantageous prejudices with him to the Governor's chair," Chessman asked in a letter to the governor's clemency secretary. "Will you kindly ask the Governor and then inform me in writing if he does not consider himself wholly disqualified from acting on the case?"[37] Brown called such outbursts evidence of Chessman's "heckling his keeper" and professed to do his best to ignore them. He may have protested too much: he thought enough of Chessman's letters to save them for the rest of his life and pass them down to his son.[38]

Tempting though it was—politically, at least—to let the Chessman execution take its course, Brown labored over the question of whether to do so, in part because the legal situation was murky. Chessman was convicted on eighteen counts in connection with a series of rapes and robberies—prosecutors alleged that he had accosted couples in their cars, robbed the occupants, and forced the women to perform oral sex on him. Under California's so-called Little Lindbergh law, criminals who transported a victim and inflicted "bodily harm" on that victim were subject to the death penalty. Chessman was alleged to have dragged one woman from her car and driven another from the scene of the robbery. By the time he was scheduled for execution that law had been repealed, but the repeal was not retroactive, so Chessman was facing a sentence that would not have been handed out had he committed his crimes, which he denied, under the current state of the law.

Was Chessman improperly convicted? Perhaps. He defended himself at trial and did so poorly, passing up advice to take a plea and ham-fistedly mishandling witnesses. He had requested and been denied, without explanation, a daily transcript of the proceedings, an error that bothered the officials and judges who later reviewed the case.[39] And Chessman was so candid in his memoir about what he had done wrong that he seemed believable when he denied the charges against him.[40] Then there was the question of punishment. Even if he was guilty, did Chessman deserve the death penalty? Under today's standards, certainly not, and even the standards in place at the time of his crimes feel stretched by the circumstances. Dragging a victim from her car is undeniably brutal, but it is hard to regard it as "kidnapping" in the manner of the Lindbergh case.

However one answers these questions, they are certainly difficult. When Chessman's case came to him the previous fall, Brown confessed his angst to his diary. Deciding Chessman's fate, Brown wrote, would be the "toughest decision I will make," and though he leaned toward clemency at that point, he was determined to keep an "open mind."[41] Then Brown attended Chessman's clemency hearing and thought again. On October 19, four days after telling his diary he leaned toward clemency, he announced publicly that he would let the law run its course. "I have searched the record, and my conscience, for some sufficient basis for resolving this issue in favor of clemency," he said in a statement released by his office while he was in Chicago. "I have been unable to do so."[42] Brown mentioned the psychological damage to one of Chessman's victims, and Chessman, true to form, sneered. "He has now emerged not only as Presidential timber, but as a psychologist," the inmate told reporters.[43]

But that did not end the matter, and Brown was still torn the following February, alone in the governor's mansion, when the phone rang. It was around 9:00 p.m., and it was his son on the line.

Full of vim and armed with three years of instruction by the Jesuits, Jerry Brown felt so compelled to speak to his father about Chessman that he called him from a pay phone in Berkeley. He argued strenuously that his father could not in good conscience allow the execution to go forward, that in the "simple and direct world of morality" his father could not sanction such a punishment.[44] Their common faith respected life. Ignatius spoke of mercy and peace. "Avoid anything that would cause the shedding even of a drop of blood," the founder of the Jesuits had offered centuries earlier. Generosity and humility were integral to the spiritual world from which Jerry had so recently emerged.

Jerry Brown knew his father's world, too, layering on a political argument. Although both Browns understood that the state supreme court was required to recommend Chessman's commutation and already had rejected it, Jerry Brown suggested that his father could grant a sixty-day reprieve. In the interim, the governor could lobby the state legislature to overturn the death penalty. That, Jerry Brown argued, would buy his father time and allow him to work the case politically, where he was most adept. True, there wasn't much chance the legislature would abolish capital punishment on such a deadline. "But Dad," Jerry persisted, "if you were a doctor and there was one chance in a thousand of saving a patient's life, wouldn't you take it?"[45]

Pat Brown had been bogged down with Chessman for months, morally and intellectually hamstrung by the demands of the case. Now his son proposed a course that seemed to offer an escape. He grabbed it. "You're right," he said. "I'll do it."[46]

As generations of California leaders would later come to realize, Jerry Brown was a hard person with whom to argue. In political terms, however, his advice that night can at best be regarded as poor—at worst, it was painfully naive. Pat Brown's staff certainly thought so. His aides were blindsided and convinced that Jerry's suggestion would prolong and deepen the debate. Nevertheless, Pat accepted his son's advice. He stayed Chessman's execution for sixty days and urged the legislature to take the matter up. REPRIEVE! read the eight-column headline in the next day's *Los Angeles Times*.[47] (Below the headline was a picture of Bernice Brown and Richard Nixon at the Olympics.) Chessman's prosecutor called the decision a "travesty of justice" inspired by Communists.[48] He also foresaw, correctly, that the same state legislature that had upheld the death penalty less than a year earlier would not suddenly reconsider.

At Brown's request, the legislature did review the death penalty, but as Chessman's prosecutor predicted, it refused to overturn it. Chessman died, his mouth twisted into a pained sneer as the pellets were dropped and he gasped for air in California's lime-green gas chamber.[49]

By the time it was over, Brown's handling of the case alienated just about everyone: advocates of the execution saw him as weak for suspending it; supporters of Chessman blamed him when Chessman was put to death. The boos for Governor Brown at the opening of Candlestick Park came from those who wanted Chessman executed and were outraged by the delay. They would soon be joined by those who saw Brown as a functionary of capital punishment, even the murderer of an innocent man. "The walls of Jericho fell down on me," he complained.[50] For decades, Bernice Brown lamented the fact that she and Kathleen attended the Olympics. Had she been home, Bernice said, she would have intercepted Jerry's call, and her husband might have escaped one of the worst political moments of his administration.[51]

For Pat Brown, the lessons of Caryl Chessman were humbling. He followed his conscience, incompletely, and attempted to navigate politics, unsuccessfully. Chessman would contribute to the nagging impression that he was indecisive, "a tower of Jell-O," as critics came to deride him. He regretted to the end of his days his handling of the case. In his eighties, Brown remained convinced that Chessman was guilty and that he had contributed to the public sentiment against him. "I also believe," he wrote, "that I should have found a way to spare Chessman's life."[52]

For Jerry Brown, the lessons were no less lasting or complicated. He might have seen the damage done to his father in that episode and hardened. It would have been politically expedient simply to abandon the demands of faith and conscience and mercy, to acquiesce to politics' more reliable standards—accountability and vengeance. To his credit, Jerry Brown did not follow that course. He remained conflicted his entire life about the competing demands on a high official charged with the grave responsibilities of assessing guilt and protecting the public, while acknowledging the human qualities of frailty, capacity for growth and understanding. He argued for Chessman's reprieve and saw the price his father paid for listening to him. He stayed that course anyway. Like his father, Jerry Brown would confront questions of life, death, and a politician's power over them into his eighties.

Pat visited Jerry Brown just a few weeks after he agreed to his son's pleadings and granted the Chessman reprieve. He was proud of his son and justifiably so. But his note to his diary reflects some of what it was to be young Jerry Brown's father. Jerry, the elder Brown wrote, was a "fine boy but too intense."[53]

# 3

# Quiet Rivers, Rushing Waters

Jerry Brown was still carrying the teachings of the seminary—and by
then the more roiling debates at Berkeley—when, in 1961, he attended a symposium entitled "Man and Civilization: Control of the
Mind" at the University of California, San Francisco. It was a major gathering held at the medical center's main auditorium. Joseph Alioto, the
soon-to-be mayor of San Francisco and soon-to-be rival of Brown,
hosted. The featured speaker was Aldous Huxley, recently diagnosed
with laryngeal cancer and confronting his mortality even as he wrestled
with grand notions of human potential and capacity. Speaking at lunch
that day, Huxley criticized Western education and values, not so much
for their deficiencies as for their insufficiencies. There is another part of
humanity that needs to be educated and nurtured, Huxley stressed—the
affective, intuitive, and spiritual foundation of man, which requires education just as surely as his intellect does.

Following the lecture, Jerry Brown, all of twenty-two years old,
had the temerity to approach the great and fearsome Huxley. Brown
stared up at the much taller Huxley, grand but rumpled in an overcoat. "How could I find out more about this other way of educating?"
Brown asked.

Huxley looked down at him. *"Zen Flesh, Zen Bones,"* he replied
without explanation. Jerry Brown left the hall and rushed out to pick up

the book, a collection of stories and koans central to Zen Buddhism and Zen practices.[1]

Brown read the book. Sort of. "I read part of it," he said later. "I read enough of it to know that I liked the stories."[2] Mostly, however, its effect was to lure him to others, to seek out the offerings of Zen. That led him first to Zen theory and practice and later to the San Francisco Zen Center.

Brown's route to the center was circuitous—he read and considered the ideas that infuse Zen for years before seeking out the center's California establishments, including mountain retreats and the San Francisco center, in Hayes Valley. But once Brown landed at the center, the discovery proved propitious. Few establishments—save, perhaps, for Yale Law School—would more greatly enrich Brown's intellect or cultural and political circle than the center, which drew casual and serious adherents from across California and beyond. It hosted retreats, most notably at its spectacular Tassajara Zen Mountain Center, near Carmel, just outside the tiny town of Jamesburg.

In the early 1960s, when Brown discovered Zen, the center was under the leadership of Shunryu Suzuki Roshi, a thoughtful and hugely influential scholar and teacher who arrived in San Francisco in 1959, establishing the center just as the city's counterculture, then in the form of the beatnik poets and their admirers, took hold.

"What I liked about Zen," Brown said later, "was the freshness. You ask: 'What is the meaning of life?' The Zen master responds: 'Have a cup of tea.' I loved that surprise. There's an aliveness about it…the lack of dogma, the lack of 'You must believe X.'"[3]

Those sound like the reflections of a young man fresh from rejecting the strictures of the Jesuit monastery, and in some ways Zen was just that—a fresh, dogma-free alternative to the Jesuit novitiate. But it would be a mistake—one that many observers of Brown would make—to conclude that his fascination with Zen represented a clean break from his Catholicism or that Brown was rejecting structure altogether. That was the route of the hippie; Brown was a student of the priesthood, not a hippie. Zen represented not a rejection of Catholicism but a fresh path of inquiry back into it. For Brown, it was an extension of that faith and an inquiry into the soul and mind, not by abandoning structure but by reexamining it.

Brown had practiced the discipline of Saint Ignatius, the methodical stripping of attachments—physical, intellectual, and otherwise—for three years in Los Gatos. He had practiced self-denial and mortification as deliberate challenges to excessive worldly attachments. Now, as he delved into the practices of Zen Buddhism, he discovered a parallel command. "In the Zen world, attachment is the central problem…We say: 'Delusions are endless. I vow to cut them down.'"

To Brown, practicing Zen meant returning to a familiar grammar, imbued with a fresh vocabulary. The Jesuits meditated on the life of God and Christ. Zen Buddhists sought to erase images from their meditation. But both sought liberation from the limitations that blocked their connection to a larger spirituality.

"From the nonattachment of Buddhism to the 'inordinate attachment' of Ignatian exercise," he said, "I found great similarity."

As he considered the question further, those similarities enchanted Brown: "Our lives are routinized, full of distractions, allurements, pleasures, pains, melodrama. That's a very active movie in which we play our part," he said. "In Catholicism, what they're saying is: 'You have to leave that all aside and focus on God or the life of Jesus,' so that you reach, you attain, what they would say is 'perfection.' In Zen, they would say 'enlightenment.' You cut through all these illusions and just be. They say: 'The rivers are the rivers. The mountains are the mountains.' Most of us have some reaction to it. We have an experience of a mountain that is our ego. Our self, our sense of us and our pettiness and our particularity. Zen is trying to get to a clarity."[4]

Over time, the sturdy rope that ran from Saint Ignatius to Zen shaped Brown's appreciation for the great ideas of politics—notions otherwise as disparate as capital punishment, nuclear weapons, and climate change—all of which had in common a necessary humility before fearsome powers such as death, destruction, the earth itself. Those issues later informed Brown's politics, but the foundation, in the combined strictures and practices of Catholicism and Buddhism, was well under construction when he was still a very young man.

In the words of the Zen master: "The rivers are the rivers."

And in those of Saint Ignatius: "Do what you are doing."

Phil Burton did not give a hoot about Zen. He cared about politics and people and the ability of politics to deliver for people. He was big, and both soft and hard—a soft touch for those who needed help, a hard sell for those who would deny the government's responsibility. While Jerry Brown was contemplating attachment and spiritual freedom, Phil Burton was a few blocks away, building a political machine.

Phil Burton was a presence, a loud man and a hard drinker who rode roughly over the feelings of colleagues and sometimes even friends. He was also gifted with a brilliant sense of politics, a nose for power and how to use it on behalf of the neediest. He was, in the words of his biographer, "in the fraternity-party atmosphere of the time, often a stick-in-the-mud. He rarely wanted to talk about anything other than politics or legislative business. He liked to drink, but even when drunk he was usually all business."[5] Burton was that rare force in American democracy: a ruthless ideologue. He came up through the competitive ranks of political infighting in San Francisco, where cultural forgiveness masked bitter, hand-to-hand political struggle.

As a member of the state legislature, Burton would leave his lasting mark on California and its politics by immersing himself in that most arcane and consequential aspect of political power: redistricting. Burton figured out early that drawing district lines meant far more than determining which neighborhood got to vote in which assembly race. The erection of district borders did not just distribute political power but also entailed a kind of risk. The person drawing lines could make one legislator safe and put another in peril. He could decide which areas of the state—and which philosophies and inclinations—would grow in influence and which would lose that influence.

Burton was a member of the legislature when the 1960 census allowed California to redraw its internal boundaries. The state was undergoing enormous demographic change at the time, growing by leaps. It was ripe for reshaping by a smart legislator to reshape its power dynamics. That legislator was Burton.

Nominally, it was Jesse Unruh, the powerful liberal legislator elected as speaker in 1961, who controlled the redistricting process. Born poor and driven, Unruh bulldozed his way through California politics, and in 1961, he wielded as much power as any man in Sacramento. He was called Big Daddy, a nickname he hated, but it stuck because it fit. He was physically imposing, charismatic, and hardscrabble tough.

Naturally, then, Unruh took the lead in the redistricting effort, focusing especially on the state legislature, his base. Burton, however, elbowed his way into the machinations, for reasons both personal and political. Personally, he wanted a way forward to Washington, so he manipulated the lines of his congressional district, in San Francisco, to maximize his opportunities there. Of more significance, though, was his quiet insertion into the legislative reapportionment process. "Unruh did not get reapportionment," Willie Brown, a politician who was one of the beneficiaries of Burton's involvement, said years later. "Phil understood it better than any computer."[6]

Burton approached the process with two goals: first to redraw lines in San Francisco, which was being forced to give up a seat, in such a way as to preserve liberal strength there at the expense of the city's dwindling conservative core and second to protect liberal interests in Los Angeles, which was growing and therefore needed to adopt the opposite strategy—namely, to add a district and distribute liberal voters in such a way as to ensure that the new seat attracted the right type of legislator. For Los Angeles, Burton turned to the emerging political might of Henry Waxman and Howard Berman, two early masters of that city's young liberal coalition. In San Francisco, Burton handled matters himself.

The process took months, and as the time for a crucial vote approached, Burton affected surprise to discover that the legislative map was one district short, having been drawn for seventy-nine seats instead of eighty. Pretending to work hastily, he drew one more for San Francisco and presented the final map to Unruh. Unruh agreed, in part because the new map protected an ally, Ed Gaffney, an old-school liberal of the era, "strong with unions but weak with minorities," as one journalist summed him up.[7] With Unruh's approval, the legislature approved the package, and San Francisco had a new assembly district, one Burton-made for a minority candidate.

Enter Willie Brown. Brown's career would span decades, outlasting and outmaneuvering governors and infuriating opponents. California today has term limits largely because conservatives could not figure out another way to dislodge Brown from his commanding post in Sacramento, where he became speaker himself years later. In the long period when California would bump around from Pat Brown to Ronald Reagan to Jerry Brown and beyond, Willie Brown would anchor the state's growing Left. He would nurture its promising talent, protect its vulnerable members, raise and dole out millions of dollars to secure and protect seats. But in the early 1960s, he was an untested activist from San Francisco, an immigrant from Texas who found liberal politics while growing up in the city's rough neighborhoods. He signed up for classes at San Francisco State University—"dodging the draft," he joked later—and was lined up alphabetically next to a fellow student: John Burton, another politically charged liberal and the younger brother of one Phil Burton.

They grew up in liberal politics together, and when Burton had the chance to muscle an opening in San Francisco, he came up with a district that suited Willie Brown well. And as for its occupant, Gaffney, he summed up the notion of a challenge from Willie Brown thusly: "I have a little nigger running against me."[8]

That was, roughly speaking, the last time anyone in California politics wrote off Willie Brown. He came within one thousand votes of beating Gaffney in 1962, but, he said, "I had been told at the outset that it might be a two-year proposition." Two years later, Gaffney latched on to a ridiculous proposal to route a new freeway through San Francisco's beloved Golden Gate Park, and Brown thumped Gaffney for supporting it. Brown discovered friends he didn't know he had. "I didn't know anything about environmentalists, but they lined up for me," he said with a laugh.[9] The freeway was stopped, and Brown won a seat in Sacramento. It would take a political movement to get him out.

\*    \*    \*

As the 1960 presidential campaign took shape, its implications for California and its senior political leaders were evident. On the Republican side, California's Richard Nixon, the vice president attempting to claw his way from under Ike's shadow, led a field of GOP contenders that ranged from New York governor Nelson Rockefeller to unreconstructed racist Strom Thurmond, once a Democrat, now more comfortably in the fold of a party drifting away from its integrationist roots. The Democrats, as per their usual practice, had numerous options but none that clearly stood out. Adlai Stevenson remained the party's great intellectual, his wisdom unceremoniously steamrolled not once but twice by Ike's likers. Massachusetts senator John Kennedy had youth, charisma, and money. Lyndon Johnson was the Senate majority leader and its unrivaled power source. Hubert Humphrey thrilled the hearts of northern liberals, and Missouri senator Stuart Symington, heir to Truman's Senate seat and blessed to have been derided by Joe McCarthy as Sanctimonious Stu, hoped for a deadlock among the more prominent leaders.

California had another important piece of the action: this was an era when conventions actually selected candidates, and the 1960 Democratic National Convention was to be held in Los Angeles, giving Brown not only a major state at his command but also a local spotlight to manipulate. Part of Jerry Brown's advice to his father in 1957 as Pat was considering running either for the US Senate or for the governorship of California was to make the most of his chance to direct the California delegation at the 1960 convention. But when the time came, Pat vacillated and ended up damaging himself.

At first, Brown allowed himself a little fantasy, one common to elected officials at all levels: why not be president? He could run as a "favorite son" in California and be reasonably assured of winning. That would give him a significant pile of delegates—eighty-one votes divided among 162 delegates, second only to the New York delegation in those days. If no Democrat won on the first ballot, why not Brown as a compromise deeper in the scrum? Kennedy's team, especially Bobby Kennedy, viewed that possibility with alarm, and Jack briefly considered challenging Brown in California's primary in order to head off the possibility. Brown, however, privately assured the Kennedys that he would throw his weight behind JFK when the time came, and after some initial skepticism, the Kennedys agreed to the tenuous deal: Kennedy would skip California, while Brown would run, win, and, when the time came, transfer the support of California's delegation to JFK.

Publicly, however, Brown affected neutrality. All candidates, he proclaimed, would "have a fair chance to get the California delegation when and if I release them," he told the Associated Press in January.[10] To emphasize the point, Brown had breakfast with Symington that morning, followed by lunch with Kennedy; the next day, he lunched with Humphrey and paid a call on Johnson. Brown figured that he would have a better hold on his delegation, a diverse collection of Democrats, if he were seen as uninterested in the office himself.

The seeds of the problem were thus sown. Loyalty barreled down one track, respect down the other. The Kennedys expected Brown to deliver, and the delegates expected Brown to cede the path. Just as the convention prepared to open, they crashed.

With the convention scheduled to begin on July 11, Brown primed the pump. "I am going to make a little statement in Los Angeles Sunday," he told reporters on Friday. "And that's all I'm going to say now."[11]

Reporters guessed correctly that Brown was prepared to declare his support for Kennedy, but he would pay the price for his long equivocation. By the time Brown endorsed Kennedy, JFK—and, more important, Bobby—had grown tired of fencing with a governor whose hold on his own state's politics seemed weak. And the California delegation, as if to reinforce that point, refused to follow the governor's lead.

When Brown met with the California delegation, he urged the delegates to join him in supporting Kennedy, only to have Stevenson supporters wage a surprising counterattack. Brown aides "tirelessly canvassed the delegation," the *Los Angeles Times* reported, but struggled to win converts. Brown, realizing that he could not deliver the entire block of votes to Kennedy, reset his sights, aiming to at least produce a plurality for the senator on the first ballot.[12] Even that went down hard. One rogue batch of delegates so adamantly insisted on its independence that it went to court to demand that Pat Brown cast the California delegates for himself on the first ballot, a move that would deny Kennedy a swift victory and open the door to a challenge from Johnson or Stevenson. The lawsuit was dismissed almost as soon as it was filed, and Brown denounced it as a "wild, publicity-seeking move."[13]

True enough, but delegates did not rebel this way against the Richard Daleys or Lyndon Johnsons of the political world. When the first ballots were tallied, Brown met his lowered threshold for success but telegraphed his lack of control: he delivered a very bare plurality for Kennedy—33.5 votes to 31.5 for Stevenson. Brown himself picked up half a vote. Sizing up the situation, the *New York Times* reported that national Democrats were surprised to find Brown so hamstrung. "He is being berated within his delegation and chided without," the newspaper said. One unnamed California delegate summed the matter up more sharply: "This is one more nail driven into Pat's political coffin. This one could be disastrous for him."[14]

A poll taken at the convention's conclusion succinctly stated the damage: "The political popularity of California Democratic Governor Edmund G. 'Pat' Brown appears to have declined sharply among California voters." The survey director, Mervin Field, noted that Brown had been "beset" by a "series of political troubles." Chessman loomed large, as did Brown's handling of the convention. Once seen as a possible candidate for president, he now seemed vulnerable to a challenge for the governorship. Some California insiders thought Brown was finished, that he "could not be elected a precinct committeeman."[15] Only time and forgiveness would permit him a return to power.

Jerry Brown graduated from UC Berkeley in 1961 and, after dabbling with the idea of a career in psychiatry, made his way to law school—again, in partial emulation of his father, who managed to secure a law degree, though, in his case, without ever having attended college. For law school, Jerry Brown chose Yale—elite, of course, as well as philosophical and expensive. On the latter point, however, tuition was not a concern. Louis Lurie was a real estate developer and theater aficionado who came to San Francisco after World War I and became rich along with the city—buying up and developing large chunks of downtown real estate while famously anchoring a lunch table at Jack's, a Sacramento Street bistro that was San Francisco's second-oldest restaurant. Lurie, said at one point to have built nearly three hundred buildings in San Francisco, was a generous philanthropist and a smart one.[16] Although he was a lifelong Republican, he saw plenty of reason to be on good terms with politicians of all stripes, so his foundation helped subsidize schooling for the children of California officeholders. That included the governor, of course, so Lurie's foundation paid for Jerry Brown to go to Yale (and, later, for Jerry's sister Kathleen to attend Stanford).[17]

Yale was a natural for Brown, who enjoyed its emphasis on the theoretical aspects of law—he remained more interested in philosophy than legal practice. He thrived, though more on the evening conversations with colleagues than on the daytime learning.

One favorite sparring partner in those years was Brown's roommate, Dan Greer, an Orthodox Jew from New York so devout that he stocked his refrigerator with kosher food.[18] Greer and Brown would go at issues for hours at a time, recalled Tony Kline, another former classmate and longtime friend of Brown. When it came time at Yale to hold a moot court (a staged legal confrontation in which students advocated before faculty judges), the case involved two students who were kicked out of a Catholic school for entering into a civil marriage. Brown represented the students; Greer the school. They argued fiercely and ended on good terms.

"The thing that impressed me about Jerry Brown in those days—that was in 1962—was his inquisitiveness and his willingness to challenge conventional views," said Kline. Even as a young person, Kline observed, Brown was a "contrarian."

Brown did warm to some of the institution's more prosaic ambitions. He enjoyed constitutional law and discovered labor law, filing away lectures on the shift of power from shop stewards to labor lawyers as workplace disputes moved to the courts.

Perhaps most important, he met people and developed great admiration for legal minds, those educated at Yale in particular. Once given the opportunity to place people in positions of influence—cabinet secretaries, personal advisers, judges, and justices—Brown inordinately relied on Yale Law School. In his final years as governor, three of his four picks for California Supreme Court justiceships were graduates of Yale: not one of the four had ever served as a judge before taking a place on the second most important supreme court in the United States, but they had gone to Yale.

In his final year or two in office, Jerry Brown took to professing that governors have no legacies. "Can you tell me the legacy of Goodwin Knight? Or Governor Merriam? Or Deukmejian?" Brown cantankerously asked the Sacramento press corps on January 10, 2018. "Governors don't have legacies. That's my No. 1 proposition. Look, we have a whole political system that judges our executives by the state of the economy, over which they have virtually no impact. So, you figure it out."[19]

Brown's protestations arose in part from mischief. He was annoyed by the suggestion that he was building a bullet train and providing for a rainy-day fund in order to burnish his place in history. When journalists pressed him about his "legacy," he prickled, as he was wont to do, and tossed out the premise of the question. The other reason was practical: major projects looked more selfless through the lens of California's future than as tools of Brown's personal aggrandizement.

One thing is clear: Brown didn't really believe that governors had no legacies. Of course, it's possible to wonder what the legacy of George Deukmejian or Goodwin Knight was, but just because some governors don't leave much of a legacy doesn't mean that none does. For all his insistence that gubernatorial leadership was ephemeral, he never had the temerity to suggest that his father failed to leave a legacy.[20] That's because Pat Brown did make a mark on California, and Jerry knew it.

Pat Brown had weaknesses as a political leader. He was too genial, too willing to say yes to too many people. But he changed California, in particular through two projects that still stand, sometimes a bit unsteadily, as concrete evidence of his time in office. He built California's system of higher education and developed the waterways that make its cities viable.

The threshold moment for the water system arrived early in Pat Brown's tenure. The same ballot that would make John Kennedy president in

1960—though Kennedy would lose to Nixon in California—featured a bond measure to pay for a gigantic reconfiguration of the means by which California secured water. That such a measure was necessary was a by-product of some of the state's most elemental and historic characteristics.

In California, ever since the end of the gold rush, the people have congregated mostly along the coast, and the rain has fallen mostly in the Sierra Nevada. That leaves those responsible for a sustainable water system two choices: either persuade the people to move inland or find a way to bring water down from the mountains.

Los Angeles recognized those imperatives early and chose to capture water to secure its growth. After secretly buying up property in the Owens Valley, in the eastern Sierras, at the beginning of the twentieth century, Los Angeles fallowed that land and absorbed the water rights, a move with several ramifications: it ended any chance the Owens Valley had to become a farm community, instead converting it to a vassal-state of the Los Angeles Department of Water and Power; it secured the water future for Los Angeles, making possible its rise to the status of the nation's most diverse and culturally interesting city; and it angered generations of residents of the valley, who felt swindled. It was nearly one hundred years before a Los Angeles mayor, Richard Riordan, would dare to set foot in the valley. Protesters greeted his visit, and in the helicopter on the way home, he laughed and said: "We stole it fair and square."[21]

The Owens Valley water supply gave Los Angeles most of what it needed, but much of Southern California still thirsted. And Northern California, though more blessed with rainfall, suffered its own version of that peril. San Francisco secured its water supply by damming the Tuolumne River, in the Hetch Hetchy valley of the Sierra Nevada, but its suburbs were dependent on less reliable sources. Finally, the vast and bounteous farmlands of the Central Valley, some of the most productive agricultural land on earth, whipsawed from plenty to parched: reliable water would serve large and small farmers and bring forth the bounty of the land.

Brown, ever the builder, proposed a solution: a state-funded water project that would dam rivers and build aqueducts, principally to ship water from east to west and north to south. The essence of the project was the construction of a dam in Oroville, California, where the rushing waters of the Feather River would be blocked and diverted into tunnels and from there to aqueducts that would move the water south. With that as the anchor, the projects would proceed—dams, waterways, generating stations. Estimates of its cost seemed to grow by the month. "We didn't know exactly the cost of the project," Brown conceded decades later. "But we figured there would be other sources of water. So the question was, we could get $500 million and build the Feather River Dam and get the project started. Then you had to complete it."[22]

The project would provide flood control in some Northern California counties—five years earlier, a cascading Feather River had killed forty people in Yuba County and Marysville, thirty miles south of Oroville, but the bulk of the benefits would flow south. Brown was not the first to suggest such an audacious harnessing of California's water; plans for the system dated back to Earl Warren's years in Sacramento (indeed, more farsighted visions extended back to the nineteenth century). But the grandeur appealed especially to Brown—the New Deal sense of enlisting workers to make nature serve society, the swarms of scientists and laborers needed to divert the course of a river, to bring water to the thirsty and crops to the hungry.

Against Pat Brown's visionary optimism stood stubborn California sectionalism. The people of Northern California, to an overwhelming degree, regarded Southern California's designs on their water as predatory. They would not be easily moved to support a proposal that would divert Northern California rivers to Southern California cities and farms.

Through the spring and summer of 1960, Brown cajoled and selectively mined data in support of what became known as the Burns-Porter Act, the bill that would funnel state money to the project, provided voters would approve. The governor worked individual legislators while also building broader support for the bill, picking up endorsements from state water agencies, mostly in Southern California. Support in northern counties was harder to get, but Brown worked for it, pledging fish and wildlife protection as well as jobs and economic development to sports-men who worried about the effect of dams and to workers who longed to build them.[23] The state's leading newspapers drew lines: the *San Francisco Chronicle* regarded the notion as theft and opposed it vigorously; the *Los Angeles Times* saw it as necessary for the future and supported it without reservation. Interviewing two state water experts in April, the *Times* headlined its front-page story, which led the Sunday paper, BASIC QUESTIONS ON STATE'S WATER PROBLEMS ANSWERED.[24]

With substantial help from Brown, the financing measure passed the legislature in June and headed for the November ballot. Its prospects were uncertain. Even Brown privately acknowledged that the cost estimates were underreported, and the politics were tough and sectional. Brown grew frustrated at times, particularly by the opposition from organized labor, which had backed him in 1958. Opponents of the measure, he complained as Election Day drew near, were "irreconcilables, doubters, quibblers and sectionalists."[25] Political analysts recognized that the bond measure, which had grown to $1.75 billion—the largest state bond in the history of the United States—would lose in most of Northern California (Brown had hopes for Butte County, where the first dam would be built, but the rest of the region was a washout), so it needed to tally a huge victory from Santa Barbara south to the border. And yet until the very last moment, the Metropolitan Water District, which provided most of Southern California with its water, remained gingerly opposed to the bond, fearful that an influx of state water would jeopardize its standing with other western states vying for a share of water from the Colorado River. Brown worked that angle, too, and the Met came on board just before the election.

On October 27, consultants to the project released their final assessments of its financing and feasibility. Interpretations varied by region. FEATHER RIVER PROJECT GETS SOUND RATING IN TWO REPORTS, the *Los Angeles Times* declared. STATE WATER PLAN CALLED IMPOSSIBLE was the *San Francisco Chronicle*'s headline.[26]

Results on election night were painfully close. Proponents believed it had failed that Tuesday. As expected, it lost resoundingly in Northern California: San Francisco defeated it by 62,000 votes out of 280,000 cast, while Placer County, near Sacramento, trashed it 13,362 to 6,717. It carried in Yuba County, where flood control promised to save lives, but even there it succeeded by barely one hundred votes. But the measure's salvation came from the south. As the votes trickled in from gigantic Los Angeles County, defeat turned first to hope on Wednesday afternoon, then to victory that night. Proposition 1 triumphed, propelled by more than 250,000 votes in Los Angeles (a margin nearly as large as the entire San Francisco electorate).

Proposition 1 laid the foundation for one of the most spectacular engineering feats of all time. With construction starting in 1961, the Oroville Dam was erected to block the Feather River. Then tunnels channeled the water to the Sacramento–San Joaquin Delta, then a 444-mile-long aqueduct carried it south and over the Tehachapi Mountains. Other dams, aqueducts, and canals followed, forming a vast web of water infrastructure. The costs—not only in construction but also in energy to run the growing system—were astonishing: at one point, planners proposed building a nuclear power plant merely to hoist the water from the Central Valley into the Los Angeles Basin. Although water generates energy as it passes through turbines, it also consumes vast amounts of electrical power. But that water made the Central and San Joaquin Valleys bloom and provided an assured water supply that allowed Los Angeles and its endless suburbs to grow in confidence. Years later, when Jerry Brown was governor, backers proposed that the backbone of the project, the state aqueduct, be named for Pat Brown. At first, and somewhat churlishly, Jerry objected, arguing that any such dedication should only come after his father had died. Pat couldn't understand why, and Jerry relented. In 1982, just before concluding his second term as governor, Jerry presided over the dedication of the Governor Edmund G. Brown California Aqueduct.[27]

Engineers, environmentalists, developers, and historians will long debate the merits of the California State Water Project. What they will not dispute—what even Jerry Brown does not, in his heart, dispute—is that it is a legacy of the governor who built it.

The State Water Project made it possible for California to grow, to become a nation-state. People need water, and civilization cannot exist without it. But society needs more than just water to grow and prosper, and Pat Brown viewed the other essential requirement as education. Brown, who never graduated from college, wanted an education system that would be the envy of the world—a center of intellect and a path to prosperity for young Californians, beneficiaries of becoming adults in a place that could afford to help them.

Few people would accuse Pat Brown of insecurity. He radiated confidence and ebullience, had no qualms about asking questions or seeking input from everyday people. He did, however, have a slightly sore spot about never having graduated from college. Whereas he was secure in his thoughts on water, say, he was less sure-footed about how to educate young people and how to elevate California's higher-education system into the world's greatest. For that, he turned to Clark Kerr.

A native of Pennsylvania, son of an erudite apple farmer, and graduate of Swarthmore and Stanford, Kerr began his career as a labor negotiator before moving, in 1945, to take over UC Berkeley's Institute of Industrial Relations.[28] Witty and urbane, and deeply political, Kerr attracted attention at Berkeley and was promoted to chancellor of that university, the state's flagship, in 1952.

It was under Kerr's leadership—and at Brown's urging—that the state of California sought to bring order to an educational system that was growing, competing with itself, and searching for a coherent identity. How were the state's community colleges and its university system to best serve students? Where would research be performed? And what about the state-college system?

Answering those questions was the mandate of the state's Master Plan for Higher Education. Implementing those answers would become the mission of the Donahoe Higher Education Act. It was Kerr who developed the fundamental structure of the plan: the University of California would be a research institution and educational provider for the state's most successful and promising students; the state-college system would provide quality undergraduate education but not confer graduate degrees or host research; the vast community-college system would offer entry-level education to any student and would provide transfer opportunities to the state-college and university systems. None of the schools would charge tuition, and no student would be turned down for an inability to pay.

The result was not just the most highly regarded public education system on earth but also a profound commitment to egalitarianism. Californians, regardless of means, could count on their state for education. No one need fear the denial of opportunity on that basis. "The campus is no longer on the hill with the aristocracy but in the valley with the people," Kerr wrote.[29]

By the end of 1961, then, Pat Brown had reason to be confident. He had persuaded voters to overhaul the state's entire water system and had persuaded legislators to do the same with education. He had bungled his role at the 1960 Democratic convention and had taken a beating over his handling of Chessman, but he'd moved on, and most Californians appeared willing to forgive those fumbles.

Then the boom fell. Richard Nixon, fresh from his humiliating 1960 defeat by John Kennedy, sulked for a while, unsure how to return to politics. He relocated to Los Angeles, a smart tactical move should he seek to regain a political foothold, since Los Angeles represented a Republican stronghold in contrast with San Francisco. Settling uncomfortably into a private law practice, Nixon weighed his options. He could run for the Senate, but that would mean challenging Tom Kuchel, a moderate Republican sure to seek reelection. Or he could take on Pat Brown, who warily eyed his potential rival from a distance.[30]

California voter registration in 1961 was Democratic by a margin of 4 to 3, but Brown, with his mishandling of the 1960 Democratic convention and the Chessman case, had exposed some vulnerabilities within that slight majority. In the 1960 presidential campaign, Nixon carried California, not too surprising since he was a native but a reminder that he had recent evidence of political strength. The governorship, should he win it, would give Nixon a national platform, and though it would take him out of the running for the 1964 presidential campaign, the early consensus was that Jack Kennedy was a lock to be reelected. Alone with his yellow legal pad, Nixon tallied the pluses and minuses of a campaign. Democrats prepared for battle: Alan Cranston, the state controller, brought down the house at a Democratic gathering when he noted that California had only recently rid itself of the "death grip" of Nixon, Knight, and Knowland. "We are resolved that not one of these three shall ever again hold public office." James Bassett, covering the event for the *Los Angeles Times,* said the applause "was so thunderous that nearby baked Alaskas collapsed like Hubert Humphrey's presidential boomlet."[31]

In September, Nixon conferred with his family, Dwight Eisenhower, and Kyle Palmer, then the retired political editor of the *Los Angeles Times*.[32] Nixon initially yielded to Pat Nixon's urging that he remain in private life. She relented, however, and agreed to support a return to politics. With that, Nixon announced his candidacy for governor of California on September 27, 1961. "The government...is in a mess and someone needs to clean it up," Nixon said. Of Brown, he added that the governor was an "amiable but bungling man."[33] Nixon also warned that while he declined to respond to attacks as a presidential candidate "because of the high dignity of the high office for which I was running," he intended this time to respond forcefully, promising his critics "the fight of their lives." He aimed, Nixon said, to "beat Pat Brown to a pulp."[34]

He did not. Hamstrung by a challenge from his right during the Republican primaries and, more important, by the voters' nagging suspicion that he didn't really want to be governor—they correctly concluded that, for Nixon, this was just a stopover on his presumed return to the White House—Nixon's campaign sputtered, then stumbled, and finally fell. Bored by domestic issues, Nixon dredged up old habits and suggested that Brown was a "do nothing" in the face of a growing Communist threat. It was transparently an attempt to invigorate his campaign, and press coverage saw through the charade. A clumsy ad by the self-proclaimed Anti-Communism Voting League accused Brown of being "insufficiently qualified on the issue of national survival" and attempted to press the matter, but it did little to affect the outcome. It was one thing to run against Brown as an amiable dunce; to suggest that he was an agent of communism was laughable.

As the campaign entered its final weeks, the Cuban Missile Crisis gripped the nation and thwarted any chance Nixon might have had to tighten the race. With one eye always on politics, Kennedy sent Air Force One to bring Brown to Washington during the crisis for consultation, an easy gift to a fellow Democrat against a common enemy.[35]

On the morning after the election, Brown was gracious and at ease. He thanked reporters for their coverage of the race, looked forward to returning to work. Nixon seethed. He watched his press secretary, Herb Klein, addressing reporters, then decided to address them himself. Riding down in the elevator at the Beverly Hilton, he observed: "Losing California after losing the presidency—well, it's like being bitten by a mosquito after being bitten by a rattlesnake."[36]

Reporters were surprised by Nixon's entrance as the bedraggled candidate replaced Klein at the microphone. "Now that Mr. Klein has made a statement," Nixon began, speaking without notes, "now that all the members of the press I know are so delighted that I lost, I would like to make one myself." He concluded:

> As I leave you, I want you to know, just think how much you're going to be missing. You don't have Nixon to kick around anymore because, gentlemen, this is my last press conference and it will be one in which…I have welcomed the opportunity to test wits with you. I've always respected you. I have sometimes disagreed with you but, unlike some people, I have never canceled a subscription to a paper and, also, I never will.
>
> I believe in reading what my opponents say. And I hope that what I have said today will at least make television, radio and the press first recognize the great responsibility they have to report all the news and, second, to recognize that they have a right and a responsibility, if they are against a candidate—to give him the shaft. But also recognize, if they give him the shaft—to put one lonely reporter on the campaign who will report what the candidate says, now and then. Thank you, gentlemen, and good day.[37]

In Washington, Earl Warren and President Kennedy were together the next day, and they chuckled over the reports of Nixon's demise.

Pat Brown was no less delighted. Asked whether he had said Nixon would "regret [his remarks] the rest of his life," Brown insisted he had said no such thing publicly. Pressed, he admitted he might have said it to Bernice.

Pat Brown entered his second term with the world on his plate. He had first dispatched Knowland and now Nixon; pundits were calling him the giant killer. True to Cranston's word, none of the state's once dominant Republican trio—Knight, Knowland, or Nixon—would ever return to state office.

# 4

# The End of the Beginning— From Protest to Rebellion

The House Un-American Activities Committee had, by 1960, become a little stale. Joe McCarthy flared in the 1950s, crushing lives and careers, until President Eisenhower outflanked him and ultimately shut him down. After 1954, McCarthy was a threat to no one other than his loved ones. He drank himself to death. Few mourned.

But the committee labored on, perversely hoping to resuscitate its power to destroy, and in the spring of 1960, it lumbered into a not-too-sympathetic town to do its business. As usual, that meant identifying and harassing Americans who affiliated with—or were suspected of affiliating with—the Communist Party.

HUAC's hearings were scheduled to begin on May 12, 1960. A month to the day after the debut of Candlestick Park, this event was slated for a different venue—the chambers of the San Francisco Board of Supervisors, housed at city hall, San Francisco's grand edifice, austere and cool. If Candlestick looked toward the future, city hall spoke to San Francisco's past—marble floors and a circular staircase hinted at opulence and privilege. Baseball built Candlestick. Gold built city hall.

In the run-up to the scheduled hearings, Californians chose sides: the American Council of Christian Churches commended the committee for its work exposing and excising "the cancer of communism," while 250 members of the Berkeley faculty deplored HUAC's "insidious and harmful" efforts.[1] Students rallied against HUAC; schoolteachers warned of Communist efforts to misdirect those same students.

The first morning of the hearing, men and women, most of them young and well dressed, assembled to register their discontent. At first, the jostling was gentle, even polite. Protesters lined up for tickets, hoping to be admitted to the proceedings and to take their seats by permission.

HUAC had issued subpoenas to forty-eight witnesses: one of them, a Berkeley sophomore named Douglas Wachter, was discovering his own activism. He had, among other things, held a vigil in protest over the pending execution of Caryl Chessman, whose sentence, as of that morning, Pat Brown had postponed, though not for long.[2] Prior to the hearing, Wachter had been quoted in the *Daily Californian,* Berkeley's student paper, pledging to "fight" the committee. When he took the stand and was questioned about his comments, Wachter refused to answer, invoking his First Amendment right to associate politically without interference from the government. He also refused to answer a question about participation in a 1959 gathering of Communists, insisting on his rights under the Fifth Amendment, protecting him from giving evidence against himself.

Mike Tigar, a Berkeley law student destined to become a leading counterculture lawyer, helped organize students to protest the proceedings, including the grilling of Wachter. Tigar and most of his compatriots were prohibited from entering, and six of them who did get seats were expelled after another witness loudly protested the committee's work. They grumbled through Wachter's morning testimony, then stirred during the lunch break. Some chanted, "Let us in." Some sang "Battle Hymn of the Republic." Yet just as violence seemed imminent, both sides retreated, and the afternoon closed without serious incident.

The next morning, however, protesters and police arrived in force and keyed for action. Tensions gathered. At around 1:15 p.m., the battle began.

Police, increasingly angered by the voluble students, declared a "general riot" and attempted to disperse it with fire hoses. Students at first held fast, donning overcoats to repulse the water, but the pressure from the hoses combined with the building's slippery marble floors took their legs out from under them. They scattered like leaves across corridors and down a flight of stairs into the building's grand rotunda. One student was "beaten into submission" by five officers. Others were also beaten, some bloodied, and at least one officer lost his nightstick and was clubbed with it by a demonstrator.[3] In that exchange, Robert Meisenbach, a twenty-two-year-old Berkeley student, was charged with attacking Officer Ralph Schaumleffel. Meisenbach denied being the aggressor and later sheepishly admitted that he was so frightened he peed in his pants.

Sixty-two protesters were arrested and charged with participating in a riot, disturbing the peace, and resisting an officer—charges they denied but would regard with pride in later years.[4] Bail for most was set at $210. The rotunda at city hall lay in three inches of water.

The May 13 fracas came to be regarded as the first student protest of the 1960s. It involved students from UC Berkeley as well as other Bay Area colleges. It pitted young middle-class men and women against what they viewed as the agents of a repressive and discredited elite. In the view of those students, Communist witch-hunters were the first rank of that flailing era, which would soon come to include the police, the FBI, the military, and, before it was over, many mystified and worried parents. It began with the use of timeworn tools, the exercise of speech and assembly, and as the years passed—as civil rights turned to Vietnam and as the Southern Christian Leadership Conference was challenged by the Black Panther Party and the Weathermen and, ridiculously, the Symbionese Liberation Army—protest would yield to violence, and oppression would find new ways of expressing itself. Much of that struggle, both peaceful and violent, would play out on the periphery of the Berkeley campus and in the neighborhoods of South Los Angeles. Before it was over, bullets would shred both, and the smell of tear gas would be hard to wash from uniforms, blankets, and beards.

California had long been a center of protest and extremism—and not of just one stripe. In the 1950s, the John Birch Society, popular in Orange County and anchored in Pasadena, saw Communists in every walk of life. Not even such estimable figures as Earl Warren and Ike were immune from their paranoid fantasies, as IMPEACH EARL WARREN signs once blanketed the landscape of Warren's native California. Bob Dylan got the idea, imagining himself a member of the society, "looking every place for them goldarned Reds."

Yes, the Birchers could and did seem laughable, but they were a force in California politics, threatening Republican candidates who coveted their enthusiasm but shrank from their outrageous accusations. Each in his time, Knight, Nixon, Knowland, and Reagan would all walk the fine line between encouraging Birch support and being saddled with its extremism.

Activist conservatism at the extremes did not end with the Birchers. California would become known in the 1970s and again in the 1990s for nursing conservative populist movements that championed such causes as property tax reduction (Proposition 13), criminal justice reform (the three strikes law), the elimination of affirmative action and bilingual education, and the imposition of harshly deterrent measures intended to deny public benefits to immigrants who live in the country illegally (Proposition 187).

The Left had its own targets and struggles, especially as the 1960s blossomed. Liberals questioned HUAC and welcomed its demise but did not always appreciate images of students confronting police, even when the police generated much of the violence that ensued. Student protest was influenced by music and drugs, splintering the Left along establishment and counterculture lines that would sometimes intersect but at other times clash, sometimes violently.

As the decade unfolded in California, the right wing fought for property rights, even the right to discriminate by race; it demanded lower taxes and patriotic public servants. The left wing rallied for coastal protection, drug legalization, and civil liberties, among other things. It got worse before it got better.

Jerry Brown would participate in his share of student protests, but not in the battles at San Francisco City Hall or on the streets of Berkeley. "I wasn't one to get arrested," he said in 2015.[5]

In 1960, Brown expressed his growing activism by showing solidarity with farmworkers in California. He joined a day in the fields, in Stockton, sleeping on the floor of a church and demonstrating on behalf of workers who were seeking stronger labor protections from the state—which is to say, Brown's father. Dorothy Day spoke to the demonstrators. Day's work was, Brown recalled, "spiritual. It expressed a deeper dimension."[6]

Dorothy Day played an important role in Brown's development, helping to bring the liturgical Catholicism of his training to the living spirit of his politics. Brown and his fellow novices had access to *The Catholic Worker* inside the seminary, and Brown read it often. Day's causes in the 1960s, when Brown first read her work, included protest over the development and spread of nuclear weapons. She and *The Catholic Worker* also championed civil rights and opposed the Vietnam War.

To Brown, she was an archetype and example—and a writer who affected him, especially as he wrestled with questions about hierarchy and liberty. Dorothy Day was a charismatic force within the larger structure of the Catholic Church, a useful example of compassion for the poor—a subject of particular interest to Jerry Brown. After Day's talk during the Day in the Fields, he approached her and inquired about her concept of utopia, what it meant in practice and what he could read to better understand it.

"I was interested in freedom and boundaries," Brown said. "She suggested that I read *Paths in Utopia* by Martin Buber. He talked about the utopian Socialists…and about how, outside of government, people organize themselves." For Brown, those models would create a limiting principle around his vision of government, distinguishing him from more conventional liberals by his refusal to regard government as a solution to many social and societal ills.[7]

A few years later, Brown joined fellow Yale law students on a trip to Mississippi. Then, too, he was with the movement but not quite of it. While there, he reached out to the segregationist governor, Ross Barnett, urging him to integrate the state's university. Barnett was neither impressed nor moved and warned Pat Brown of his son's meddling. Pat thanked his counterpart for the alert; Jerry Brown headed home.

\* \* \*

In the 1960s, the battle lines of populism and enlightened liberalism took shape around the issue of housing discrimination. Pat Brown had come to office determined to eradicate California's tolerance of discrimination in the workforce and housing, and he doggedly pursued both, first winning approval to establish a Fair Employment Practices Commission and then turning to housing. The bill that sought to eradicate racial discrimination in housing was introduced by assemblyman Byron Rumford, a black pharmacist who represented liberal Berkeley and who had endured a lifetime of discrimination. Rumford's bill, which would make it illegal to refuse to sell or rent a house to any person based on his or her race, creed, or national origin, bumped around the legislature for months, until in May of 1963, it neared an important hurdle: the state senate's Governmental Affairs Efficiency Committee, a notoriously tough stop for liberal bills.[8] On the eve of that vote, Brown acknowledged the "hard fight" ahead while wholeheartedly expressing his support. "It is my honest view, that California has taken steps—and is taking steps—which, if they do not falter, will indeed make our state a model and a leader for the nation."

Passed by the legislature in the eleventh hour of the 1963 session, the Rumford Fair Housing Act was poised to become law until California's penchant for nasty populism—and its vulnerability to special-interest machinations—kicked in. Real estate interests and landlords who had unsuccessfully fought the Rumford bill turned to California's ballot-initiative process to get from voters what they had lost from legislators. Although the initiative did not directly address the Rumford Act, it sought to prevent the government from denying any person the right to sell or rent property "to any person as he chooses," thus framing discrimination as freedom, as the proponents of discrimination often are wont to do. Once qualified for the ballot, the measure received the useful title of the California Fair Housing Initiative and was assigned a number, making it Proposition 14 on the November 1964 ballot.

Like populist initiatives before and since, Proposition 14 at first did not much trouble the state's leadership. Brown regarded it as so beyond the pale that he openly disparaged its supporters as racists, risking the ire of those who believed they were supporting owners' rights rather than outright racism. Matters were further clouded by the mirror-image aspect of the initiative. A yes vote on Proposition 14 meant rejection of the Rumford Act—meaning that no meant yes and vice versa, at least in terms of housing discrimination.

Support for—and opposition to—Proposition 14 cut along familiar demographic lines. Majorities of Asians, blacks, and Latinos all opposed the initiative, and support tended to fall off among poll respondents with the highest levels of education. Democrats opposed the measure, while Republicans supported it.[9] Opponents included church groups and librarians, the president of Joseph Magnin department stores, and the state's leading Democrats. Supporters were quieter, reluctant to be labeled racists. As Election Day neared, Pat Brown raged against the measure, dropping his customary good cheer and attacking proponents of Proposition 14 with vigor. And yet not only did Proposition 14 win, it also won by a landslide, with two-thirds of Californians supporting it. It passed in Los Angeles and San Francisco, in Sacramento, Fresno, and San Diego. It was a wipeout for Brown and the progressives, a triumph for California's periodic explosions of conservative protest.

UC Berkeley in the early 1960s was not the Berkeley of uprising and dissent. Yes, there was the protest at San Francisco City Hall, but the university campus was largely quiet, more likely to be disrupted by water balloon fights than tear gas. But the rumblings of change could be heard: *Brown v. Board of Education,* in 1954, written by Berkeley alum Earl Warren; Rosa Parks and the Montgomery bus boycott, in 1955; the forced integration of Little Rock Central High School by a reluctant but determined Eisenhower, in 1957. Berkeley students were not at the center of those events, but they wanted to discuss and debate them. A Berkeley student group, SLATE, helped organize the HUAC protest in San Francisco, and the ensuing trials radicalized many of those who participated. Berkeley was eager to engage, unsure how to do so.

Then, in 1963, an unlikely leader arrived on campus. Mario Savio was born in Manhattan and grew up in Queens. Brilliant, handsome, high-strung, Savio suffered from a stammer that would overcome him when he spoke to people in power. He wanted to be a priest but was fascinated by science. He yearned to understand the universe.[10]

Drawn to Berkeley by the hunch that he could find himself there, Savio arrived in 1963. "I just had a feeling, a good feeling, about the place, that somehow real things were going on there."[11] Rarely has the admonition to trust one's gut been more roundly fulfilled.

He started with civil rights, traveled to Mississippi, helped form the Council of Federated Organizations, confronted white nationalists, organized blacks, was beaten up by the Klan. Returning to Berkeley, he sought to politicize a campus still shaking off the 1950s. Emboldened by the tactics of the civil rights movement, Savio and his compatriots sponsored lectures, invited controversial speakers, and asserted the right to leaflet and demonstrate along what was known as the Bancroft strip. It seems so small in retrospect: the right to hand out leaflets at the corner of Bancroft Way and Telegraph Avenue, at an entrance to the campus.[12] And yet. The regents had barred political activity on campus—an attempt to insulate academic pursuits from political distraction—so this was a provocation, intentional and consciousness-raising.

It was a challenge that took California's liberals by surprise. Pat Brown welcomed the support of active young people. Clark Kerr had given them their Master Plan for Higher Education, intended to secure a quality education for every young person in this bustling, energetic state. Who were these young people to rebel and protest?

And so it began: liberals mystified by leftists, young people exasperated by age and power. One side asked, How could the beneficiaries of such well-intentioned largesse and love fail to appreciate those gifts? The other responded, How could such privileged and insulated people not hear the rising voices? They spoke past each other, their enmity solidifying with each confrontation.

The clash that crystallized it began on a sunny morning in Berkeley— October 1, 1964. Jack Weinberg, a member of CORE (the Congress on Racial Equality) set up a card table in the prohibited area. It was stocked with leaflets and other forms of political advocacy. When questioned, Weinberg refused to identify himself or leave. He was arrested. Within minutes, protesters, drawn by the police presence, began to gather. Weinberg was in the back seat of the squad car, and demonstrators massed around it, chanting, "Release him!" Images of students surrounding and leaping on the car would quickly become emblems of a new assertiveness on campus, a determination not to accept incremental progress or good-faith assurances. Protest morphed into combat. The conflict stretched through the fall as demonstrators held their ground and the administration struggled to blend tolerance for speech and protest with discipline and order.

On December 2, 1964, Savio delivered his response. Analogizing the university to a machine governed by a board and driven by the necessity to produce a product, he memorably refused to go along.

"There's a time when the operation of the machine becomes so odious, makes you so sick at heart, that you can't take part, you can't even passively take part," Savio yelled into a microphone at Sproul Plaza, his stutter overcome by his intensity. "And you've got to put your bodies upon the gears and upon the wheels, upon the levers, upon all the apparatus. And you've got to make it stop. And you've got to indicate to the people who run it, to the people who own it, that unless you're free, the machine will be prevented from working at all."[13]

Jerry Brown wasn't much for this kind of protest. He was on the Berkeley campus in 1960 but off at Yale by the time the movement gathered force. Always skeptical of broad strokes, he was surrounded by confrontation politics but apart from them as well. His father was the governor, and as Savio and other demonstrators turned increasingly against Pat Brown, Jerry was conflicted. He met Savio and even arranged for Savio to speak with Pat Brown one day on the phone. It did not go well. "Savio compared the students' treatment with the Vietcong," Brown remembered. The comparison struck Brown as overwrought and self-indulgent. "That's why I had no interest in student politics at the time."[14]

The exchange captures something of both Browns at that moment. Pat Brown's distress with the student protests was obvious: students at the university that he had built and nurtured had suddenly turned against him. They resented being part of the "machine," and he was one of its operators. Naturally, that upset and angered him.

Jerry Brown's reaction was more complex. He shared his fellow students' anxieties about the war in Vietnam and their commitment to social justice for minorities and farm workers. He already had demonstrated his independence from his parents by seeking out the seminary and could easily have bolted against his father now. Imagine the impact of young Jerry Brown joining Mario Savio on the steps of Sproul Hall, denouncing a university leadership that included his own father. Jerry Brown did not do that. He was not a radical, and not inclined to be swept up in the passion of a moment. He was not and never would be an extremist.

Instead, he attempted to broker a truce between Savio and his father. Failing that, he attached completely to neither. He kept his distance from Savio and maintained a guarded independence from his father. For a man who later would defy liberals in his own party and annoy conservatives with his success, those days in the early 1960s were formative indeed.

Much, maybe too much, can be said of the familial impulses that connected and divided Pat and Jerry Brown. They loved and admired each other. Pat was proud of his son and sometimes bewildered by him. Pat did not imagine raising a priest for a son, nor did he imagine that his boy would someday become governor. For Jerry, his father was an object of appreciation and exasperation—he shrank from the retail politics that Pat practiced, the reaching and touching, the phone calls during dinner, the petty and insistent demands of those pleading for assistance. And yet he could not help but admire his father's achievements and the affection he inspired. Pat and Jerry, like many a father and son, circled one another, their relationship filled with admiration and rebellion, bewilderment and love.

Brown graduated from Yale in 1964 and returned to California to study for the bar and launch his legal career. His father helped Jerry land a clerkship with Justice Mathew Tobriner, who was happy to accept the son of his good friend and patron (it was Pat who placed Tobriner on the court). Jerry went to work at the supreme court in San Francisco, commuting from the East Bay with a group of former law students that included Kline.

Brown suffered one embarrassing setback during that time. He failed the bar—the first time anyone could recall that a Tobriner clerk had done so. Chastened, Brown set about studying again, this time ensconcing himself on the third floor of the governor's mansion in Sacramento, where he would pore over his reading materials while his father conducted business downstairs. It was the only time that Jerry Brown lived in the governor's mansion—with his father. One encounter above all others would stand out for him from that period. He was stretching his legs during a break from studying when he heard voices wafting up the stairs. They were raised in argument, and he cocked an ear, straining to pick up words.

Pat Brown and Jesse Unruh were fighting. Unruh believed he had a promise from Brown that the governor would step down after two terms, clearing the way for Unruh to make his bid. Brown denied any such commitment and refused to clear the way. The two fought tenaciously.

Jerry listened, out of sight of the two men, who were on a couch in the mansion's living room on the first floor while he eavesdropped from the staircase. It was, Jerry Brown reflected years later, a powerful jolt, realizing that his father was defending his own place in politics and that the outcome of the conversation would shape the lives of countless Californians, not to mention that of Brown's own father. If there can be said to be a moment when Jerry Brown first imagined the governorship for himself, that was it.

Jerry returned to his studies. He passed the bar the second time around.

Student protest at Berkeley was provocative but largely, at least at that point, peaceful. Not so elsewhere. On a hot night in August of 1965, Officer Lee Minikus of the California Highway Patrol—Brown's highway patrol—pulled over Marquette Frye, suspected of drunken driving, in Watts, just south of downtown Los Angeles. Minikus administered a sobriety test, which Frye failed. As he did, a crowd, including Frye's mother, gathered. She began to shout at her son while others turned on the officer. A tense situation deteriorated, and when Minikus pulled his gun to force Frye into his squad car, the crowd, by then roughly two hundred people, erupted. Protesters threw "wine and whisky bottles," according to the *Los Angeles Times,* as both Frye and his mother were arrested and taken away.[15]

"An estimated 1,000 persons rioted in the Watts district Wednesday night," the morning *Times* reported. Fueled by rumors that the Frye family previously had been victimized by police, demonstrators "attacked police and motorists with rocks, bricks and bottles before some 100 officers" sealed off the area.[16]

By Friday the thirteenth, the dimensions of the crisis became clearer. NEW RIOTING, the *Times* bannered that morning. The subhead: STORES LOOTED, CARS DESTROYED. Predictably, the paper's coverage focused on the riot's impact on white people: the front page featured two large photographs, one of a white firefighter with a wounded ankle, the other of a white police officer "stoned by the mob."[17] By then, the *Times* estimated that seven thousand people were rioting and seventy-five people were injured, including thirteen police officers and two firefighters.

Pat Brown was on vacation in Greece. Rather, he was attending a "Greek-American convention," thin cover for an overseas junket with his family. Pat Brown cabled his confidence in the LAPD. "We are going to maintain law and order in California so long as I am governor," he insisted.[18] He rushed home and huddled with close advisers, including Los Angeles lawyer and future secretary of state Warren Christopher. Jerry Brown listened in, wondering with the rest of the state how his father would cope with this sudden onslaught of violence. His father and Christopher, young Jerry thought, were too cautious, uncertain about the landscape and its changing character.[19]

The Watts riots were profoundly destabilizing in their violence and unsettling in their message, to liberals in particular. Lyndon Johnson had traveled a long way on civil rights. Once a not-so-unusual Texan who liberally used the word *nigger* and appealed to a southern base, by 1965 Johnson was the champion of the Great Society, a collection of programs he had first begun proposing in 1964. Intended to address a range of American issues, the Great Society's most ambitious element was its stated goal of eliminating poverty, a notion that Johnson and others, including Pat Brown, believed would have its greatest and most positive impact among American minorities. Viewed in that admittedly paternalistic context, Watts was not just violent but ungrateful.

Johnson's remarks about the riots, delivered a week later, captured that ambivalence. "Who of you could have predicted 10 years ago, that in this last, sweltering, August week thousands upon thousands of disenfranchised Negro men and women would suddenly take part in self government," Johnson asked, "and that thousands more in that same week would strike out in an unparalleled act of violence in this nation?"[20]

Brown was similarly baffled and sought answers to the violence by appointing a commission to investigate the causes of the riots. He named John McCone, a Republican former director of the CIA and a leading businessman, to chair the panel. Among McCone's key deputies was Christopher, destined for preeminence in Los Angeles and Washington. Pat Brown charged the commission in August, and it returned its report on December 2.

The report began by emphasizing the limited nature of the violence: out of some 650,000 black residents of Los Angeles County, "about two per cent were involved in the disorder." Still, the commission conceded, "this violent fraction, however minor, has given the face of community relations in Los Angeles a sinister cast."[21]

Summarizing the events that led to the riots, the commission identified disappointment with the pace of the "Federal poverty program"; the failure of authorities to confront rioting elsewhere, thus encouraging more uprisings; and the passage of California's Proposition 14, which affirmed discrimination in housing. The commission also took pains to assert that Watts was not a race riot per se but rather a violent uprising that swept up many blacks—"Negroes," in the vernacular of the day. Nevertheless, the McCone Commission sensed something deeply amiss in the city and did its best to sound a warning, however abstractly:

What has depressed and stunned us most is the dull, devastating spiral of failure that awaits the average disadvantaged child in the urban core. His home life all too often fails to give him the incentive and the elementary experience with words and ideas which prepares most children for school. Unprepared and unready, he may not learn to read or write at all…Frustrated and disillusioned, the child becomes a discipline problem. Often he leaves school, sometimes before the end of junior high school…He slips into the ranks of the permanent jobless, illiterate and untrained, unemployed and unemployable. All the talk about the millions which the government is spending to aid him raise his expectations but the benefits seldom reach him.[22]

That language was eloquent, correct—and oddly unhelpful. What could Los Angeles or even California do in the face of such crushing and endemic problems? The McCone report was widely admired, but very little of what it proposed lent itself to action. It went the way of many such documents, destined for a shelf. In this case, however, it would find new life in the hands of its vice chairman, Warren Christopher, when he had the opportunity decades later to examine the Los Angeles Police Department. Then, as they did not in 1965, his recommendations would have a profound and lasting impact.

The violence that gripped Los Angeles in August of 1965 was baffling and far-reaching—and part of a larger discontent that expressed itself across American life. Though dwarfed by what was to come, crime rates began a steady upward march in the decade, giving liberals a chance to point to the effects of poverty, racism, and alienation even as conservatives lamented the shredding of family values and traditional mores. Crime would become a consuming issue in American politics by the end of the decade, when Richard Nixon would win the presidency based in large measure on his promise to reestablish civil order.

Violence on campus, in the streets, and even in the ballpark. With Los Angeles still smoldering from the Watts riots, the Giants and Dodgers met for a tense series in San Francisco. The biggest crowd of the season, 42,807 fans, gathered for the August 22 meeting of the two rivals, by then well ensconced in their lives as California teams. Each club fielded its ace for the Sunday afternoon game: Sandy Koufax took the mound for Los Angeles, Juan Marichal for San Francisco.

There was already rancor between the two teams. The Dodgers had taken two of the first three games that weekend, both tense extra-inning contests bracketed around one easy Giants victory. With the clubs locked in competition for the title, both teams also played rough: pitchers brushed back batters and defended their own players from such insults. Marichal was vocal in his criticism of the Dodgers, whose catcher, John Roseboro, vigorously defended his teammates.

That was the state of affairs when Marichal came up to bat in the third inning. Koufax, who wielded one of baseball's most intimidating fastballs but was reluctant to throw it at opposing players, pitched his rival closely but fairly. Roseboro, frustrated that Koufax would not deliver a message, took it upon himself to do so. He threw back to the mound very close to Marichal's ear, ticking it, according to Marichal. Then, in what the *New York Times* described as "a burst of uncontrollable temper," Marichal wheeled on Roseboro and clubbed him on the head with his bat.[23] No words were exchanged, merely fury. Roseboro was hit at least twice, and one of the blows opened up a two-inch gash in his head. Benches emptied over this astonishing display of baseball violence: fistfights happen, but beatings with a bat do not. Eventually, the two sides were pried apart by peacemakers—Willie Mays played an instrumental role in restoring calm—but only after a shocking eruption of rage that seemed all too appropriate in a period so racked by confusion and riven by violence.

The protests of the early 1960s were only a warm-up to the Vietnam disturbances of the late 1960s and the 1970s. But even these early flare-ups left Pat Brown and his fellow Democrats baffled and frustrated. They believed in progress and sought it, but every advance seemed to invite more frustration. Civil rights led to progress but also to impatience. Victories on the ground in Vietnam did little to discourage the enemy and only seemed to deepen questions at home about the conflict.

And so, as the 1960s turned from protest to violent conflict, California's politics missed a chance at inclusion and instead calcified. Brown was the governor who coddled students at Berkeley and allowed riots in Los Angeles. The Right grew first alarmed and then rigid: conservatives would stand in defense of a social and political order even as it careened away from them. The fiscal Right railed about taxes and government interference; the religious Right called for government interference to block society's embrace of abortion and drugs and sexual freedom. The Center-Left, which Pat Brown personified, was breaking into factions: New Deal Democrats soon would find themselves cobbled together with more radical elements—an unstable coalition, as time soon proved.

The Democratic Party's tent stretched to its limits and then beyond. Organized labor, civil rights demonstrators, feminists, and antiwar activists would soon find themselves immersed in their micropolitics, sometimes overlapping, sometimes oblivious to one another, and sometimes fighting each other for the leadership of the Left. Tom Hayden had no more in common with Richard Daley, who arrested him, than with Ronald Reagan, who mocked him. The coalition of the Left confronted the Right with a unified commitment to change, only to fracture over what that change should look like.

The center collapsed.

# 5

# California Culture, Circa 1965

*She and his father would never seem to get it through their heads that things were changing in Sacramento.*

—Joan Didion, *Run River*

*Run River* was published in 1963—a year before Berkeley, two before Watts. Didion wrote it in New York in a "raw" yearning for her native California—Sacramento, with its levees and ranchers, its winter floods and summer heat. "I sat on one of my apartment's two chairs...and wrote myself a California river," she reflected many years later.[1] From that chair, Didion wrote herself into the history of her place and re-created the lost art of writing about and above one's youth. It marked Didion as a significant new literary presence, one rooted squarely in California.

No author since Frank Norris had more forcefully channeled the currents of the American West, and none had done so with such a deliberate voice. Joan Didion gave California a position: serious, sober, and curious at a time when much of the country thought of it as anything but those. She wrote about California, but more important, she wrote as one who knew California. She and her neighbors killed rattlesnakes as a favor to one another. She puzzled over gangs and uncertainty, waded skeptically through the currents that swept up others. She thought with care and intelligence and would come, much later, to examine her own life and family with the same heartbreakingly clear eyes that defined her body of work. Through Didion, California connected Ronald Reagan and the Donner Party, the Grateful Dead and El Salvador. Didion, who visited the California governor's mansion as a young girl in the era of Earl Warren, would become, in due course, a chronicler and friend of Jerry Brown.

More than just announcing a new literary talent, *Run River* encouraged a writers' movement, creating a more self-consciously California literature on a more abstract foundation. The Beats already had established a beachhead in San Francisco, where, in the early 1960s, poet Gary Snyder built upon the ideas of his predecessors and brought a deeper immersion in Japanese literature and Zen to his simple and moving verse. Snyder's work, which would affect Brown deeply, bridged the Beats and an avant garde period that came to be known as the San Francisco Renaissance.

Meanwhile, a few miles south, Wallace Stegner, a great writer of the American West, gathered some of the talents of a generation around him at Stanford University. Ken Kesey, whose *One Flew over the Cuckoo's Nest* introduced him to the world in 1962, was part of that band, though he would eventually grow estranged from Stegner. For Stegner, California was "the edge of the continent, and he thought you were supposed to stop there," Kesey remembered. "I was younger than he was and didn't see any reason to stop, so I kept moving forward."[2] Kesey was part of an extraordinary class of writers that year at Stanford, including Wendell Berry, Ken Babbs, Larry McMurtry, Ed McClanahan (a.k.a. Captain Kentucky), Gurney Norman, and Robert Stone.[3] Together, they put down a literature of fields and wars, drugs, liberation and reflection, fiction and nonfiction, New Journalism and inventive flights.

The visual arts exploded, too. Andy Warhol launched his career in Los Angeles in 1962 with an exhibition at the fabled Ferus Gallery. Irving Blum, director of the gallery, sold five of Warhol's thirty-two paintings (Campbell's sold thirty-two flavors of soup) individually before realizing that their power emanated from being displayed together. He managed to reclaim the sold works, including one from actor Dennis Hopper, and eventually donated them to the Museum of Modern Art in New York.[4] Their appearance at Ferus meant more than just the emergence of a new talent: it signaled a shift away from abstract expressionism—Barnett Newman, Mark Rothko, Franz Kline, Philip Guston, Willem de Kooning, and Clyfford Still all showed at Ferus—and toward something new, more playful and interactive, more drawn from streetscapes than from landscapes, more a conversation than a speech. At first, critics called it commonism. "Happily that didn't stick," Blum recalled.[5] Later, it became known as pop art. That one stuck.

Warhol was a New Yorker, notwithstanding his California show, but the Ferus Gallery was just one hub of a growing California presence in the visual arts. Richard Diebenkorn, a native of Oregon but a Californian since the age of two, made a breakthrough in 1964 after a trip to the Soviet Union exposed him to the great works of the Hermitage.[6] Diebenkorn, who relocated from Berkeley to Los Angeles in 1966, began his dreamy, arresting Ocean Park series that year. Influenced by Matisse, the Ocean Park paintings were magical, impossible to process without a skip of the heart. Though he defied cultural trends—Diebenkorn moved from figuration to abstraction just as Warhol and the pop artists were headed in the other direction—his influence spread wide, in part through his work and in part through his position as a teacher at UCLA.[7] The *New York Times* described the series as "one of the most majestic pictorial achievements of the second half of this century, in this country or anywhere else."[8] And *Time* magazine proclaimed that Diebenkorn had joined the grown-up table of artists: a retrospective of his work proved that Dienbenkorn was not, "as the condescending tag once read, a California artist, but a world figure."[9]

Talent took note. John Baldessari and Ed Ruscha stood out, their works demanding attention from critics accustomed to looking to New York and inclined, as *Time* noted, to label artists from California as something less than those from New York or Paris. The Ferus Gallery provided a center. As the *Guardian* wrote: "Ferus was founded in 1958, preaching a gospel that had tenets in common with pop art and the

Fluxus movements in New York, and reacting in its own diverse ways to the long shadow of abstract expressionism. [The curator Walter] Hopps quit Ferus in 1962 to run the Pasadena Art Museum, where he curated landmark shows by Marcel Duchamp (1963) and Man Ray (1966), both of which profoundly influenced the Ferus group."[10]

Given California's vast spaces and outdoor orientation, it seemed natural that architecture would flourish, and it did. In midcentury, Southern California was known for residential innovation, while the northern part of the state was more distinguished by public works, a distinction that would grow less pronounced over time. Frank Lloyd Wright made a mark in Los Angeles with his Hollyhock House in 1921 and his sublime La Miniatura, in Pasadena, two years later. But his greatest impact was realized by those influenced by his work.

In the 1960s, Richard Neutra pulled the leading oar of modernism in residential architecture, propelled in part by his inclusion in an influential MoMA exhibition in 1932. His work, along with that of Charles Eames and Pierre Koenig, among others, was sponsored by *Arts & Architecture* magazine, which, over the course of two decades, made possible the construction of the Case Study Houses, concentrated in Los Angeles though with a few in San Diego, one in Phoenix, and one in Northern California.[11] The case study houses persist in the modern imagination in part because one of them was captured by the work of another brilliant artist, photographer Julius Shulman. In Shulman's photograph, two women are seated in the glassed-in corner of a Pierre Koenig case-study home, jutting out beyond a ridgeline, the lights of Los Angeles outside and below.[12]

That one image conveyed precariousness and playfulness, the edge of a continent and the beginning of something new. Few photographs have communicated modern Los Angeles more fully or concisely.[13]

In San Francisco, meanwhile, the standard for public architecture was set—and never matched—by completion of the Golden Gate Bridge, in 1937. It was a mark so defining that it became synonymous with San Francisco's entire persona—its orientation to the west, its welcoming of the new and the foreign.

Nothing would surpass the bridge, but many greats succeeded it.

Having built homes in Los Angeles, Frank Lloyd Wright made a memorable impression in the hills north of San Francisco, where his Marin County Civic Center displayed his brilliance for horizontal lines and landscapes. The architectural firm founded by William Pereira, builders of the Theme Building at Los Angeles International Airport as well as that city's Times Mirror headquarters, countered by exploring San Francisco's vertical potential, a source of nerves ever since the 1906 earthquake leveled the city. Emboldened by advances in earthquake engineering, the firm's architects designed and built the world's largest pyramid, home of Transamerica, begun in 1969 and completed in 1972.

The California 1960s-era project with the most profound cultural and political impact was, by contrast, almost hidden from public view, a collection of private and public structures built along the coast north of the city. The Sea Ranch, designed by Charles Moore, Donlyn Lyndon, William Turnbull, and Richard Whitaker as the firm of MLTW, along with a small army of consultants and land-use advisers, was tastefully dramatic, hugging the cliff lines of the Northern California shore. It was intended to melt into natural hedgerows that dotted the coastal plain, leaving stretches of grass and timber unmolested.[14] In those ambitions—to "live lightly on the land," as one early designer insisted, borrowing language from the area's native settlers[15]—the Sea Ranch reflected California's emerging environmental sensibilities and offered a community uniquely harmonized with its surroundings. At the same time, the Sea Ranch sparked debate about access to the coastline, about whether developers and owners had some special right to California's beaches. The Sea Ranch managed to be both a masterpiece of community design and a warning about environmental encroachment. It helped propel adoption of the California Coastal Plan, completed under then governor Jerry Brown in the 1970s. And it would require the intervention of the California legislature to sort out the project's responsibilities for providing coastal access.

In music, the Beach Boys moved from local band to national phenomenon, supplying a sound track for surfing (in 2018, surfing would become California's official sport, for what that's worth). Raised in Hawthorne, California, and battle-readied by an abusive father, Brian,

Carl, and Dennis Wilson, along with a cousin and friend, produced a musical style that was distinctly Southern California—soft harmonies and light themes, including their 1962 phenom album, *Surfin' Safari*. Never mind that the Beach Boys weren't really surfers; they tapped a yearning for warm sand and girls in bikinis.

In 1965, the Grateful Dead, initially known as the Warlocks, performed their first concerts as a jug band before sliding into a trippier groove and landing a spot at Kesey's Acid Tests in La Honda, a tiny hamlet in the hills above Palo Alto, where Jerry Garcia gave guitar lessons at a music store on California Avenue. One of his students, a lost teenager named Bob Weir, went on to become the Dead's lead singer and rhythm guitarist. Like Didion and Kesey, Warhol and Diebenkorn, the Dead would lead a hearty band of followers and imitators, in their case anchoring a San Francisco music scene that would host the Summer of Love in 1967.

California's interior, often a trailer in cultural innovation, made its contribution to the music scene as well. North and east of Los Angeles, along the eastern edge of the Central Valley, Alvis Edgar "Buck" Owens held down a regular gig at the Blackboard, a honky-tonk bar that became the hub of the "Bakersfield sound" in country music. Starting in 1963, Owens wrote and performed Number 1 country hits for six years in a row, with some of his signature numbers covered by bands more popular on the coast, from The Beatles to the Grateful Dead. As in literature and other arts, success bred success; Owens would continue to record in and from Bakersfield for decades, joined there in 1960 by Merle Haggard when Haggard was paroled from San Quentin prison, and much later by Dwight Yoakam, a Kentucky native drawn to California by the Bakersfield sound, which he modernized in the 1980s and rechristened the "Bakersfield beat."

Led by those artists and writers, California's counterculture snowballed, and the nation's cultural center of gravity shifted west, tracking the movement of politics and baseball. By 1965, Los Angeles rivaled New York in the visual arts, attracting and developing talented painters and experimental artists who longed for its freedom and the quality of its air, the soft light of Venice near the beach and the filtered hills above Hollywood. And San Francisco, led by the Dead, was on its way to becoming the center of the country's music and drug culture. The Haight, just a short walk from where Jerry Brown grew up, would soon shed its quiet, middle-class sensibility in favor of becoming a wellspring of hippies, free concerts, and LSD.

Ah, LSD. In Jerry Brown's youth, marijuana was California's edgy drug of choice. It was bad enough—an "evil weed" thought to provoke insane reactions in those who smoked it. LSD was another step altogether: mind-altering, subversive, and outright weird. Users lost all touch with normalcy, flung themselves into music and color, drifted away from reality itself. The sight of young men and women on acid, distracted by hallucinations, dopey with euphoria or lost to reverie, frightened those outside its orbit.

LSD first began showing up in the Bay Area in the early 1960s, introduced by nothing less than a CIA-funded project known as MKULTRA, intended to test the effectiveness of hallucinogens as truth serums by giving them to subjects at a Menlo Park veterans' hospital. Kesey volunteered to be a subject of the experiments, which allowed interrogators to squeeze out secrets from subjects under LSD's hallucinogenic influence—a spooky merger of Cold War and drug culture. For Kesey, one result was the central figure of *Cuckoo's Nest*. According to Kesey, the inspiration for the book's elusive and arresting narrator, an American Indian named Chief Broom, came to him while on peyote. Though Kesey rarely wrote while on drugs, they supplied ample inspiration, and he happily spread the word. As he recalled:

The first and best [LSD] I ever got came to me by the very reliable way of the Federal Government. They gave me mine—paid me and quite a few other rats both white and black $20 a session in fact to test it for them, *started it* so to speak, then, when they caught a glimpse of what was coming down in that little room full of guinea pigs, they switched the guinea pigs out, slammed the door, locked it, barred it, dug a ditch around it, set two guards in front of it, and gave the hapless pigs a good talking to and warned them—on a threat of worse than death—to *never* go in that door again—and if you still think they should give you yours after careful examination of the rot-minded, chromosome damaged results of these little experiments begun ten years ago, then I think you should demand they either give you yours or award all those poor guinea pigs the Purple Heart.[16]

No one ever accused Kesey of brevity.

Kesey volunteered at the hospital where the hallucinogen experiments were performed, and that gave him access to a set of keys he used to open the doctor's office and lift acid after hours, sharing it with chemistry-minded friends. Thanks to them, acid began leaking into the counterculture. It took a while for the authorities to catch on, and by then, LSD was solidly a part of hippie consciousness, from Timothy Leary's studied explorations to San Francisco's rowdier adoption of the drug. On November 27, 1965, Kesey hosted the first Acid Test. Held at his La Honda property, it was a rambling concert and group trip. Attendees dropped acid, played with Day-Glo, and grooved to the Grateful Dead and unorganized sounds of the Merry Pranksters, a band of hippies gathered around Kesey.

The question of the hour became, Can you pass the Acid Test? Thousands tried. Acid found adherents across the cultural landscape— in the teachings of Leary, the massive visions of Richard Serra, the poetry of Allen Ginsberg, the syncopation of Charles Mingus. And acid would prove remarkably persistent, inflecting the visions of such diverse talents as Chance the Rapper, RuPaul, and Steve Jobs, among others.[17]

To those who imagined themselves holding fast to a social order, LSD seemed to be loosening society's grip. On the night of March 25, 1966, at a dance at UC Berkeley's Harmon Gym, those two factions got a whiff of each other and realized how far they'd grown apart. It was a Friday evening, and the event was billed as a Peace Trip, part of the Vietnam Day Committee's effort to raise money and consciousness about the war. This event featured the Jefferson Airplane and boasted "psychedelic lights" among its many attractions.

This was not what straight America had in mind for its children. Couples were writhing—some having sex, others staggering about under the influence of LSD. The room stank of sweat and vomit. "There was a strong sweet, sickening odor which I immediately detected as marijuana," one officer reported. Colored lights provided a backdrop, and several bands played at once. This debacle, a subcommittee of HUAC concluded, was the logical conclusion of a permissive university administration and a society that fostered "an anything-goes atmosphere."[18]

Many Californians agreed, and one pointedly posed the question on many minds: "How could this happen on the campus of a great university?" The man asking that question was Ronald Reagan.

# Part Two

## Into Politics

# 6

# Whipsaw: The Reagan Years

From the time that Jerry Brown emerged from the seminary to the moment he became governor, only two men held that office. One, of course, was Brown's father, who shaped his son in ways direct and indirect, by setting examples to follow and others to rebel against. The other was Ronald Reagan, and his tenure presented Jerry Brown with far different lessons—of media and politics, pragmatism and principle. Jerry Brown naturally spent his life in comparison to his father—it impossible to consider either's service without reference to the other. Oddly, however, Brown's governance in some ways more resembled that of a man he barely knew and with whom he had little in common personally or philosophically. For Reagan, though remembered today mostly as a lion of the national conservative movement, was in fact a moderate California governor—one who raised taxes, supported abortion rights, and led a consequential campaign for gun control.

Jerry Brown spoke a different language from Reagan's—more spiritual, grander, sometimes goofier. He was not exactly Reagan's heir, but to a surprising degree, they governed from a similar place—practical and moderate rather than ideologically rigid. And both men were ever conscious of the television camera.

Ronald Reagan made his fame in Hollywood—first as an actor and later as a spokesman for General Electric. He was married, twice, in California, and raised his children there. He rose to prominence in Hollywood's Screen Actors Guild and secretly worked with the FBI to root out subversives in his chosen industry and his adopted state.

And yet Reagan was not a Californian. Like so many who found themselves in the sprawl and dynamism of California, he arrived from elsewhere, looking to make or find himself. Reagan was born during a blizzard in Tampico, Illinois, on February 6, 1911, the second son of Nelle and Jack Reagan. He grew up here and there, his father an alcoholic who moved about, his mother the object of his worship. His most formative memory was his work as a lifeguard, where he achieved small-town renown for fetching flailing swimmers from the Rock River. He attended Eureka College, where he was a student activist galvanized by an administration plan to cut courses and faculty. In 1937, he arrived in Hollywood.[1]

Reagan's time as an actor made him famous, and his tenure with the Screen Actors Guild and General Electric hardened his politics. Once a self-described New Deal liberal, Reagan drifted rightward through the 1950s. In his role with GE, he traveled extensively, honing a motivational speech that he seemed to absorb as he refined. He believed in the power of individualism. He opposed Medicare, denounced the United Nations and foreign aid, bemoaned America's weakness in the face of communism. He was smart and funny, irresistible. By 1964, his journey was sufficiently complete to inform his delivery of the speech "A Time for Choosing" to the GOP convention in San Francisco in support of candidate Barry Goldwater. Decrying "a little intellectual elite" in Washington that was dragging humanity toward the "ant heap of totalitarianism," Reagan warned: "Regardless of their sincerity, their humanitarian motives, those who would trade our freedom for security have embarked on this downward course."[2] And what a course it was. "You and I have a rendezvous with destiny. We'll preserve for our children this, the last, best hope for man on earth, or we'll sentence them to take the last step into a thousand years of darkness."[3]

Reagan's speech—and Goldwater's nomination—marked a reckoning for the Republican Party. It had defeated the voices of moderation, the

Eisenhowers and Rockefellers, even the Nixons. The GOP was purified, degreased of compromise. And it was now prepared to do battle with the Democrats, with their statism and pink communism, their treacly feints to the poor. The "time for choosing" had arrived.

Lyndon Johnson decimated Goldwater in November, one of the most thorough lambastings in American political history. Johnson won more than 60 percent of the popular vote and carried every state outside the Deep South and Arizona, Goldwater's home. It was more than a defeat—it was a humiliation, a stark and convincing repudiation of the ideas that Goldwater and Reagan advocated. And yet America's children survived their sentence to a thousand years of darkness, and Reagan persevered as a voice in the wilderness. He was emboldened by his own words, dandified as the spokesman of a righteous cause, albeit one that few Americans had signed up for. Easy on the eye and ear, favored by the camera, he now had substance, too. A new future suggested itself: politics.

But how to begin?

As 1964 ended, there seemed no obvious route to the presidency. Johnson occupied it, and Reagan's forces had been wiped from the field. But Reagan was, at least for a time, a Californian, and California's politics were in flux. Governor Brown had fumbled the 1960 Democratic convention, to the irritation of the Kennedy and Johnson forces; the Chessman case hung over him. Drugs and counterculture swamped old-style liberalism and left Brown unsettled. Liberals were unfulfilled by Pat Brown. Conservatives were downright furious with him.

Reagan initially was not sold on the idea of challenging Brown. Legend has it that Reagan's campaign was hatched by two Goldwater supporters, Walter Knott (of Knott's Berry Farm) and John Gromala, who were searching for a candidate to carry the fight forward. "The idea hit us each about the same time," one recalled. "Why doesn't [Reagan] run for governor?"[4] Lou Cannon, the great Reagan chronicler, shrewdly sized up Reagan's strategic ambivalence: determined not to be a politician yet drawn to the office and ultimately eager to be part of history's stream. Once he decided, however, he committed body and soul. "Now I have come to a decision that even a short time ago I would have thought impossible for me to make, and yet I make it with no lingering doubts or hesitation," Reagan, speaking to a television camera, said on January 4, 1966.

Underestimating Reagan started early. On the same day that Reagan announced, Pat Brown dismissed him as "untried in politics," and George Christopher, Reagan's likely competitor for the Republican nomination, argued that voters wanted someone with "proven ability." Christopher, himself a former actor but one whose résumé was bolstered by a well-regarded run as mayor of San Francisco, offered the conventional wisdom of the moment, wisdom shared by Brown, that if Reagan were to win the nomination, Brown would "decisively beat" him.[5] A few weeks later, the *San Francisco Chronicle* summed up the reaction of the state's elites: Reagan's "performance" as a citizen-politician, the paper sneered, was "not his fault. It was simply a flagrant example of mis-casting."[6]

Reagan was easy to underestimate and difficult to pigeonhole. In 1966, he was the natural standard-bearer for California's surly right wing—its cranky defenders of a crusty culture, united by anticommunism and uncomfortably allied with the John Birch Society and its tentacles. And it's certainly true that Reagan had his bona fides with the right: he paid his dues for Goldwater, wowed crowds with "A Time for Choosing," and even went lightly on the Birchers: "In voting for me, a voter buys my philosophy," he noted in his announcement address. "I don't buy his."[7]

But Reagan was always a bit sunny for the right—more impish Irishman than glowering evangelist. And his later deification as an untarnished conservative papers over some of the subtleties of Reagan as California candidate and governor. As he set out to win his first political office, his tone was softer than many would remember, less angry and more wistful. "A great society must be a free society," he said, "and to be truly great and really free, it must be a creative society calling on the genius and power of its people."[8]

And so Reagan and Brown squared off, Brown foolishly welcoming the opportunity to take on the man he believed to be the weaker of his foes, playing defense to Reagan's offense. Reagan in 1966 was new and loose, handsome and cheerful. Brown sagged from the weight of eight years in office and was a bit flummoxed by an opponent who understood the election cycle's new technologies—sophisticated voter analysis and, especially, television—far better than he did. Those issues might not have been enough to sink Brown, but a "fratricidal primary fight" with conservative Los Angeles mayor Sam Yorty and an "ineptly managed campaign" dug Brown's hole even deeper.[9] He later confessed to feeling wearied by the whole affair.[10] He won the Democratic primary, but garnered just 52 percent of the vote, a sure sign of weakness.

Reagan, meanwhile, started strong and built momentum. He passed and pulled away from Christopher, winning the Republican primary with nearly two-thirds of the votes cast, and he beat the former San Francisco mayor in all but four of California's fifty-eight counties. Where Brown limped out of the primaries, Reagan emerged stronger and more credible.

Reagan was not a perfect candidate. During the race against Brown, he struggled to explain his position on racial covenants in housing, especially after it was discovered that he had once sold a home with such a restriction, and he exaggerated the extent of unemployment in California, telling an audience that 15.1 percent of state residents were on welfare when the real number was 5.1 percent.[11] Reagan's campaign managers spotted the danger: for any candidate, explaining is losing, but for one whose experience and even intelligence were at issue, miscues took on even graver significance. The campaign withdrew to Malibu for three days to brief Reagan. Reflecting both his skill as an actor—including a willingness to take direction—and his underappreciated intelligence, he absorbed the material and returned to the campaign with renewed confidence and energy.

There were no more significant mishaps, though Brown continued to hammer, even mock, Reagan in the campaign's final weeks. "What has Ronald Reagan ever done for the state of California in his entire life," Brown asked at a candidate forum a week before Election Day, "other than make a motion picture—*Bedtime for Bonzo* or *Ladies on Probation* or *The Last Stand of Custer*?"[12] One particularly ill-advised ad featured Brown reminding a group of students that John Wilkes Booth killed Lincoln. And Booth, he added archly, was an actor. It was terrible politics.

By contrast, Reagan continued to build his arsenal. Reagan was good at listening. He learned from audiences and noticed that whenever he mentioned the student protests at Berkeley, it got a rise from the crowd. He began to talk about it more and forced Brown into the uncomfortable position of defending protesters he did not really support. As the Free Speech Movement turned darker, Reagan denounced "filthy speech" and was rewarded for it by voters.

Near the end, ABC News described the race as a duel between "the actor and the old pro," a contest Reagan won handily[13] by a margin of nearly one million votes out of 6.5 million cast. Brown carried only three counties, including his native San Francisco County and Alameda County, across the bay.

Reagan's governorship was both entirely as promised and utterly unexpected. He cut some social services—notably, California's system for treating the mentally ill—in keeping with his promise to limit the growth of government. That proposal, over which Reagan equivocated, had enduring effects on the future of California health care, little anticipated at the time and still felt today. The shocking rise of homelessness in California is at least in part a consequence of Reagan's actions in the 1960s and Brown's unwillingness to reverse them in the 1970s.

And yet Reagan also was capable of surprise and of surprisingly nimble adjustment to changing circumstances—attributes that Jerry Brown would come to appreciate and emulate. Nowhere was that more evident than in his recognition that he could not effectively govern without a substantial tax increase. The political risks of such an increase were extreme—Reagan had campaigned on the promise to reduce taxes, not increase them—but the new governor's pragmatic side triumphed over his conservatism. In that effort, he had the surprising support of the legislature's most powerful figure, Democrat and dealmaker Jesse "Big Daddy" Unruh. Unruh wanted higher taxes for the services the state could provide and also welcomed an opportunity to ding the new governor. Moreover, both Reagan and Unruh saw the benefits of a property tax decrease, which a hike in other taxes—income taxes, sin taxes, and levies on financial institutions, among others—could help pay for. And so Reagan, the suave Republican in the corner office, bargained with the ball-busting Unruh, and they agreed to bring forward the largest tax increase ever proposed by an American governor.

Reagan fought on one curious point: he maintained a loathing of tax withholding, the process by which the government siphons off small amounts of money every paycheck rather than collecting it all at once. But he understood that minimizing the personal impact of taxes also minimized opposition to them. Unruh understood that, too, and he ultimately prevailed.[14]

Nor were taxes Reagan's only departure from orthodoxy. In one case, the confounding twists of racism and radical politics turned Reagan into a leading advocate of gun control. The tale speaks volumes of the period.

The largest armed insurrection ever waged against the United States government was that of the Confederacy, which rose in treason and in defense of slavery (shrouded in the veil of states' rights). The resulting war devastated both sides but left a united nation, one that would thenceforth refer to itself as a singular United States rather than a plural collection of entities.

By some measures, the second-largest armed rebellion against that American government was waged by the Black Panther Party, along with its allies and affiliates. Born in Oakland, California, in 1966, the Black Panther Party for Self-Defense arose in opposition to the Oakland Police Department and widespread allegations of abusive, racist policing by its officers. The Panthers were led by the charismatic and fearsome combination of Bobby Seale (chairman) and Huey Newton (minister of defense). They soon adopted the provocative tactic of arming members and shadowing on-duty police. The Panthers, originally six members and then many more, published Chairman Mao's "little red book" and used the money to invest in guns. They were, as Seale said of his friend Newton, "ready to organize the black brothers for a righteous revolutionary struggle with guns and force."[15] The gun, according to Panther ideology, "is the only thing the pigs will understand."[16]

Their brazen willingness to take the fight to the police grew out of an inspired piece of legal research by Newton, who discovered that California law permitted the brandishing of a firearm so long as it was not concealed. The Panthers were not the sort to conceal anything, so as they patrolled the police, they displayed their guns on their hips. They were looking for a confrontation, and they got one on the streets of Oakland in 1967, when police spotted a group of armed black men and suspected the worst. The two sides squared off, shouting at each other. Newton would not back down, demanding that an officer recognize his right to carry a gun in public. Seale said later that he was convinced in that moment that Newton was the "baddest motherfucker in the world."[17]

The Panthers' show of force rattled California politics and scrambled its allegiances. Suddenly, conservative supporters of gun rights were confronted with those rights being exercised against their friends and allies. Gun rights looked great when wielded by white men in suburbs: they were a little less appealing in the hands of a defiant Huey Newton.

So the legislature descended to ts basest instincts. It took up a bill, introduced by a Republican assemblyman from Oakland, Don Mulford (whose legislation would thus be known later as the Mulford Act), that would make it illegal in California to carry a loaded firearm in public. Debate was set for Tuesday, May 2, 1967.

As the legislators prepared to discuss the bill, there was a commotion outside the building. Twenty-six Black Panthers, all of them armed, strode onto the grounds of the capitol to pronounce their opposition to the proposal. Seale read a statement calling "on the American people in general and the black people in particular to take careful note of the racist California legislature."[18] He then turned to his comrades and said, "All right, brothers, come on," then headed inside for the state assembly room, though the group was briefly sidetracked by the fact that none of the Panthers knew where the chambers were. Finding them, the Panthers entered calmly, weapons loaded and held high, followed by a scramble of camera crews.

Rarely in history has the assembly's green chamber—the "color of money," one wag once observed—come to a more startled halt. Legislators were confronted with "a band of armed Negroes," as the *Los Angeles Times* put it, and responded in outrage and fear.[19] The Panthers were hauled away as security frantically tried to determine the safety of the governor. As it happened, Reagan had been scheduled to enjoy a fried-chicken lunch with a group of schoolchildren on the capitol lawn that morning, but a last-minute change in plans caused him to miss the spectacle of armed protesters barging their way into the rooms outside his office. Lyn Nofziger, the governor's able press deputy, shuddered at the thought of a confrontation between his boss and the Black Panthers; it was averted only by luck. Once police had the Panthers in custody, they searched for a reason to arrest them, but the offending Panthers had broken no law. Eventually, they were released and their weapons were returned to them.

The assembly, still shaken from its brush with the Panthers, narrowly passed Mulford's bill. The senate split evenly, but that was enough to get it to Reagan's desk. He signed it into law on July 28. In giving his approval, Reagan noted that he saw "no reason why on the street today a citizen should be carrying loaded weapons."[20]

At the same time that the Mulford bill worked its way through the legislature, elected leaders took up another piece of legislation that would challenge Reagan and, in later years, puzzle his conservative acolytes. In this case, the issue was abortion.

Reagan was never a hard-liner on abortion. His conservatism was not religious, and his personal life did not radiate old-school rectitude—he was the first divorced man to become president, and Nancy Reagan was pregnant when the two were married. He came of age in Hollywood, where abortions were the source of endless gossip and tabloid coverage but were not the subject of intense moral opprobrium. Still, Reagan's supporters included many with pitched views on the subject, and they assumed that his allegiance with them on other issues implied agreement on abortion as well.

That notion was tested in the spring of 1967, when the legislature, following the lead of Colorado and North Carolina, considered liberalizing its abortion rules. Up to that point, abortion was legal in California only in cases where it might save the life of the mother. Under a bill proposed by state senator Anthony Beilenson, it would be permitted in those cases and in cases where the mother was the victim of either forcible or statutory rape as well as instances in which the pregnancy might "gravely impair" the mother's mental or physical health. By the standards of abortion law in the days before the Supreme Court decided *Roe v. Wade,* in 1973, that language was enough to put California among the most permissive states in the union.

Reagan didn't like it. He debated the measure up until the final day. At the signing ceremony, he opened by saying, "I've changed my mind," and put down his pen. Reporters were briefly taken aback, then realized the governor was joking.[21] Reagan complained that the bill might make California a destination for women seeking abortions, and he confessed to worrying that the legislation was "full of loopholes." Nevertheless, with the pen back in hand, he signed. Supporters were relieved. "I'm glad it's all over," one said.

In two pivotal months of 1967, then, Ronald Reagan, who would become the guiding symbol of Republican conservatism, made it easier in California to get an abortion and harder to brandish a weapon. He was, in the end, more pragmatic than ideological, at least as governor.

As if drawn to the flame of Reagan, young people found their way to California in 1967, some to do battle with the combative governor, others merely to goad him by being there. "It was the largest migration of young people in the history of America," one documentary announced, a claim as intriguing as it is unprovable.[22] What is beyond dispute is that in the spring of 1967, hippies, as they were called, trooped into San Francisco, sometimes happily, sometimes dopily. Many could not even say for sure why they came, just that they felt the need to be there.

There was no organizer of the Summer of Love. It was, in a sense difficult to appreciate today, spontaneous, the outgrowth not so much of intention as of devotion. People drawn to the counterculture—centered in San Francisco's Golden Gate Park, with Haight and Ashbury Streets at one end, and radiating outward—experienced the mid-1960s as a time of discovery, of reconsidering established values. And of drugs. Notably, LSD.

It was a messy period of imagination, much of it grounded in music. Jefferson Airplane, Quicksilver Messenger Service, the Lovin' Spoonful,

Big Brother and the Holding Company (featuring Janis Joplin), the Charlatans, the Paul Butterfield Blues Band, and Santana were among the musical acts that came from or to San Francisco in that effervescent period. Joan Baez straddled folk music and politics. The Grateful Dead hosted the whole affair, and Jerry Garcia played the reluctant hippie king. The Beatles gave their final scheduled public performance at Candlestick Park in 1966. Los Angeles was home to important music and musicians—the Byrds were one leading act, and the Doors would soon follow, with the community of artists based in and around Laurel Canyon following soon after that—but San Francisco was music's first California mecca. It was teeming with music and drugs, each fueling the other. "We're all people that knew each other," one musician from those days recalled. "We all bought dope from the same guys."[23]

Beginning in early 1967, young people began arriving in San Francisco. Some of it was politics. The Vietnam War was inflicting its damage on American culture, exacerbating deep distrust of the government and institutions. Some was music: the Monterey Pop Festival was held from June 16 to June 18, and many of those who attended drove up to San Francisco at the conclusion to the keep the music going. Some of it was drugs. Not until October 6, 1966, was LSD made illegal in California—the Dead marked the occasion by dropping acid—and that served more to criminalize youth than to eliminate the drug. In a larger sense, however, the appeal of the counterculture and San Francisco, of hippies and flowers and antiwar demonstrations, was that they suggested a different way of living—a more communal, natural, and positive deployment of human energy. As the Summer of Love played out in sunny San Francisco, young men and women arrived in search of something different and better. For a time, they had it.

Eventually, the crush of young people overwhelmed that promise. The city's jails filled; clinics strained to keep pace with overdoses. Desperate mothers and fathers pleaded with their children to come home, and many did, though some followed Timothy Leary's famous advice to "turn on, tune in, and drop out."[24] Even the Dead decamped for Marin County, north of the city.

The Summer of Love did not change American life, at least not permanently, certainly not in the way that Reagan would. But for a brief few months in the summer of 1967, the polarized wings of American life squared off in San Francisco: hippies and cops, Reagan and Garcia, drugs and the defenders of a groaning social order. It wasn't Goldwater's vision of a "time for choosing," but it was one of taking sides. One who didn't was Jerry Brown.

# 7

# Up the Ladder

Jerry Brown skipped the Summer of Love. Too young, too skeptical, too liberal to join up with Reagan's team, too old, too straight and too Catholic to enjoy the counterculture, he was outside the poles staked out in 1967 California. Brown was a newly minted lawyer looking to make a name for himself, invariably dressed in a jacket and tie, the furthest thing from a hippie though just as many miles away from an establishment conservative. And so while his contemporaries, at least those a shade younger, drifted from Monterey to the Haight, Brown wrestled with a far more establishment challenge: how to make his way into the arena of politics. His first steps were opportunistic and guided principally by his ambition.

Having completed his clerkship with Justice Tobriner, Brown's first decision was where to work. He chose Tuttle and Taylor, a boutique Los Angeles law firm, for several reasons. It was a prestigious and exciting firm, new and challenging to the city's established institutions. It would give Brown a foothold in a part of the state with which he was unfamiliar. And it would immerse him in the company of distinguished colleagues, including the firm's litigation partner, Bill Norris, a Southern California kingmaker and later a judge on the United States Court of Appeals for the Ninth Circuit. Norris would become one of two senior lawyers, both loyal to Pat Brown, who helped guide Jerry Brown through his political ascent. The other was Stephen Reinhardt, then a Los Angeles labor lawyer and later a distinguished and proud liberal also on the United States Court of Appeals for the Ninth Circuit. Both would leave their marks on the young politician—helping seal his allegiance with labor and forging a sense of legal and political courage that he might not otherwise have acquired, at least not at such a young age.

Brown was a curiosity in the Tuttle and Taylor offices. He practiced litigation and was friendly but not particularly outgoing, remembered Raymond Fisher, yet another lawyer from the firm who went on to serve on the Ninth Circuit. The young lawyers ate together many days, usually at a spot called the Yorkshire Grill, a deli on 6th Street. Fisher recalled two memories of those meals: Brown would always take time to chat with the waiters and busboys at the restaurant. "And I would always pay," he said.[1]

In one case, Brown was teamed with senior lawyers at Tuttle and Taylor as well as some from O'Melveny and Myers, a much bigger and politically connected institution. The lawyers in the case were debating whether to challenge the judge assigned to it. O'Melveny's great lion, Warren Christopher, was cautious by nature and reluctant to risk offending the jurist. Norris, by contrast, urged a more aggressive position. "Go for it," he said. Brown followed Norris.[2] The motion to recuse was filed, and the Ninth Circuit gently urged the judge to step aside.

Brown chafed at some of Tuttle and Taylor's norms. The firm generally opted to try cases in front of judges, who could be relied upon to dissect intellectually rigorous, sometimes legally dense arguments. Brown took on pro bono criminal cases, and argued them in front of juries, where he believed his powers of persuasion would be more effective. "Jerry spoke to juries," said Eli Chernow, who worked with Brown in those years.[3] And Brown enjoyed using his talents to help. One time, a secretary in the firm was despairing that her boyfriend had lost his driver's license; Brown intervened with the Department of Motor Vehicles and got it back. No other lawyer at Tuttle and Taylor would have thought that to be part of his responsibility.

Brown was consummately a bachelor. He kept odd hours, often

arriving for work late in the day and working well into the night. Handsome and exotic, he drew the attention of office secretaries, who vied to work for him. He leaned on older colleagues and their wives to supply him with the trappings of home. He was a regular guest at the Chernows' for dinner, sometimes calling at the last minute and announcing that he was on his way over. And he could be both blithely inconsiderate and touchingly thoughtful. He would spot a newspaper on a colleague's desk and walk away with it without thinking to ask. But then he could surprise with a charming gesture. Eli Chernow had a Picasso print in his office that he treasured. Brown took it one day without explanation and returned it a few weeks later, framed.[4]

Jerry Brown may have struck some people as fringe, as young and Californian and crunchy. But in California, during the summer when some young people of Brown's age were preparing for the Summer of Love, or during the following year, when Tom Hayden and company were arrested on the streets of Chicago, Brown was engaged in the meticulous work of an up-and-coming member of the establishment. He was charting a career in politics.

He got his start from Kenneth Hahn, a liberal icon of the Los Angeles County Board of Supervisors—Hahn was famously the only elected official willing to meet publicly with Martin Luther King Jr. after the Watts riots in 1965. Hahn, long friendly with Pat Brown, nominated Jerry to the Los Angeles County Delinquency and Crime Commission.[5] Breaking with his father, Brown also took a spot as finance director of Eugene McCarthy's presidential campaign, an early indication of Brown's discomfort with the Vietnam War.

Because of his father, Brown was a minor celebrity in the McCarthy campaign and was sometimes called upon to speak in public. He did, and he found he enjoyed it. He and his father even staged a mock debate over their respective candidates, with Jerry Brown arguing that McCarthy was needed to correct a wayward war machine in Washington and Pat Brown suggesting that party loyalty to Johnson was important at a time of such stress.

Their disagreements would seem small as the campaign unfolded.

First was the assassination of Martin Luther King Jr., in Memphis. Then Johnson's announcement that he would not seek reelection. Then, on June 4, Senator Robert Kennedy's victory in the California Democratic primary, followed minutes later by shots ringing out in the cramped kitchen of the Ambassador Hotel in Los Angeles. Kennedy fought for life at Good Samaritan Hospital. Twenty-five hours later, he died. The convention in Chicago was marred by violence, and the party, torn by dissension and assassination, staggered into the general election against Nixon, who promised to restore the forces of order against those of rebellion and dissent.

Hubert Humphrey, the Happy Warrior, was out of place in 1968, when an angry and frightened America sized up Nixon and the Minnesota Democrat. George Wallace's independent candidacy kept Nixon from winning a majority—and highlighted the racial divisions that added to the campaign's drama—but Nixon won the Electoral College handily. Nixon, the bane of Earl Warren and Pat Brown, was elected president of the United States on November 5, 1968.

Then, as the year turned to 1969, an opportunity arose for Jerry Brown. California had decreed that each county should elect a board to supervise the community colleges within its borders. Thus commanded, Los Angeles County scheduled elections. Despite reservations from some of his mentors, who worried that it was too soon for him to establish an identity separate from his father, Brown seized the opportunity and announced his plans to run. He joined forces with another neophyte politician, a journalist named Tom Quinn, who was putting together a slate mailer—a collection of endorsed candidates who paid for the privilege of getting their names into mailboxes—to promote his own candidacy and those of other contenders. Quinn sought out Brown, figuring he could break even on the mailer and put his name beside that of the governor's son. Jerry Brown was motivated and signed up.

Their plan was nearly foiled when, on the weekend before the election, Dwight Eisenhower died and President Nixon declared a national holiday, halting mail services, but Quinn hustled to the post office and got the slates in the mail before the service shut down. Brown was impressed, and a lifelong friendship was formed.[6] With 133 candidates on the ballot and seven open seats, voters made their first round of choices on April 1, 1969. Brown finished first—with 186,901 votes, he tallied fifty thousand more than the second-place finisher, Mike Antonovich[7]—a testament to his name far more than his program, yet it was the most exciting moment of his life up to that point.[8] The results of the first round selected fourteen winners to advance to a second election; Brown won that, too. Quinn finished out of the money in his race, ending his career in elected office before it began but propelling him toward life as a trusted political adviser to Brown and others, including Mayor Tom Bradley. For Brown, it was a thrill, a validation of his decision to run and a successful launch.

Brown proved a quixotic member of the board. At the first meeting, he was nominated to serve as chair, but he realized he would not win, and instead set out to make his mark as a provocateur.[9] That proved prescient. As a trustee, he was strangely dogmatic on public safety questions, proposing that no student who had been found guilty of campus disruptions within the past three years be allowed to enroll in LA's community-college system. He supported a motion from the board's conservative bloc to recommend an investigation into "possible public offenses" during protests in East Los Angeles. Even more oddly, he advocated a helicopter-based task force to patrol the district and swoop in at signs of protest. Brown could send off contradictory signals: He criticized some student protesters for their disruptions, but when National Guard troops killed students at Kent State University, in Ohio, he supported a motion to lower campus flags to half-staff. Determined to appeal, as he said, to "the hard hat worker and the black man in Watts," Brown sometimes antagonized both.

Brown also showed his early prickliness over government spending. He voted against creating offices for the board members, then waged a silly campaign against giving them "new wooden desks," as if that were an unconscionable luxury. He opposed hiring a media-relations specialist and voted against paying for a colleague to attend a conference. Those votes did little to endear him to his colleagues, just as his later frugality would earn him enemies in Sacramento.

During his tenure, several teachers faced disciplinary actions for classroom speech. There, Brown was more reliably liberal. Deena Metzger, a Los Angeles Valley College English instructor, read a poem she had written, "Jehovah's Child," to her class after another teacher, Leslie Hoag, had tried it out on hers. The poem included some banal vulgarities, "so-called Anglo-Saxon four-letter words," as a judge later put it. After receiving complaints, the community board voted to dismiss Metzger, but Brown fought strenuously in her defense, and a court ordered her reinstated. Brown also stood with Hoag, as did the court, over the objections of the board majority.[10] Those cases prompted a broader review of the district's tenure practices.

Brown's debut year in politics, 1969, was a signature period in the life of the nation and a tragic, violent one in California. Nixon, whose political identity was forged in California, became president in January. The Stonewall Inn riots, in June, announced the emergence of a gay rights movement unwilling to quietly accept harassment. Apollo 11 put the first man on the moon in July. The Black Panther Party, whose aggressive wielding of firearms had made Reagan an unlikely gun-control advocate, shot it out with the LAPD on December 8; the gunfire raged for five hours, wounding three officers and six Panthers.

Nixon's inauguration and the Black Panthers shoot-out bracketed the year, but it was the summer that defined 1969 in California. In Los Angeles and San Francisco, the summer of 1969 was one of dread and terror.

Tex Watson drove three young women to a house on Los Angeles's Cielo Drive late on the night of August 8. Five people, including actress Sharon Tate, were inside. Watson shot down one, and the group then entered the house, murdering—butchering, really—the occupants. Tate, who was eight months pregnant, begged to be allowed to live. "Let me have my baby," she pleaded.[11] Her killers stabbed her to death. Before leaving, one of the intruders, Susan Atkins, smeared the word *pig* on the inside of the front door. She used Tate's blood for the message. The Manson murders were under way.

Charles Manson directed a second killing the following night, and his followers lit upon the home of Leno and Rosemary LaBianca. They, too, were dispatched in buckets of blood: Leno was stabbed twenty-six times, Rosemary forty-one times. The killers again left their message: DEATH TO PIGS.

SECOND RITUAL KILLINGS HERE, the Los Angeles Times announced in an extra edition on August 11. "Residents of the Los Feliz neighborhood clustered in curious but frightened groups on their lawns in the post-midnight hours," the Times reported. In the days and weeks following, the city was riveted by the police investigation into what was described as a "motiveless mass murder." Without suspects or a motive, the threat was ubiquitous. The moon landing and war in Northern Ireland displaced the murders from the front page, but only briefly, as police publicly fumbled with false leads—believing initially that the killings were drug-related.

Fear around the Los Angeles killings was amplified by another chilling set of murders, these in San Francisco. The so-called Zodiac killer, who boasted of his killings with regular missives to the San Francisco Examiner, taunted authorities. "School children make nice targets," he wrote in October. "I think I shall wipe out a school bus some morning. Just shoot out the front tires and then pick off the kiddies as they come bouncing out." By fall, his toll had reached five, and he remained at large.[12]

Not until December did police announce arrests and a theory in the Los Angeles murders. WILD CULT BLAMED IN TATE SLAYINGS, the Times reported. Suspects already were in custody, including one Charles Manson, who, the Times said, "refers to himself as 'God' and 'Satan.'" The Manson "family," as it was then first described, was "willing to do his bidding without question."[13] By then, the Zodiac killer had claimed seven victims.

Manson was arrested, tried, and convicted. He died in prison in 2017. The Zodiac killer has never been found.

As 1969 became 1970, Brown was growing tired of his board service and looking to climb another rung on the political ladder. He had attracted attention as a community-college trustee, but that post was never going to contain him. And so, with the help of his new friend and adviser, Tom Quinn, he searched for an office that would expand his horizons, give him the opportunity to develop a statewide profile, and introduce him to donors and political heavyweights. He settled on the sleepy but promising post of secretary of state, until then known mostly as a sinecure for a father-and-son combo of California political veterans, Frank C. Jordan and Frank M. Jordan, who between them held the office from 1911 to 1970 with just one three-year interruption.

Unlike the school board, this post was the real thing of state politics: a full-time position with statewide jurisdiction. The secretary of state didn't do much, true, but he had visibility and reach. For a politician looking to establish a beachhead, it was ideal.

Brown announced his candidacy for the office on March 2, pledging to police campaign contributions, especially those from special-interest groups; such contributions, he said, were "inherently corrupting." Brown, who took a leave from Tuttle and Taylor to run, was identified in some press coverage on first reference not as a college trustee or a Los Angeles lawyer but rather as the "son of the former governor."[14]

Pat Brown had, by 1970, settled into comfortable and lucrative retirement from public office. After his loss to Reagan in 1966, he and Bernice bought a house in the wealthy neighborhood of Benedict Canyon, and Pat entered private law practice. He still harbored thoughts of a triumphant return to office, but for the moment, he was content to ride out the Reagan years. His son's foray into California politics was both exciting and unsettling, suggesting the possibility of a family legacy but also marking the end of his own era and the commencement of another. At Jerry's insistence, Pat kept his distance from his son's labors. His son, the elder Brown told reporters, had warned him: "Dad, don't interfere with my career, please."[15] Nevertheless, it was his name that made Jerry Brown a story in this race, and he knew it. And then Brown caught an early break. Just weeks after he announced his intention to seek the office of secretary of state, its holder, the younger Frank Jordan, died at home after a long convalescence from a stroke. Suddenly, the field was clear.[16]

Brown had no particular interest in the office itself. In a 2015 interview, he acknowledged, without equivocation, that "it was a path." He was aiming for bigger things, and the secretary of state position was useful. Brown did not say that at the time.

In 1970, he campaigned as a reformer and, amusingly, as an outsider. He first fought off a shallow Democratic field and then, in the general election, faced Republican James Flournoy. Thoughtful, deliberate, and gentlemanly, Flournoy made a curious adversary. He was black—in fact, he was the first black candidate nominated by either party for statewide office in California—and a defender of the establishment, offended by Brown's suggestions that special interests and corporations wielded too much influence. It made for a puzzling race: the son of a former governor took on the status quo while an African American lawyer defended it. Brown won, but not by much: three hundred thousand or so votes separated the two on election night. Brown later would call Flournoy "a wonderful man and a true gentleman."[17]

To administer the oath of office, Brown called upon a family friend. He was thirty-two years old and entering a fairly insignificant post, but Jerry Brown was given the oath by Earl Warren, chief justice of the United States and, up to that point, the longest-serving governor in the history of California.[18] Brown was proud to stand next to Warren that day and would find ways to mention it for the rest of his life. "Not many people know it," he said in 2019, when he was eighty years old and had surpassed Warren's gubernatorial record. "Earl Warren swore me in."[19]

Brown's service as secretary of state had moments of significance—no small feat for an office that has little actual authority and given that Brown was relatively isolated in Sacramento. As an elected official, he served alongside Governor Reagan, not as a member of the governor's cabinet. As a result, Brown and Reagan eyed one another but interacted rarely, with Brown charting his own political course, indifferent or even hostile to Reagan's interests.

Brown tangled with Nixon, an easy foe, accusing an aide to the president of falsely notarizing the document donating Nixon's prepresidential papers to the National Archives in return for a sizable tax deduction. The aide, actually a partner in the law firm of Nixon's personal attorney, had, according to Brown, backdated the agreement in order to take advantage of a tax break that had since been eliminated. The effect, Brown said, was to save Nixon around $250,000. Brown's only recourse, as secretary of state, was to revoke the partner's powers as a notary, reflective of the limitations of Brown's office.[20] Still, it was emblematic of Brown at that stage—fighting for justice with one eye firmly on his press clippings. He was inclined, one former aide remarked, "to turn litigation into a press release."[21]

As that suggests, Brown was focused on using his office as a platform, both to draw attention to issues he considered important and to raise his profile. In both those spirits, he taunted President Johnson over the war in Vietnam. In March of 1972, he derided Johnson as a "hustler," eliciting a pained reply from Jack Valenti, then president of the Motion Picture Association and Johnson's ever-loyal deputy. "I know it is now fashionable and politically chic to count L.B.J. as a leper, to dismiss him as a non-person," Valenti wrote. "That gets laughs and applause from the crowd. But you strike me as a man who doesn't court popular fads."[22]

Brown was unusually acquiescent. In a letter to Valenti, he acknowledged that he was wrong to call Johnson a hustler but stood fast on his criticism of the president. "When I think of the suffering of the Vietnamese people, the maimed and killed soldiers on both sides, the drain on our economy for years to come and the division and alienation in our country, I cannot help but conclude that it would have been better to sacrifice some of the social programs sponsored by the President in exchange for the avoidance of the Vietnam build-up."

If sparring and making news were Brown's main ambitions as secretary of state, he nevertheless did put in some real work, too. Brown's chief achievement during those years was to win passage of California's Political Reform Act, a set of regulations intended to reveal and limit sources of money in politics and to create the state agency to monitor those rules, the Fair Political Practices Commission. Even before moving into his new position, Brown understood the political power of reform, using it to underscore his image as someone outside the mainstream of California politics. As secretary of state, he turned to two associates,

Dan Lowenstein and Bob Stern, a pair of sharp, deceptively easygoing lawyers, to draft the measure itself.

There was a twist, however. Brown asked Stern to write the bill—actually three bills that interacted with one another—in such a way that the legislature would reject the package. The theory, Stern recalled years later, was that Brown wanted the measure on the ballot and wanted to use it to run as an outsider. To do that, he needed to run against the legislature, not with it. Stern and Brown set to work and enlisted the support of Howard Berman, a friend and ally in the assembly and Phil Burton's old comrade from the redistricting days. Berman agreed to introduce the bills with the paradoxical determination to see that they were defeated.[23]

As drafted, the legislation sought to achieve several goals: it placed limits on campaign spending for all statewide offices; it required elected officials to submit regular updates on their assets and investments; it prohibited lobbyists from contributing directly to campaigns and from giving more than $10 a month in gifts; it prohibited anonymous or shadowy contributions to campaigns by requiring contributors to identify themselves; it created the Fair Political Practices Commission, which was charged with policing the provisions of the act. As the campaign unfolded, much attention was focused on the $10-a-month limit. That, Brown said, ought to be enough to buy a politician "two hamburgers and a Coke." Later, when Brown met with Reagan to discuss the governorship, Reagan served him a hamburger and a Coke.

Organized labor strongly opposed the measure, arguing that it would curb the power of unions to support elected officials, an argument that proponents dismissed as inaccurate—labor could, they noted, contribute as before; it merely would have to disclose its donations. Labor leaders and others hired the PR firm of Whitaker and Baxter, a powerhouse in California politics, to shepherd the campaign against the measure. An ad that appeared on radio and television just before Election Day argued that Proposition 9, as it was called, infringed on free speech and expression. The proposal, it said, "is not political reform…It is political repression."[24] Proponents were led by Brown, happy to have his name associated with the proposition as his own election approached. The Sierra Club, the California Coastal Alliance, Ralph Nader, and Common Cause joined the ranks of supporters. The *Los Angeles Times,* which rarely found itself allied with Nader, nevertheless supported Proposition 9, saying that its enactment would give California "the strongest laws in the nation to enforce integrity and responsiveness in government and politics."[25]

One last bit of cleverness accompanied the bill. It required the approval of voters, which suggested that it would appear on the November ballot. Brown, however, persuaded legislators to put the initiative before voters in June. That was key for Brown, who by then was angling to run for governor and who anticipated a crowded, difficult Democratic field. Having his own initiative on the same ballot would help turn out his natural supporters, a nifty bit of political maneuvering that would remind rivals that for all the talk of Brown as dreamy or intellectual, he was also a shrewd tactician.

Jerry Brown had imagined himself as governor ever since the day he listened from upstairs at the governor's mansion—then his father's house—as Pat Brown and Jesse Unruh discussed strategy in the breakfast room. As 1973 turned to 1974, Brown resolved to run while his father's reputation could still buoy him and while his own political profile was in ascent.

A campaign for governor would be big, complicated, and expensive. Not everyone wanted him to do it. In fact, among the doubters was Pat Brown, who briefly considered running for his old seat, only to have Bernice talk him out of it. Pat corralled Tom Quinn and invited him to lunch at the Polo Lounge in Los Angeles. Jerry was not ready for the campaign, Pat warned. He was too young, too untested to take on the field that was coalescing around the governor's race, one that included San Francisco mayor Joe Alioto, assemblyman Bob Moretti, businessman and civic activist William Roth, and congressman Jerry Waldie. In Pat Brown's world, governors worked their way to the office—Reagan, of course, was an aberration. Jerry risked running and losing, throttling his potential before he ever had a chance to develop it. "You're going to ruin his career," Pat Brown told Quinn.[26]

Jerry Brown would not be talked out of running, and Pat Brown would come around. As commentators speculated on his potential as a governor through 1973, Brown, with his father's help, quietly amassed more than $400,000 for a possible run. He then took a deep breath and made it official: California, he announced on January 28, 1974, can have "blue skies, a prosperous economy and an educational system second to none."[27] That was typical. Brown was determined to take full advantage of his solid name recognition and his thin résumé—a combination that made him well known while also hard to attack. He vaguely touted clean air and rapid transit, good schools and jobs, all part of "a new spirit of activism" somehow consistent with fiscal discipline and the insider-outsider positioning that allowed him to be both the son of a former governor and a new face at the same time.

He was also the beneficiary of events. On June 17, 1972, a security guard at the Watergate office and hotel complex in Washington, DC, noticed a strip of tape across the latch of an office door. The office inside was the headquarters of the Democratic National Committee. The burglars, it would soon be revealed, were a motley collection of four Cubans and a former CIA operative. The address books of two of the burglars included the name of Howard Hunt, another former CIA operator who was working for the Nixon White House.

The tentacles of Watergate were long and complex. Before the scandal had played itself out, it would reveal base violations of the law—conspiracy, break-ins, obstruction of justice, violations of privacy, and misuse of government power, to name a few—by the highest officials in American government, including President Nixon himself. Among the scandal's casualties was a blow to confidence in government itself, a wound reinforced by Vietnam and one from which the nation has yet to recover. It also recalibrated the tone and effectiveness of American politics. Once a contest of experience and judgment, politics then often became a race to prove oneself an outsider, a candidate untainted by the institutions he seeks to join or lead.

In such an environment, Brown's political reforms found a natural constituency.

Despite a flurry of last-minute campaigning directed by Whitaker and

Baxter, including a deluge of advertising in the final week, proponents carried the day easily, winning nearly 70 percent of ballots cast. Brown's gubernatorial bid was, as hoped for, boosted as well—with the ballot measure helping to reinforce Brown's distance from old-style politics and his reputation as a reformer.

The overlapping campaigns for political reform and the governorship were smothered by Watergate, but another event, more distinctly Californian, shadowed the races as well. Like the confrontations with the Black Panthers, this had its roots in the state's radical Left, which flourished in the 1960s and 1970s, mostly though not exclusively in the San Francisco Bay area.

On February 4, 1974, less than a week after Brown announced his candidacy for governor, members of the Symbionese Liberation Army burst into a Berkeley apartment complex and clubbed two of its residents, hauling off one of them, the nineteen-year-old member of a rich and well-connected California family. The kidnapping of Patty Hearst would dominate news coverage in the state and beyond for the next nineteen months. HEARST HEIRESS KIDNAPPED, the *Los Angeles Times* blared across its front page. All other news—save for a brief update on a truckers' strike being negotiated by the White House—was pushed back in the paper. The abduction, during which UPI said Hearst had been "dragged screaming from her duplex apartment and dumped into the trunk of her kidnapers' car," led papers from Redlands to Santa Rosa to Santa Maria.

The ensuing drama—the manhunt, the barely coherent "communiqués" from the SLA, the shocking images of Hearst, then identified as Tania, wielding a gun during a bank robbery—captivated the nation, especially California, for months. The SLA's demands were extravagant and ludicrous. In a tape recording delivered to radio station KPFA on February 12, the group's leader, Donald DeFreeze, who went by the name Cinque, announced the findings of the "Symbionese War Council, the Court of the People," which is to say, himself and a few self-important comrades. Before negotiations could commence for the return of Patty, Cinque proclaimed, the SLA required a "show of good faith" by the Hearst family. That was to take the form of a food give-away, "$70 worth of meats, vegetables, and dairy products" to anyone in California qualifying for various types of assistance. To be clear, Cinque added, the food had to be distributed from at least five stores in various communities and it had to be "of top quality." He gave the Hearsts one week to organize the effort.[28] In response, Randy Hearst, Patricia's father, formed an organization called People in Need and charged it with coordinating a food giveaway, though one less comprehensive than the SLA initially demanded.

The first distribution took place on February 22, and it was, like most things connected with the Hearst kidnapping and its aftermath, a mess. Five thousand people lined up at the Oakland distribution point, and when the trucks were late in arriving, the crowd turned surly. As trucks finally attempted to unload, they were set upon by the impatient crowd, the giveaway disintegrating into a riot. People clambered aboard trucks and threw food into the crowd. More than twenty people had to be hospitalized.[29]

The hunt for Patty Hearst consumed law enforcement for months, and authorities tracked the SLA to Los Angeles in the spring. On May 16, SLA member Bill Harris pocketed a bandolier at Mel's Sporting Goods in Los Angeles. The clerk caught him in the act and confronted him as he attempted to leave without paying. But Harris was armed and on the run. Patty Hearst was waiting outside in a van, and when she saw the store owner and clerk tackle Harris, she reached for the weapons she and her comrades/captors were carrying. Hearst opened fire with a machine gun, hurting no one but loudly alerting police to the SLA's presence in Los Angeles.[30] Hearst and Harris—with his wife, Emily—fled, but the LAPD was engaged. The following day, May 17, the LAPD cornered leaders of the group at a modest Victorian-style stucco home in South-Central Los Angeles. Hearst was believed to be inside.

SLA HIDEOUT STORMED, 5 DIE, read the banner headline in the *Los Angeles Times* on Saturday morning.[31] The paper reported in dramatic detail the siege carried out by five hundred police officers, highway patrol officers, sheriff's deputies, and FBI agents, who descended on the house on 54th Street, first pumping thousands of rounds inside, then standing by as tear gas caught fire and burned the structure to the ground. The battle was carried on live television and was featured on the front page of virtually every newspaper in America the following day. Although the SLA released a hostage, its members refused to surrender, dying in the fire. Patty Hearst was not among them.

Hearst remained at large for another six months, and initial sympathy for her morphed into public contempt as she seemed to acquiesce to the will of her captors. She eventually was apprehended—or rescued, depending on one's perspective—without much incident on September 16 in a San Francisco apartment across the bay from where she was abducted. Booked at the San Mateo County jail after her initial arrest, Hearst was asked her occupation. She responded: "Urban guerrilla."[32]

What did that mean for politics? In one sense, nothing. The SLA never wielded influence in the way that, say, the Black Panthers did. But the Hearst kidnapping was a monumental distraction at precisely the time that the California candidates for governor, including Brown, were attempting to establish themselves in the public consciousness. Breaking through the Hearst coverage was nearly impossible: for those candidates who did not already enjoy widespread recognition, the attention given to Hearst was attention taken away from them. Only one candidate, Brown, entered the race with universal name recognition, largely a gift from his father; only he benefited from the kidnapping and the public's fixation on it.

Moretti tried to get Brown's attention. In April, he accused Brown, as secretary of state, of a conflict of interest: overseeing the election in which he was a candidate. Brown's campaign literature and conduct in office, Moretti charged, were "clearly unfair, certainly unethical and apparently illegal." Brown ignored him. Three weeks later, a Field poll showed Brown and Moretti as front-runners, and Moretti pressed Brown for a debate. Brown ignored him again—exploiting the luxury of positive name recognition during a busy time.[33]

With the public looking elsewhere, Brown did the careful work of building his campaign, winning over some constituencies and neutralizing others. In that last mission, Stephen Reinhardt, then a labor lawyer working in Los Angeles, delivered an invaluable service. Reinhardt's assignment was to win the backing of labor or, failing that, at least to negate its influence, given Brown's uneasy relationship with that vital Democratic constituency (labor, as noted, was opposed to Proposition 9 and political reform generally, so its support for Brown was hard to come by). Reinhardt had connections to the state's leading unions, and he called in chits for Brown. "I was running against Joe Alioto," Brown remembered. "By every right, he should have gotten labor's support." But Reinhardt reached out to one Herman "Blackie" Leavitt, who ran the Hotel and Restaurant Employees and Bartenders International Union. Blackie knew people, and he persuaded the leadership of the AFL-CIO to deliver an "open endorsement" in the primary, effectively depriving Alioto of that crucial support. Reinhardt was pleased: "I got labor not to endorse Alioto," he reflected decades later from the federal courthouse in Los Angeles, where was then a veteran member of the bench. To sweeten his commitment to Brown, Leavitt arranged for the unions to raise $100,000 for the Brown campaign.[34] Brown was grateful and invited Leavitt, his fiancée, and his sister to dinner to express his thanks. Brown forgot to bring money, and Leavitt ended up getting the check.[35]

When Pat Brown was ushered into private life by Ronald Reagan, he returned to a world he had long put behind him, the private practice of law. He had no clients and no real legal specialty, having spent more than two decades working as district attorney, attorney general, and governor. He accepted an offer from an old friend, Joseph Ball. Brown and Ball met in 1940 on the train that was bearing the California Democratic delegation to the party's national convention in Chicago. "He and I were alternate delegates," Ball wrote decades later. "From that point forward, we became friends."[36] Two Democrats en route to a Democratic National Convention, they nevertheless shared a deep admiration for Earl Warren, then California's attorney general, a Republican in the early stages of a career of immense national significance.

Ball, Brown, and Warren would go on to overlapping careers in the decades after that first encounter. Brown and Warren struck up a friendship that was close and politically advantageous, especially for Brown, who received Warren's subtle but helpful support in his campaign against Richard Nixon. Ball would serve as staff counsel to the Warren Commission when Warren was charged with the grueling assignment of investigating the death of his friend John Kennedy. Brown would tempt Ball not once but four times with offers of a spot on the California Supreme Court, Ball declining each time.[37] And Ball would chair two of Brown's three campaigns for governor. Having lost his third attempt, Brown then accepted Ball's offer to join Ball, Hunt, and Hart, and Ball agreed to add the governor to the firm's named partnership. Brown insisted on being listed first: "I'm the governor of the state," he told Ball. "I've got to be first."[38] Ball agreed, and for a time the firm was called Brown, Hall, Hunt and Hart (later, it became Ball, Hunt, Hart, Brown, and Baerwitz). The firm had offices in Los Angeles, Beverly Hills, and Long Beach and did all manner of legal work as well as dabble in politics. But the firm's bread and butter was its lucrative representation of oil and gas interests.[39] Brown worked out of the Beverly Hills office, just a few miles from his house in Benedict Canyon.

The firm's oil and gas practice included domestic and foreign clients, and Pat Brown helped land a lucrative addition to the firm's stable: the government of Indonesia. Hired by the Indonesian state-owned oil exploration firm, Pertamina, Brown set out to help the company secure loans from American banks to expand its work. In return, he received both direct compensation and a share of Pertamina's concession for importing oil to California.[40]

Brown's relationship with Pertamina—the company's California affiliate would later be called Perta Oil—was replete with significance for his life and family. For starters, it made him rich. Once oil revenue began flowing in, he shared it with his family, doling out shares of stock in the company to his children, though never to Jerry, according to Brown and others close to him. In addition, because Jerry would go on to hold the governorship himself, the Perta Oil money specifically and Pat Brown's oil interests generally would occasionally arise as sources of conflict and controversy. In the 1970s, father and son would take opposite sides in the crucial debate over rules regulating California's coastline, and Pat's investments and oil income would cause some critics to wonder about the Brown family's trustworthiness on issues related to energy and fossil fuels years later.

In the meantime, Perta and its reach would create complications for the up-and-coming Jerry Brown. In his 1974 campaign for governor, he accepted contributions from Perta Oil Marketing, which his father chaired and which ran the oil importation business for Indonesia in California. Perta gave $21,000 to the Brown campaign that year, and executives of the company pledged and contributed thousands more. The donations came to light when one of Brown's opponents in the Democratic primary discovered them and alerted reporters. Brown handled the ensuing kerfuffle poorly. At first, he insisted that there was nothing wrong about the contributions and that they did not suggest any allegiance or obligation to the oil industry. Joe Alioto, Brown's chief rival at that stage of the campaign, didn't buy it. Backed by Indonesian oil and confronted with serious questions about the price of gas and California's energy future, Brown could not be trusted, Alioto said, adding: "With those contributors, he is not going to wage a fight against oil monopolies."[41]

That was convincing, and Brown knew it. A week later, he insisted that two Perta executives withdraw their pledged support of $15,000 each, suggesting that he did, in fact, see a problem with the contributions, at least in terms of public perception and political expedience. Brown's campaign spokesman was uncharacteristically curt in response to questions about the canceled pledges. "It was Brown's decision," he said. "He thought they had contributed enough. And that's that."[42]

Easier said than done. Campaigns love to call a halt to coverage only to discover that reporters aren't taking direction. That was the case with Perta. Brown's relationship to the company, through his father, haunted him for decades. It fueled conspiracy theories—that Brown, for example, opposed nuclear power because it threatened the sale of oil; later, that Brown supported fracking—or, more precisely, opposed a ban on it— because unspecified oil interests favored it. Brown's handling of the relationship didn't help. By suggesting in 1974 that there was no reason whatsoever to question contributions from the company, he appeared defensive, especially for a candidate who claimed electoral rectitude in other regards. It seemed fair to ask how Brown could simultaneously believe that officeholders could be swayed by a $20 dinner and that he was immune to the inducements of a $21,000 contribution. His later insistence that he had no connections or obligations to Perta—or to his father—similarly stretched credulity.

The bottom line is that Brown did get help from Perta and, of course, from his father. But there is no evidence that such help ever influenced any decision, much less those as grave as the ones involving nuclear power or fracking. Such contributions and connections might have influenced another candidate, and Brown was not wrong to champion reforms that limited influence and required disclosure of contributions and gifts. Those ideas might seem inconsistent, but they found harmony in a candidate who had deep confidence in himself and little trust in others—a fairly concise description of Jerry Brown.

Brown's family was under no illusions, nor were they conflicted, about the effects of Perta's money. Jerry's sisters and their children welcomed it. At a celebration of Pat Brown's eighty-second birthday, his children and grandchildren composed a couple of ditties to honor him. One was entitled "Gonna Climb a Mountain," and it poked fun at his garrulousness and love of swimming. It also recounted the roots of his nickname. And the song took special note of his debt to Indonesia:

> *He adores his cupcakes*
> *Takes them out to lunch*
> *And now we all would like to say*
> *To Perta Oil, thanks a bunch.*[43]

On the day of the primary, Brown's Proposition 9 won handily and imposed its limits on California politicians from that point forward. Brown was one of them, because he won the primary, too, doubling the vote count of his nearest rival, Alioto. On the Republican side, Houston Flournoy, no relation to the Flournoy whom Brown had beaten four years earlier, took his party's nomination. Flournoy, the state's respected if uninspiring controller, was a political science professor and family man, a study in stability and predictability in contrast to Brown.

Brown pivoted into the general election campaign with a comfortable lead in the polls, but the race tightened in the final weeks. The Brown camp was concerned, because voters seemed to grow tentative at the idea of electing a candidate so young, so untested, so clearly there because of his family connections.

"Jerry's just unsafe in a lot of people's minds," Tom Quinn said as Election Day drew near and Brown was dropping about one percentage point per day in opinion polls.[44] Faced with the end of his career barely after starting it, Brown stepped up the tempo. He stumped the state with vigor, canvassing by car and plane. He hosted press briefings and candidate events and framed the choice for voters as between "a new spirit in Sacramento" or "recycling Reaganism."

If the campaign had lasted another two weeks, Brown might have lost. But it didn't. He won in a squeaker. Jerry Brown was governor-elect of California.

# 8

# Rebellion to Revolution

B rown's election in 1974 capped a lurching and chaotic period, one that combined elements of vision and violence as forces in California and beyond talked past one another and, all too often, screamed at one another. It did not begin or end with Brown's election, but it framed his rise to power, underscoring the bitter polarization of the period and helping to explain the desire for new approaches and ideas outside the normal range of politics. That worked to Brown's advantage: He represented something new at a time when much that had been accepted was suddenly in doubt. Before considering Brown's governorship, then, it is worth pausing to reflect on the tumult that gave rise to it and that surrounded his early tenure in a swirl of protest, disenchantment and determination to try to new things.

The Free Speech Movement, to take just one example, started with booths on a Berkeley plaza and ended with students overturning police cars and occupying buildings. Pleas segued into demands. Protesters moved from quiet disagreement to active confrontation. The next turn was even more dramatic: the two sides went to war. And then, most unexpectedly of all, that atmosphere—of daring and defiance, experimentation, intellectual adventurism, freedom—gave rise to the revolution that would most change California and the world. It all happened quickly, but not quietly.

In the early years of the 1960s, civil rights held the field as the leading cause of demonstrations in California and beyond. The great struggles that *Brown v. Board of Education* helped encourage propelled a noble movement that also produced landmark legislation—the Civil Rights Act of 1964, the Voting Rights Act of 1965. Though the center of gravity of that movement lay south of the Mason-Dixon line (what Thurgood Marshall used to call the Smith-and-Wesson line), California saw its share of demonstrations and sent more than its share of students to those battles. David Harris, Tom Hayden, Al Lowenstein, and even Jerry Brown, with his distaste for theatrical confrontation, all contributed to and took risks to advance that historic campaign.

By 1965, though, all other causes on the front lines of dissent were giving way to one: the war in Vietnam. In California, the pace and intensity of resistance to the conflict gained steam in 1965, as Ronald Reagan, then still a candidate for governor, made headway with moderate voters by taunting student protesters, whom he derided as spoiled children unwilling to sacrifice for their country and sponging off the generosity of their parents and a soft government. California had abundant young people, a tradition of confronting authority, and a governor worth confronting. The result was a season of conflict, escalating as it went.

Like the protests against it, the Vietnam War began slowly. Its earliest glimmers can be detected in the Eisenhower years, when Ike reluctantly agreed to dispatch a small contingent of American advisers to a country where the French had abandoned a long, fruitless colonial effort, culminating in a catastrophic defeat at Dien Bien Phu in 1954—a defeat made more bitter by Eisenhower's refusal to commit American troops to reinforcing the doomed French garrison.[1] When Eisenhower left office, at the end of 1960, the United States had roughly nine hundred soldiers in Vietnam.[2]

Under Kennedy, the American presence in Vietnam slowly increased, though still without widening to a full-scale invasion. Advisers were drawn more deeply into combat, and South Vietnam pleaded for ever-increasing support. Kennedy boosted troop levels to more than ten thousand before being assassinated, on November 22, 1963. Then came

Johnson. Lyndon Johnson hated Vietnam. He wanted to defeat poverty, and Vietnam claimed resources. He wanted to advance civil rights, and the cause was overwhelmed by the war. Vietnam proved the ruination of his presidency—and, tragically, he watched it happen.

Johnson believed that American prestige and credibility depended on victory, but no matter how he tried, he could not achieve that victory. In the end, he committed tens of thousands of American lives to a cause that was not his own in a country that he could not understand. In 1963, 16,300 American soldiers were in Vietnam. That number grew to 23,300 in 1964, 184,300 in 1965, 385,300 in 1966, 485,600 in 1967, and 536,100 in 1968, the last year of Johnson's presidency.[3] As the American force ballooned, domestic opposition to it increased as well. The chant "Hey, hey, LBJ, how many kids did you kill today?" would haunt Johnson to his grave.

Protesters who began by gently urging a reconsideration of the war—through teach-ins, nonviolent demonstrations, petitions, and the like—became increasingly desperate as their pleas were ignored and their friends and classmates sent away. The example of Berkeley captures the arc of protest for the period.

In 1965, antiwar activists in Berkeley set aside a day—Vietnam Day, they called it—to express their opposition to the escalating conflict. For thirty-six hours, from May 20 to May 21, speakers engaged students with their critiques of Johnson, who had just authorized one of his many significant increases in troop strength and launched the bombing campaign known as Operation Thunder. Some ten thousand students showed up for the teach-in, which featured such speakers as I. F. Stone, Dr. Benjamin Spock, activist and *Ramparts* magazine reporter Robert Scheer, author Norman Mailer, and Mario Savio. The teach-in was intermittently attended: the *San Francisco Examiner* estimated around 2,500 students during the dinner hour, growing to about eight thousand as the night went on. Speakers mostly denounced the war and called for American withdrawal. The *Examiner* treated the whole affair as an amusement, labeling it the Camp Meeting at Berkeley. "The 'community meeting' is scheduled to continue until about 7 o'clock tonight and those who stick it out deserved an accolade of some sort—something more, perhaps, than grass stains on the bottoms of their jeans," the paper wrote on its front page after the first day of the gathering.[4]

That was 1965, early in the era of Vietnam protest. Another gathering two years later in nearly the same spot would illustrate the effects of an escalating war, an impatient public, and, especially in California, a surging desire to confront the agents of the war and their defenders, including Governor Reagan.

This time, the protest was billed as a demonstration of resistance to the draft. Part of a national "Stop the Draft Week," the Bay Area's events included gatherings at the San Francisco Federal Building— where young men were urged to turn in their draft cards—and a blockade at the induction center in Oakland. This was not to be a Camp Meeting. Demonstrators who attended that event were warned in advance that they "should expect arrest."[5] It began on October 16, and among the first to be arrested was Joan Baez, along with her mother and more than one hundred other demonstrators. That was merely to set the stage.

Hearing of the arrests, thousands of demonstrators descended on Sproul Plaza on the UC Berkeley campus that night, preparing for the main event: the next morning's march to the induction center. They began the short march at dawn, but when they arrived at the center, at 1515 Clay Street in Oakland, they were met by an enraged police force. This is how the *Examiner* recorded it:

A flying wedge of helmeted police, wielding clubs and spraying tear gas, routed a crowd of thousands of anti-draft demonstrator[s] from the streets in front of the Armed Forces induction center in Oakland this morning.

About two dozen of the crowd of 3500 fell or were clubbed to the pavement during the initial, seven-minute blitzkrieg. 20 demonstrators were subsequently taken to hospitals, as was one Highway Patrol officer. At least 17 persons were arrested.[6]

Governor Reagan was in the Virgin Islands but released a joint statement with the acting governor, Robert Finch. They saw the event somewhat differently from those at the scene. "The officers displayed exceptional ability and handled themselves with great professional skill," the two said. "Their quick action is a tribute to the high caliber of training they have received and reflects a fine spirit of cooperation between city, county and state law enforcement agencies."

Stunned by the ferocity of what some demonstrators called Bloody Tuesday, the protesters limped back to the Berkeley campus and held two more days of quieter events. Then, on Friday, they returned in force, this time prepared for a fight. What the *Examiner* called a "wild melee" erupted when police attempted to forcibly remove protesters from the area in front of the induction center and demonstrators responded with force of their own. They donned helmets to protect themselves, then rolled cars into the street, letting the air out of the tires and disabling the engines so they could not be moved. They dragged wooden benches from bus stops and upended concrete tubs containing trees; they piled up garbage cans and newspaper racks. The barricades of Paris appeared in Oakland, blocking 14th and 15th Streets. Police battled back, seizing control at one intersection and shepherding a busload of inductees into the center. The battle raged back and forth—protesters grabbing territory, police fighting to reclaim ground.

Until that day, demonstrators always had been on the defensive: once police determined to break up a protest, they would be the ones to command the streets, driving off those who came to express grievances. This day was different. It was the demonstrators who fought off police. As the *Examiner* noted: "The offensive today was taken by the anti-draft demonstrators, rather than police."[7]

This was not merely protest. This was deliberate, violent confrontation. A page turned in the annals of the antiwar movement.

At the birthplace of much of this tumult, Berkeley, tempers rarely subsided and occasionally boiled. That seething sense of rage, of impulsive and determined intention to resist power, of independence from established ways, found expression repeatedly through this period. Berkeley was often at the center, as it was in the spring of 1969.

The scene this time was a scrubby patch of ignored property adjacent to the university campus. The University of California acquired the land, about one-third of an acre between Dwight Way and Haste Street, in 1967, intending to use it for student housing. The following February, residents of the property were evicted, and houses on it were razed. The university, however, was short of money to begin construction, so the lot went fallow. The result was an eyesore, and in early 1969, the surrounding community decided to take the blight into its own hands. "In a Telegraph Avenue coffee shop," one participant wrote, "an idea sprang up among a group of locals. 'Why not turn that vacant lot into a park? Lots of people are showing up in Berkeley, hanging out, sleeping in the street. They need a nice green place to be.'"[8]

The revolution, it has often been said, was an endless meeting, and the meeting over what then became known as People's Park was just that. Residents gathered in informal, continual conversations, debating improvements to the property and embarking on them without the formalities and inconveniences of city and university approval. One group would seize upon the idea of a pool. "The next morning would see dirt flying from a widening hole," recounted one person. Then others would warn of the dangers of a pool. "Heads would nod and the dirt would fly right back in the hole."[9]

It was messy, chaotic, leaderless—like so much of that period. And it unfolded under the wary, suspicious eyes of the university leadership and the state's governor, Ronald Reagan. This was university property, a violation of Berkeley building and permit rules—exactly the type of affront to authority for which Berkeley already had become known. Reagan had defeated Pat Brown in no small measure because Brown tolerated combative expression. Reagan would not cotton to it on his watch.

At 4:00 a.m. on May 15, 1969, a fencing company—a nonunion fencing company, as one scholar of the episode archly points out—arrived in darkness to seal off the park.[10] They posted fifty-one NO TRESPASSING signs and blocked access.[11] The park's community champions arrived that morning to find their project taken from them during the night. Predictably, they were outraged, and rage turned to protest, which turned to violence. Police were armed with bird shot and used it to fire into the crowd. A total of thirty-two people were shot in that fashion, three of them seriously injured, on the first day of confrontation. The National Guard, deployed for the first time by Governor Reagan, arrived with bayonets. They surrounded the park on the ground and flew overhead in helicopters, spraying the protesters from above with tear gas. Protesters rushed for shelter in campus buildings but were locked out.

By the following afternoon, the *San Francisco Examiner* described the scene on Berkeley streets as "open guerrilla warfare."[12] "We're going to do everything we can to defend that park," said one protest leader, "and destroy a university that would try to take it away from us."[13]

The language was typical of the period and reflected the hardening of positions that had become commonplace by 1969. Protesters were no longer simply attracting attention to a cause or a message. They were actively in conflict, seeking confrontation, using it not just to challenge but also to destroy institutions that practiced or symbolized dominant oppression. Reagan dismissed the dissent over the park as a "phony issue" and "an excuse for a riot," but that proves his misapprehension of the seriousness of a movement that by 1969 was eager for a riot. Violence was no longer a by-product of dissent. It was an end in itself.

The conflict at People's Park left scores wounded and supplied history books with yet another chapter involving guardsmen, hippies, tear gas, and bird shot. Protesters waved bloody banners and showed up topless at the park perimeter, taunting guardsmen. They called the day Bloody Thursday, and with some good reason.[14] One protester, James Rector, was hit with a shotgun blast and suffered wounds to his stomach, spleen, and other organs; he died of heart failure on May 19.[15]

The would-be settlers of the park mourned its takeover. "For all of us, hip and straight, the Park was something we had done, something that drew our community together," one epitaph for it read. "The Park was common ground."[16]

Campus protests peaked in 1970. One infamous confrontation, at Kent State, left four dead, two of whom were merely walking to class when National Guardsmen opened fire on demonstrators. Three months later, Chicano activists in Los Angeles declared a moratorium on the Vietnam War and took to the streets. Sheriff's deputies responded with cruel force, killing three demonstrators, including journalist Ruben Salazar, who was hit by a tear gas grenade.

As violence escalated on campus and in American streets, some of those at war with the government took their action further. The eighteen months comprising 1969 and early 1970 represented the apotheosis of a certain type of violent frustration, rare to that point in the nation's life: bombings. At a hearing in the summer of 1970, a US Senate subcommittee counted 1,188 bombings and attempted bombings from January of 1969 through July 9, 1970; the list of bombings filled thirty-four pages of the *Congressional Record*.[17] And there were signs of things getting worse. The subcommittee investigation concluded that the bombings increased in frequency in 1970, jumping from 1.6 bombings per day in 1969 to 3.1 per day in 1970.[18] Those bombings left dozens dead and caused millions of dollars in damages. They also fueled long-simmering suspicions about conspiracies and international villains, as if Americans could not possibly be responsible for such heinous acts without provocation from abroad.

The demonstrations against Vietnam accomplished a breathtaking feat: they ended a war. They did so by brazenly, rashly, sometimes violently confronting American leaders with their miscalculations and forcing them to consider a deeper morality than anticommunism or Cold War balance. Violence in the service of ending a war is paradoxical, and its effects were at best mixed. At least as many Americans were repelled by the bombings as were persuaded by them to reconsider the war in Vietnam or the failings of advanced capitalism. Still, the combination of nonviolent protest, violent rage, public weariness, and establishment confusion produced precisely what demonstrators fought so hard to achieve. On April 30, 1975, North Vietnamese forces captured Saigon, ending two decades of war in Vietnam and the terrible carnage of that long conflict. A war that killed or wounded some three million Vietnamese and 58,193 Americans ended with South Vietnam's defeat.[19] In the united Vietnam, Saigon was renamed Ho Chi Minh City.

While that struggle gurgled to a boil in 1970, another revolution was under way, also rooted in California's contrarian countercultural traditions and history. And although the antiwar movement would achieve its significant ends, this one would go far, far further. It would change the world.

Two groups of computer scientists stood at opposite ends of a wobbly hookup at 10:30 p.m. on October 29, 1969. One group was at UCLA, the other at the Stanford Research Institute, in Palo Alto, California. Charlie Klein, a researcher at UCLA, sat down as if he were a local user at the university's Scientific Data Systems Sigma 7 computer, but this time he sought to log on to Stanford's Programmed Data Processor machine, some four hundred miles away. To do so, he needed to send a message from the Sigma 7 through an Interface Message Processor, a router the size of a refrigerator, to a similar router in Northern California and from there to Stanford's computer. The two routers had been installed in the weeks before this test and were connected by a communications link.

At UCLA, Klein began to input the letters *login* but only got as far as *lo* before the Stanford system crashed. Still, two letters traveled from Southern to Northern California, briefly linking the computers, each the size of a small house, on the two campuses. As UCLA computer scientist Leonard Kleinrock later put it, the internet had just uttered its first word, *lo*, "as in 'lo and behold.'"[20]

The internet could have ended up being nothing more than a few links between a few computers. The Defense Department oversaw the Advanced Research Projects Agency, where a remarkable leader, Bob Taylor, supervised a supremely talented team of computer visionaries. But the failed connection between UCLA and Stanford at the end of 1969 hardly shouted that a new era was at hand, and in 1972, the DOD considered unloading the project to a private entity. Xerox and AT&T both weighed bidding for the network but passed. It was a fateful mistake for those companies but a lucky one for the world. "A corporate owner would likely have exerted more control over who could join and might also have adopted a more rigid definition of acceptable behavior," Leslie Berlin, a Silicon Valley historian, wrote.[21] *Control* and *rigid* would not be words later associated with the internet.

\* \* \*

The technological center now known as Silicon Valley did not exist until the early 1970s. Before that, it was a region of orchards and vegetable farms, then a few subdivisions—bedroom communities for San Francisco and, to a lesser extent, San Jose. And there were a few tech companies, now viewed as ancestors of what became Silicon Valley, then outlier businesses in computer development, often with connections to the defense industry. Hewlett-Packard was the foremost of those. What the area also had, it is important to note, was Leland Stanford Junior University, sometimes confused in its early years for a junior college given its namesake, Leland Stanford Jr. And it was close to San Francisco and Berkeley and all that suggested, especially as the first generation of tech companies became the second.

The initial eruption was led by an especially controversial, even disreputable, scientist named William Shockley. Working at Bell Labs in the 1940s, Shockley contributed to the company's development of the transistor while antagonizing his colleagues with his determination to be seen as foremost in that effort. Shockley left Bell after publishing *Electrons and Holes in Semiconductors with Applications to Transistor Electronics* in 1950. In 1956, he founded the Shockley Semiconductor Laboratory in Palo Alto. He recruited scientists from Stanford and elsewhere and then proceeded to torture them with his erratic management and behavior, which seemed to grow increasingly demanding and autocratic after he received the 1956 Nobel Prize in Physics. As his mind deteriorated, Shockley became preoccupied with eugenics and descended into racism. His colleagues, meanwhile, saw both the potential in his early discoveries and the impossibility of working with him further. In 1957, a group later known as the Traitorous Eight fled Shockley's employment and founded Fairchild Semiconductor. It was to become the germinating seed of the semiconductor industry, the first wave of Silicon Valley.

By 1970, the semiconductor business was well established in the area between San Francisco and San Jose. But it was far from the industry that occupies that space today. Early Silicon Valley was largely funded by the government and closely linked to research for the Defense Department. Fairchild gave rise to National Semiconductor and Intel, among many others. Hewlett-Packard grew into a mainstay of life on the peninsula.

Xerox sponsored breakthrough research. Each of those was a pioneering and historically significant company in the development of our modern era, and each was affiliated with national security and defense. Government contracts helped seed the Valley, but the generation that followed those pioneers arrived with a different temperament. There was a reason that California hosted the technology revolution, that it didn't happen outside Boston or in North Carolina or Texas or Washington, DC. As Jerry Brown reflected, it was some combination of the music, the sense of rebellion, and the drugs.[22] There, in the cradle of the protests against HUAC and the Vietnam War, an earth-shaking revolution took hold.

That had implications not just for the world but for California, too. Until that point, California's economy rested on familiar pillars: agriculture, tourism, entertainment, trade. Then an entirely new business sprang up and eclipsed them all. Silicon Valley nurtured a culture of staggering gyrations. It represented nothing less than the greatest accumulation of wealth in human history, but it also swept in periodic collapse, innovation, retrenchment, and frustration. All of which would define Brown's gubernatorial tenure, along with California more broadly and then America itself in the years to follow.

Play ball.

# Part Three

## Governor

# 9

# The Rush to Change

Transitions for chief executives—whether presidents or governors or mayors—follow a reasonably familiar pattern. The newly elected leader appoints a transition committee, headed by a person of stature and guided by a close personal confidant. The committee sets about identifying promising candidates for positions throughout the government; the newly elected official sifts through résumés, meets with the most appealing contenders, and makes a series of announcements, gradually filling up the administrative ranks in time to launch on inauguration day.

Not Jerry Brown. Following his November election, Brown went through the motions. He appointed the committee, set out his priorities, reserved office space in downtown Los Angeles, hired staff. But the real business was done elsewhere and by others. Brown asked two close associates—one good friend and one trusted aide—to run his transition. Tony Kline, his old friend from law school, took one oar, while Gray Davis, who joined the campaign after his own bid for state treasurer failed, picked up the other. Kline and Brown were close; Davis and Brown less so. But Brown admired Davis's sense of organization and his reliability. Davis was also a determined fund-raiser, complementing Brown in an area where Brown was uncomfortable and still learning.[1] They set up shop in Brown's modest Laurel Canyon home, purchased with help from his parents.

Laurel Canyon was a happening. The narrow, steep streets of the neighborhood were home in the late 1960s and early 1970s to Joni Mitchell and Jackson Browne, members of the Eagles and James Taylor. Crosby, Stills, and Nash wrote there, trading band members with the Byrds. David Geffen trolled for talent there and found plenty. Joni Mitchell set "Ladies of the Canyon" in those hills; she and Graham Nash lived together for a while, and he wrote "Our House" about that time. They had a fireplace. Frank Zappa had a duck pond.[2] Brown's house had a pool. The neighborhood was hip and stylish, mellower than the big mansions of Bel Air or Beverly Hills, groovier than the Valley, on the other side of Mulholland Drive, which snaked along the crest of the Hollywood Hills. The little enclave sat just above the Sunset Strip, where the Whisky a Go Go featured girls in go-go boots in a cage. The Roxy and the Troubadour were reliably rock and roll and folk, respectively; the Melody Room was jazzier.

Surrounded by the musical culture of the 1970s, tasked with building an administration for the nation's largest state, Brown removed himself from both. He took the occasion to study political philosophy. "He was trying to figure out Ludwig Wittgenstein," Kline recalled.[3]

Brown had long been interested in the philosopher, regarded as among his century's most significant thinkers. Wittgenstein's preoccupation with the logic and influence of language, his quest for moral perfection, and his study of the relationships between perception and reality all spoke to Brown as he faced great opportunity and hard reality. Brown also was reading Oswald Stengler, and his decision to tackle those difficult philosophers at this crucible moment in the governor-elect's life reflected his determination to lead differently—to advance a politics of ideas, not just favors and service.

"Politics is practical, tactical, transactional," he said in 2016. "But it also is a framework of ideas and in a framework of the good and bad." Beginning with the 1974 campaign, he added, "I [was] always trying to look beyond the first level of the obvious and say: 'Okay, what are we going to do?'"[4]

Brown approached the governorship with his spiritual well-being under consideration as well. After the primary, he journeyed to the

Abbey of Our Lady of New Clairvaux, a Cistercian abbey, or Trappist monastery, in the Northern California town of Vina. And then, after his victory in the general election, he traveled to Tassajara, the Zen retreat in the mountains above Carmel. At each, he paused quietly, far from the news he was at the center of, and reflected. He was drawn, Brown would say later in life, to the monastic—to quiet and detachment—and to the freshness of the insight it allowed.[5]

Brown used his own freshened eyes to consider ancient ideas. He was not one to "drop out" or to find new perspectives in drugs or altered consciousness. Influenced by his religious studies, his exploration of Zen, and his immersion in classics, he walked a path of tradition while also inviting discovery. That tension—contradiction, some might say— helped reinforce his detachment from the currents of the day. He could seem to outsiders so utterly modern, with his youth and girlfriends and talk of space exploration and technology, yet he was not and never would be a modernist. While others plotted political strategy and reveled in showing Reagan the door, Jerry Brown read Wittgenstein and sat quietly in monasteries, rising early, saying little, thinking deeply.

Brown, Kline, and Davis were joined by a fourth member of the team. Jacques Barzaghi—French by birth, an actor and filmmaker by trade, an enigmatic and windy philosopher by inclination—filled the undefined role of sidekick and adviser to Brown. Brown and Barzaghi met at a party around 1971, when Brown was California's secretary of state. Brown was, of course, a well-known figure in California even then. Barzaghi was unimpressed. He did not recognize Brown and took the occasion to lecture his party companion about the fate of the Navajo. Never afraid of an argument, Brown took note of Barzaghi. It was hard not to. Dressed in his self-styled uniform—beret, aviator jacket, and boots, all black, of course—Barzaghi presented himself as a quasi-Marxist philosopher and man of earth. Over the years, many of Brown's associates would come to dislike Barzaghi and distrust his relationship with Brown, but the two of them hit it off immediately, and Brown hired him as an adviser without a specific portfolio. Barzaghi would run errands, pick up laundry, and act as chauffeur, maid, valet, and mystic. He was ubiquitous yet never servile; he and Brown would discuss French literature and furniture and history.[6] "Don Quixote had Sancho Panza and Richard Nixon had Bebe Rebozo," the *New York Times* observed later. "Jerry Brown…has Jacques Barzaghi."[7]

As one Brown friend said, "I thought he [Barzaghi] was some kind of houseboy, but I did not make the mistake that some did of treating him as such."[8] Crossing Barzaghi from that point forward would prove dangerous for Brown intimates. It seemed to many that accepting Brown's novel companion became the price of admission to Brown's friendship. Smart friends learned to accept Barzaghi or, at least, pretend to. Brown and Barzaghi spent more than three decades as friends and confidants before eventually parting ways. During those transition days, they were rarely apart.

As for the more mundane business of building an administration, Brown set out to recruit officials from unlikely places. He courted business leaders and environmentalists and selected a large number of lawyers, particularly drawn from public-interest law firms. He was determined to recruit young people, and he was committed to ethnic and gender diversity with a zeal unknown by any of his predecessors or even many of his contemporaries. "I wanted to open up new pathways," he said in 2016. "I got energetic young people. I was young once."[9]

His top priorities, Brown said on the day after his election, were to fill the positions of finance director, secretary of food and agriculture, and secretary of transportation and to appoint a newly created energy commission charged with the responsibility of choosing locations for electrical plants.[10] "I wasn't that worried about experience," he said later. "I thought these jobs could be learned."[11]

Brown did not at first highlight an entity that would prove to be one of his most lastingly significant. The California Air Resources Board had come into existence under Reagan and was charged with supervising the state's air-quality efforts, including its work under the parameters of the federal Air Quality Act. Brown named Tom Quinn, his loyal and capable campaign manager, to oversee CARB. That was a position of significant influence, though some wondered whether it was a slight to Quinn to be passed over for chief of staff, a position that went instead to Gray Davis.

If Quinn considered it a demotion, he did not let on. On the contrary, he would use his position to help Brown achieve some of the most lasting and far-reaching change of the governor's first two terms.

Quinn was to head the five-member board, but he needed colleagues, especially when two Reagan appointees, realizing that Brown was not likely to reappoint them, decided to resign. For one of those slots, Brown met with Mary Nichols, a twenty-nine-year-old public-interest lawyer who, like Brown, was a graduate of Yale Law School. Soon after Brown's election, Nichols, visibly pregnant, met with Quinn and, having secured his approval, made the trip to Brown's Laurel Canyon home and there met the governor-elect for the first time.[12]

Brown announced her appointment after taking office, and Nichols would prove to be both an exceptionally capable board member and an ardent, effective advocate for clean air. Her tenure spanned Brown's first terms in office. Gov. Arnold Schwarzenegger brought her back to the job during his time, and she served yet again under Brown during his second stint, twenty-eight years after the first. Under her leadership, California would become the nation's foremost force in addressing first air pollution and later climate change. A section of the Clean Air Act, passed in 1963 and significantly broadened in 1970 (the 1970 act, among other things, extended pollution controls to automobiles), explicitly gave California permission to adopt more rigorous standards than those applied to the rest of the country, an acknowledgment of the smog that had become a defining feature of the Los Angeles Basin. In her position as a member and later chair of the California Air Resources Board, Nichols would leverage that special authority granted to California to effectively set pollution standards for the nation. The auto industry screamed in protest, but so many cars were sold in California that the state's standards became those for the nation; Nichols weathered protests but held her ground.[13]

Brown had not promised much during the campaign. He'd run as an outsider and benefited from both Watergate and the Hearst kidnapping. He had avoided issues and concentrated instead on themes: change, activism, energy, youth, clean and constructive government.[14] He almost lost, but, having won, he had the luxury of assuming office without a confining set of campaign promises to fulfill. As he approached his inauguration, then, he did so with a relatively blank slate, though with a firm determination to be different. So firm, in fact, that he sometimes seemed a parody of himself.

On the eve of the inauguration, Brown canceled the traditional celebrations: the times were too demanding, he said, to warrant such extravagance. Pat and Bernice had looked forward to the event and were disappointed. Jerry paid them no heed. And, as always, he improvised: he was drafting his inaugural address the night before he delivered it, sorting through past inaugural addresses and finding none, including those of his father, particularly impressive. Nevertheless, the next day, he opened with a nod to his family. "I wasn't sure I was going to make it," Brown began. "My father thought I wasn't going to make it, either. But here I am."[15]

Speaking casually, almost flippantly—"I'm not going to give you a for-malistic address," he said. "I just want to tell you what's on my mind"—Brown opened, as he often did and would in years to come, with a warning about the state of society. In this case, he was worried about the election's low turnout and what that suggested about a wounded belief in government.

"More than half of the people who could have voted, refused," he noted, "apparently believing that what we do here has so little impact on their lives that they need not pass judgment on it. In other words, the biggest vote of all in November was a vote of no confidence."

Those were not exactly the words of a governor looking to make friends with the legislature, and he compounded his criticism of its work by pledging to implement his own Proposition 9, with its restrictions on campaign contributions and lobbyist gifts—pointedly, to members of that same legislature.

Scolding done, Brown promised to cooperate with the federal govern-ment on job programs and to work with the private sector as well. He stressed the need for clean air and water, foreshadowing his commitment to environmental protection. And in another preview of his tenure, in this case the frugality that would come to define him as an unusual

Democrat, he pledged budget cuts, starting with those that would affect his own office, which he vowed to trim by 7 percent.

Brown closed by turning to what he believed he could do with the office he had just assumed. Here, too, he sketched themes, explicitly and implicitly, that would become familiar over time. He promised little, instead offering goals that were achievable and focused, within the reach of politics and yet remarkable considering the history of his state.

"It is time that we treat all workers alike, whether they work in the city or toil in the fields," Brown said. "All workers, whoever they are, and wherever they are, should be strongly represented and have an effective voice in the decisions that affect their wages and working conditions."[16]

The whole speech took less than eight minutes. The *Los Angeles Times* credited Brown with setting "exactly the right tone for his administration and for the new Legislature."[17] But a columnist for the *San Francisco Examiner* came closest to echoing Brown's self-appraisal. "Any speech that short," he wrote, "can't be all bad."[18]

Brown announced some of his appointments during his transition, others in the days and weeks after taking office. Throughout, Brown rewarded loyalty and recognized talents. Tony Kline was given the position of legal secretary, overseeing Brown's selection of judges, among other things. For secretary of agriculture and services, Brown reached back to his days at Berkeley and picked a brilliant young lawyer and fellow member of International House: Rose Elizabeth Bird. Brown's appointment made her the first woman ever to serve in a California governor's cabinet. And with the economy at the center of the state's politics, Brown placed great emphasis on jobs, so he chose a former campaign worker, Jim Lorenz, to head the state's Department of Employment.

At Brown's behest, Lorenz spent the administration's early months attempting to create a jobs plan. He ran into the usual obstacles—bureaucratic interference, struggles for turf and leadership—along with those that Brown introduced: uncertainty, vagueness, lack of overt support. Working for Brown, Lorenz concluded early on, was humiliating, an exercise in self-sacrifice on behalf of an egocentric and unfocused leader. Lorenz soldiered on, composing a long memo to outline his ideas on employment, only to have a copy of that memo leaked to the *Oakland Tribune* on June 19. The *Tribune,* then a sternly conservative voice, headlined its exclusive: BROWN'S SECRET WORKER STATE, THE SECRET JOB REVOLUTION.[19] Brown distanced himself from the report and the plan, leaving Lorenz hanging out to dry. "The artful dodger was at it again," Lorenz later wrote in *Jerry Brown: The Man on the White Horse,* the first tell-all insider look at the early, chaotic months of Brown's governorship. First through deputies and then directly, Brown urged Lorenz to resign. Lorenz would not. A month after the story appeared, Brown fired him.

> He had no commitment one way or another. He didn't care. The sole concern he had was expressing the popular will successfully enough to be reelected governor in 1978 and president in 1984. Jerry was the totally democratic man. Like the proverbial weathervane, he turned in whichever direction the winds blew him. For as he himself said to me one day long before we were to reach a parting of ways: "Popularity is the only currency of the realm around here."[20]

Lorenz's book is not altogether fair, nor was it intended to be. It was written, after all, by a man Brown had fired. Yet it highlighted an aspect of Brown's leadership—the elevation of ambition beyond all other values— that would fuel Brown's most severe critics, from Lorenz to Pete Wilson to Bill Clinton and beyond. Brown himself lent credence to the view of himself as unprincipled with his penchant for glib deflection. Early in his governorship, he compared his approach to governing to that of guiding a canoe—"You paddle a little on the left, you paddle a little on the right, and you paddle a straight course," he remarked.[21] That became known as Brown's "canoe theory of politics," and it did him a disservice. Brown was not balancing for the sake of balance: he was practicing something closer to what the Jesuits call discernment, exploring ideas by looking at them individually and assessing their moral foundation, their appeal to what the Jesuits sometimes call a "reasoning heart." Such an exploration is not ideological or even fundamentally political, and as such it can produce ideas that do not readily comply with political norms. That is a serious undertaking, and Brown attempted to put it into practice, but it required too much explanation to survive conventional scrutiny. He opted for a slogan, "Paddle left, paddle right," and undermined his own seriousness of purpose. Lorenz, without quite grasping it, called Brown on it. Brown had only himself to blame.

Others fared better, often in novel posts. Brown asked poet Gary Snyder to head the California Arts Council. Stewart Brand, publisher of the *Whole Earth Catalog*, received the title of special assistant to the governor: in that happily vague role, he met regularly with Brown and brought in speakers to enlighten him and the staff. At Brand's invitation, Jacques Cousteau paid a visit. So did Buckminster Fuller, Herman Kahn, Ray Bradbury, Ken Kesey, and Carl Sagan.

Brown thought big. He proposed that California invest in satellites, a suggestion that drew scorn. He created an Office of Appropriate Technology and named an architect he had met at the San Francisco Zen Center, Sim Van der Ryn, to head it. Van der Ryn would pioneer a host of innovations, some mocked in their time, that would eventually become commonplace: the smart building, solar installations, biofuels, drought-resistant plantings.

Van der Ryn, a native of the Netherlands who trained as an architect at the University of Michigan, would prove one of Brown's most lastingly influential appointees, both as the founding head of the Office of Appropriate Technology and as state architect. Van der Ryn examined people in their environments and designed buildings to suit human needs. Those ideas would become commonplace in architecture in later years, but Van der Ryn was at the leading edge of an environmental design movement. At the time, his ideas struck some people as just odd.[22]

It began with just Van der Ryn and one assistant and a budget of $25,000, housed in what had been a Mexican restaurant in downtown Sacramento. Van der Ryn half-jokingly called it the Office of Commonsense Technology and described its mission as reaching the public "with workable ideas on what people can do to save money and energy."[23] One early participant in the office's creation said its goals were to "document, proselytize, demonstrate."[24] As it grew, the office could be irritating to the bureaucracy—it swelled to more than forty staff members who weighed in on state projects and buildings, recommending a drought-resistant garden in one instance, modern insulation in another. The office touted experimental waste-treatment systems, composting, biofuels, and solar energy. Its architects and planners wrestled with the right balance between ventilation and heat conservation—an especially pressing concern in the years following the Arab oil embargo and its destabilization of energy supply and price.

Van der Ryn felt no compunction about using his dual positions as state architect and head of the new technology office to intercede in ongoing projects. In 1976, he was shown plans for a pair of proposed government towers to be built in Sacramento. "I went through some of this stuff about 'The era of cheap energy is over,'" he said later. "That we can't think about the first cost of buildings anymore. We have to think of [the] cost of the use-life of the building, what the energy consumption is going to be…Buildings that are responsive to Sacramento climate have huge overhangs, passive solar systems that act as supply wheels, the way adobe works…Just a lot of commonsense design stuff. In two days, I was able to undo a $40 million office building project. In two weeks, we've done schematic plans for basically a kind of Mediterranean style that would be a frame state office building with an interior court."

The building opened in 1981, supplying office space to the state's Department of Developmental Services, Health and Human Services, and others. Its then avant-garde features, including passive heating and cooling systems beyond those employed up to that point, made it a "flagship for the state's Energy Efficient Office Building Program," a General Services Administration spokesman said decades later.[25]

All that may have sounded spacey to some critics, but the Office of Appropriate Technology proved as conservative as it was revolutionary. "The principles of appropriate technology are bipartisan, fiscally conservative and applicable in both institutional and personal choices," said Bob Judd, who succeeded Van der Ryn as the office's director. By 1981, the office had a staff of nearly forty people and a budget of more than $3 million a year.

\* \* \*

Did Brown's appointments or innovations revolve around any organizing principle, or were they merely the haphazard work of a philosopher-prince suddenly turned into a governor? Some wondered about that question, to the point where even Brown joked about it. "The only way a person can get a job in this administration is if he's a poverty lawyer, a kook, or a priest who was with Cesar Chavez," Brown said soon after taking office.[26]

But Brown was not hiding his ideas or short-circuiting serious thinking. He read voraciously and intelligently, and he made no secret of what impressed him. That was most evident in his enthusiastic embrace of the work of economist and philosopher E. F. Schumacher, whose admirers included Van der Ryn.

Brown touted Schumacher's important book *Small Is Beautiful: A Study of Economics As If People Mattered* with the zeal of the converted. He quoted from it, handed it to visitors, carried it in public. Schumacher's premise, the idea that spoke so eloquently to Brown, was that economic systems needed to work within limits. The tenets of that system included moderation, preservation of resources, gradual change, and fulfillment. Its values centered on health, beauty, and permanence. All that appealed to Brown's most passionately held notions and gave coherence to ideas Brown had been approaching since childhood, first in terms of religion, later intellectually, and then in his developing sense of unity with the environment. "Small is beautiful" became the Brown administration's semiofficial motto, and the son of California's builder-governor became a prophet of limits, conservation, and deference to nature and God.

There was another, deeper intellectual influence at work on Brown. This one reached him first through writing and, later, through personal example—an influencer whose thinking on specific subjects, the university in particular, would shape Brown's approach to policy matters. More important, this man's worldview informed Brown's temperament and relationship to those around him.

Brown's first exposure to Ivan Illich occurred in the late 1960s, when he came upon an article that mentioned *Deschooling Society,* an extended challenge to modern institutions and assumptions. Illich, an Austrian

Catholic philosopher whose ideas have largely slipped out of modern conversation but whose work was seriously debated in the 1970s, was foremost a skeptic. To Illich, education as provided by contemporary Western society was worse than harmless: it was deceptive, lulling society into the myth that it was providing knowledge and mobility when it was rather an industry of control. "It was something," he told Brown later, "like engineering people."[27]

*Deschooling Society* spoke to Brown on two levels: it reinforced his uneasiness with the architecture of public education in California, which he regarded as wasteful and unproductive. And, much more deeply, it stoked his suspicions about institutions in general. Brown had rejected the retail politics of his father and opted for deeper things, the study of God and immersion in Ignatian meditation. Emerging from the seminary, he discovered Zen, whose parallels to the teachings of Saint Ignatius he welcomed and in which he discovered new foci for meditation along familiar paths.

This exploration, the defining intellectual exercise of Brown's life, was marked by a unifying theme: skepticism. Illich touched that deep place in Brown, the unwillingness to accept what others believed with conviction but without proof. "I am skeptical," Brown happily acknowledged in 2016. "I always have been. I don't know where it started, but I don't believe most things that people say."[28]

Illich gave philosophical heft to that instinct in Brown, who was captivated, as many of that era were, by the freshness and vivacity of Illich's writing. Education, Illich argued, did not elevate or enrich. At a time when the pursuit of equal educational opportunity was commonplace across much of American society, Illich would have none of it. "Rather than calling equal schooling temporarily unfeasible, we must recognize that it is, in principle, economically absurd," he wrote in *Deschooling Society*. "To attempt it is intellectually emasculating, socially polarizing, and destructive of the political system which promotes it."[29] In place of such fraud and destruction, Illich proposed skill exchanges and "learning webs," rejections of modernity and innovation and a return to the wisdom of instinct.

His analysis was not limited to schooling. Modern medicine, Illich argued, did not cure or heal, as the opening line of *Limits to Medicine* memorably declared. "The medical establishment," Illich wrote, "has become a major threat to health."[30] He believed what he wrote: Illich nursed a tumor for years, calling it his "mortality" even as it protruded from the side of his head.[31] Educators and doctors were not necessarily complicit in a fraud, he argued, but rather were swept up in a system that they could not see beyond. Illich questioned the premises of systems— the university, the judiciary, politics—more than did the participants in those systems. To understand Brown, his friend Nathan Gardels observed, one has to understand Illich.

Brown's appreciation of Illich helped explain one of the great mysteries of Brown's first terms as governor: Why, many observers asked, was Brown so hard on the university system that his father did so much to build and nurture?

The glib answer, heard often in Sacramento and on campuses, was that Jerry Brown was tough on the university precisely because Pat Brown had loved it so much. That was nonsense, an example of critics making a connection based on a single point of data—the relationship between father and son. In fact, Brown was stingy with all state departments, not just the university, though university officials were more bitterly disappointed than most, in part because they thought Brown would return them to the largesse of his father, especially after the lean years under Reagan.

Brown's first state budget was typical of his relationship with the university. He provided for a 4.6 percent increase in funding, enough to allow himself to argue that he had been generous but far less than university officials, starved by Reagan, felt was needed to help them recover. Brown also denied the university money it sought for new construction. To make matters worse, he seemed to hold professors and university officials in some contempt. University officials needed to "wake up and realize these are hard times," he said.[32] The university was a "pretzel palace" of complexity, barely connected to truth, he argued. Brown questioned the commitment to teaching and students, wondered why money mattered so much to administrators and teachers. Wasn't there "psychic income" to be derived from teaching, he asked.

Brown's taunting of the university did not do much to change it. But he liked to shock a system—the judiciary was about to find that out—and the university was no exception. His first round of appointees to the university's board of regents included a conservative financial manager and veteran of the Reagan administration, Vernon Orr; the president of the Mexican American Legal Defense and Education Fund, Vilma Martinez; and Gregory Bateson, an anthropologist once married to Margaret Mead whom Brown met at the San Francisco Zen Center and who wrote about topics ranging from cybernetics to ecology. Bateson would regularly report back his disappointment with the system to Brown, and the two would commiserate about an educational infrastructure that offered too many choices without enough learning, one that seemed to measure student success by the wrong metrics and seemed to do less teaching than posturing.[33]

Bateson would prove especially influential, at least in regard to his impact on Brown's conception of the university's mission. "Bateson talked about how the university was not studying the eternal verities," Brown said years later. "He thought we had to deal with fundamental principles. That was what the university should do."[34]

Through four terms as governor—and during that entire time, as a regent of the University of California—Brown would never be convinced that the university lived up to that ideal. Its array of offerings was exciting but lacked an overarching unity, he believed. Instead, Brown harkened to a more classical, conservative sense of the university's mission, one that was more focused intellectually and modern technologically. He never quite was able to achieve that.

Bateson's influence on Brown extended beyond the latter's role as a regent. The anthropologist wrote deeply and broadly on notions of ecology—connectedness between organisms—and these thoughts echoed Brown's explorations of Ignatius and Zen. Bateson, perhaps influenced by his experimentation with LSD, drew those connections and challenged readers, including Brown, to question fundamentals of perceived reality. Bateson was a warm man and a demanding teacher. He and Brown formed a friendship that lasted to the final days of Bateson's life. On July 3, 1980, Bateson lay dying at the San Francisco Zen Center. Jerry Brown, young governor and old friend, came to visit his dying comrade. Bateson could barely speak. He seemed deep in thought. But when Brown entered, he responded. "Gregory recognized him and stretched out his hand to greet him," Bateson's daughter recalled.[35]

Bateson and Brown sat together, quietly, on the bed. And Bateson whispered something to the governor. Those gathered around him could barely hear, but Brown heard clearly. "Are there more angels?" Bateson had asked. Brown did not know how to respond. "It's okay," Bateson said.[36]

Bateson died the next day, July 4, in San Francisco.

Brown's move to Sacramento meant setting up not just business in the town where his mother and father had once reigned. It also meant moving his personal life from Los Angeles to the capital. He announced himself as a bachelor and ascetic.

First and most famous was his refusal to live in the new governor's mansion, in Carmichael, around ten miles from downtown Sacramento. The mansion was completed in 1975 after having been commissioned by his predecessor, Reagan. Dubbing it the House That Reagan Built, Brown announced that it was too grand for him, "not my style," as he carefully put it, lest he offend those who appreciated its look. Joan Didion, taking stock of the unoccupied residence overlooking the American River, understood the significance of that description. "The house is not Jerry Brown's style…and it is a point which presents a certain problem, since the house so clearly *is* the style not only of Jerry Brown's predecessor but of millions of Jerry Brown's constituents." The House That Reagan Built was, Didion added at the end of her essay, "evocative of the unspeakable."[37]

Brown stayed away from the house—he privately derided it as having all the character of a supermarket, and it sat vacant through his tenure— and instead lived as a frugal, monkish figure with no need of luxury. He rented an apartment near the capitol—it occupied the top floor of a building at 1400 N Street; the other apartment on that floor was kept vacant for security reasons[38]—and put a mattress and box spring on the floor (it was not, as legend later came to have it, a futon). He eschewed the official state Cadillac provided for governors and opted instead for his blue Plymouth, though he accepted a chauffeur. He rarely carried money and often asked passersby or guests to pick up a tab or lend him change for a cab or a phone call. He flew commercial and coach. He traveled with little security, sometimes none at all.[39]

And there was the question of Brown's sexuality. Opponents had long hinted that Brown was gay. At thirty-seven years old, handsome, well dressed, and conspicuously unmarried, it was a believable possibility at a time when being gay could have been hurtful to Brown politically—on a national stage if not necessarily in California. Brown never denied rumors of his homosexuality, later explaining privately that he saw those rumors as neither damaging to him—it would have been hurtful for him to suggest that it was somehow wrong to be gay—nor worthy of a reply.[40]

In the absence of a comment from Brown, the state's newspapers came amusingly close to speculating outright about his sexuality. In a 1975 profile just before Brown's inauguration, the *Los Angeles Times* reported that a "long-time friend" said "any inferences that Brown may be less than normally attracted to women are 'not true, ridiculous.'" Another friend reported that Brown had had several "traditional" relationships, adding, almost boastfully: "He has a whole lot of them now."[41] Those who knew him best knew well that he was heterosexual, but they were bound by confidences. One associate from those years recalled that on the campaign trail, Brown would sometimes break for a "nap" with an attractive young woman. Another remembered that he once quietly slipped away with a very young woman who caught his eye while she was registering to vote.[42]

Of those who needed no convincing that Brown liked women, some were eager to find him a companion. His correspondence from early in the first term includes a number of letters in which the senders tried to set him up with dates. "To quote an old adage: 'All Work and No Play Makes Jack a Dull Boy (or Dull Governor),'" wrote one helpful correspondent. She suggested that Brown look up her daughter, a nutritionist working in Sacramento. "Not only is she very pretty, but she is very intelligent," her mother added.[43]

And then he showed up with Linda Ronstadt on his arm. Ronstadt would quickly become part of Brown's lore—and he of hers—in part because she was at least as well known as he was inside California, and she was certainly more famous outside the state. The two had met in 1971 at a deliciously low-end Mexican restaurant in Los Angeles called Lucy's El Adobe Cafe, where Brown ate frequently and Ronstadt ate occasionally. They spoke that evening, then Brown asked her out. They dated discreetly through the early 1970s, but their relationship attracted new and widespread attention once Brown became governor and Ronstadt released her breakthrough album, *Heart Like a Wheel,* which went on sale just weeks before Brown's inauguration. Brown visited her at her homes in Malibu and Windsor Square, a pricey Los Angeles neighborhood, and Ronstadt occasionally joined him in Sacramento, though she did not much like it there. "We didn't go out in public that much," Brown recalled in 2016. "It was a pain in the neck."[44]

Instead, they cohabited in Los Angeles and Malibu. And though Ronstadt disliked politics, she enjoyed the social life around it. She accompanied Brown to parties and gatherings, usually in Southern California, and she occasionally acted as unofficial First Lady. During a visit by Princess Margaret to Los Angeles, Brown annoyed the princess by announcing that he would not be staying for the full meal—a glaring breach of royal protocol. The two were seated next to each other, and when the food was served, Ronstadt dropped by their table, putting one hand on her boyfriend's shoulder and the other on the princess's shoulder. Ronstadt, dressed in white miniskirt and red boots, snatched a piece of food off Brown's plate and asked, "What are we having to start?" The princess was horrified.[45]

At least the princess got dinner. When Prince Charles visited Brown in Sacramento, in 1977, Brown served him cold cuts and sprouts on bread; they talked about solar energy and space exploration over their spare lunch.[46] Charles returned to Windsor Castle, Brown to the mattress on the floor.

Brown could be an attentive companion—many associates from those years recall him interrupting meetings to take a call from Ronstadt or checking in with her from faraway locations—but he could be absent-minded and self-absorbed, too. They were at home one more morning in Malibu when the phone rang. Ronstadt was in the shower, and Brown answered. It was Joe Papp, the Broadway director and producer. As Ronstadt toweled off, Brown informed her that a producer had called with a proposal for her. Brown got the production wrong, and Ronstadt had to straighten it out later. Soon, she was starring in *The Pirates of Penzance*.[47]

Brown dated other women—at various times, he was linked to actress Natalie Wood and photographer Pamela Fong—but those who spent time with him and Ronstadt sensed a genuine connection. "They really like each other," Assemblyman Willie Brown gleefully reported to *Newsweek* magazine. "He's a different person when he's with her. There's a side the public never sees. He's flirty, flippant and very funny. And he's as interested in her physically as I'd like to be."[48]

# 10

# Rights and Opportunities

Brown's impressively brief inaugural address stayed away from specifics and resisted binding obligations. As a result, the few promises that he did make stood out. In effect, they boiled down to two versions of the same commitment: bargaining rights for agricultural workers and for state employees. To deliver, Brown turned to two very different and able associates: Rose Bird was entrusted with securing rights for farmworkers, while Raymond Fisher, Brown's Tuttle and Taylor colleague, was given the job of developing those same rights for public employees.

Pat Brown came to office as a supporter of farmworkers, convinced that they deserved a fairer shake from California's vast and concentrated agricultural industry. He proposed a state minimum wage that would have delivered hefty raises to farmworkers. But he lost that battle, and, as was occasionally his habit when delivered a defeat, he pouted. Moreover, as his governorship unfolded, he developed closer ties to some of the state's leading growers, further attenuating his relationship to workers. By 1966, when a young Cesar Chavez led a march to Sacramento to draw attention to a farmworkers' strike and to encourage a boycott of table grapes, the marchers regarded Pat Brown as an adversary. Chavez asked to meet with the governor on Easter Sunday; Brown, vacationing with his family at Frank Sinatra's estate in Palm Springs, turned him down.[1]

Jerry's support for farmworkers was less ambivalent and his ties to growers less meaningful. And the young governor was, in his early years, always eager to prove his independence from his father. The result was that Jerry Brown embraced the cause of farmworkers far more enthusiastically than had his father. Among Jerry's first acts was to ask his new agriculture secretary, Rose Bird, to draft a state labor law that would extend collective bargaining rights to farmworkers. Bird set out to do so, even as Brown, prodded by the United Farm Workers, reached out to Chavez behind the scenes.

Though Bird later would become a problematic appointment for Brown, her assignment to this first task suited her well. Born to parents who worked as chicken ranchers in Tucson, Arizona, and raised by her mother after her father left the family when she was five, Bird grew up poor and determined. Her mother took the family to New York after her father's departure and subsequent death, and Rose attended Long Island University on a scholarship. She then came west for law school at Berkeley's Boalt Hall. She lived at International House, and there met Jerry Brown during his brief time at Berkeley. Even as a student, she was celebrated for her skills as an advocate and writer, graduating with honors in 1965.[2]

Bird impressed Jerry Brown during the campaign, and it was proof of his confidence in her that he entrusted her with one of his most pressing priorities. In part, that was because Brown appreciated Bird's willingness to challenge him. Once, during a cabinet meeting early in the first term, Brown glibly dismissed the need to give state workers a raise. Why should they receive one? he asked. "They don't do anything." Most of Brown's colleagues just let his bursts of temper pass. Bird did not. "That's garbage, Jerry," she responded.[3]

When it came to hammering out a deal for farmworkers, Bird's focus and fearless resolution proved to be valuable strengths. She had the job of producing a package that neither side was likely to appreciate, and it helped that she had little interest in being loved. With her as a bullish broker, farmers and farmworkers staked out their ground: farm owners believed workers were best treated as temporary seasonal employees, not permanent workers entitled to the protections of a union. Farmworkers, under Chavez's leadership, argued the opposite. Chavez and the United

Farm Workers produced a wish list for their goals in the form of a bill that they entrusted to assemblyman Richard Alatorre, a young liberal representative from Los Angeles. Farmers drafted their model bill and asked state senator Ken Maddy, a Fresno Republican, to carry it.[4]

While the principals searched for allies in the capitol, Bird conducted running negotiations, demanding that farmers, farmworkers, and their respective allies focus their efforts on her talks as the centerpiece of the debate. That frosted some of Brown's friends—and many of his critics— in the legislature, which felt excluded from the drafting of a signature, even historic, bill. "It was outrageous," assemblyman Willie Brown said later.[5] But it was effective. On April 10, Howard Berman, the Democrats' floor leader, introduced Brown's bill in the state assembly. It had clear benefits for the union, including the promise of secret-ballot elections and the right to strike at harvest time, but growers were allowed to hire strikebreakers, a major concession to their side. That gave the illusion that the bill was doomed. The proposal "won no immediate praise from any of the competing groups in the farm labor struggle," wrote George Skelton of the *Los Angeles Times*.[6]

In fact, Chavez and Brown were meeting out of view, and Chavez already had given his private support for the compromise. The UFW intentionally withheld its public support for the bill in order to reinforce the notion that it, too, was being forced into a deal against its interests— and thereby to head off any efforts to make it concede more. The strategy was intended to freeze the growers and Teamsters, a rival union with its own ideas for organizing farmworkers, into supporting the deal on the table, but it required the UFW to place great trust in Brown. It had to rely upon his promises to protect farmworkers even when agriculture and the Teamsters threatened to bolt the deal. Brown held fast, and in doing so he earned Chavez's profound respect.[7]

Bird, meanwhile, led the public fight. Despite the bill's lack of outward support, Bird warned legislators not to tamper with it. It was, she said, enough to satisfy, if not please, all sides. The legislature's job, she haughtily informed California's elected leadership, was to approve in its entirety the first substantive bill introduced by the state's thirty-seven-year-old governor in an area that had eluded the efforts of two previous governors, one of whom was his father. Legislators swallowed hard but yielded to the brash governor and his deputy. Ten days after it received Brown's bill, the legislature adopted it, sending it back to him for his signature. He signed it into law on June 5. California became the first state in the nation to provide such labor protections for farmworkers.

Adoption of the act was, as Brown said at the time, "a beginning rather than an end." Among other things, the act gave him the authority to name a five-member board, and his appointments immediately infuriated farmers, who felt double-crossed. Brown chose members clearly sympathetic to labor, including LeRoy Chatfield, a former administrative director of the United Farm Workers; Joe Ortega, a lawyer and Mexican American activist; and Roger Mahony, the auxiliary Catholic bishop of Fresno and ardent defender of farmworkers, who was granted a leave by the Church to handle his new government duties full-time.[8] Brown made Mahony the board's chair. Some growers complained, saying the "nominees were not selected on the basis the governor had promised" and were tilted in favor of labor over farmers.[9]

The board got off to a rocky start: the United Farm Workers competed with the Teamsters to organize workers, hold elections, and win certifications. Chavez complained of unfair practices; he and others blamed the board's staff for confusion. "The operative word is paralysis," the *Los Angeles Times* editorialized in October.[10]

All that would complicate the act's place in history. Indeed, it would prove a mixed blessing even to the man who seemed to benefit from it most. Cesar Chavez won a great victory with the passage of the act, and it seemed to cement his place in the history of American labor. It was Brown, however, who best understood the peril that victory posed for Chavez. "Once you snatch the gold ring, the game is over," Brown whispered to Kline. "Cesar's now got to find another struggle."[11]

Brown's administration could sometimes seem a jumble of voices—Gray Davis's steady baritone, Jacques Barzaghi's French-accented utterances, Brown's own insistent directives. But one voice found little purchase. Pat Brown, once governor himself, now sat firmly outside the new governor's inner circle.

News coverage naturally compared the two and probed—sometimes gently, sometimes less so—at hints of friction. A 1976 cover story in *Family Weekly*, a light newspaper insert of the day, was cheerful in tone but undergirded with bite. "Jerry wasn't particularly sensitive as a child," Bernice Brown, his mother, was quoted as saying. Jerry has "alienated some governors," his father added. Looking back at Jerry Brown's upbringing, the author noted: "The Brown children all vividly remember fiery discussions at the dinner table, and in particular, Jerry's debates with his father. Pat calls them 'rousing conversations,' but Jerry—at 12 and 13—decided they were tests of his mettle. His father thought he was helping him to find his identity. Jerry thought he was being squelched."[12] Pat Brown's assessment of his son: "He has that mass appeal. Not individual appeal—he's an introvert—but mass appeal."[13] What may be most noteworthy about the *Family Weekly* piece is not so much its significance—it appeared in *Family Weekly*, not a serious political or news journal—but the fact that Pat Brown saved it. It sits with his papers today at the Bancroft Library at UC Berkeley, his son's alma mater.

Some thought Jerry was downright mean to his father. Pat would call, day after day, and get stuck with Davis or some other aide, Jerry too busy to talk with his father. That was a shame, because Pat Brown knew the gubernatorial ropes—he was, after all, the only living Democrat ever to have held the office, and under other circumstances, he might naturally have been called upon by a young Democrat to help him understand and master the bureaucracy. Gray Davis recalled that Pat Brown would sometimes offer a useful suggestion, but Jerry, would ignore it if he knew it came from his dad. Instead, the way to get Jerry Brown to listen to it was to pretend that it was someone else's idea, at least long enough for Jerry to mull it over.[14]

Jerry Brown did not hide his occasional differences with his father, and at times he enjoyed telegraphing his independence. But he took care not to stray too far, stressing that the two had governed at different times and that different times demanded different types of leadership. When *Playboy* magazine sat down with Brown in 1975, the interviewer, Bob Scheer, opened by asking about Brown and his father. "On the night of your close victory, you were quoted as telling your father, 'I almost lost because of you.'"

Scheer allowed Brown to edit his responses, and Brown used the unusual opportunity to soften the impact of that and other questions. "I was joking," he jotted in response, an answer that was further refined by the time the magazine was published. "I was kidding him because he seemed to be taking so long at the microphone, and I was getting restless," the ultimate answer read.[15] Asked to compare their styles, Jerry Brown initially was critical of his father, calling his father's approach to politics appropriate for his period but "a bad anachronism" in the current political climate. He added, of his father's approach: "It is also one that I think needs to be tempered with a serious commitment to the hard work involved in the job." Reading that, Brown did not like the way it sounded, so he amended his response. He cut out the critical language and replaced it with a harmless banality. "I guess we are different," he wrote. "What can I say?"[16]

The sanitized version of the interview appeared in the April 1976 issue of *Playboy*. It stirred the impression that Brown was preparing to run for president, as he was, and gave readers a deeper look at his blend of Catholic structure and liberal idealism. His father was barely mentioned, just as Brown's edits had ensured.

Private correspondence between father and son hinted at Pat's unhappiness at being held at bay. He peppered his son with suggestions for appointments and well-meaning if sometimes bossy advice in areas as far-flung as home rule and forced busing.[17] Pat's notes usually were direct and intended to dole out ideas or insights. Sometimes, however, they verged on plaintive. Writing to his son near the end of 1975, Pat offered some thoughts on how to handle the Teamsters and closed with a father's plea: "Please let me know your plans. I always let you in on mine."[18] There is no record of a reply from Jerry.

Jerry Brown and William F. Buckley made for an odd pair of adversaries. Both were graduates of Yale—Buckley attended as an undergraduate, Brown as a law student—and both were deeply invested in their Catholicism. But in 1975, when Buckley invited Brown to appear on the former's television program, *Firing Line,* Buckley must have imagined he was setting up a lightweight for dismantling. Pretentious and smug, Buckley relished intellectual combat that he could win, and Brown, young and glib, seemed easy pickings, a novice to Buckley's master. They met on October 3 to discuss "the practical limits of liberalism," seated knee to knee in matching armchairs mounted on swivels, as if prepared for chess, which, in a sense, they were. Buckley was dressed in a peach jacket, Brown in a gray vested suit with a burgundy tie. Young men and women in shirtsleeves and blouses sat cross-legged at their feet.[19]

Buckley moved first, sending forth a pawn of condescension. "The governor of California is a young man whose father was also governor, the interregnum having been presided over by Ronald Reagan. He defeated his opponent narrowly in a race ignored by the majority of California's voters."

Brown squirmed a bit in his chair. Buckley riffed through Brown's background, describing his term as secretary of state as being notable in that "he proved adept at attracting the attention of the press." Brown chuckled sardonically at that.

Buckley launched into a question about busing as a means of achieving racial integration in schools, and Brown countered. He would, Brown said, "leave it to the courts."

The two parried for a few minutes over that and other topics, moving from constitutional interpretation to congressional authority in the area of the Civil Rights Act and the Voting Rights Act. Buckley expressed his surprise, his amazement, that Brown would defer to the Supreme Court, comparing acknowledgment of its judgment to "internal assent." "They're asking us to treat the Supreme Court more or less as Catholics are asked to treat the papacy," Buckley said.

Brown would not be out-Catholiced by Buckley. "That seems to be changing, too," he responded. "The doctrine of what is ex cathedra and what is not is rather difficult to define. It used to be every encyclical. Now it is very hard to identify what is subject to the doctrine of infallibility and what is not."

Buckley never recovered his position. Brown took over the conversation and articulated an "ecology" of civil and religious principles—

from busing to property taxes to segregation and the "lack of hope that is available to all." "We have to find a structured set of roles and jobs," Brown argued in language that Buckley himself might have uttered had Brown not beaten him to it. Buckley instead fell back on a rote critique of the Warren and Burger courts, sneering at decisions over school prayer and abortion. Brown was flying at a higher altitude. Buckley fiddled with his pen and flushed bright red. Beads of sweat gleamed from his forehead and upper lip.

It was Brown, not Buckley, who emphatically declared the significance of boundaries, and, within those constraints, stitched together his faith, his environmentalism, and his fatalism. "Freedom is totally impossible without limits, without structure," Brown said, music to the ears of any conservative, then pivoted to an application welcomed by liberals. "There are limits to the planet…The idea that government has some omnipotence or omniscience is completely absurd and counter to all the thinking that went into this country. There are many things that cannot be solved. There are many things that lie beyond or beneath government. And there is an overblown rhetoric and an overblown expectation that if there is a problem, there must be a program to solve it."

That, Brown added, twisting the knife, was the failing of Vietnam. "We were beaten," he said, ignoring Buckley's attempt to interrupt, "not because we lacked technology, not because we didn't have the hardware, not because we didn't have the systems analysis at the Pentagon. We lost because we lacked the political will to carry out a particular objective."

Appearing beside America's most ostentatious conservative, Brown had just trumped Buckley's religious faith and adherence to limits—and had done so to advance a theory of environmental protection and to repudiate the Vietnam War.

Checkmate.

Jerry Brown prepared to address the legislature and people of California in early 1976. He had been governor for a year. In that time, he had scored a historic victory for farmworkers and established himself as a novel and enterprising governor. His life—the car he drove, the mattress he slept on, the women he dated—was widely reported on, and he was the center of national attention as he moved California into its post-Reagan era.

But as he rose to speak on January 7, Brown had other ideas. Determined to keep his State of the State address short—it clocked in at eleven minutes and was uninterrupted by applause—he nevertheless wanted to say something larger about government and society. For a young governor of a major state on a roll, Brown sounded fed up, disillusioned, even angry:

> Throughout much of our recent past, the economy and the environment generated a surplus out of which new social programs could be financed. Growth was so rapid that relatively few hard choices had to be made. It was an era of guns and butter, of escalating benefits and few questions, a time when new programs were added and few old ones eliminated.
>
> That time is no longer. We have just completed and lost the most disastrous war in our nation's history. The oil boycott has shown that our economic machine is dependent on the resources of others. We began the last decade with great expectations about ending poverty and providing equal opportunity to everyone. Glib statements were made about protecting the environment.[20]

With the indignance of the betrayed, Brown pronounced that a new time was at hand, one of choices, when good ideas had to vie against one another for attention and resources, when not all problems could be solved. These were not the words of a Pat Brown or even a Ronald Reagan, whose leadership Brown implicitly repudiated with those comments. There was no sunny optimism, no false hope. This was the speech of a Jesuit steeped in self-denial, one of a close reader of Schumacher and Illich. It was delivered by the son of a woman who saved coupons throughout her husband's governorship. Brown lamented failure and deception and announced the coming of a new period in the life of his state and nation.

"In short," he said, "we are entering an era of limits." It would not be easy. "We are now forced to make difficult choices. Freeways, childcare,

schools, income assistance, pensions, health programs, prisons, environmental protection—all must compete with one another and be subject
to the careful scrutiny of the common purpose we all serve."

Brown made some news with his speech, proposing to eliminate state
income taxes for those making less than $5,000 a year along with his
promised flat-dollar across-the-board pay hike for state workers and an
increase in state support for educational opportunity programs (Brown
ignored the hard choices implied by those government gifts). Those
proposals overshadowed his darker passages in the next-day coverage of
his address, which focused on the tax proposal. Still, newspapers found
a way to register their puzzlement. THE BROWN '76 RESPONSE: "IT'LL
DO…NOT SO HOT," read the headline in the *San Francisco Examiner*.[21]
From the *Long Beach Independent*: GOVERNOR CAME LATE, SPOKE
BRIEFLY, LEFT FAST.[22] A *Los Angeles Times* editorial the next day treated
Brown more generously, but did so by assuming that Brown did not
mean what he said. The proposals within the speech, according to the
*Times,* "belie his own exhortations over the past year that Californians
must lower their expectations."[23] In other words, the *Times* supported
Brown so long as the governor did not mean what he said.

Legislative reaction was no kinder. Senator George Deukmejian, a
Long Beach Republican and senate minority leader with a future ahead
of him, called Brown's speech "totally vacant of any specific solutions to
the problems confronting California." Assemblyman John Vasconcellos,
a San Jose Democrat, credited Brown with providing "insight about
society's failures" but faulted him for neglecting to suggest what to do
about them.[24] Assembly speaker Leo McCarthy, a Democrat, agreed,
blaming Brown for offering "no specific solutions" to the state's problems. Republican assemblyman Eugene A. Chappie called it "a whole
bunch of pablum."[25]

And yet the "era of limits" would come to define Brown for
two, perhaps three generations of Californians. It set him apart from
peers and critics and established the devotion to frugality that would
characterize the Brown years. Many politicians detest choosing, picking
one constituency over another; they prefer growth and expansion and
doling out its benefits. Not Brown. Guided by the conviction that his

predecessors had gulled a gullible public, he determined to choose, a course that would often result in collisions with his fellow liberals and that would consistently set him apart, sometimes as a party of one. Tough politicians learn to say no; truly unusual ones enjoy it.

State employees did not enjoy the romance of farmworkers. They lacked a charismatic leader in the form of Chavez. They had the respect, but not the deep loyalty, of the governor and legislature. But Brown was committed to the principle of collective bargaining and labor organization; state workers were not to be an exception. To further that agenda, he turned to Ray Fisher, his former colleague from Tuttle and Taylor and a savvy, insightful lawyer and strategist who would leave a significant mark on Los Angeles, California, and the United States over the course of his long and important career.

Like many Brown intimates, Fisher at first found the new governor difficult to pin down. Fisher recalled flying from Los Angeles to Sacramento one morning for a midday meeting with Brown. Arriving, he was told that the governor was running behind schedule. Fisher waited all day, then repaired to a hotel and returned the next morning. Again he waited, until finally Brown emerged to ask whether Fisher would accompany him to the airport and back to Los Angeles. The two, Brown suggested, could talk in the car and on the flight. Fisher of course agreed, but Brown was distracted again in the car, discussing a bill that had landed on his desk and that he was unsure whether to sign. The highway patrol officer driving the car wryly confided to Fisher that when Reagan was governor, he would typically sign ten bills on the way to the airport; it was rare for Brown to finish even one.

Fisher and Brown boarded the flight, and Brown continued to work on other matters. Finally, after disembarking, they dropped by the Radisson hotel near LAX and talked. It was after midnight. Brown asked Fisher to be his special assistant for the collective bargaining issue. Fisher agreed, bringing that protracted conversation to an end. At least, he thought, he had it better than some: it was not unusual in those days for men and women invited to speak with the governor to bring a sleeping bag; they would camp in the capitol corridors while waiting their turn.[26]

Fisher had hoped to work from Los Angeles but quickly realized he needed a base in Sacramento. He rented a modest hotel room—"I think they charged by the hour," he remembered—and began by examining where support lay in the legislature. There was good news and bad. Bob Moretti, the assembly speaker, had put together a bill that was comprehensive and thoughtful. It created a Public Employment Relations Board, akin to the panel approved for farmworkers, and established a structure for union organizing and representation. But Brown, who had run against Moretti, didn't like him.[27] More important, Brown and his staff were flush from the farmworker victory and believed that the lesson of that struggle was that the legislature could be ignored with impunity.[28]

Then there were internal disputes. "Rose isolated me," Fisher recalled of Rose Bird. She consigned Fisher to a remote office and a shared secretary, determined to squelch his access to the governor and impede any success that might diminish her own achievements. Fisher waited his turn.

Once the farmworker bill had become law, Fisher—again working with Howard Berman—advanced the legislation for state employees. It did not follow the dogmatic approach of the farmworker bill: this bill received hearings and was open to amendments. One fierce critic was San Diego mayor Pete Wilson. The ambitious Wilson, who was facing reelection that fall, claimed that allowing public employees the right to organize and strike would "remove from local elected officials the ability to make those decisions we were elected to make" and result in "enormous" costs to taxpayers.[29]

At Fisher's urging, Brown traveled to San Diego to explain his support for the idea. Brown met with a local civic group. "He dazzled them," Fisher said. "It neutralized their opposition."[30] Wilson's opponent in the mayoral campaign favored the collective bargaining bill, but Wilson beat him soundly in September, propelling the San Diego mayor into contention for statewide office, perhaps even in position to challenge Brown in 1978.

Meanwhile, the public employee bargaining bill struggled in Sacramento. It was killed outright at one point—Fisher blamed Brown, in part, for feeling overconfident after the farmworker victory and not doing enough to lobby for public employees—and then split into two bills, one covering teachers and one for other state and local workers. The first bill, backed by California teachers' unions, made it through and extended bargaining and organization rights to California's 360,000 teachers, while the other legislation remained moribund, at least for a while.

In 1977, behind the leadership of assemblyman Ralph C. Dills, the legislature at last approved collective bargaining for state workers, adding another 90,000 to 100,000 workers to those covered by Brown's promises and the legislature's actions. The act specifically permitted state workers to form and join unions and required state officials to "meet and confer" with representatives of those unions. It also created the Public Employment Relations Board, which, like the farm labor board, had authority to supervise and enforce the provisions of the act. Brown signed the bill on September 30. A union leader praised Brown's "political courage" but warned that critics would remember his action. "There are sharpshooters in the hills ready to fire at anyone who comes to the aid of public employees."[31]

California's coast may be its most distinctive and defining feature. From San Diego beaches to the rocky, wooded shores of Del Norte County, California's oceanfront extends 840 miles and supplies the state with recreation, tourism, and industry. It is also fragile and vulnerable— susceptible to damage from pollution, as demonstrated by the Santa Barbara oil spill in 1969, and to development, as illustrated by the construction of The Sea Ranch along the northern coast in 1970.

Under Ronald Reagan's watch, Californians passed their first coastal protection act, using the ballot-initiative process to circumvent a divided legislature under the influence of development and energy-exploration interests. A coalition of environmental groups came together as the California Coastal Alliance and qualified Proposition 20 for the ballot in 1972. It passed, creating a protection zone that extended the entire length of California's coast, reaching three miles out to sea and one thousand feet inland.[32]

The new law did not, however, complete the job. It authorized creation of a commission to study the coastline and return with comprehensive recommendations for protection, all of which would need to be codified into law. That task fell to Jerry Brown in 1976, and it was a difficult one—the state senate had defeated every attempt at coastal protection for nearly a decade. Anthony Beilenson, who chaired the senate finance committee, called it an "extremely difficult" undertaking.[33]

Brown's support was assumed but not guaranteed. His environmentalism suggested it, but the interests arrayed against comprehensive protection were powerful and varied. Oil companies wanted permission to drill. Developers wanted permission to build, and labor did, too—new homes require construction workers to build them. That meant that Brown would be squeezed from his right and from his left. In his State of the State address that year, the speech in which Brown introduced his "era of limits," he endorsed "reasonable rules to control the use and development" of the coast, but that merely begged the question of what was "reasonable."[34]

Over the ensuing seven months, the governor and legislature, with special interests from all sides pulling levers, attempted to fashion a comprehensive bill. It was tough sledding. Lobbyists representing business interests—including real estate developers, port users, and commercial boating firms—joined with representatives of local governments angered by the intrusion on their authority to fend off various proposals.

So determined were foes of the plan that they enlisted the support of an influential lobbyist sure to get under Jerry Brown's skin. Pat Brown, famously or infamously representing Indonesia's oil interests, took charge of the California Council for Environmental and Economic Balance, a group fighting the plan, and thus placed himself in rare public conflict with his son.[35] The elder Brown nearly prevailed. In June, the assembly's Resources, Land Use, and Energy committee killed the key bill. But Jerry Brown was in no mood to lose on a procedural vote or to be outmaneuvered by his father. He rushed back from out of state to intervene, reviving the temporarily dead bill the following day.

Brown's efforts put the negotiations back on track. Splintering the legislation into several separate bills also helped break down the opposition. Two dozen bills wound their way through the process during the summer. One created a permanent coastal commission with the power to oversee development within one thousand yards of the ocean; another established rules for environmental-impact reports; still another provided for the acquisition and improvement of parkland along the coast; yet another created a special commission to originate and review plans for the Santa Monica Mountains, in Southern California. One bill extended the lives of six regional coastal commissions as part of the state's overall structure for review of development proposals, giving them four more years under the new law. Labor objected, and Brown agreed to trim that back to two years in return for labor withdrawing its objections.[36] In the end, it took a total of twenty-one bills to patch together a framework for coastal oversight and protection.[37] Brown signed the package of bills on September 29. He had outfoxed development and oil interests, including those represented by his father—a testament to mastery of the issue's complex insider politics. The winner was the environment.

It was, Brown said, a historic step toward protecting "one of the most beautiful spots on the planet."

The Giants and Dodgers initiated California's embrace of baseball, arriving in 1958 and debuting their respective ballparks in 1960 and 1961. They opened the floodgates, and California's weather and population distribution made it a perfect place for Major League Baseball. The California Angels joined the American League in 1966, followed by the Oakland Athletics in 1968. The San Diego Padres, a National League team, began playing in 1969. By the beginning of the 1970s, California, without a team for its first one hundred years, had more than any other state.

The Athletics, known as the A's, were mostly shadowed by the Giants, across the bay, but the A's came to life in the 1970s. With their brightly colored uniforms, imposing mustaches, and devastating pitching, they drew crowds and commentary. And they won. In fact, the A's strung together an extraordinary run of World Series, first in 1972, then again in 1973 and 1974. The A's of that era—*Dynastic, Bombastic, Fantastic* is the title of Jason Turbow's history of the team—were a swaggering and colorful collection, befitting the early 1970s and highlighting much of California's mood.

Baseball came to California in 1958. In the 1970s, it was head-quartered there.

The fight for California's coast occupied much of Brown's time in 1975 and 1976. The campaign for state workers to receive union protections stretched across three years. In the midst of it, Brown was pulled away from California by his ambition on an adventure that captured the rambunctious, ambitious, and unorthodox aspects of his personality. It began late on a Friday afternoon as Brown was casually meeting with a few reporters in his private office at the capitol.

Brown was taking questions when one reporter asked whether he would consider a run for president. Brown's feasibility as a national candidate had been much discussed during his 1974 gubernatorial bid, but as that contest closed and Brown barely eked out a victory, it largely subsided. Then came the victory in the farmworker debate, and his star rose again. When the topic came up this time, Brown seemed casual. As a matter of fact, Brown answered, he was planning to become a favorite-son candidate in California—meaning that he would run not necessarily with the intention of winning but rather to control a bloc of delegates and have influence over the convention. "The philosophy I've been talking about should be articulated," Brown said to the bewildered group of journalists, none of whom had been warned to expect any announcements that day, much less a declaration, for the presidency. "The people have a right to hear as wide a debate as possible."[38]

And even as Brown offered himself as a possible favorite son, he declined to rule out running in other primaries, too. Suddenly, Jerry Brown, governor for barely a year and just thirty-seven years old, was a candidate for president—and joining a race that already was well under way. Why did Brown enter the race so unconventionally? "Because I really couldn't think of a good reason not to," he answered later.[39]

Journalists were not the only ones taken by surprise. One aide, over-hearing the governor's remarks, rushed to Gray Davis's office. Davis was as surprised as the reporters. He called Mickey Kantor, a Los Angeles lawyer with deeper national political experience than anyone on Brown's

Sacramento team. Davis asked Kantor to come to Sacramento right away. "Jerry's just announced for president," Davis told him.[40]

Kantor hustled to Sacramento only to be put on ice for hours while waiting to get in to see Brown. Whiling away the time, he chatted with Barzaghi, and the two wandered over to Frank Fat's, a legendary Chinese restaurant a short walk from the capitol. Eventually, Brown joined them and opened by asking Kantor, "Would you put this together for me?" Kantor, flummoxed by the haphazard announcement and proposal, nevertheless agreed, and they cobbled together a message that would combine environmental protection, political reform, and diversity— three notable strengths of the still young Brown administration.

Complicating their task was the state of the primaries. By the time Brown backed into the campaign, ten states had already voted in Democratic primaries, with the Georgia governor, Jimmy Carter, showing the greatest strength. Filing deadlines had passed for more than a dozen more. As the newly minted campaign team scouted out the calendar and map—and consulted with Tom Quinn and others—the most promising possibility for Brown's debut seemed to be Maryland. It was still open for joining and had a particular advantage for Brown: it was the home state of his friend Nancy Pelosi, and her father and brother were both former mayors of Baltimore. Quinn reached out to Pelosi, and she assured the Brown team that the governor could expect a warm welcome there. He got one.

Arriving in Baltimore soon after announcing his candidacy, Brown was welcomed at the airport by the governor, Marvin Mandel, and an enthusiastic crowd. They traveled to a local Hilton hotel, where 2,500 more people greeted Brown. "People today are looking for a new spirit," Brown told that gathering. "I want to capture the initiative people had when Jack Kennedy was president."[41] Onlookers swooned, and politicians took note.

And so it was that Jerry Brown set out to become president of the United States.

The campaign was a strange event in the history of American politics— part shrewd strategy, part windy adventurism. It featured Warren Beatty, with his daffy attempts to hit on women and entertain crowds (the former were successful, the latter less so), and Mandel, Maryland's rough governor, who saw Brown's bid as a chance to strike back at the annoyingly moralizing Carter. Brown thrilled some crowds and left others wondering what had hit them. He could be playful with reporters and then turn curtly dismissive, sometimes so abruptly that it was hard to know when he was playing and when he was being serious. He spoke Latin often and seemed at least as much of a sort-of Jesuit evangelist as a committed candidate for president. Do what you are doing, Ignatius suggested. Brown did.

And yet Brown was coldly serious, too. He beat Carter in Maryland and almost beat him in Oregon as a write-in candidate (finishing third there to Frank Church). He won Nevada, where he also was a late entry, and California, to no one's surprise. He was able thus to claim correctly that he beat Carter in nearly every state where they ran head-to-head.

As the convention approached, Brown could point to significant victories, but he also had to concede that Carter, with his earlier start, had the delegates to win. Still, he enjoyed suspense and mischief and practiced a little of each in the closing weeks of the primaries. Out of the blue came the offer of an endorsement from the Louisiana governor, Edwin Edwards, a southern governor as enjoyably shady—he would later serve time in federal prison—as Brown was scrupulously clean. Brown might have turned it down. Edwards's support came too late to make a difference, and he was not Brown's kind of politician. But Brown was feeling impish. "Why not?" he asked when Tom Quinn told him that Edwards wanted him to pay a visit.

Brown and his entourage traveled to Louisiana to scoop up the unlikely endorsement. Landing in New Orleans, Brown was shuttled to Baton Rouge to spend the night at the governor's mansion. The rest of the group stayed behind for dinner in New Orleans and arrived late in Baton Rouge. The next morning, more than a few reporters attended the endorsement press conference nursing headaches. One dared to ask Edwards how he could possibly find political common ground with Brown, given their obvious differences in style and approach. "Jerry Brown and I have identical political philosophies," the governor responded to disbelieving ears. "States' rights!"[42]

At the convention, held in New York, Brown got more buzz than traction. He and his supporters camped out at the Hotel McAlpin, a fleabag on the verge of closing. They battled rats and roaches while crafting strategy and hosting events, improvising with abandon. There was a mariachi fund-raiser on Tuesday night and another fund-raiser on Wednesday.[43] Brown attended both, joining Cesar Chavez on Wednesday in the hotel's ballroom for one last passing of the hat. Tickets cost $10 each, with proceeds going to the UFW. Jane Fonda, Tom Hayden, Jerry Rubin of the yippies, Elaine Brown of the Black Panthers, and senators Alan Cranston and John Tunney were among those present as the throng greeted Brown with "wild cheers."[44]

Later that night, Brown's name was placed in nomination by Chavez and seconded by congresswoman Yvonne Burke as well as by Edwards. For those keeping score, that meant Brown's most prominent supporters included a revered Latino labor leader, a breakthrough African American woman, and an aging and slightly disreputable white southern governor. It is safe to say that no other American political figure could have attracted that trio of backers.

Chavez's remarks were happily received, especially by the UFW contingent that accompanied Brown to the convention and greeted his appearances with the union's trademark symbol: a black eagle against a red background. "There's a great deal to be done in this nation," Chavez told the delegates. "We have to give people a sense of purpose. We need to excite hope in the people for the future."[45]

Burke came next and lauded Brown as "truly the voice of a new generation." Insightfully, she described that voice as one "that demands that we examine, search, question and continue."[46]

Brown asked the Carter team whether he could be allowed to endorse Carter from the podium and turn his delegates over to the nominee there. Carter, by then wary of Brown, denied him the chance. Brown stayed with the California delegation on the floor as Carter mopped up the win. Brown headed home.

His quixotic quest for the American presidency was over. For the moment.

# 11

# The Earth

*Bring me men to match my mountains.*
—Sam Walter Foss, "The Coming American"

S am Walter Foss, one of the great popular American poets of the late
nineteenth century, imagined men of the future strong enough to
weather storms and settle lands, men of vision and purpose, "Men whose
moral currents sweep / Toward the wide enfolding ocean." Foss's voice
found willing ears in California, where his signature line, of men and
mountains, is etched into the pediment of the Jesse M. Unruh State Office Building, one of Sacramento's main government halls, hinting at the
connection between California and nature, a connection older than California's life as a state and one that transcends its politics and
demographics.

Inhabited first by native people who settled into its abundance,
colonized next by missionaries who struggled to tame its resources, then
opened to the world in a rush for its treasures, California has been
defined by its land, with its staggering bounty and humbling rigor. California gazes across the Pacific Ocean and gives rise to Mount Whitney,
whose summit is higher than any other mountaintop in the Lower 48.
It boasts more and richer farmland than any place on earth as well as

brutal deserts, including Death Valley, which reaches farther below sea level than any other spot in North America. California's protected lands include Yosemite National Park and parks that are home to the northern redwoods, while its cities depend on a water-relocation system that would have made Rome blush.

Nature in California is at least two things at once: it is defiantly dangerous—just ask the members of the Donner Party—yet paradoxically fragile. The humans who can be thwarted by its peaks, parched by its deserts, or drowned in its seas can do stunning damage, often by accident. And they have.

Late one Tuesday morning in January of 1969, with Richard Nixon freshly sworn in as president of the United States and Ronald Reagan ensconced as governor of California, pressure began to build in a pipe beneath the surface of the ocean off the coast of Santa Barbara. Workers scrambled to contain it but failed. At 10:45 a.m., the pressure became so intense that the pipe blew, shattering drilling equipment and cracking the seafloor around five miles from the beach. Oil and gas spewed forth into the water and came gurgling and swirling to the surface. Union Oil owned the well, which was drilled from a rig known as platform Alpha.[1]

It is sometimes said that the Santa Barbara oil spill gave rise to the environmental movement. That's not precisely true. John Muir campaigned for wilderness protection long before anyone thought of placing oil platforms within sight of Santa Barbara's beaches, and Rachel Carson warned of the dangers of pesticides in the food supply seven years before oil washed up on that shore. Bob Dylan released "A Hard Rain's A-Gonna Fall" in 1963, lamenting "seven sad forests" and a "dozen dead oceans." Its bleak imagery of wounded souls included the narrator's walk through a black forest, surrounded by empty-handed people, "where the pellets of poison are flooding their waters." Aldo Leopold, whose book *A Sand County Almanac* was and is an enduring landmark of environmental consciousness, was widely read on college campuses in the 1960s, and nuclear weapons testing had raised alarms about fallout and related damage: the Nuclear Test-Ban Treaty, championed by biologist Barry Commoner and others, was adopted in 1963. Paul Ehrlich's influential book *The Population Bomb* was published a year before the Santa Barbara spill. Though it turned out to be mostly wrong, Ehrlich's work generated intense debate about the capacity of the earth to support humanity.

Nature showed signs of stress. The Cuyahoga River, in Ohio, caught fire on June 22, 1969—not for the first time, but this time to public distress. Smog began its creep across American cities, especially Los Angeles, by the end of the decade. Warnings were sounded, and the reaction, by 1970, was under way. Young people—some, at least—were trying to find their way "back to the land," and a consciousness about nature's fragility had gripped many people, young and old.

But if the oil spill did not create the movement, it did have a profound effect on it, especially on the politics of environmentalism. Those ramifications would be reinforced time and again in California even as their lessons were lost elsewhere. Santa Barbara was vivid and public—and unifying. Birds covered in oil and beaches fouled by tar and slime stirred the souls of Republicans and Democrats alike, especially in California.

The first reports that January indicated a problem but gave little hint of what was to come. The Coast Guard spotted the slick drifting south and west of platform Alpha and reported a problem, though at first it was unclear how serious that problem was. A modest ten-paragraph story in the *Long Beach Independent,* which followed coastal issues closely, noted that an oil slick between twenty-five and seventy-five square miles in area was spreading in the Pacific, drifting southwest from a leak in the Santa Barbara Channel.[2] The short article concluded with a note from a Santa Barbara County supervisor saying that company executives had assured him that the well was protected against any serious spill.[3]

That account was overtaken by events within hours. The slick at first drifted out to sea, but a change in the wind direction began to push it back toward shore the following day. By Sunday, the *Los Angeles Times* warned in a front-page caption that "miles of state's beaches…are threatened by the huge oil slick," and the paper's lead story examined the colliding political and cultural forces whose "free-for-all battle…could affect the entire offshore oil industry in California."[4] Indeed.

The oil gushed for eleven days at a rate of one thousand gallons per hour, ultimately fouling thirty-five miles of coastline and coating eight hundred square miles of ocean. More than three thousand birds died after being drenched in the viscous fluid. Union Oil's chief did himself no favors when he professed to be surprised at the public reaction. "I am amazed at the publicity for the loss of a few birds," he unwisely remarked.[5]

President Nixon visited the Santa Barbara area a few months after the spill and lamented the breadth of the disaster. He walked the beaches in a suit and oxfords—even on a beach, he was Nixon—and ignored a nearby knot of protesters. He seemed sincerely moved. "What is involved is the use of our resources of the sea and of the land in a more effective way and with more concern for preserving the beauty and the natural resources that are so important to any kind of society that we want for the future," he told reporters. "The Santa Barbara incident has frankly touched the conscience of the American people."[6] And he promised to respond: "We are going to do a better job than we have done in the past."[7]

Nixon, both a Republican and a Californian, was unashamed of his environmentalism, as his record would attest. Moved by the oil spill and the damage to California's coast, he declared the 1970s the "decade of the environment." In his State of the Union address in 1970, the first after the oil spill, Nixon spoke at length about the environment and proposed to take action to protect clean air and water. He called on both parties to join him. "Restoring nature to its natural state is a cause beyond party and beyond factions," he said.[8]

The following year, Nixon went further. He proposed six goals for America. One of them was "to restore and enhance our natural environment." He proposed measures to clean up air and water; to expand parks, recreation areas, and open space; and to fight noise. He delivered. As president, Nixon supported environmentally minded legislation, including the Clean Air Act and the Clean Water Act, and he founded the Environmental Protection Agency. Republicans joined him in all those efforts. Under Nixon's watch, the federal government even intervened to relocate a proposed Florida airport that would have had an impact on the Everglades.[9]

Not until environmental protection confronted the existential threat of climate change would Nixon's party flinch, at which point Republicans in California would face a difficult political decision: stick with the party or remain with the state. Jerry Brown would put that test to them in his second iteration as governor.

For Jerry Brown, the evolving challenge of environmental protection stirred a deep intellectual craving—the grappling with an absolute that evoked the study and gravity of God. "God is not mocked," the apostle Paul declares in Galatians. Nor is the earth. "Some of the certitudes of pre–Vatican II Catholicism fell away," Brown said in 2015. "In their place I saw ecological certitudes."[10] In that, Brown was echoing Paul, whose exhortations in Galatians sought to elevate his listeners from trivialities and falsehoods and restore their confidence in God and Christ. When one confronts an absolute, one adjusts oneself, not the absolute.

Like many environmentalists of his time and place—midcentury California—Brown's respect for nature at first assumed the form of protecting wild spaces from intrusion. The coastline needed protection from oil spills and development. Wilderness was threatened by development, too, as well as by recreation, agriculture, ranching, and mining. Brown responded. His admiration for *Small Is Beautiful* and his embrace of "an era of limits" both reflected a determination to reorient the relationship of humanity to its planet. As Schumacher wrote: "Man, whether civilized or savage, is a child of nature—he is not the master of nature. He must conform his actions to certain natural laws if he is to maintain his dominance over his environment. When he tries to circumvent the laws of nature, he usually destroys the natural environment that sustains him."[11] Brown wholeheartedly agreed and absorbed Schumacher's environmentalism into his own growing sense of a unity of things—a set of convictions that would come to bind his Catholicism, Zen Buddhism, and exploratory intellect. In this regard, Zen practice occupied a special and evolving place for Brown.

"The river is the river," Brown liked to say of his pursuit of Zen. That was enough for his critics. They heard Brown's aphorisms and tuned out, waving away the governor as a flake without bothering to consider the substance beneath his words. But just as Brown's seminary life laid a foundation for his environmentalism—God and nature both suggest absolutes—so, too, did Zen. For most people, a river is not just a river. It is a river seen through the eyes of personal experience and distraction. The river reminds us of a movie or an advertisement for a river or time spent by a river in childhood or the fear of drowning or the exhilaration of running rapids. It is replete with memory and preconception.

But the river is also a river. It exists outside the observer, independent of preconception or interpretation. It is its own thing, imbued with itself, not with the appreciation of itself. Once this is understood, it becomes clear that the river does not exist for the amusement or enjoyment of humanity. It has its own place, separate from those who appreciate it or seek to destroy it. It exists because it exists.

That is a less aggressive foundation for environmentalism than vain claims about what the earth requires. The earth, as Brown said, "will be just fine." But the place of people on the earth is precarious, temporary. That does not excuse indifference. Humanity's place is central to humanity, but placing it in the context of the universe, of the river as a thing in itself does enforce a certain humility.

The practice of Zen, with its insistence on shedding attachments and stripping life to experience rather than filtering it through interpretation, draws practitioners into closer communication with the absolutes of nature. From that communication flows respect, the modest acknowledgment that humanity is a presence but just one presence, that humanity's duties and powers are limited, that the obligation to help one's fellow man does not presume dominion but rather humility and service. "The river is the river" leads directly from "Do what you are doing."

In either tradition, the observer is commanded to see. To see clearly and comprehend both the surface and what lies below, to appreciate not just that which is obvious but that which matters. "Do you not yet understand or comprehend?" Mark asks. "Are your hearts hardened? Do you have eyes and not see, ears and not hear?"[12]

Brown was also influenced by an event in 1972—the first United Nations Conference on the Human Environment, held in Stockholm. It anticipated and influenced Schumacher, seeking to acknowledge the productive and beneficial aspects of human interaction with nature while warning of the growing peril in that interaction. "We see around us growing evidence of man-made harm in many regions of the earth," the conference's final report concluded. "Dangerous levels of pollution in water, air, earth and living beings; major and undesirable disturbances to the ecological balance of the biosphere; destruction and depletion of irreplaceable resources; and gross deficiencies, harmful to the physical, mental and social health of man, in the man-made environment, particularly in the living and working environment."[13]

The Stockholm conference not only summarized the growing threat to nature as a result of man's actions, it also sounded a note of urgency and offered a thread of hope—a balance that Brown would deliberately seek to emulate as his appreciation for the political and moral imperatives of environmental protection deepened. "Through ignorance or indifference we can do massive and irreversible harm to the earthly environment on which our life and well being depend," the report said. "Conversely, through fuller knowledge and wiser action, we can achieve for ourselves and our posterity a better life in an environment more in keeping with human needs and hopes."[14]

For an American Democrat of that period, environmentalism posed an additional challenge. This was a time when protecting nature appeared at odds with economic growth and health. The industries that threatened nature, after all, provided jobs—for miners, farmers, construction workers, oilmen. Nixon alluded to those tensions in his support for environmental protection. "The argument is often made that there is a fundamental contradiction between economic growth and the quality of life," he said during his State of the Union address in 1970, "so that to have one we must forsake the other."[15] Easy for a Republican president to say, hard for a Democratic elected official to reconcile. The constituencies most threatened by a 1970s view of environmental protection were largely contained within the Democratic coalition, so Brown's championing of the environment continually had the potential of upending his already tenuous relationship with organized labor. Perhaps as a result, Brown's embrace of environmentalism took hold gradually and, at first, in private.

He barely mentioned the environment in his campaign for the community-college board, when it would have seemed odd (though that hardly would have stopped him). He campaigned for secretary of state as an advocate of political reform and as an outsider determined to shake up Sacramento, but not in terms of its environmental policy.[16] Not until his 1974 campaign for governor did he first begin to identify publicly with environmental concerns and imagery. In that campaign, Brown proposed a nine-point program for regulating oil companies in California, a popular notion in the years after the Santa Barbara spill. His environmentalism expressed itself in issues of the day as well: during the 1973 energy crisis, California authorized drilling in some state lands after a case-by-case review; one request came from ARCO. Brown opposed the drilling while his opponent, Houston Flournoy, supported it.[17]

The environment spoke to Brown's convictions with a gravity that much of politics could not. In a manner similar to his youthful attraction to the seminary as an antidote to his father's style of politics, the environment was a counterweight to Brown's own immersion in the ephemeral practice of political discourse. "There is room in politics for diametrically opposed opinions," Brown said in 2015. People of conviction and goodwill may disagree on the death penalty or abortion or, as Brown put it: "Do you want a hamburger or a turkey sandwich? Do you want a Chevrolet or do you want a Ford?"[18]

Politics is full of such choices: proponents may have deeply felt views, but they allow for disagreement. Choices involving nature do not. Humanity may not choose to despoil nature and assume that it will bounce back; mankind may not imagine that climate change is a myth and thereby escape its consequences. Nature is real and absolute, in ways that can make one think of God. "We may not know what each law is, but we do know there are laws," Brown said of nature, though he might as well have said of God. "And they do not admit of exception." As such, humanity's opinions about nature, unlike those about capital punishment or turkey sandwiches, are irrelevant. For Brown, spiritual inquiry led to immersion in nature, to deep contemplation of its disinterested laws and the consequences that would befall those who ignore or defy them.

"For whatsoever a man soweth," Paul continues in Galatians, "that shall he also reap."[19]

The most immediate effect of the oil spill on the burgeoning environmental movement in California was the creation, in 1970, of Earth Day. From its inception, Earth Day was meant to fuse the energy of the antiwar movement with the breadth of support for the environment. It was natural, then, that Earth Day would find support from Republicans and Democrats and that it would be born in California.

Its chief founder was Senator Gaylord Nelson, a Wisconsin Democrat who recruited Pete McCloskey, a Bay Area Republican, to join him in a bipartisan campaign to ignite smoldering public concern for the environment. They hired Denis Hayes, the newly graduated head of the Stanford student body, to serve as the organization's coordinator. Hayes secured a deferment from his planned entry into Harvard Law School and set up offices in Washington, DC. (Hayes later attended Harvard's Kennedy School and received his law degree from Stanford.) With little money but an energetic and inspired staff, Hayes set the kickoff for Earth Day as April 22, 1970.[20] When the day at last arrived, the environment itself seemed pleased. Across America, some twenty million marchers— a staggering percentage of the nation's overall population—gathered under sunny skies to protest polluted air and water.

"Huge, light-hearted throngs ambled down autoless streets here yesterday as the city heeded Earth Day's call for a regeneration of a polluted environment by celebrating an exuberant rite of spring," the *New York Times,* beneath the byline of Joseph Lelyveld, declared on its front page, which gave over a six-column headline and photograph to the event. "If the environment had any enemies they did not make themselves known."[21]

Teach-ins were held at most California campuses; USC's mascot, Tommy Trojan, donned a gas mask and wore a sign reading: DANGER: POLLUTED AIR. BREATHE AT YOUR OWN RISK. IN THE KINGDOM OF SMOG, MULTITUDES HAIL EARTH DAY, wrote the Associated Press, whose story opened: "An airplane punctuated the blue sky above normally smoggy Los Angeles with the letters 'a-i-r,' while down below, thousands rallied yesterday on Earth Day for the fight against pollution."[22] Students and pollution-control officials marched together in Silicon Valley, where the *Times* of San Mateo declared: EARTH DAY IS SUCCESS.[23] In Santa Rosa, teachers and students left their cars at home in favor of more environmentally friendly transportation; the spirit was infectious. "Pedestrians spoke to each other," one columnist marveled. "Cyclists waved and smiled."[24]

There was substantive reaction as well. The California Department of Public Works, then still under Reagan, announced that it would, going forward, consider the effects of smog and noise when proposing new freeways. The state assembly voted to extend restrictions on offshore oil drilling. "Industry must be compelled to spend more and do more," the *Los Angeles Times,* once California's most reliably conservative voice, intoned.[25]

The public response demonstrated the huge shift in awareness of and concern for the environment and focused political attention on a new force in American life. "Public opinion polls indicate that a permanent change in national priorities followed Earth Day 1970," a later analysis concluded. "When polled in May 1971, 25 percent of the U.S. public declared protecting the environment to be an important goal, a 2,500 percent increase over 1969."[26] Over a similar period, from 1965 to 1970, membership in the Sierra Club more than tripled, bringing it to more than one hundred thousand.[27]

The 1970s would move environmentalism from the fringe to the center of American politics, no place more so than in California. The issues and images evolved. Concerns over smog morphed into debates over acid rain and eventually climate change. Coastal protection extended its reach from Santa Barbara to the Central Coast and Northern California shorelines, primarily to the credit of Congressman Leon Panetta, whose long fight for a coastal sanctuary off the stunning Monterey coast began in 1972 and finally was won in 1992.[28] The Apollo 17 photograph of the "blue marble" that was the earth against the black backdrop of space reoriented perspectives in 1972, reminding all those who saw it—and it was one of the most viewed photographs in history—how alone we are.

Brown would not speak for the earth, but he would, for the rest of his career, urge humanity to inhabit its planet with humility and a sense of purpose and regard. The environment may or may not have use for mankind, but it has had few better friends than Jerry Brown. His environmentalism would become a mainstay of his politics and a central aspect of his intellect and spiritualism.

Did the earth need him? Probably not. The river is the river.

Did humanity need help? Without question. Do what you are doing.

# 12

# Misjudgments

Brown believed deeply in diversity. Rare is the leader who could appreciate both the strategic Ray Fisher and the loopy Jacques Barzaghi. Brown prided himself on being able to appreciate diverse talents, and his picks reflected his intellectual curiosity, his loyalty, and his willingness to think freshly.

Brown was genuinely committed to diversity in its most traditional sense. Women and minorities found places in the administration and the judiciary in record numbers during his administration. By the middle of 1977, Brown had appointed 1,862 people to positions in state government: 31 percent were women, 10 percent were Latino, and 8 percent were African American—a sea change in the complexion of the California bench and state workforce.[1]

But Brown's commitment to change sometimes clashed with his judgment, and the tension between those impulses was tested in early 1977, when he suddenly had the opportunity to appoint a new chief justice for California. Chief Justice Donald Wright informed Brown of his intention to retire early that year; Wright recommended that Brown consider replacing him with Stanley Mosk, a giant presence on the court and a highly regarded liberal justice. Alternatively, Brown might have chosen Mathew Tobriner, another associate justice and the one for whom Brown had clerked after law school. Both were seasoned, thoughtful, and respected. Both had been placed on the high court by Brown's father, which might have seemed an advantage but may in fact have handicapped them at a stage in Brown's career when he was still trying to distinguish himself from his father.

Tony Kline, responsible for recommending potential jurists to Brown, urged him to consider Shirley Hufstedler, a graduate of Stanford Law School and a pioneering female lawyer and judge placed on the California Courts of Appeal by Pat Brown in 1966, shortly before he left office.[2] In 1977, she was serving on the United States Court of Appeals for the Ninth Circuit, a position to which President Johnson had appointed her. She would, without question, have been an experienced, talented, and universally acclaimed chief justice for California.

But Brown wanted more than that. "Jerry Brown wanted to make a statement," Kline remembered. "Jerry wanted to rattle the cage."[3]

Brown liked the idea of appointing the first woman to serve as chief justice, but he wanted someone further outside the normal legal circles than Hufstedler, who was eyeing the US Supreme Court in any event. Brown had a low opinion of the state's judiciary, complaining that judges did not work hard enough and lamenting what he viewed as their institutional conservatism. He wanted to break some norms. Change. Fast. He nominated Rose Bird.

The state's legal establishment groaned. Bird was intelligent and big-hearted. She had led the fight to win approval of the Agricultural Labor Relations Act and had helped to ban the short-handled hoe, a brutal farming tool that left those who relied on it with disabling back injuries. In the years following passage of the act, she had shepherded it into existence, briefing Brown as the UFW, Teamsters, and newly formed Agricultural Labor Relations Board settled into their roles.[4] She was strong and compassionate. But her reputation as a stiff-necked taskmaster unwilling to work with others, rigid and difficult, was also well known. And she had not served any time as a judge, a fact that hardly disqualified her as a justice (Earl Warren, among others, had demonstrated that a chief justice drawn from outside the judiciary nevertheless could be effective), but this reinforced doubts about her within the legal community. Her nomination was divisive and would face a close confirmation vote.

Under California law, justices must be confirmed by a three-member panel consisting of the chief justice, the senior justice of the state's appellate court, and the attorney general. In this case, that meant the acting chief justice, Mathew Tobriner (since the chief justice was retiring), appellate justice Parker Wood, and attorney general Evelle Younger. Tobriner, despite being passed over, was a loyal Democrat and dear friend of the Brown family; he was assumed likely to vote in Bird's favor. Wood had long opposed nominees without judicial experience, so he was guessed to be a no. That left Younger, a conservative Republican, ardent supporter of the death penalty, and likely challenger to Jerry Brown in 1978. All of which placed Younger in a delicate political position. If he supported Bird, he risked losing conservative support within his party, but if he opposed her, he faced the possibility of backlash from women, some of whom believed Bird to be the victim of sexism (though Bird herself consistently refused to be labeled a feminist). The vote was complicated further by the fact that Brown was forwarding two appointments to the commission, those of Bird and Wiley Manuel, an Alameda County Superior Court judge who, if confirmed, would become the first African American to serve on California's supreme court.

While Younger considered his options, controversy over the Bird nomination bubbled over. Particularly incendiary was a letter from Bishop Mahony, who chaired the state's Agricultural Labor Relations Board, the panel whose very existence was the result of Bird's work. Mahony respected Bird and her achievements, but he privately warned against placing her on the court. "My opposition to her appointment as Chief Justice centers on her questionable emotional stability and her vindictive approach to dealing with all persons under authority," Mahony wrote to the three-member commission. "I experienced her vindictiveness on many occasions…She has a personal temperament which causes her to lash out at people who do not agree with her."[5] Although the letter was sent in confidence, Younger released it publicly, further roiling the waters around Bird.

And yet when it came time to vote, Younger cast his lot with principle. Jerry Brown, he said, had been clear about the kinds of justices he would nominate. Bird fell squarely within that definition, and though Younger did not believe her to be the best-qualified person for the office, he nevertheless considered her qualified and within Brown's right to appoint. Younger then "reluctantly" cast his vote for Bird, clearing her for service on the California bench. Manuel also was confirmed.

Bird's swearing-in—a duty that traditionally fell to the senior justice of the court, Tobriner—was scheduled for March 27. Brown usurped him, performing the ceremony himself and underscoring both his commitment to Bird and his disdain for the traditions of the court to which he had appointed her. Justice Mosk, still bitter about being passed over, declined to attend. When Bird arrived to take up her post, Mosk could not contain himself. "I certainly cannot blame you for being here," he told her, "but I blame Jerry Brown for putting you here."[6] Neither justice ever forgave the other. Larger forces outside the court soon would bring their own, much more damaging, critique of Bird, with devastating consequences.

At first, the group of churchgoers who arrived in Northern California in the mid-1960s seemed benign enough. They were friendly and, if a bit private, at least eager to make a good impression. They espoused progressive politics, and the congregation was racially integrated and seemed open-minded. Their leader was charismatic and charming, generous and outgoing with the local and state officials whose friendship he courted. The group—roughly 140 members, half African American and half white—came from Indiana and settled in Redwood Valley, northwest of Sacramento, in 1965.

Seeking to expand and spread its ministry, especially to the poor, the church acquired property in San Francisco and Los Angeles in the early 1970s. By 1974, when Brown was elected governor, it had become a significant force in the politics of those cities, especially San Francisco. Its leaders boasted of their ability to turn out volunteers and voters on Election Day. Mayor George Moscone was a supporter, as was Willie Brown. Herb Caen, the popular columnist for the *San Francisco Chronicle,* regularly sang the church's praises. President Jimmy Carter and Vice President Walter Mondale endorsed its work. It seemed, to some, a beacon of integration and progressivism flourishing in the heart of San Francisco.

The church was known as Peoples Temple. Its leader, Jim Jones, would soon become a household name.

In 1976 and 1977, Jerry Brown was occupied with his legislative agenda, his presidential bid, his closely watched personal life. He had imposed his fiscal conservatism on California's budget and managed, through it, to advance liberal ideas while still holding the line on state spending. As a result, the state had a large and growing surplus. With all that, Brown missed, at least for a time, a brewing political movement that would come to envelop California and his remaining time as governor.

Complaints about taxes—in California, as everywhere—were hardly new. In California, those complaints often centered on property taxes, since land values had increased steadily, sometimes dramatically, in the 1960s and 1970s. Property taxes were a function of assessed value, so as values increased, taxes did, too, even without an increase in tax rates. Back in the Reagan years, Jesse Unruh's support for the governor's general tax hike at the outset of his administration was partly based on the hope that it could provide property tax relief. It did, for a while quieting the discontent.

But by the time Jerry Brown assumed the governorship, that pressure was building again. The immediate impetus came from an advocate so irascible and persistent that some regarded him as little more than a gadfly. Howard Jarvis was a lobbyist for the Los Angeles Apartment Owners Association, and he had been floating tax proposals and running for office for years—trying but falling far short in races for the US Senate and several times for mayor of Los Angeles. It's safe to say that most establishment figures in California politics did not take the gruff, slightly embarrassing Jarvis seriously. He was more like the guy who yells at city council meetings than a serious political operative.

As a result, when Jarvis teamed up with a legislator named Paul Gann to push for property tax reform, few in Sacramento initially paid much heed. Some of Brown's aides worried and warned the governor that there might be danger in the movement, but Brown, like most of his colleagues, waved off their concern. "I did not pick up the power," he said in 2016.[7] In fact, Brown's frugality, such an essential component of his iconoclastic political makeup, worked against him in the building debate over property tax cuts: he had so successfully held down the cost of state programs that California enjoyed a projected $5 billion surplus in 1978. Why, voters asked, should they pay rising property taxes at a time when the state was flush?

Jarvis was poking at warm embers. Until the late 1960s, county tax assessors in California had the flexibility to spread around the cost of taxes in their areas. In general, that caused them to increase taxes on businesses in order to accommodate homeowners, who made up most of the electorate. That allowed the total tax burden to be met while serving the politically expedient goal of pleasing most constituents. In 1965, however, San Francisco's assessor was caught granting relief to business donors. Homeowners were outraged and sought revenge. Jarvis, somewhat belatedly, gave them an opportunity.

Compounding the political forces were economic ones. California property values soared in the early 1970s, and the value of homes in some areas more than doubled. What that meant is that even without increases in property tax rates, tax bills sometimes doubled. For homeowners, especially those on fixed or limited incomes, this represented a significant and unanticipated new cost of living, one incurred merely by staying in their homes. The system appeared both crooked and unfair.

Jarvis's response was to propose a sweeping decrease and reexamination of California's property tax structure. His initiative started by proposing to roll back all assessments to their 1975 levels, so the increases of the previous three years would disappear. Beyond that, the initiative would cap taxes at 1 percent of a property's value and would limit annual increases to 2 percent a year. Only if a home or business were sold would its assessment be brought up to date. One other detail that would come to have long-range consequences: the initiative proposed that any government in California thereafter that sought to raise general taxes would need to secure a two-thirds vote, either of the elected body or the public, for the increase to take effect.

Most of this was heresy to Sacramento, a wholesale grab of what had traditionally been the authority of state and local government. What's more, it would both instantly strip away billions of dollars in state revenue and subsequently make that revenue exceedingly hard to replace. To lawmakers, this was ludicrous. Only when Jarvis announced that his initiative had gathered the necessary signatures and qualified for the June 1978 ballot as Proposition 13 did the state leadership finally snap to attention and realize that doom was at the door. Brown proposed an alternative tax relief measure, but it went further than Democrats in the legislature were prepared to go; they rejected it and produced one of their own.[8]

Rushing, the legislature passed its rival measure, Proposition 8, intended to deliver some tax relief without the pain that Proposition 13 promised to inflict. That introduced some confusion into the election planning but did little to take the steam out of Proposition 13's momentum. Brown endorsed Proposition 8 and opposed Proposition 13. He believed through the spring that Proposition 8 would be enough and that Proposition 13 stood little chance of passing. Tom Quinn tried to warn the governor. As Quinn and the governor sat by Linda Ronstadt's pool, Quinn tried to persuade Brown to be worried. He wouldn't bite. "It's not going to pass," Brown insisted.[9]

Proposition 13 appeared on the ballot on June 6, 1978. So did Jerry Brown, running for reelection in the Democratic primary for governor against token opposition. He had no concerns for his own race—it was in the bag—and believed Proposition 13 would fail. He was half right. Brown won his primary with more than 77 percent of the vote, but Proposition 13 surged to victory, though less spectacularly than its proponents hoped. Interestingly, in fact, Proposition 13, which imposed a two-thirds requirement on future California tax increases, fell just short of that threshold itself, an anomaly that would irritate lawmakers for a generation.

On the Republican side, Evelle Younger, who had cast the deciding vote for Rose Bird, won a plurality of his party's votes, giving him the nomination but emphasizing the difficulty he would face in the general election against the better-known Brown. Younger attempted to boost his fortunes by seizing the momentum behind Proposition 13, but Brown, in one of political history's swiftest about-faces, immediately announced his conversion. He was, he said, a "born-again tax cutter," and he vowed to implement Proposition 13 immediately.

The next day, Brown addressed a special session of the state legislature. Elected leaders, in a "somber, crisis mood," listened as Brown urged them to heed the message of the initiative and return the state surplus as well as cut another $300 million in spending. "We must look forward to lean and frugal budgets," he told the assembled legislators. "It is a great challenge and we will meet it."[10]

Some people at the time and afterward were shocked at the governor's abrupt embrace of tax-cutting, but it was both political and practical. Proposition 13's victims were real. School districts were hard-hit—they suffered a double blow from the combined effects of the initiative and a trio of court decisions known as *Serrano v. Priest,* which redistributed school funding in the 1970s. And city and county governments lost both money and influence as Proposition 13 shifted resources away from them and concentrated decision making in Sacramento. By imposing rigid limitations on future tax increases, the initiative also hamstrung the future to the whim of a 1978 electorate, exacerbating California's boom-and-bust budget cycles. Those were real and lasting consequences, and Brown largely was silent about them.

It is also true, however, that Brown had little ability to refuse to obey the initiative's commands. As Brown said in 2016, he had no choice but to embrace Proposition 13 once it had passed, even though it imposed immediate economic stress on the state. His job, like it or not, was to implement what the voters had commanded. Just as important, at least for Brown, was the peril in foot-dragging. He knew that Younger had little chance of beating him, but what chance the dull and uninspiring Younger did have lay in marshaling the energy behind Proposition 13. Brown's move denied Younger that opportunity.

Brown and Younger waged a spirited but civilized campaign, made easier by Younger's slim chances of winning. When Younger was stricken with a kidney stone and hospitalized over the summer, Brown graciously wished him well. "We will have our disputes, but I want you to know that my best wishes are with you for a speedy recovery," Brown wrote, addressing his note to "Ev."[11] Younger replied more formally, on state stationery and addressing Brown as "Dear Governor." Nevertheless, the cordiality between them was evident. "I am feeling fine now," Younger replied two weeks after Brown's note. "I have some advice for you: If you can avoid ever having a kidney stone, do it."[12]

Brown notched his victory over Younger on November 7, winning 56 percent of the vote and carrying all but nine of California's fifty-eight counties. It was a decisive win and a dramatic vindication, at least in political terms, of Brown's pivot on Proposition 13.

Could Brown have acted differently on Proposition 13? Certainly he and others could have done more to see it coming. He could have spent some of the surplus that offered Jarvis such an inviting target. He could have prevailed on the legislature to deliver a more satisfying alternative tax-relief package, one that might have quenched voters' thirst without imposing the long-term restrictive provisions of Proposition 13. He could have changed the subject or proposed some appealing government program that might have defused the energy of the tax revolt. He did none of those things. Those are legitimate what-ifs, and Californians will forever be left to wonder how history might have been different.

Once the initiative passed, Brown's options were far more limited. He could have let the California budget collapse in the face of Proposition 13's cuts, but that would hardly have qualified as responsible leadership. It would have represented a dereliction of duty and, arguably, a violation of his oath of office. He fought Proposition 13 and lost. Having lost, it was his job to make it work as best he could. It worked for him politically, but it also was his job.

Brown was not the only winner on November 7. The ballot that fall included one of California's periodic divisive and hostile initiatives, in this case a measure backed by John V. Briggs, a conservative state senator from Orange County, then still the heart of California's right wing. With help from Anita Bryant, famous for her orange-juice advertisements and later for her antipathy toward gays, Briggs qualified an initiative to outlaw teaching in public schools by anyone who engaged in "public homosexual activity." The measure's language provided that a schoolteacher or other school employee could be terminated if the employee engaged in gay sex that was "not discreet and not practiced in private" or if he or she was engaged in "advocating, soliciting, imposing, encouraging or promoting" private homosexual sex.[13]

Although Briggs conceded that he came up with the proposal in part to boost his own candidacy for governor, the measure was presented as a protection for children. "We don't allow prostitutes to teach," Briggs proclaimed in one debate with a gay teacher. "If they're not good enough for the church, for the Army, if they're not good enough to get married, how are we to support the notion that they're to serve as role models (for schoolchildren) when they can't bear children themselves?" On May 1, 1978, Briggs and his allies turned in five hundred thousand signatures to the Los Angeles County registrar, more than enough to qualify the measure for the November ballot. It became Proposition 6, and its proponents argued that the legislature and governor lacked the will to solve the pressing problem of gays in the classroom. That left it, they argued, for the people to assert their will.

Brown did not lead the campaign against the initiative, but he was unequivocal in his opposition. He denounced the initiative as "McCarthyism" and remained steadfast even as Briggs accused him of pandering to gay interests. "As far as people's private lives—religious, sexual, political," Brown said, "I believe that the right of privacy is a very important protection, and I think that it ought to be very vigorously enforced at all levels."[14]

Even for critics of gay rights, the measure was a tough one to support. Its vague restrictions on "advocating" homosexual activity raised obvious free-speech questions, and Briggs's sanctimony offended secular conservatives. As a result, it was a broad coalition that gathered against Proposition 6. One leading opponent was San Francisco supervisor Harvey Milk, the nation's first openly gay elected official ("self-professed homosexual," as reports in those days often referred to him). Another was Ronald Reagan, the state's former governor, then eyeing the American presidency—and even Reagan, despite his reservations about the gay power movement, was offended by the naked discrimination of

Proposition 6. Still, populism can have an energy of its own, and on the eve of Election Day, opponents of the bill were concerned that a surge of antigay sentiment could swamp their efforts. They needn't have worried. Californians, by a margin of two to one, defeated Proposition 6, protecting the rights of gay men and women to teach and, by extension, recognizing their humanity and rejecting those who viewed them as a threat.

The first signs of tragedy trickled out on Saturday, November 18. Congressman Leo Ryan of San Mateo, just south of San Francisco, was leading a delegation to Guyana. He had been asked to visit the country by families with relatives who were members of Peoples Temple, which was building a commune in the jungle. The temple had friends in high places: Jerry Brown had spoken at its San Francisco headquarters, and the city's liberal elite—including the assembly speaker, Willie Brown; the mayor, George Moscone; and supervisors Harvey Milk and Dianne Feinstein—had all voiced their admiration for the congregation and its leader, Jim Jones, at one time or another.

But the temple also had skeptics, who were growing in number and in concern. Some families complained that their loved ones were being held in the jungle against their will. Ryan had agreed to visit to investigate those claims and, if they were true, to bring home anyone who wanted to leave. The commune was known as Jonestown, named for the temple's recognizable leader, the sunglasses-wearing Jones.

Ryan was not warmly received. Previous visits by the American embassy in Guyana to Jonestown had yielded little information, and diplomatic officials were curt with Ryan. They offered little assistance when he arrived, on November 15, in Georgetown, Guyana's capital.[15] While there, Ryan also met with temple officials and representatives, trying through blandishments and threats to gain entrance into the jungle city that Jim Jones and his followers were busy creating. After much negotiating, temple officials gave their blessing, and Ryan was allowed to go and take a small group with him.

He and his assistants arrived on Friday, November 17, and, after conferring with Jones, Ryan summoned most of the news reporters and photographers to join them (Jones forbade one reporter, from the *National Enquirer,* from entering Jonestown). The initial visit went well. Ryan was greeted with suspicion but Jones and some of his followers fielded questions and declined invitations to return to the United States with the Congressman.[16]

Then, overnight, a group of followers escaped. Plans for a return visit by the media on Saturday were delayed. Ryan himself continued his business, even as a terrific tropical storm washed over the compound. He met with a group of would-be defectors and offered them seats on his plane if they wanted to leave. Twenty-six of Jones's followers asked Ryan to take them with him. As they prepared to leave for the airstrip, one man tried to board the truck to leave with his child. His wife screamed at them to stay. Jones twitched nervously. Ryan stood by in a pavilion. Then, without warning, one of Jones's followers leaped at the congressman, drawing a knife to his throat. "Motherfucker," he said, "you're going to die." Guards pulled him off, but Ryan was shaken, and his shirt was stained with blood. Until that moment, temple authorities had hoped the congressman would return to the United States with an upbeat assessment of life in Jonestown. Now they could not count on that.[17]

Ryan, members of his staff—including Jackie Speier, his chief of staff and, later, US congresswoman—and members of the media were driven to a nearby airstrip, where they and the would-be defectors arrived in different vehicles. Two planes touched down, and Ryan's team sorted out reporters and defectors, deciding which of the thirty-three people wanting to leave would occupy the twenty-four seats available between the two aircraft. A devoted Jones follower, Larry Layton, lurked nearby, plotting to stop the escape in any way possible. As the groups were sorted and the passengers began to board the two planes, a tractor-trailer bearing a group of Jones loyalists barreled toward the airstrip. They were carrying rifles and shotguns. Pulling up near the planes, they opened fire.

Eight members of Ryan's group, including the congressman and Speier, were struck and either killed or badly wounded. Three others, including *San Francisco Examiner* reporter Tim Reiterman, were hit as well. They scrambled off into the surrounding jungle, defenseless and desperate for cover. The attackers took brief stock of their work, then fled back to Jonestown, leaving the dead and wounded behind.

REP. RYAN SLAIN, AMBUSH AT GUYANA AIRPORT, read the banner headline of the Sunday edition of the *Examiner*.[18] The first reports could only identify four of the dead, but the *Examiner* stressed that others, including Reiterman, still were unaccounted for. Also unknown were the fates of Jones and his followers. Although the first dispatch said that "Guyanese troops were reported to have secured the tiny airstrip in the interior and had moved in on the church's 27,000-acre agricultural mission at Jonestown," it gave no hint as to the status of the mission or its members.

The mind-boggling details flowed in over the next twenty-four hours. On Monday, the *Examiner*'s lead story reported that Jones and his wife, along with 381 others, had died in "suicide-murders." By the next day, the *Examiner* was reporting details of the event: that babies had been the first to die; that corpses covered the ground of the compound, many still dressed "in finery" for Ryan's visit; that cyanide was used to poison hundreds of men, women, and children, including full families locked in deathly embraces; that Jones himself had died from a gunshot wound.[19] Later, tapes made by Jones would capture the last moments of his congregation: "We didn't commit suicide," he could be heard saying at the end. "We committed an act of revolutionary suicide protesting the conditions of an inhumane world."[20]

The reported number of deaths proved heartbreakingly incorrect. The Guyanese soldiers first on the scene counted the corpses they could see, not realizing that there were layers of dead beneath them, already rotting in the jungle. All told, 918 people died that day, some by gunfire, most by poison. Parents were encouraged to kill their children first so that they would find it easier to kill themselves. A popular and insensitive myth is that the followers "drank the Kool-Aid." In fact, there was no Kool-Aid. They either drank punch mixed with poison, under threat of death, or were shot.

San Francisco, home to many members of the temple and its supporters, was left to weep. No words could capture the city's anguish over those days, waiting for reports of survivors that did not come, wondering how so many could have been gulled by Jones and his evil designs.

It was a little before 11:00 a.m. on November 27. Mayor Moscone was at work at the city's grand city hall. He had just been through a tough period. On top of Jonestown—which stunned him even more than it did most San Franciscans, given his relationship with Jones—Moscone had been wrestling with a delicate matter. One of his fellow supervisors, a thirty-two-year-old former police officer and firefighter named Dan White, had resigned his post, saying he needed to get back to work full-time because he needed the money.[21] White then came under pressure from his supporters and had second thoughts; wavering, he asked Moscone to reinstate him. Moscone also hesitated—he did not like saying no to people—but White had given him an opportunity to secure a liberal majority for the board, and other members, notably Supervisor Milk, urged Moscone to stand firm. That left some tense days of indecision. With everyone made nervous by Jonestown—there were reports of hit squads waiting to retaliate in San Francisco, rumors of a so-called "White Night" during which Temple followers would fan out across the city with a list of political leaders and assassinate them—White continued to show up at his office, bedraggled and desperate.[22]

As of that morning, the mayor had decided to take Milk's advice. He had turned down White's request and was intending to name another, more liberal, candidate, Don Horanzy, to replace White.[23] The issue, Moscone believed, at last was behind him. His office already had begun distributing copies of the statement announcing Horanzy's appointment and turning the page on the White escapade.

But the issue still burned for Dan White. He had been up all night, stewing about the decision and wondering whether it was too late to get Moscone to reconsider. He dressed for work, putting on a suit with a vest and dark tie. He called for an aide to pick him up. She did and dropped him at city hall at around 10:30. Unbeknownst to her, White was carrying a .38 special beneath his jacket. He had loaded it with hollow-point bullets, and he snuck in through a basement window on McAllister Street to avoid the metal detector.

White went straight to Moscone's office, passing Willie Brown, who was on the way out. Moscone was puzzled and irritated by the sight of White, but the affable mayor invited him inside anyway. They argued. White pulled the gun from his holster. He shot Moscone in the shoulder and chest, then stood over him and shot him twice in the head. White reloaded, left the office, and headed for the office of Harvey Milk. Dianne Feinstein, another member of the board, saw White in the hall and called for him. He brushed her off and bee-lined for Milk's office. White shot Milk five times as well, the last at point-blank range into Milk's skull.[24]

The shots were deafening, and witnesses abounded. Feinstein rushed from her office, fearing White had killed himself, and smelled the gunpowder.

Feinstein was no stranger to violence and death: that year alone, she had received death threats from the New World Liberation Front, which had shot thirteen holes into her beach house eighteen months earlier.[25] Her husband, a brain surgeon, died earlier that same year. Feinstein now knelt beside Milk and felt for a pulse, instead finding a bullet hole. Her hand came away covered in blood.[26] She knew then that there was no hope. "There's no mistaking dead," she recalled four decades later.[27] One of Milk's aides reached for the phone but could not speak. Feinstein gently took the receiver from him and placed it in its cradle.

White got out of city hall in the confusion and, around an hour later, turned himself in to the SFPD's Northern Station, four blocks away. "He just walked in the door, put his hands up and turned himself in," one station officer said.[28] Some police, hearing that the liberal Moscone was dead, cheered. A grim and telling joke made its way through the ranks within hours: "What did Mary Ann [White's wife] tell Dan after she heard about the shootings?" the set-up went. Her answer: "No, Dan, I said to get milk and macaroni, not Milk and Moscone."[29]

In Moscone's office, Feinstein was joined by the police chief, Charles Gain. They emerged at 11:20 a.m. Feinstein was shaking so badly that the chief supported her.[30] But after Moscone's death, Feinstein was the city's acting mayor by virtue of her position as president of the board of supervisors, and she quickly recovered. Possessed of an inner strength built on tragedy, she willed herself to composure. None who witnessed her that day would ever forget it.[31]

Reporters had gathered at city hall for Moscone's expected announcement of White's replacement. Now they were frantic. First thoughts went to Jonestown. Were cult fanatics reaching back from Guyana to exact revenge in San Francisco? How many people were dead? Was the killer at large? Feinstein called an impromptu press conference in the city hall rotunda, just feet from where her colleagues had been murdered minutes earlier.

"As the president of the board of supervisors," she began, her voice steady, "it is my duty to make this announcement: both Mayor Moscone and Supervisor Harvey Milk have been shot and killed."

Reporters gasped. One shrieked. Another shouted, "Jesus Christ!" Feinstein tried to continue but was drowned out by shouting. "Hold it, hold it," one person yelled, attempting to let her speak. "Quiet! Quiet!"

Breathing hard but remaining composed, Feinstein added the shocking, mystery-solving, mind-bending note: "The suspect," she said, "is Supervisor Dan White."[32]

# 13

# "Moonbeam"

Jerry Brown would never be accused of readily accepting conventional wisdom. His most consistent leadership strategy was to question—to refuse to accept what others regarded as settled facts. Liberals were expected to spend. He cut. Catholics were expected to obey. He challenged. He advocated environmental protection to his liberal secular admirers while framing his devotion to nature as commitment to God. Politicians were optimists. He contemplated the end of the world, cheerfully. "It's about being in the inquiry," he liked to say, particularly as he grew older.[1] Asked to justify salting away money for a rainy-day fund at the height of California's 2018 prosperity, Brown responded: "What's out there is darkness, uncertainty, decline and recession. So good luck, baby."[2]

By 2018, Californians were used to Brown's pronouncements, but in his early governorship, his unwillingness to conform to even the most casual political traditions could take observers aback. Consider the once hot issue of fluoridation. During the Reagan years, advocates of fluoridating California's water had been stymied. Fluoridation was a bugaboo of the John Birch Society, which spied the government's malevolent intent in doctoring the water supply. Although the society was already in decline during Reagan's governorship, the suspicion lingered on—somewhat as resistance to vaccination does today. For advocates of fluoridation, Reagan's departure and replacement by Brown represented a triumph and an opportunity. Finally, a forward-thinking liberal would hear them out and, surely, recognize the medical benefits of adding small amounts of the chemical to tap water in order to prevent tooth decay.

A group of the proponents secured a meeting with Brown and confidently presented its recommendations. Brown listened, then began to ask questions—not Birch Society questions but those of a Jesuit, a reader of Illich, a skeptic. Did he understand correctly? the governor asked. These advocates believe that children who eat too many sweets or fail to brush their teeth will benefit by the government's putting a chemical in their water? Why, Brown asked, should the government intervene to solve a problem of family order and discipline? Wouldn't the better solution just be for parents to make their children brush their teeth?

The advocates shook their heads in disbelief. This, they thought, was supposed to be an easy sell. Brown continued to ask questions and eventually dismissed the group without an answer. He assigned the matter to Dr. Jerome Lackner, who headed the state's Department of Health and was known for his skepticism about fluoridation. California did not order statewide fluoridation of its water until 1995, a full twenty years later, and then under Republican governor Pete Wilson.[3]

Brown's refusal to embrace orthodoxy extended to all aspects of his life as governor. This was evident in his first gubernatorial budget, in 1975, and it became all the more so as he wrestled to adjust to the havoc wrought by Proposition 13's passage, in 1978.

Brown represented a youthful, vigorous vision of the future— unspecific, to be sure, but emblematic of a California ready to be rid of the aged Reagan and his white Republican friends and cronies. Reagan mocked the counterculture, stoked California's fear of its young. Brown spoke of the arts and space and technology. He was new. Modern.

And then Brown got to work. "The economic uncertainty now facing the people of California requires that new state spending be held to a minimum," Brown wrote as he opened his budget message in

1975, immediately after taking office. Continuing, Brown outlined three principles of budgeting:

> We cannot spend more than we take in.
> Better government does not always require more spending.
> This budget recognizes no sacred cows.

That hardly sounded like the return of Pat Brown. Indeed, Jerry Brown's determination to ride herd on state budgets would come to define his leadership and distinguish it—and him—from most of his Democratic peers, colleagues, and predecessors. He would always watch the bottom line, searching for opportunities to fund innovation and protect the poor while refusing to indulge in deficits (though occasionally, in the area of state bonds, pushing obligations into the future). Brown's budget for 1975–76 contained all those hallmarks. While holding down overall state spending and emphasizing frugality, he found room to increase spending for the University of California, the state university system, and elementary and high school education. He boosted expenditures for welfare, expanded job programs, and significantly increased money for environmental protection.[4]

His budgets for the following three years reflected those same instincts. In 1976, he declared that he was submitting "a budget for an era of limits," language drawn from *Small Is Beautiful,* which would become synonymous with Brown. The spending plan he introduced that year began the slow buildup of the state surplus while continuing to reject tax increases. He proposed a $65-a-month salary increase for all state workers, meaning that low-wage workers disproportionately benefited. "Groceries," the governor wrote, "are purchased in dollars, not percentages." He held his own office budget flat and found ways to increase spending for migrant housing, college scholarships, and early childhood education. He also proposed the creation of the California Conservation Corps, a work program for young people that would stand as one of his proudest achievements.[5] And, with the creation of the Agricultural Labor Relations Board, he funded that first-of-its-kind agency.

Brown's pattern—overall respect for limits, with modest increases for top priorities—hit the skids in 1979, after Proposition 13 passed and went into effect. The state's emergency actions that summer had only begun to absorb the impact. The budget, he said, "reflects the clear mandate of the voters for a leaner government."

That year's budget, for the first time, included a heading: "Reductions in Low Priority Activities." Department by department, the governor listed those things that government once did but would do no longer. The California Highway Patrol ended its noise-reduction program; the Department of Motor Vehicles cut ninety-three positions from the unit that collected unpaid parking tickets; the Seismic Safety Commission was abolished; the Department of Health Services cut 165 positions; the School Improvement Program was cut by $38 million. And so on.[6]

Those cuts were softened by dipping into the state surplus, then more than $6 billion. But the surplus was dissipated within a year, and the real pain would soon begin.

Brown continued to be stingy with money and praise for the University of California, which practically begged for his attention and approval. In 1979, his ire focused on the university's relationship to the nation's nuclear weapons infrastructure. Brown, driven by a combination of principled opposition to nuclear proliferation and canny counterpositioning to President Jimmy Carter, decided to sever the long-standing relationship between the university and the national weapons laboratory at Los Alamos.

The university's connection to Los Alamos ran through the Lawrence Livermore Laboratory, located in the hills east of UC Berkeley. The laboratory was—and is—an important research center in the American nuclear weapons program. By the late 1970s, neither the university nor the US Department of Energy, which supervised the weapons program, was entirely satisfied with the arrangement. Under a contract between the two entities, the Department of Energy paid the university $3.5 million a year as a "management fee." In return, the university kept up the lab and provided the opportunity for scientists to conduct weapons research.[7]

An Energy Department study group concluded in May of 1979 that there was "faltering in the relationship" and blamed California and the university for failing to address investment needs at the lab. At the same time, a growing public sentiment, led in part by former RAND Corporation employee and iconic whistle-blower Daniel Ellsberg, questioned the propriety of the university's contributing to the weapons program at all. Ellsberg derided weapons stockpiling as naive and called on the university to break its connection to the lab and its work. Advocates for such a severance coalesced as the UC Nuclear Weapons Labs Conversion Project, which staged a series of demonstrations in the spring and summer of 1979.

Brown was sympathetic. Weapons research, Brown argued, "does not particularly serve anything in the university interest." In his role as a regent, Brown proposed that the university sever its relationship to the lab and agree only to fund research unrelated to weapons. He made that idea public in May, acknowledging at the time that a majority of regents did not support him but setting to work rounding up votes for the board's July meeting. Members of the conversion project were ebullient. Others less so. "Some people would say that Gov. Jerry Brown took a bold leap on the side of the angels last week," one columnist wrote. "We would say that the regents should tell the governor to go fly a kite."[8]

The regents took the matter up on July 20. Brown knew he was likely to lose—vote counts on the eve of the meeting showed him behind— and he used the occasion to goad the university's governing body. The vote, Brown said, offered the regents an "opportunity to redeem some of their past mistakes."[9] Gregory Bateson, in one of his last acts as a regent, voted with the governor, but the majority declined Brown's invitation to redemption. It voted to maintain the relationship.

George Kieffer, then the board's alumni regent, who would go on to chair the board during Brown's return to office in the 2010s, voted with the governor in 1979 but came to believe he had made a mistake. It made more sense, he concluded in retrospect, to have the university administer the lab and have influence over its work and direction. It took decades, but among those who agreed, looking back, was Brown.[10]

*　　*　　*

Brown's reelection had been a snap. Governing in its wake had not been. Proposition 13 scrambled everything in state finances. The period had not been bad for him politically, however, because his transformation from Proposition 13 opponent to "born-again" tax cutter played well nationally as the tax revolution spread outward from California. As 1980 approached, Brown took the measure of his own popularity, compared it to President Jimmy Carter's faltering electoral strength, and thought another run for the presidency was worth a try.

Tom Quinn initially was enthusiastic. Carter was weak—the Arab oil embargo was stressing the economy, inflation was on a tear, and Carter seemed overmatched by the office—and Brown already had shown strength against him in 1976. An earlier start and a more focused campaign, Quinn and others thought, could propel Brown to the Oval Office. Brown, who had proposed a California satellite, entered the campaign with enthusiasm and hope, captured by his uniquely Jerry Brown slogan: "Protect the earth, serve the people, explore the universe."

And he kicked it off in fine fashion: Brown and Ronstadt visited Africa in the spring of 1979, a voyage that neither bolstered Brown's presidential prospects nor helped his relationship with his girlfriend. Ronstadt was irritated by the press coverage and by repeated inquiries as to whether she and Brown were engaged. "Would you marry somebody you'd known for just two years?" she asked at one stop. "I know some rock stars have reputations for whirlwind romances, but I don't."[11] Brown used the trip to visit African leaders and discuss environmental issues on the continent. Ronstadt's week included twenty-four hours at a game reserve; most of the rest of the time "she spent shut up in her cottage" in a Nairobi hotel, according to one report. Brown and Ronstadt spent his forty-first birthday together in Monrovia, where they were spotted holding hands.[12]

Back in the United States, Brown trudged off to Iowa and New Hampshire, wooing picky voters with a combination of personal conservatism and liberal friends. He chastised smokers for burdening the nation's health-care system, demanded frugality of the kind he had practiced in California as a means for balancing the federal budget (he argued for a constitutional amendment to force such an approach if necessary), and railed against nuclear power at a time when Three Mile Island had made the nation sensitive to the risks of that technology. He appeared with Jane Fonda and Tom Hayden, neither accustomed to the granite hills or coffeehouses of New Hampshire but both celebrity activists and friends of Brown.

Brown's ideas managed to be spacey, prescient, and sensible in ways that it took time to appreciate. "People are not listening," he said, "because conventional politicians are not talking to basic issues."

Brown addressed those issues. "Our true security interests lie in a greater unity of the American people," he told Bill Moyers. Brown called for "rejuvenating our productivity and our technological capacity" and re-investing in "the space program, agriculture, aerospace, computers…the things that we are best at."[13] On balancing the budget, Brown resisted the notion that an amendment would, in Moyers's words, put the nation's economy in "constitutional chains." Instead, Brown drew upon his asceticism and his gubernatorial experience: "I don't consider balancing your budget some economic theory. I consider that a political, moral commitment to pay one's bills on a rational, agreed-upon schedule, and I think the persistent resort to a deficit reflects the inability of the American political system to muster a governing coalition."[14] Only Jerry Brown could frame the deficit as a moral demand; he alone argued for a balanced budget as an imperative of a religious liberal.

Brown's faith did not include heavy doses of forgiveness. He hectored Carter. When Carter suspended grain exports to the Soviet Union in retaliation for the Soviet invasion of Afghanistan—an unpopular move in states such as Iowa, which holds an early caucus—Brown fired off an impertinent note to the president. He posed a series of questions to Carter about the embargo, then closed with: "Because of the substantial adverse impact of your decision within this country, I would appreciate a response today."[15] Carter did not oblige. When Carter dropped out of a debate in Iowa, saying he needed to tend to the hostage crisis in Tehran, Brown accused him of ducking. "I find it shocking that he would use the hostages as an excuse to insulate himself from political discussion," Brown said. "He's not going to get the hostages home one day sooner by hiding in the White House."[16]

Brown's campaign rolled with a rollicking sense of improvisation. As the Africa trip suggested, the candidate was loose and irreverent, his backers mostly young and excited. The crowds that came to hear him didn't know what to expect. Many craned their necks for glimpses of the celebrities that gathered around the governor. Would Jane Fonda or Linda Ronstadt make an appearance? How about Warren Beatty or Jackson Browne or one of the Eagles?

Brown's campaign was complicated by a nagging problem at home. Unlike some states and the federal government, which select their chief executive and his alternate—vice president or lieutenant governor—California elects its top officers separately; they do not run as a ticket, and sometimes, as in 1978, they are antagonistic. The result: On the same ballot on which Brown was reelected in 1978, Californians had selected as their lieutenant governor a record-industry maverick named Mike Curb. Curb, a Republican who ran in part because Reagan urged him to, clashed with Brown from the first, and he made Brown's life just a little more miserable by asserting that he had the right to make gubernatorial decisions when Brown was out of state on the campaign trail. Thus Brown would head to Africa or New Hampshire or Iowa, and Curb would pounce, issuing executive orders and, in one case, nominating a judge. Brown objected to this naked showmanship, and the two sides duked it out in court. On December 27, 1979, the California Supreme Court split the baby on the constitutionality of that awkward entanglement: it concluded that Curb could act as governor during Brown's absence from the state but that Brown could revisit Curb's decisions upon returning to California.[17] Curb's determination to nettle Brown did just that, but it was more nuisance than impediment.[18]

One highlight of the 1980 campaign jumped the rails from politics to culture, where it has persevered. Linda Ronstadt hated politics and avoided most contact with that part of Brown's life, but when he announced his campaign for president, she relented and did her part. She helped organize two concerts, raising money for the campaign and delivering a memorable cover of "My Boyfriend's Back," dedicated to Brown.[19] Jimmy Carter was not going to match that.

Brown's political strategy was to position himself as the Democratic alternative to the failing Carter, a viable approach given Carter's evident political weakness. That strategy, however, depended chiefly on one thing: Senator Edward Kennedy not entering the race. Kennedy, as Brown's team recognized, would pose a liberal threat to Carter and could swamp Brown's attempt to position himself as the Democratic alternative to the president.[20] Unfortunately for Brown, Kennedy dangled the possibility of a campaign for months and then, in September of 1979, announced that he was withdrawing his endorsement of Carter and considering a campaign himself.

Brown should have realized that the jig was up. It was one thing to fight Carter, another to simultaneously fend off Carter to his right and Kennedy to his left. "If Kennedy is in, Brown is out," said California's AFL-CIO chief, John Henning. "His situation would be pretty good if it were just him and Carter, but with Kennedy in there, he'd better start thinking of running for the Senate in 1982."[21]

Nevertheless, Brown soldiered on, hoping first to register an upset in New Hampshire and, failing that, to beat Carter and Kennedy in Wisconsin, establishing himself as a candidate who could win outside California. It did not work out that way. As the campaign turned to primaries and caucuses, Brown effectively withdrew from Iowa, then scored less than 10 percent of the vote in New Hampshire (Carter won New Hampshire with just 47 percent of the vote, a weak showing that validated Brown's strategy, but Kennedy finished second with 37 percent, proof that voters disenchanted with Carter were heading to Kennedy, not Brown). The next batch of primaries was uncontested by Brown, and he didn't break 5 percent in any of them. He instead invested his resources in Wisconsin, whose voters were scheduled to go to the polls on April 1.

To make his final case to the voters of Wisconsin, Brown leaned on one of his many gifted supporters, movie director Francis Ford Coppola. Coppola created a multimedia presentation that was aired by the campaign on March 28. In theory, it brought together taped and live elements in what was intended to be a riveting display of video technology and the candidate of the future—"The Shape of Things to Come," as it was immodestly billed. Less than twenty seconds into the event, there was trouble: Brown's appearance was billed as "live from Madisno [*sic*], Wisconsin." Then Brown appeared, dressed in an overcoat and making his way to a microphone amid strange background voices. As he spoke, the images and sounds were out of sync, and the lighting mysteriously ebbed and flowed. Coppola later acknowledged that the presentation "looked as if it were a transmission from some clandestine place on Mars."[22] It would have been trouble for any campaign, but for a fading one premised on the transporting possibilities of technology, it was a killer. Jodie Evans, Brown's young campaign manager, understood the damage. She cried. Brown retreated back to California wounded.

Brown's campaign for president in 1980 didn't do much for him personally or politically. He lost the race, of course, and suffered some uncomfortable moments with Ronstadt. Most lastingly, however, the 1980 campaign branded him with a nickname that he would never shed.

The originator of this moniker was a Chicago newspaper columnist, a great one. Mike Royko, then at the *Chicago Sun-Times,* was tough and fun. He wielded a sharp pen and used it with humor and wit. He was not, it must be said, always fair. He wrote fast and trusted his instincts, good qualities in a columnist if not always in an political analyst or a human being. In April of 1979, he got a bee in his bonnet about Jerry Brown, and he let Brown have it, throwing in California just for the fun of it, too.

"Among its strangest exports," Royko wrote of California in the spring of 1979, "are its politicians." He ticked off a few, naming Nixon as "the national wart." And then he turned to Brown. "California," he wrote, "is threatening us with Gov. Jerry Brown, the position-leaping, buzz-wording, tripe-talking, science-fiction candidate who wants to bring his moonbeam ideas into the White House."[23] There it was: "Moonbeam." Royko knew he had something there, and he leaned on it. "I long ago gave up trying to figure out what Gov. Moonbeam stands for or believes in, besides getting his pretty mug on TV and confusing people into voting for him."

Royko went on in that vein for a while, and he intuitively poked

Brown's most tender weaknesses. Brown was vague and vain, a "presidential aspirant gadding about," an "intellectual hustler," a man whose main gifts were his looks and the ability to "jabber so nimbly that nobody can figure out what he's talking about." Royko hammered him for dating Linda Ronstadt, "a famous female person he's not married to," and nastily suggested that Brown had scoped out the politics of that relationship. Brown's advisers, Royko said, "probably told him not to worry because there are more rock fans and lecherous 41-year-old men than prim, disapproving old ladies." Royko concluded by noting that he'd just seen *Invasion of the Body Snatchers*. It was set in California, and he said he was "still convinced that it was a news documentary." The *Los Angeles Times* carried Royko's column under the headline SHOULD AMERICA FENCE OFF CALIFORNIA?[24]

It was biting, funny, and withering. Brown knew he'd been gotten. Royko himself seemed taken aback, particularly over time, by the column's lasting impression. Brown's subsequent campaigns invariably identified him as Governor Moonbeam, and no significant interview with him for the following four decades would fail to bring it up. It will, no doubt, appear in any obituary to be written about Brown.

Royko was embarrassed at having coined the moniker and tried his best to walk it back. "He got that nickname because a guy in Chicago was stringing some words together one evening to earn his day's pay and tossed in what he thought was an amusing phrase," Royko wrote in 1991. "And if he had it to do over again, he sure as hell wouldn't."[25] That wasn't true. Royko hadn't used the nickname once, "one evening." He'd used it repeatedly and to continuing effect. And he'd jabbed at Brown in other contexts, too. Near the end of 1979, Royko wrote about a now happily forgotten discussion about whether Chicago mayor Jane Byrne had undergone cosmetic surgery. Royko used the occasion to revisit his critique of California and its governor. Responding to a question from a California writer about Byrne, Royko chastised the writer for calling the procedure a face-lift, saying he should have known better, since "there is more plastic surgery done per square inch of human skin in your scatterbrained state than anywhere else in America, or possibly the world." As for Brown, Royko said: "He should have a brain lift."[26]

None of that was fair, of course, but it was good writing, the stuff of columns produced quickly and not meant to last. To the chagrin of all concerned, this one did. From that point forward, Jerry Brown would be known, at least by some, as Governor Moonbeam. It was a high price to pay for his ill-advised presidential campaign.

# 14

# Crime, Justice, and a Fly

A strong theme of Brown's first two terms as governor—alongside environmental protection and fiscal restraint—was his continuing interest in criminal justice, which would occupy his attention for the rest of his life, though he would strike a notably different tone in his twenty-first-century return to office.

For many liberals concerned with justice in the 1970s, determinate sentencing was an appealing social reform—essentially a long list of prescribed sentences that would be applied by judges in lieu of individual judgments based on the defendants before them. Under that approach, offenses would drive punishment, rather than attempting to assess the offender and his—or her—capacity for learning and growth. The driving impulse was the concern that judges and parole boards had acquired too much leeway in sentencing defendants and holding inmates in custody. Discretion allowed for inequality, and critics viewed the system as rife with opportunities for judicial officials to sentence poor and minority defendants to longer terms than other defendants and then deny them opportunities for early release. A system already tilted toward those with advantages was made more so by discretion. It was no surprise, then, that Jerry Brown ran for office in 1974 by promising to reform California's criminal justice system, suggesting that he would take aim at the state's indeterminate sentencing system without quite saying how he would go about it.

For conservatives, meanwhile, determinate sentencing meant nearly the opposite, yet it was curiously appealing to them as well. Those critics believed that lenient judges and parole boards were too quick to allow dangerous criminals back into society. For them, the perils of the existing system were that latitude led to leniency and permitted crime to flourish. In short, liberals wanted consistency, and conservatives wanted to lock in longer sentences. Tellingly, during the 1974 campaign, Flournoy had embraced sentencing reform as well.

Notably, however, support for these reforms came from centrists in both parties. More ideological members—at both ends of the spectrum—were cautious, again for mirror-image reasons: Some conservatives feared that sentences prescribed by the Left would be too lenient, and many liberals worried that fixed sentences would lend themselves to abuse over time, as new outrages inflamed the public and the Right pushed for longer prison terms.

Faced with that wobbly array of views, the solution that the two sides lit upon was to limit discretion without eliminating it entirely, and the vehicle was known as determinate sentencing. Any solution that seemed to fulfill such disparate ambitions was worrisome, and Brown had reservations. He supported the liberal goals of determinate sentencing— and he was pleased to be regarded as tough on crime as well—but he initially argued that those goals would be better met through a pilot program or a more modest approach. "I didn't want to sign a law," he recalled later.[1]

Still, he wanted some changes to the system and assigned his legal secretary, Tony Kline, to spearhead the effort. Guided by Kline, reformers in the legislature drafted SB-42, introduced by a Walnut Creek Republican and former district attorney named John Nejedly. The bill rejected California's system of indeterminate sentencing and virtually all the premises upon which that system rested: that criminals should be sentenced based on their capacity for growth; that their time in custody was designed to rehabilitate them; that parole boards should grant release to those prisoners who provided evidence of growth and understanding; and that, once released, former inmates should be supervised for extended periods in order to monitor the success of their rehabilitation. By contrast, SB-42 called for long sentences based on offenses, not individual cases. It curtailed the ability of parole boards to grant early releases, and it was predicated upon the notion that prison was meant to punish, not rehabilitate.[2]

Although he privately supported the principles behind SB-42 and was represented by Kline in the drafting and lobbying of it, Brown did not immediately signal his feelings about the bill as written, and legislators went to work without a clear sense of where Brown would come down. Not until March of 1976—and then only with a casual remark from the attorney general, Evelle Younger, indicating that his office and Brown's were working together on the bill—did Brown's support for the proposal become known outside a small circle of Capitol insiders.[3]

Brown's backing helped bring Democrats into the fold on the issue, and the rickety coalition of liberal reformers and tough-on-crime conservatives steered the bill through the legislature. Two court cases helped move that process along. In 1975, the California Supreme Court held that authorities could not constitutionally justify holding for twenty-two years a prisoner convicted of fondling a young boy; the following year, two inmates successfully challenged the parole board's handling of their cases. Those cases suggested that the legal architecture of indeterminate sentencing was giving way, and helped reinforce Brown's already-expressed view that changes were needed in the system.

With the Brown administration working from the sidelines to support imposition of some sentencing rules while reserving judgment on a final proposal until those rules were articulated, legislators honed the bill through the spring of 1976. SB-42 ultimately created four prison ranges—sixteen months to three years, two to four years, three to five years, and six to seven years. It also provided for life sentences and the death penalty. Judges were directed to sentence inmates within one of those ranges and were allowed limited discretion to modify them to account for factors that might mitigate or enhance the sentence. Once in custody, inmates were able to shave sentences slightly by accumulating "good time." Parole remained, in theory, but was sharply curtailed—

inmates could not be released prior to serving their prescribed sentences minus whatever "good time" they had accumulated. Brown succeeded in rebuffing several attempts by Younger and conservatives to lengthen the sentences in the bill, and that was enough to persuade liberals to go along. Overall, most sentences decreased under the legislation, though early releases also were essentially eliminated. The bill, which was introduced on the first day of the legislative session, passed with just twelve minutes remaining before the midnight deadline on August 31. One opponent, Republican assemblyman John Briggs, who would lead the effort to drive gays from public schools, warned that "this will release a bloodbath on the citizens of California." The speaker ignored him, and the motion passed.[4]

That ended the debate for the moment, but for Brown it went on for years. Once given the structure of determinate sentencing, advocates of stricter punishment had an apparatus with which to tinker. Every term thereafter, beginning in 1977, legislators would introduce measures to adjust the sentencing ranges set out in statute. As liberals had feared when the matter first came before the legislature, those proposed amendments almost always would stiffen sentences, upsetting the delicate balance of leniency and rigidity that characterized the compromises of SB-42. Prison populations grew, eventually to the breaking point, a problem that would dominate much of Brown's attention in his third and fourth gubernatorial terms.

By 2018, Brown had long since become disenchanted with the results of his 1970s sentencing reform. Successive legislatures had added so many sentencing enhancements that the package's original goals had slipped away.[5] Enhancements, he said, had so distorted the original designs of determinate sentencing that unraveling it was beyond comprehension. Under the 1976 approach, he recalled, sentencing was supposed to be "swift, certain, and fair." Over the years, it had become more swift and certain but less fair. Did Brown regret his endorsement of the sentencing reforms of the 1970s? Not exactly. He still believed that the original scheme had merit and that it did address legitimate concerns about equity in criminal justice. But it had become unwieldy over time, especially in reaction to certain crimes. "You can never punish enough for whatever the crime of the decade is," Brown said in 2018, sitting on a couch in the office he had occupied forty years earlier. First it was drugs, then sex crimes, then clerical abuse of children. Going back further, he reflected, it had been criminal libel or honor crimes. Humanity, he noted, "has a strong instinct for punishment."[6]

Brown's 1980 presidential campaign was effectively over after April 1. That left nearly two years of his term, and, since term limits in California had yet to be enacted (voters would approve them in 1990), Brown had the option of seeking a third term as governor. In other words, he had plenty of time to reestablish himself inside California and reimagine his future in the state's politics. He did not. Brown instead lapsed into torpor. He and Linda Ronstadt drifted apart after the presidential run, leaving a hole in his personal life. And politics began to become oppressive.

The effects of Proposition 13 took time to be fully felt in California, mainly because the state's large surplus in 1978 helped cushion the blow. At Brown's urging, the state had dispensed funds in 1978 and 1979 to ease the gap in local and school funding created by Proposition 13's cuts. Brown, arguing that he was heeding the will of an electorate frustrated by high taxes, had further supported reduction in state income taxes. The result was that by the end of 1980, California's surplus had disappeared.

"For this reason," Brown wrote in early 1981, "the moment of truth is upon us."[7]

Addressing the legislature on January 8, he warned that California had reached a crucible moment. "For the first time since World War II," he said, "state government spending will clearly not keep pace with inflation."[8] Brown's address to the legislature seemed emblematic of his parsimony. It was nine minutes long.

Brown's plans for 1981 did not curtail all state spending. He managed modest increases in criminal justice, and he insisted on continuing to build up the California Conservation Corps. "I only wish we could enroll thousands more," he lamented.[9] But the overall message was of reduction, of living within new limits, politically and otherwise. Legislators did not all approve of Brown's austerity. David Roberti, the liberal senate Democratic leader, accused Brown of going "too far" in heeding the fiscally conservative mood of the electorate and of trimming state spending to prepare for yet another run for the presidency, this time in 1984. "Maybe the drive for tax relief has gone far enough," Roberti said.[10]

With Democrats pulling away and suspicious, Brown's programs that year faced unusually hard sledding. In June, both versions of the budget passed by the legislature raised spending above the levels Brown had recommended in January. Moreover, conservative elements of the legislature struck out as well, inserting language into the spending plan that attempted to curtail state funds for abortion. The effect, noted assemblywoman Maxine Waters, would be to curtail abortions for poor women while permitting them for those who could afford them. "If all women have a right to make that decision, then poor women should have a right to make that decision as well," she said.[11] It took months and much legislative maneuvering, but Waters, with Brown's help, ultimately prevailed.

In the end, the budget balanced, barely. Brown's painstakingly built surplus disappeared, dropping to $0.3 million—effectively nothing—by year's end. The newly inaugurated president, Ronald Reagan, wasn't delivering much help to the states, even his old home, California. Education at the elementary school and high school levels was cut, as was higher education. Health and welfare got a tiny increase, and legislators dribbled out a bit of additional tax relief.[12]

State planners hoped economic performance would keep California out of a deficit, but they acknowledged that the once deep well of reserves and surpluses had run dry. Like consumers who spend money when times are good, Californians faced the difficult task of scaling back their spending in response to decreased revenue. "Eventually," the state budget analysts explained, "they must adjust their living standard to correspond to their monthly paycheck."[13]

For all its controversies, the Brown administration had escaped scandal for nearly eight solid years. Brown famously turned down gifts—though his Proposition 9 had created an exception for books—and his fierce

SEMINARIAN: Young Jerry Brown entered the Sacred Heart Novitiate in Los Gatos, California, on August 14, 1956. He would spend the next three-and-a-half years studying to become a Catholic priest. *(Photo courtesy of Jerry Brown and Anne Gust Brown)*

THE GOVERNOR AND HIS FAMILY: Although novices were restricted to the seminary, Brown was allowed to leave to join his father and family when Pat Brown was inaugurated as governor of California in 1959. Pat and Bernice Brown are seated in front; standing are Jerry, Kathleen, Cynthia, and Barbara. *(AP Photo/Clarence Hamm)*

PLAY BALL!: California celebrated on April 12, 1960, when Candlestick Park opened in San Francisco, bringing baseball to its new outpost on the West Coast. Dignitaries at the game included San Francisco mayor George Christopher, accompanied by his wife, Tula; California governor Pat and Bernice Brown; and vice president Richard Nixon, also a native Californian. (*Bob Campbell,* San Francisco Chronicle/*Polaris*)

CALIFORNIA ROYALTY: A hunting trip in the early 1960s brought together a former, current, and future California governor. Pat Brown is on the left, with former governor Earl Warren and future governor Jerry Brown on the right. Second from left is Wally Lynn, a friend of Warren's. (*The Papers of Chief Justice Earl Warren, 1951–1970. Archives, University of Virginia Law Library*)

FREE SPEECH: The 1960s erupted across California. Mario Savio is taken away during a Berkeley rally on December 7, 1964. The following year, riots in Watts added to the sense of disquiet among many Californians and contributed to doubts about Pat Brown's leadership. *(AP Photo/Robert W. Klein)*

A NEW FORCE: Pat Brown was thwarted in his attempt at a third term as California governor by a newcomer to elected politics, actor Ronald Reagan, shown here with his wife, Nancy, on election night, 1966, in Los Angeles. *(Courtesy of Ronald Reagan Library)*

PANTHERS WITH GUNS: On May 2, 1967, members of the Black Panther Party, exercising their right under California law to carry a loaded firearm in public so long as it was not concealed, stormed the California Assembly, bringing debate over a gun control bill to a stunned standstill. The bill passed, and Reagan signed it, making the governor an early and vocal supporter of gun control. *(Sacramento Bee/Tribune News Service via Getty Images)*

MUSIC IN THE STREETS: The Summer of Love drew thousands of young people to San Francisco, home to a bustling combination of drugs, politics, and music. Central to that culture was the Grateful Dead, shown here at the celebrated intersection of Haight and Ashbury. Outside California, Jerry Brown was sometimes lampooned as a hippie, but that was never accurate; he skipped the Summer of Love. *(Photo by Herbie Greene)*

MODERN ENVIRONMENTALISM: Oil washed up on the beaches of Santa Barbara, California, in January of 1969, gushing from an offshore leak at a Union Oil well. The company's chief executive professed himself "amazed at the publicity for the loss of a few birds." Jerry Brown embraced environmental causes early and throughout his career. *(Bettmann/ Contributor/Getty Images)*

REBELLION TO REVOLUTION: As protest in California moved from civil rights to Vietnam, it became more confrontational and violent. Here, protesters at UCLA face off against officers from the Los Angeles Police Department and the Los Angeles Sheriff's Office. California's deepening divide over the war and, later, disenchantment with Watergate, helped clear the way for Jerry Brown's gubernatorial victory in 1974. *(Los Angeles Times Photographic Archives, Collection 1429. Library Special Collections, Charles E. Young Research Library, UCLA)*

RISING TO POWER: Brown first ran for public office in 1969, winning a seat on the board of the Los Angeles Community College, then won statewide office in his first try, becoming Secretary of State in 1971. Earl Warren, then chief justice of the United States, administered the oath. Behind Warren sat his wife, Nina, and Brown's parents, Bernice and Pat. *(AP Photo)*

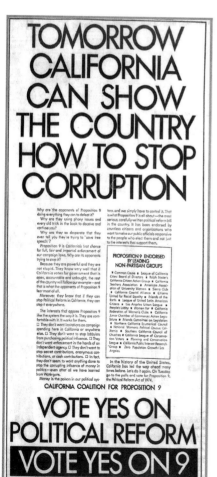

REFORM POLITICS: Elected as a political reformer and spurred by Watergate, Brown sponsored Proposition 9, which sought to limit what he described as "the poison in our political system," money. The measure was approved by voters in 1974, on the same ballot that Brown won the Democratic nomination for governor.

GOVERNOR-ELECT: Fresh off his 1974 gubernatorial victory, Brown met with reporters at his Los Angeles campaign headquarters. *(Los Angeles Times Photographic Archive. Department of Special Collections, Charles E. Young Research Library, UCLA)*

PRESIDENTIAL AMBITIONS: Barely had he settled into office before Brown ran again, this time for president. Here, he joins reporters on the bus as they travel through Massachusetts. *(Owen Franken/Corbis via Getty Images)*

BACHELOR: As governor, Brown dated Linda Ronstadt, who occasionally and reluctantly lent her great talents to his political ambitions. Here, Ronstadt and Brown join the Eagles onstage at a Brown fundraiser on May 14, 1976. *(Richard E. Aaron/Redferns/Getty Images)*

TRAVELS WITH RONSTADT: Brown and Ronstadt took time off from the 1980 campaign for president to visit Africa. They are pictured here on April 11, 1979, when they visited a United Nations program in Kenya. *(AP Photo/Mark Foley)*

BIRD AND FEINSTEIN: Rose Bird, left, was Jerry Brown's first pick for the California Supreme Court in 1977 and the first woman removed from that court by voters, in 1986. Here, she administers the oath of office to another icon of California politics, San Francisco supervisor Dianne Feinstein, who became mayor of San Francisco following the 1978 assassination of George Moscone. *(AP Photo/Sal Veder)*

TAX REVOLT: The populist uprising that became the Property Tax Revolution of the 1980s that helped bring Reagan to the White House began in California with Proposition 13. Spearheaded by a curmudgeonly gadfly named Howard Jarvis, the initiative took Brown and other political leaders by surprise. Here, Jarvis shows off boxes of letters supporting the measure, which passed in 1978. *(Erhardt E. Krause,* Sacramento Bee*/Center for Sacramento History)*

MOTHER TERESA: Brown's travels during his years out of office included a stay with Mother Teresa in Calcutta, India. Although his time with her was brief, it left a deep impression on Brown and became a significant part of his identity. *(Photo courtesy of Jerry Brown and Anne Gust Brown)*

REFLECTION: Jerry Brown left office in 1983 after losing a bid for the US Senate. He traveled abroad, including a stay in Kamakura, Japan, where he studied Zen Buddhism and worked on his writing. In early 1987, two *Los Angeles Times* reporters caught up with him, and he reluctantly posed for this photograph. *(Kenneth Reich,* Los Angeles Times. *Used with permission)*

THE BREACH, AGAIN: Back from abroad, Brown was elected chairman of the California Democratic Party, a role ill-suited to him, then ran yet again for president, a role he enjoyed. His debates with Bill Clinton were spirited and sometimes biting, but this one, hosted by Phil Donahue, was a civilized exchange. *(Cynthia Johnson/Liaison/Getty Images)*

RIOTS: Racial tensions in Los Angeles boiled over in April 1992 after a Ventura County jury acquitted four Los Angeles police officers on all but one count in the 1991 beating and arrest of Rodney King. The subsequent riots left scores dead and caused more than $1 billion in property damage. Los Angeles was left reeling. *(Steve Dykes/Los Angeles Times via Getty Images)*

MARRIED AT LAST: Famously a bachelor, Brown met Anne Gust in San Francisco in 1990, and they dated for more than a decade. They were married in 2005 at Oakland City Hall. Feinstein, by then California's senior US senator, officiated. *(John Storey,* San Francisco Chronicle/*Polaris)*

UNCERTAIN TIMES: As Brown climbed back up through California politics in the 1990s and early 2000s, the state struggled through a difficult period. Gray Davis, once Brown's chief of staff and later California governor, was recalled from office in 2003 and replaced by Arnold Schwarzenegger, a civic-minded action hero. When Brown took over from Schwarzenegger in 2011, it was the second time he followed an actor in office. Reagan was the first. *(Mario Tama/Getty Images)*

RETURN: Brown returned to the governorship in 2011. Anne Gust held the Bible, and Tani Cantil-Sakauye, California's chief justice, administered the oath. *(Justin Sullivan/ Getty Images)*

GOVERNOR, ACT 2: Brown, accompanied by Anne Gust and their dog, Sutter, walked to work on the first day of his historic third term, twenty-eight years after he had departed the governorship in 1983. *(Robert Gauthier/*Los Angeles Times *via Getty Images)*

ADVISER: Brown's third and fourth terms were more focused and productive than his first two, a credit to his own experience and maturity and to his staff, led by Nancy McFadden. Here, she heads the table in the governor's office while Brown declaims. McFadden died near the end of the fourth Brown term, succumbing to cancer. *(AP Photo/Rich Pedroncelli)*

CLIMATE: No issue more profoundly shaped Brown's time in office than the environment, and his final terms were devoted to confronting climate change, which afflicted California with more intense wildfires and decreased snowpack, compounding the state's droughts, among other plagues. President Donald Trump and Governor-elect Gavin Newsom joined Brown for a tour of damage caused by a 2018 fire. Trump bemoaned the damage to the town of "Pleasure" — it is actually named "Paradise" — and urged California to do a better job raking its forests. Newsom and Brown suffered Trump's visit to Paradise that November mostly in silence, if also, as here, through clenched teeth. Below: Boats crowded for space as water levels on state lakes dropped. *(Above: AP Photo/Evan Vucci, File; below: Mark Ralston/AFP via Getty Images)*

HOME: Anne and Jerry and their dogs — Cali is pictured here — wrapped up their lives in public service in 2019 and relocated to their property in Colusa County, on land that Brown's ancestors bought and that has been in the family for more than 100 years. They live there today. *(Melina Mara/*Washington Post *via Getty Images)*

attacks on the influence of money in politics established him as a critic of government corruption Then, suddenly, he was hit with a serious charge: "Gov. Edmund G. Brown is using state funds to compile massive lists of his political supporters and to install a sophisticated computer mailing system to make use of the lists."[14] Those allegations, first reported by the *Los Angeles Times*, rocked Brown's staff just as the governor was returning to his duties from his 1980 presidential campaign.

The creation of such a list, which Brown was accused of ordering and taking a personal interest in, seems mild by contemporary standards of campaign chicanery, but the charge arose at a time when such violations were novel. The use of a computer—"a sophisticated computer mailing system"—gave it an additional air of intrigue. And compounding the potential damage was Brown's own rectitude: it is especially wounding when a critic of corruption is seen as tainted by it.

The allegations were serious enough for the Fair Political Practices Commission, which Brown, after all, had established, to join the calls for an investigation of the governor. Brown promised cooperation, but aides resisted, and the scandal mushroomed in typical fashion, with charges of a cover-up overtaking the initial allegations of misuse of funds. One staff member altered a memo; others seemed evasive or unavailable. Prosecutors took note. Sacramento's DA looked into the matter. Attorney general George Deukmejian investigated, as did Los Angeles district attorney John Van de Kamp, the former a prominent Republican, the latter an up-and-coming Democrat.

Little by little, the scandal melted away. The FPPC could find no criminal wrongdoing, nor could the attorney general. In Los Angeles, Van de Kamp pursued the investigation into the fall, probing allegations that Brown aides had destroyed evidence. But that line of inquiry went dead, too.

Brown simultaneously admitted error and professed innocence at an exhaustive news conference in July. "The governor's office—and I include myself—is guilty of bad judgment, mistakes, and sloppy practices," Brown admitted. After listing some of those practices, however, he added: "I do not believe that anyone in my office made a mistake of such gravity that it would merit dismissal. By now, most of the people accused in newspaper stories and the FPPC report have suffered more than from any reprimand."[15]

As to the essential question left at the end of the inquiry, "There was no cover-up," Brown insisted. "There is no conspiracy."

Neither Brown nor any member of his staff was held criminally responsible.

On June 5, 1981, the *Los Angeles Times*'s coverage of the budget machinations in Sacramento was the lead item on page 3 of the newspaper. Tucked beneath it, less prominently, was a short item about a forthcoming report from the Centers for Disease Control, in Atlanta. The report, according to the *Times,* examined five mysterious cases of pneumonia. Wayne Shandera, a CDC epidemiologist from Los Angeles, said researchers were puzzled by the cases, which included one death, and that the symptoms resembled those found in cancer or transplant patients whose immune systems had been catastrophically compromised. The story's headline read: OUTBREAKS OF PNEUMONIA AMONG GAY MALES STUDIED. Why would the cases center on gay males? Shandera told the reporter, "The best we can say is that somehow the pneumonia appears to be related to gay life style."[16]

Brown was at least two things at once in the late 1970s and early 1980s. He was a promisingly young new face in American politics, appealingly fresh and unconventional. And he was governor of America's largest state, a position that carried conventional duties and responsibilities, a position most recently held by Ronald Reagan.

That created a tension in Brown's life, one that was evident in his relations with institutions such as the California judiciary and the University of California and in his efforts to confront certain issues. One such issue was that of nuclear power.

The antinuke movement gathered steam in the late 1970s. It represented a convergence of themes—revulsion at the threat of nuclear war, anxiety about threats to the environment, and distrust of the government institutions that sanctioned, promoted, and licensed nuclear power plants. Brown shared many of those misgivings, and so "no nukes" reached him at the level of his skepticism and courtesy toward his friends, many of whom were sympathetic to and involved in the movement. Brown had tried in 1979, unsuccessfully, to break the university's relationship to nuclear weapons research: his proposal to denuclearize the Lawrence Livermore lab failed at a vote of the university regents that July.

In addition, he supported limitations on nuclear power and expressed reservations about it through the late 1970s, but he also nodded to its potential on occasion, noting, for example, that it was preferable in some respects to burning oil or coal, with the resultant air pollution. His calls for a moratorium on new nuclear plants was enough to anger advocates of nuclear power while falling short of the actions demanded by its critics, who wanted existing plants dismantled. Speaking at an antinuke rally in Washington in the summer of 1979, Brown was introduced by Jane Fonda and greeted warmly when he urged protesters to demand action against nuclear power at a local level. But when he called for "a moratorium on new nuclear power plants," some in the audience booed: "Shut 'em down in California, Jerry, shut 'em down."[17] When it came to nuclear energy, the center was a difficult place to stand.

In the summer of 1981, antinuclear activists in California prepared to confront one of the state's leading utility companies. Pacific Gas and Electric owned the Diablo Canyon nuclear power plant, near San Luis Obispo, along California's Central Coast. PG&E had begun construction of its Diablo Canyon generating station in the Reagan gubernatorial years, and the reactor was up for commissioning in the early 1980s. That was a federal process over which Brown had little say as governor, but it raised the question of his position on nuclear power and forced him to choose between a significant sector of his support and a major contributor to the California economy and power supply.

Protesters set their sights on a confrontation, and PG&E girded for it. "The blockade of the Diablo Canyon Nuclear Power Plants, which has been announced by the Abalone Alliance and other opponents of the plant," the utility's chairman, Frederick Mielke, wrote to Brown on July 29, "requires your immediate attention and action."[18] Mielke's letter barely concealed the executive's frustration with Brown. "Your opposition to the Diablo Canyon plant," he wrote, "has given moral

214 • JIM NEWTON

support to those who are organizing the blockade." Mielke urged Brown to mobilize the National Guard and to prepare to respond in force. For its part, PG&E pledged to do all it could "to assure that there is not violence and that no harm comes to anyone."[19]

Not exactly. Even as PG&E promised to avoid violence, it prepared to wage it: the utility erected a firing range outside its reactors. "Uniformed guards have been pumping ammunition into silhouettes of human bodies," the *Wall Street Journal* reported.[20]

Unbeknownst to PG&E, Brown already was taking steps to guard against a disruptive or violent confrontation. In late June, the California Highway Patrol confirmed its plans to deploy four companies, approximately two hundred officers, to a camp in San Luis Obispo. Local law enforcement was alert to the need for reinforcements under mutual aid agreements with the state, and plans to call in the National Guard were prepared and ready to be activated.[21] In the end, Brown approved those agreements and called up the National Guard while still maintaining his opposition to nuclear power. When the protest began in September, Brown appeared at the demonstration and, after some hesitation on the part of organizers, was allowed to address the gathering. At the same time, he authorized the use of the National Guard as well as state and local law enforcement to ensure access to the plant.

The action began on September 15 with a "sea blockade" along the periphery of a safety zone established by the Coast Guard. Another contingent of protesters arrived at the plant's main gate that afternoon, some climbing inside the facility using assault ladders. At around 4:00 p.m., law enforcement began making arrests. Pursuant to the arrangements Brown had authorized, 560 people were arrested that first day. Some were booked at nearby Cuesta College, others at a Department of Corrections facility. Protests continued for weeks, as did arrests. By September 22, 1,483 people, including the musician Jackson Browne, had been taken into custody. Over the course of the following several days, the protest petered out, but not before another two hundred arrests were made, on September 28, and not before a series of court hearings, at which most charges against most demonstrators were dropped, had taken place.

Brown emerged both as a foe of nuclear power and an agent of the state. "Jerryfoolery," one columnist called it. "Nuclear power is a difficult one," Brown said, reflecting on the standoff and emphasizing that he did not have the luxury of acting as a mere protester. "I was governor, too."[22]

The Mediterranean fruit fly is a nasty little creature. It is around one-quarter of an inch in length. Its torso is black and silver, and its wings have orange patches. Its head is topped by an ugly, bulging set of red eyes. It lays its eggs in fruit, and they hatch a few days later, destroying the fruit as they grow into larvae for another week or so, then emerge as flies to repeat the cycle. The medfly causes trouble because it voraciously infests apples, apricots, avocados, bell peppers, cherries, all types of citrus fruits, coffee, eggplants, figs, grapes, kiwifruit, mangoes, olives, papayas, peaches, pears, persimmons, plums, pomegranates, tomatoes, and walnuts, to name a few. The United States Department of Agriculture considers it "the most important agricultural pest in the world."[23] Once infected, fruit falls early and decays, ruining it for market. Moreover, the flies breed rapidly and spread widely, so infestation can quickly overcome whole regions and the entire yield of some crops.

The fly is a perennial threat to California and other Mediterranean-climate growing areas, so farmers and agricultural inspectors vigilantly look out for it. On June 5, 1980, two of the critters turned up in the backyard of a home in San Jose. (The same day, a single fly was discovered in Northridge, a suburban community in the San Fernando Valley, part of Los Angeles, but that infestation received far less attention, perhaps because the area included less farmland and was farther from the state's breadbasket, the Central Valley.)[24] Within days, more flies were found in the Santa Clara Valley, near where Brown had briefly been in college—at the time of the infestation it was the heart of both Silicon Valley and a dwindling but still important mélange of farms and orchards. State officials hastily conferred, then ordered a quarantine on crops from three counties in the Santa Clara Valley while they struggled to devise a broader response.[25]

Brown hesitated. The interests on both sides were powerful and loud. Agriculture demanded swift action: spread of the bug could devastate

216 • JIM NEWTON

crops and shut California markets to imports for fear of spreading the infestation. Environmentalists were equally impassioned: aerial spraying, which farmers demanded, could expose hundreds of thousands of Bay Area residents to harmful pesticides, chemicals strong enough to damage the paint on cars and kill fish in streams. Brown was naturally sympathetic to environmental arguments, but he could hardly ignore agriculture, one of his state's most significant and influential constituencies—and one, given Brown's support for the United Farm Workers and the Agricultural Labor Relations Act, that was already wary of the governor.

Brown's quandary was ratcheted up by Washington, where the newly elected president, Ronald Reagan—a familiar foe, both of Jerry and his father—was installed. Reagan's Department of Agriculture insisted that California take strong action to thwart the medfly lest the pest find its way into the state's export crops and take hold in other states. By the end of July, federal officials had placed their own quarantine on a 105-square-mile area in and around the Santa Clara Valley, prohibiting any farm goods from that zone from entering interstate or international supply chains. The quarantine was economically devastating and swept up even those farmers whose crops were not susceptible to the medfly. Farmers begged for permission to override existing pesticide bans so that they might fumigate fields to eradicate the bug. More complicated was the question of how to eliminate the pest from the residential and commercial areas that covered much of the affected area.[26]

The crisis grew. Traps throughout the area yielded more of the flies through 1980. Brown continued to hew to a middle course between farmers and environmentalists, authorizing the release of millions of sterile fruit flies intended to disrupt the medfly breeding cycle. Ground crews stripped fruit from trees, and ground spraying attempted to debug infested areas. But Brown stopped short of what agricultural experts clamored for: aerial spraying of the chemical malathion.

Medflies did what medflies do: they multiplied. By the end of 1980, it was clear that trapping and sterilized breeding were not stopping the spread of the pest. On Christmas Eve, Brown declared a state of emergency in Santa Clara and Alameda Counties, the two suburban communities on opposite sides of the San Francisco Bay that had become hubs of the crisis. Brown's action freed his prized California Conservation Corps to join other agencies in stripping trees of fruit and deploying ground crews to spray. The National Guard was left on hold, prepared to join a regionwide campaign to remove every piece of potentially infected vegetation. A voluntary removal program was already under way, but Brown announced on December 24 that the government would begin its full efforts on January 6.[27]

Brown continued to fight growing pressure to approve the aerial spraying, but the federal government weighed in heavily on the side of farmers. The US Department of Agriculture expanded its quarantine area and in July of 1981 threatened to place all of California under its restrictions. Brown howled in protest. "The action of the Reagan administration in threatening a quarantine is sabotage," Brown complained.[28] Finally, on July 10, he folded. Spraying by helicopter began at midnight that night.

The various sides continued to squabble. Brown felt cornered, demanding federal help while rejecting federal demands. B. T. Collins, then serving as Brown's chief of staff, tried to reassure residents that malathion wouldn't hurt them, so he chugged a glass of it in front of reporters. "I am firmly convinced that the stuff is not bad for you," he insisted. Observers were more horrified than impressed.[29] Brown proclaimed that the problem was "beyond the control of the state." Federal officials were miffed. "I think everything may be served better for a few days if the governor wouldn't make so many statements," Richard Lyng, the second-ranking official in the Department of Agriculture, said on July 16. The *Los Angeles Times* headlined its story the next day with: FIGHT MEDFLY AND BE QUIET, BROWN TOLD.[30] Brown said he had merely used boilerplate language to request federal assistance.

But once the helicopters took off, the essential battles—between Washington and Sacramento, environmentalists and farmers—were over. Brown had agreed to spray. All that was left was to argue about details—whether the area qualified for disaster relief, where the helicopters would be based. Farmers went away mad that Brown had dawdled. Environmentalists were furious that he had caved. Homeowners worried for their pets and cars. Brown had fought and lost.[31]

Decades later, with just months left in his fourth and final term as governor, Brown and I sat in his office in the capitol, sparring as usual over language, the lessons of politics and philosophy. I asked him at one point whether he was enjoying his final months, and he challenged my question. Of course he was enjoying himself, Brown said; he was eighty years old and serving as governor of his home state, the largest and most important in the union. We laughed and squabbled. But when the topic turned to history, Brown became more serious. We discussed moments when he regretted his actions or might have acted differently. Looking back at the medfly crisis, he said, "I should have sprayed immediately."[32]

Brown approached the end of his second term with his state tiring of him. His most loyal base, in Northern California, was shaking off malathion and feeling cross. Three years of implementing Proposition 13, along with periodic gestures to the tough-on-crime lobby, had worn out the Left. Plus Brown himself seemed tired of the work. The medfly had done to him something like what Chessman had done to his father—his tacking between positions alienated both sides of an impassioned debate, leaving him without friends.

Brown's answer to that: try something new. What that meant, in this case, was to pass on a bid for reelection and instead run for a seat in the United States Senate, where Republican S. I. Hayakawa was considering retiring in the face of uneasiness in his own party after his one undistinguished term. Republicans spent much of 1981 searching for their best option to retain the seat. Representative Barry Goldwater, son of the iconic standard-bearer from 1964, staked out the Right; Representative Pete McCloskey, an environmentalist and Nixon challenger from way back, looked to corral what was then a still-viable liberal wing; and the San Diego mayor, Pete Wilson, a genial moderate whose politics would harden in later years but had not yet begun that migration in 1981, elbowed for the center. A private poll in August showed Wilson faring best against Brown, beating the governor by four-teen points. Hayakawa finished a dismal third, reinforcing doubts about his electability.[33] Through the fall, Brown remained coy about his plans, even as the Los Angeles mayor, Tom Bradley, another Democrat, moved to run for governor on the assumption that Brown intended to move to the Senate.

By the beginning of 1982, Brown was acknowledging that his eyes were on the Senate seat, but California showed signs of not caring much. A January Field poll revealed that just 23 percent of Californians approved of Brown's performance, compared to 41 percent who disapproved. The economy was soft, and the legislature was wrangling over reapportionment and other issues. One especially cranky bunch of legislators wanted to haul in Brown's transportation director under subpoena for having the temerity to push public transportation over freeway construction. The capitol felt chaotic and unfocused. Wilson's San Diego seemed a calm contrast. As the campaign solidified, Brown faded. By June, Wilson led Brown by twenty-two points, and pundits were calling the race—one of the most expensive in Senate history—over.

Until the very end. Mysteriously, Brown bounced back in the campaign's closing weeks. "I feel unaccountably good," Brown told reporters on the last day of October. A new poll showed him within a point of overtaking Wilson. Wilson, by nature cool, shrugged off the surge but refused to predict victory, offering only that he was "cautiously optimistic."[34] His caution was habitual; his optimism was rewarded.

Wilson beat Brown handily on November 2, part of a Republican triumph in California that defied a generally good night for Democrats nationally. George Deukmejian scored a surprise victory over Tom Bradley in the governor's race—a win that has preoccupied pollsters ever since, because Bradley seemed a lock. Analysts have attributed Deukmejian's victory to causes as varied as racial bias in poll respondents to the presence of a gun-control initiative on the state ballot that may have drawn out conservatives in opposition.

Brown's loss was less of a mystery. He had trailed from the beginning, surged at the end, but still fell short. Reflecting on the defeat many years later, he said his bravado in those final hours had been more of an indication of campaign euphoria and exhaustion than careful analysis. "I was tired," he said.[35] It was time for Brown and California to take a break from each other. He even said as much publicly: "I believe the people of

California would like a respite from me," he told a reporter from the *Los Angeles Times*. "And in some ways, I would like a respite from them."[36]

But even as he left, Brown made it clear that it was not forever. "I'll reflect and come back again some day," he predicted to reporters who pressed him on the morning after he had been shown the door at the ripe old age of forty-four. "I shall return. But not for a while."[37]

# Part Four

# The Time Away

# 15

# Years of Darkness and Reflection

Jerry Brown and California parted ways in 1983. Brown returned home to Los Angeles, which became his base for a journey of reflection and discovery, with an occasional look over his shoulder. California plunged into a dreary decade. The years that followed were a period of crime and retribution, recession and despair, bitter race relations and death on a sweeping, terrifying scale as California led the nation into the worst health crisis in modern history, one more compromised by politics than any that had come before.

From the barest hints in the early 1980s—the June 5, 1981, CDC alert that raised questions about gay men dying from pneumonia; the mysterious reports of immune systems compromised in ways not previously seen—an epidemic quietly slipped into America's blood. By the time AIDS became part of the English language, which it did when Rock Hudson announced that he had the disease, in 1985, no corner of the country was safe. And no city was in more peril than San Francisco.

The decade began rambunctiously and confusingly for California's cultural capital and its rapidly growing—and increasingly assertive—gay population. Harvey Milk's election to the board of supervisors, in 1977, was a triumph for gay rights. Liberation and political identity were magnets and reinforced each other. Gays flocked to San Francisco in those years, gaining power and drawing more transplants to the city; by the end of the 1970s, two of every five men in the the city were gay.

Gay political power grew commensurately. The defeat of Proposition 6 in 1978—and by such a resounding margin—proved that, at least in California, voters were unwilling to accept the banishment of gays from public schools. Milk's assassination, just a few months later, staggered San Francisco, but his work outlived him. In 1980, Jerry Brown declared Gay Freedom Week for the entire state, reinforcing the growing influence of gays in the state's politics and the state's growing acceptance of that influence. Four years later, Democrats held their presidential convention in San Francisco. It was held, appropriately, at the center named for George Moscone, killed in 1978 alongside Harvey Milk: one hundred thousand people marched to call attention to AIDS, a powerful demonstration of unity and force. Gays were by then the linchpin of San Francisco politics, a force in California and a burning ember in the nation's social conscience.

But political power was no match for the scourge that was invisibly infecting that same community. AIDS began to make itself known in gay enclaves around the world in the early 1980s, before the disease had a name. First came the handful of cases of *Pneumocystis carinii* pneumonia (PCP) in Los Angeles that infected five gay men between the ages of twenty-nine and thirty-six.[1] Then came outbreaks of "gay cancer," as some called it, a previously rare ailment known as Kaposi's sarcoma, which dotted an alarming number of gay men with purple lesions, puzzling doctors from Copenhagen to San Francisco.[2] More mysteries abounded: previously healthy men, many of them young, complained of lethargy and diarrhea. With increasing frequency, they succumbed to pneumonia, resisting treatment that should have easily restored them to health. They withered and died, leaving loved ones heartbroken and doctors at first perplexed and then frantic.

The prevalence of these disorders among gay men was striking. Epidemics do not tend to single out any one demographic group— rich people or blacks or Catholics or liberals. They often concentrate on geographic areas (which sometimes has demographic implications), but social clusters do not usually lend themselves to disease transmission.[3]

This collection of ailments, however, was unbounded by geography—evidence was surfacing in Africa, Europe, and the United States—and was showing a distinct affinity for gay men. By 1981, the correlation between these deaths and gay men was so strong that the first name for the disease was GRID, short for gay-related immune deficiency.

AIDS's concentration among gays supplied the contours of the political fight to fund research into the disease through the early 1980s. Despite pockets of infection among hemophiliacs, other transfusion recipients, and Haitians, AIDS was largely a gay disease, and those communities who harbored ill will toward gays—the religious right, especially—showed little concern as the death toll climbed. No less than the Reverend Jerry Falwell, head of the self-proclaimed Moral Majority, declared: "AIDS is the wrath of God upon homosexuals."[4] Politicians, especially on the Right, took note. By the year of Ronald Reagan's re-election, 1984, some seven thousand people had died of it, and Reagan had yet to mention the word *AIDS*. It fell instead to two liberal Californians, congressmen Phil Burton and Henry Waxman, to secure the first funding for AIDS research, $15 million in 1982 for the Centers for Disease Control and the National Institutes of Health.[5] Year after year, those congressmen would scrape for pennies in research, dreading opposition from sanctimonious conservatives all too willing to let gay men die.

That changed in 1985. Long the ruggedly handsome leading man, Rock Hudson grew gaunt and frail in front of the world. He appeared with Doris Day in Monterey on July 15, 1985, to promote a new project of hers; he shuffled in late, and his waxen complexion and hollow cheeks drew audible gasps from those present.[6] The following week, Hudson arrived in Paris, where he was seeking an experimental treatment. He collapsed in the lobby of his hotel, further fueling concerns about his health and rumors that he was suffering from AIDS. His publicists announced only that he was battling liver cancer.

Though he had never said so publicly, Hudson was gay. His career rested on a 1950s image of masculinity, and though Hudson wrestled with coming out, he never did. That left gay men and doctors ambivalent about the hoopla over Hudson's illness in the summer of 1985. Attention to AIDS was tragically overdue, but that it would only come once the disease touched a famous masculine faux heterosexual was bittersweet. Hudson's renown was such that his old Hollywood friend Reagan called him that summer—Reagan's wife, Nancy, joined in on the phone even though, as was learned decades later, she had refused to intervene to help Hudson get the Paris treatment for his illness.[7] Reagan called merely to wish his friend well, but that was a grace note Reagan had denied every other victim of the illness thus far.

At the end of July, with his health precipitously failing, Hudson returned to Los Angeles—he chartered a 747 airliner for $250,000 in part because he and his advisers were afraid of how he would be treated by other passengers on a commercial flight—and was shuttled by helicopter to the UCLA Medical Center. Once he was admitted, doctors there provided the first medical confirmation of what the world knew. "Mr. Hudson is being evaluated and treated for complications of Acquired Immune Deficiency Syndrome," said Dr. Michael Gottlieb, the UCLA immunologist who grasped AIDS's dimensions long before the world understood. "His condition is serious but stable."[8]

Ten weeks later, Hudson died, as one writer noted, "after completing his most dramatic role, impressing his incurable disease, AIDS, on the consciousness of the world."[9]

Reagan finished his first year in office at the end of 1981. Despite growing alarm, then fear, then terror, he remained silent about AIDS through that year and those that followed. He did not deliver an address on the subject until 1987, when Nancy helped persuade him to speak out. While Reagan waited, the world changed. At the end of 1981, 270 cases of GRID had been reported; 121 of those patients had died. Seven years later, with Reagan preparing to leave office, that tally had reached 82,362 reported cases in the United States alone: of those, 61,816 had died.[10] As of late 2017, 36.9 million people around the world were living with HIV.

The toll in San Francisco was especially harrowing. "In this neighborhood that gained renown for its culture of openly expressed homosexuality, the predominant concern of the living is now dealing with death and dying," the *New York Times* reported in 1987, the year that Reagan finally spoke out about the crisis. By then, more than two thousand San Franciscans, almost all of them gay men, had died from AIDS-related complications. The once ebullient streets of San Francisco's Castro neighborhood had become dark and reflective. Bathhouses were shuttered, stores closed, parades ceased. Many survivors could count twenty or even thirty friends who had succumbed to AIDS. A generation of young men came to San Francisco to enjoy freedom and instead found death.

Whatever else may be said for or against Reagan, his silence during those years is a blemish on his reputation and legacy, an act of manifest indifference that can only be regarded as cruelty. Reagan could have altered the course of this decimating epidemic; he instead chose politics over compassion. He elected to call his friend Rock Hudson and turn his back on the rest of those who suffered.

Jerry Brown at first kept a relatively low profile after leaving office in 1983. He gave occasional speeches, appeared at fund-raisers for causes and candidates, paid a small fine for a campaign irregularity in his 1982 Senate race, and gritted his teeth when his successor, George Deukmejian, accused him of presiding over an "era of neglect" for the state's business community.[11] He founded two think tanks, the National Committee on Industrial Innovation and the Institute for National Strategy. The two had offices in downtown Los Angeles, which Brown made his base for a time. He moved back into his house in Laurel Canyon and drove a Ford Taurus. He had a home computer—an Apple III, it was a gift from his staff—and he traveled, meeting with technology executives in Boston, North Carolina, and Silicon Valley and with intellectuals and political leaders in Mexico during the summer of 1983. Joan Didion sat on the board of the institute, as did economist Lester Thurow and Adam Yarmolinsky, an arms control expert. Nathan Gardels, a charismatic writer and shrewd policy observer who had known Brown for years, served as its executive director.[12] The institute kept its distance from universities, worried that such an affiliation would thwart its freedom to explore, and instead supported itself by charging particpants to join Brown on voyages abroad as well as by holding occasional fund-raisers, usually in California or New York.

The institute's work received strategic wisdom from an unlikely triumvirate. Pierre Trudeau, the former Canadian prime minister and a former Jesuit, liked to join conversations around the institute when he was in town, which he often was, since he was dating Barbra Streisand. Armand Hammer, the oil executive and philanthropist, was based in Los Angeles, where he headed Occidental Petroleum. He offered guidance about trips to China and the Soviet Union, two places where he had strong connections. And Richard Nixon, of all people, saw an opportunity to lend a hand to the son of his old adversary. He was, Gardels recalled, conspicuously gracious and generous with his advice.[13] "You'll do well," Nixon told Brown. "You're interesting."[14]

Brown conducted most of his work at the edge of the limelight, and Californians seemed in no hurry to have him back. BROWN'S IMAGE REMAINS LOW, read a *Los Angeles Times* headline from 1983.[15] The following year, Brown gave only two speeches in California and used one of them to deplore the quality of Democratic candidates for president—Walter Mondale, Gary Hart, and Jesse Jackson had, in Brown's words, "marginalized the political dialogue."[16]

Brown headed for Mexico. In 1983, he and Gardels traveled to Ocotepec, outside Cuernavaca, near where Ivan Illich had founded the Centro Intercultural de Documentacion (CIDOC), the extraordinary think tank and language institute. Ocotepec was no Davos, where the rich have long gone to compare notes. It was built on a rented estate and decidedly rustic: unilluminated by streetlights, it was achingly dark at night, and scorpions often found their way into guests' showers.[17]

Brown studied Spanish during the day. At night, however, he had his first extended opportunity to meet with and discuss the world with Illich. In their long talks, mutual admiration graduated into friendship.

Brown was enthralled by Illich's disconnection from orthodoxy and his ravenous interest in ideas. A serious talker, Illich was also a studious listener, convinced of the fraying of modernity but open to debate and argument. He enjoyed disagreement but not dullness. He did not, Brown recalled, "suffer fools. People with quick minds don't like to spend a lot of time with people who have slow minds."[18] Illich and Brown shared a religious background—Illich was an ordained Catholic priest, and though he eschewed much Catholic orthodoxy, he was in many respects a product and admirer of its conservative structure and tradition. In all those ways, he and Brown were alike—appreciative of structure and skeptical of institutions. They spoke long into the night, many nights, consulting the center's extensive library, spiritedly debating. To the extent that Brown was tugged between life as a politician and life as a monk, this was his abbey and this the most sustained period of reflection of his adult life.

The two struck up a friendship in those weeks that lasted the rest of Illich's life. In 1993, they met again in Cuernavaca to discuss a book on medicine, and they shared close, even intimate confidences over nearly two decades. Illich sent Brown an extended reflection on suicide in 2000, one that Brown would consult when he, as governor, considered a right-to-die measure near the end of his tenure. For Illich, then himself gravely ill, the question of how to address suicide was one of friendship, "not poison but a sign of unconditional trust."[19] Illich's prose and wisdom informed, enlightened, and sometimes haunted Brown. Beginning in 1983, Illich was never far from his thoughts.

Brown dabbled in international affairs. He visited Bonn, where he met with former chancellor Willy Brandt and discussed nuclear weapons, and Paris, where he met with Francois Mitterand and was hosted by Pierre Salinger. In England, Isaiah Berlin chatted with Brown and Gardels and offered the view that "life is just life" before Brown and company dashed off for meat pie with royalty in the Cotswolds. "This was bizarrely interesting, and sure proof that, at least in Britain, the frightful decadence of fading royalty has not seen its last day," Gardels recorded in a letter from the period.[20]

Brown visited the Soviet Union for the first time in 1984, traveling there with Gardels and other members of an American delegation. They met with Soviet officials and everyday citizens. Officials guarded his access and kept Brown from mingling freely; he was not allowed, for example, to ride the Moscow metro. But Brown was ravenously curious, asking about everyday life and gauging Russian interest in peace with the United States. "Are the people happy?" he asked while visiting Moscow.

"That's the bottom line, isn't it?"[21] Brown mused about arms control and relations between the two countries at a time when Reagan was in the White House and nuclear armaments very much on the minds of both nations.

Commenting on the arms race, Brown said he intended to devote more time to the topic, which he described as "an addictive process." Soviet officials seemed to puzzle over Brown's visit. He was, one said, "unusual and interesting." The *Washington Post* captured Brown at this moment. "His Soviet hosts," the *Post* wrote, "certainly seemed to treat him as a politician with prospects."[22] Gardels agreed: "They took Jerry seriously as a future candidate."[23]

Still another trip took them to China, where Brown and his entourage traveled up the Yangtze River to the area that is now the site of that country's enormous hydroelectric station, the Three Gorges Dam. They met with a Tibetan monk and a member of China's parliament. They traveled to Japan, meeting there with political leaders and intellectuals. Back in Los Angeles, Nicaraguan president Daniel Ortega dropped by to talk with Brown; their talk was published by the *San Francisco Chronicle*.[24]

At night, Brown and Gardels sometimes met for a late supper at Chasen's, a legendary late-night West Hollywood eatery, where Brown enjoyed the restaurant's fabled chili. Joan Didion would occasionally join them, as would author Carlos Fuentes. Another regular was Carlos Castaneda, often accompanied by one or more women; he called them his witches. Together, they would gather around a table—authors, politicos, and California's former governor—sharing literary and political observations early into the morning.

"We addressed the central issues of our time," Gardels recalled.[25]

From the moment of her appointment as chief justice of the California Supreme Court, Rose Bird had been a target for the state's conservatives. To them, her politics and association with Jerry Brown made her objectionable, and Bird did herself few favors by doing little to build allegiances, on or off the court. She was isolated and vulnerable almost from her first day on the job.

Unlike federal judges, who enjoy lifetime tenure, California appellate justices serve under a hybrid system that combines elements of appointed and elective office. Supreme court justices are nominated by the governor, then confirmed (or rejected) by a panel consisting of the attorney general, the chief justice, and the senior member of the California Courts of Appeal. If confirmed, the justice takes his or her place on the bench but must stand for retention at the next general election and again every twelve years after that. If a justice fills the unfinished term of her predecessor, she must stand for retention at the conclusion of that term.

Brown appointed Rose Bird in 1977, and she was quickly forced to confront a challenge to her retention, since the next general election arrived the following year. A coalition of tough-on-crime groups pooled efforts to defeat her but came up short. She won 51.7 percent of the votes cast. That was good news and bad for Bird: her victory preserved her place on the court, but the tightness of the race—it was the slimmest victory ever for a California Supreme Court justice—emboldened critics to think she might be vulnerable in the future.[26] That came up just eight years later: because Bird had filled an unfinished term when joining the court in 1977, she faced a second retention election in 1986. This time, the forces arrayed against her were better financed and better armed—Bird had a longer record to critique after nine years on the bench, and her critics had a better feel for what would resonate with voters who were considering whether to keep the state's first female chief justice.

The campaign against Rose Bird drew Brown back into the fight, especially once that campaign expanded to target not just Bird but also two of Brown's other appointees on the court—Cruz Reynoso and Joseph Grodin. The battle took on the character of a challenge to Brown's service and judgment, not just an attack on a single nominee. Recognizing that his defense of his own nominees might seem personal, Brown ceded that terrain to his father, still spry at eighty, who spearheaded a fund-raising effort to defend the three justices. The younger Brown, meanwhile, took the high ground of defending judicial independence. "When I made appointments to the Supreme Court, I did not look for individuals who would take the path of least resistance," Brown wrote in an op-ed piece published in the *San Francisco Examiner* in March. "I wanted those who were strong and independent…I did not want justices who followed public opinion polls."[27]

Bird's great sin, aside from being a strong woman and a difficult person, was that she had run afoul of California's business interests, consistently siding with consumers over manufacturers, tenants over landlords, workers over employers, policyholders over insurance companies. Those cases attracted far less notice than the death penalties that reached the court and that Bird deflected, rejecting every death sentence that reached the court. But the death penalty was good politics: defendants who received the Bird court's mercy were, almost always, heinous criminals guilty of horrifying crimes. The plaintiffs in the business cases were far more sympathetic but also far more costly for California companies. The result was an anti-Bird coalition that combined populist, tough-on-crime elements—police, prosecutors, victims' groups—with quiet, determined, and well-heeled special interests. It was a formidable combination.

In August, Governor Deukmejian, running for reelection, expanded his attack on the court to include Grodin and Reynoso. All three, the conservative Republican governor proclaimed, were guilty of "a lack of impartiality and objectivity" in deciding capital cases. He urged voters to affirm the service of the court's conservative members and its liberal dean, Stanley Mosk, but to cut short the tenures of Grodin, Reynoso, and Bird, all appointed by Jerry Brown.[28]

Deukmejian kept up his unusual campaign against the court through Election Day, staying focused on the death penalty and using it against his opponent, the Los Angeles mayor, Tom Bradley, whom Deukmejian regularly tied to Bird and her colleagues and whom he characterized as part of a large, soft Left incapable of making the hard decisions required to keep California safe. Election Day vindicated that strategy and upended California politics. Deukmejian won a second term, while fully two-thirds of Californians voted to toss Bird from office. Smaller but decisive margins turned out against Grodin and Reynoso. On a single ballot, Californians removed the court's first woman and first Latino justice.

With the benefit of long hindsight, Brown would come to acknowledge that he pushed too hard with Bird. "These are all learning experiences," he said one rainy afternoon in 2016. "I didn't have the knowledge that I have today."[29] In another conversation, he added that he overestimated the importance of intelligence in a chief justice and underestimated other qualities. "Rose Bird as chief," he said. "She didn't have the diplomatic skills that that job requires."[30]

Brown may have placed too much blame on himself and Bird. They faced determined and not altogether honest opposition, and the not-so-subtle challenge to a powerful woman undoubtedly hardened many against her. Still, the combination of a vulnerable candidate and motivated, moneyed opposition is almost always fatal in politics. The court's liberal wing was wiped out, and Deukmejian was given the opportunity to replace three justices in one swoop, a wholesale overturning of Brown's contribution to the court.

Brown's unsuccessful attempt to defend his appointees was followed by another dip out of the limelight. Late in 1986, he quietly departed for Japan to reflect, meditate, and write. Hunted down in 1987 by his old International House housemate Kenneth Reich, by that time a reporter at the *Los Angeles Times,* Brown said he was spending his time among the temples of Kamakura trying "to better understand and articulate my philosophy…and to ultimately set out my vision of the future."[31] The former governor, sporting a salt-and-pepper beard, was evasive in his conversation with Reich, who jauntily relayed that he only located his former classmate after "exhaustive inquiries with police and other authorities." Cornered, Brown said: "I can be reached, but I prefer not to be."

Once found, however, the former governor did talk. He lamented the loss of his judicial appointees and reflected on the history of the death penalty in California. He ruminated about a book project and pointedly left the door open to his return. "I'm certainly not shutting off any doors to the future," he said. "But I don't have a direct path that I can give to you at this moment in time."[32] Reich, delighted at having hunted Brown down and persuading him to talk, sent an unedited transcript of his interview to Pat and Bernice Brown.[33]

Before coming home, Brown had one more stop on his self-discovery travels. Near the end of January, 1987, Brown made contact with Mother Teresa in Calcutta. Her work offered Brown two opportunities: immersion in the lives of the poor and reconnection with his Catholicism. Of the latter, Brown said: "For many years, I wasn't paying a lot of attention to it, but as I have had a chance now, after office, to reflect on it, it's a very powerful part of my thinking and my background." Rediscovery of those notions, he added, "conditions those principles that I bring to any public life that I might be in."[34]

Brown's time with Mother Teresa was brief—he was in Calcutta for less than a month—but it returned him to the religion of his youth after a long trip through politics and meditation. "The work with Mother Teresa is a world of generosity, of seeing the person in front of you—the poor of Calcutta that show up at your doorstep—as the embodiment of Jesus, of God," Brown told a former aide in 1996. "There's nothing more important. Politics is a power struggle to get to the top of the heap. Calcutta and Mother Teresa are about working with those who are at the bottom of the heap. And to see them as no different than yourself, and their needs as important as your needs. And you're there to serve them, and doing that you are attaining as great a state of being as you can."[35]

California was ready to try out Brown again. The state felt precarious. The Loma Prieta earthquake, on October 17, 1989, was centered near Santa Cruz, along the Central Coast. It collapsed a section of the Bay Bridge, between San Francisco and Oakland, and was felt as far south as Orange County. It struck at 5:04 p.m., as players warmed up for a decidedly California World Series, pitting the San Francisco Giants against the Oakland A's. Chunks of concrete fell with bellowing crashes, knocking out power in the ballpark. The crowd at first seemed exhilarated and cheered, then quieted as the magnitude of the quake settled in. The series was suspended, not to resume for ten days. The A's swept the Giants in four games, never giving up so much as the lead in what became known as the Bay Bridge series, a wry if unintentional nod to the ruptured span between the cities.

Brown elected to make his long-awaited political return on board a surprising, even shocking, vehicle. The man who had demonstrated disdain for party structure, who had set a course outside political norms, and who had styled himself as an outsider notwithstanding his lineage decided to seek the chairmanship of the California Democratic Party, a position generally reserved for an up-and-coming member who has demonstrated prowess in fund-raising and is looking to establish a name.

The chairmanship in those days alternated between residents of Southern and Northern California: preparing for his run, Brown moved from Los Angeles to San Francisco.[36] As he had before, Brown leaped into the campaign late. Steve Westly, an ambitious venture capitalist carving a place for himself in California Democratic politics, had a head start in the chairmanship campaign. Brown swept him aside, offering his own far-better-known name in opposition. Brown's reemergence from the wilderness was an irresistible story line, and delegates were intrigued by the novelty though also worried about what a return to the Brown era might look like. Brown, "happier than he has been for years," according to the *Los Angeles Times,* seemed to revel in the discomfort his return caused some observers. "I guess I feel a little like Typhoid Mary," he said in late 1988. "I walk in and people want to step back a little. Ohhhh boy, it's going to be Hayden and Bird, Willie Brown, death penalty, Cesar Chavez, farm workers. Whewww!"[37]

It wasn't all that. The revived Jerry Brown brought new qualities to the table—a hint of patience, the seriousness of being fifty. And yes, there were reminders of the old Jerry Brown, too—the wry humor, the love of conflict, the squeamishness about money. Brown beat Westly without much trouble, then established himself as a skinflint spearheading the party's political fortunes, mostly in the form of raising money and organizing campaigns—two areas where his credentials were hardly sterling. His discomfort showed.

The duties of state Democratic chairman are, in theory, to provide the party and its candidates with leadership, organization, and support—to articulate unifying messages that bind the party's representatives around common themes and help advance their interests in the mind of the public and in opposition to others, mainly the Republican Party. In practice, that mostly means that the party chairman raises money and is judged by how the party's candidates do on Election Day.

Brown hated raising money, but he did it. He stumped for candidates at all levels: whether it was appearing on *Face the Nation* or addressing a crowd of 350 senior citizens on behalf of a state senate candidate.[38] He could be shrewd, urging voters to elect a Democrat from one Republican redoubt to "so shock Orange County that maybe things might change," and bombastic: "There was no crack cocaine in this state when I was governor."[39] He was more contrarian than consistent, sometimes sounding skeptical about protectionism, for example, and other times championing it. But he was undeniably committed as he worked the luncheon and dinner circuit to support his party's candidates. The same man who before and after would decry the influence of money in politics raised roughly $2 million for the party and its candidates during that cycle.[40]

# 16

# Her Father's Daughter

O ne race mattered more than most. Having run as his father's son in his early campaigns, Brown then had the opportunity to help rally the party around his sister Kathleen Brown as she made her first attempt at California statewide office. Kathleen brought her own significant credentials to the race. The youngest of the Brown children, known in her childhood as Kathy, she showed early political promise. Shortly after her father was elected governor and moved the family to Sacramento to take up residence in the governor's mansion, Kathy enrolled at Sutter Junior High School. She was new and looking to make friends and so, in a distinct nod to her father, decided one way would be to run for office. Girls were not permitted to run for class president, so she entered the race for vice president. On the night before the vote, Kathy was home at the mansion cutting up strips of cardboard for campaign signs. Dick Tuck, the famous political prankster who made a career out of dogging Richard Nixon, happened to be visiting Pat Brown that night, and he asked Kathy what she was doing. When she explained, he was appalled. Those posters, he said, would not do. He commanded Kathy not to leave for school in the morning until he could stop by.

At 8:00 a.m., just before Kathy headed for the door, Tuck arrived carrying a paper bag. In it was a pile of glossy campaign buttons bearing the slogan KATHY BROWN FOR VEEP. She handed them out at school and won in a landslide.[1] One lasting impact of her campaign: Sutter Junior High adopted campaign-expenditure limits in her wake. Pat Brown was delighted: "Kathy won primary at school," he noted in his diary.[2] Two days later, still basking in her victory, her father added: "Kathleen developing into a beautiful girl."[3]

As she grew up, Kathleen displayed her brother's willfulness and her father's exuberance. She was expected to attend the University of California, of course, but she opted for Stanford instead. Knowing her father would object, Kathleen filled out the application herself. She was accepted, but Pat Brown would not hear of it. Kathleen was determined and sought out a nun, Sister Kieran, to help make her case. Sister Kieran happily agreed: "Tell your parents to come to my office," she told Kathleen.

"My father was not intimidated by many people," Kathleen remembered decades later. But Sister Kieran was a force, a Dominican nun no more used to hearing the word *no* than the governor was. "You know, Governor," she said as Pat Brown took his seat. "Many students are admitted to the University of California at Berkeley. Not all finish. Not many students are admitted to Stanford. All of them finish. Knowing Kathleen, I would recommend Stanford."[4] Kathleen Brown went to Stanford.

Kathleen made her way into politics less forcefully than either her father or her brother did. She married George Rice, and they had three children. Smart and polished, charismatic in her father's mold, less enigmatic and more approachable than her brother, Kathleen developed a taste for politics in Jerry Brown's campaigns for secretary of state in 1970 and governor in 1974. Jerry and Tom Quinn dispatched her to California's "secondary markets," medium-size cities and areas where the arrival of a Brown was enough to attract media attention all by itself. Quinn would brief Brown on the issues that the campaign was emphasizing that week, and she would trundle off, meeting with voters and reporters, taking questions, representing her brother and her family. "I liked it," she said later.[5]

She did so despite her brother's relative indifference. Jerry always appreciated his sister, but seven years separated them, and they had grown up in different worlds. Moreover, Jerry Brown's detatchment— his studied remove from earthly cares—extended to family relations as well. He could seem distant or disinterested, more likely to warm to a philosophical debate than to a friend, colleague, or sister in need.

Never especially close, they nevertheless gravitated to a common love of politics—and, even then, they were drawn to it by different impulses. Jerry absorbed the philosophy of politics, its connection to the classics and contemplation, its relationship to history, and its susceptibility to skepticism. For Kathleen, as for their father, politics was more grounded in the lives of people, in the opportunities to help one person after another, to translate experience into governance and thus help by extension.

Kathleen Brown ran for the Los Angeles school board in 1975, in part because her children were in school and she had developed strong opinions about education by sharing their experiences. She won a "runaway victory," becoming, at age twenty-nine, "probably...the youngest board member in the Los Angeles city school district's 120-year history."[6] (No records could prove it, but no one could remember anyone younger.) Her career appeared to be launched in the mold of her brother's, which got its start in the community-college district. But Kathleen Brown then divorced and remarried, this time to newsman Van Gordon Sauter, and she left the school board when Sauter's work with CBS took them to New York—a move that disappointed some of her early supporters, who felt abandoned by her decision to walk away, even for compelling personal reasons. In New York, she went back to school herself, getting her law degree from Fordham University. Returning to Los Angeles with Sauter, she joined Warren Christopher at O'Melveny and Myers and continued a career that emphasized infrastructure, public finance, public policy, and law. And just as the county supervisor, Kenneth Hahn, had once given Jerry Brown a political jump start, the mayor, Tom Bradley, did the same for Kathleen Brown, appointing her to the city's Board of Public Works, a full-time post that gave her responsibility for the diverse challenges of maintaining Los Angeles's sprawling infrastructure. She took to the position enthusiastically, busily building and maintaining the underpinnings of a growing city even as her brother touted the virtues of *Small Is Beautiful*. Both recognized the paradox. "We argued about it," Kathleen said.[7]

While serving as a public works commissioner, Brown was visited by a pair of political consultants then making a name for themselves, Cathy Unger and Bev Thomas, whose Los Angeles–based firm, Unger/Thomas, was building a respected business advising political leaders and candidates at all levels. Unger and Thomas were eager to back a woman candidate for state office, and they saw the obvious potential in Brown. They sounded her out on a possible run for 1990, when an unusually large number of state constitutional offices were up for grabs. Brown was intrigued and drawn to the state treasurer position because it seemed to dovetail most closely with her experience and interests. In addition, the person elected to the office in 1974, Jesse Unruh, had died in August of 1987, during his fourth term. After the spot remained vacant for a time, Governor Deukmejian named Thomas W. Hayes to fill out Unruh's term. That meant Brown would face an incumbent if she ran, but an appointed incumbent was thought to be more vulnerable than an elected one, providing an opening for a relative newcomer, especially one named Brown.[8]

Before taking the plunge, Brown gathered a dozen or so politically intelligent advisers, drawing from her own list of contacts as well as some supplied by her father and brother. The group mulled the options over for a time before one of the organizers realized that Warren Christopher, the famously taciturn and wise adviser to Pat Brown, had yet to venture his opinion. "Chris, you haven't said anything," one person remarked. "What is your view?"

Speaking softly, as he almost always did, Christopher replied, "Whatever Kathleen wants to run for she can run for. She's a Brown, and it's statewide, and it doesn't really matter. She should do what she wants."[9]

Brown declared herself a candidate for treasurer on March 5, 1990. Her campaign was mostly waged on the dry terrain of government finance. Her main strategy was to criticize the incumbent for the state's "backlog of bonds," a problem barely remembered today, though she launched a sharp attack near the end on Hayes and his deputy, former Jerry Brown chief of staff B. T. Collins, for sending out a campaign mailer on official state stationery—a charge that, though true, earned Kathleen Brown the eternal enmity of Collins, who never spoke to her again. She won, and the headlines cast her victory as one not just for her but also for her family. KATHLEEN BROWN'S VICTORY REVIVES A CALIFORNIA DYNASTY, the *Los Angeles Times* wrote.[10] Few believed Kathleen Brown's political destiny would end in the office of the state treasurer.

Higher up on the ballot, the results were less gratifying for the Browns. Senator Pete Wilson, who had beaten Jerry Brown in 1982 and launched the governor into the exile from which he was only just returning, this time edged out the San Francisco mayor, Dianne Feinstein, for the governorship—the job Wilson had always coveted. It was triply bitter for Brown: Feinstein was a friend and ally; Wilson was a longtime foe and rival; and the defeat, a close one, marred Brown's tenure as party chair because he had failed to deliver the governorship back into Democratic hands. On the flip side, his sister won handily. Talk of her as a gubernatorial or even national candidate began almost as soon as the polls closed.

As critics sifted through the results of the election, some credited Brown with turning some seats and holding others despite predictions to the contrary. But he also shouldered some of the blame for Feinstein's defeat as well as the loss of the state's attorney generalship. Specifically, some blamed him for failing to invest in an aggressive get-out-the-vote effort that might have helped Feinstein on Election Day.[11]

For Jerry Brown, all that was, to some degree, beside the point. The Democratic Party chairmanship had never been a serious or lasting ambition. It rarely was for anyone and certainly wasn't for Brown. In January of 1991, he vented his frustration with critics of his performance in the 1990 cycle. "That whole thing is nonsense," he said. "Every single comment came from people involved with other candidates."[12]

He had spent two years in the position, and it had worn him out. "My job was to raise the money, and I did that," he reflected later. "I found that…working with the elite, the top 1 percent, has separated us from the majority." And it had been a drag. "The fact that you're elected chairman doesn't mean you're the boss," he said. It was more a series of obligations. Even the party's conventions were uninspiring. "It's an empty show," he said.[13]

He quit. And was reborn. The same Brown who came late to the taxpayer revolt came early to the revulsion over money in politics. He was done with courting large donors and hobnobbing with the wealthy. Brown was among the first to deplore the "1 percent" and to warn of a system that pulled politics away from those it governed. He would never be consistent on this point—Brown was scrupulous about campaign finance as a candidate, less so as an officeholder—but it would remain part of his message from that point forward.[14]

It was a strange political year in California. When Wilson won the governorship, he vacated his US Senate seat. That meant he got to appoint his own successor, and he turned to a Republican nearly as colorless as he was. John Seymour made an early fortune in real estate and went on to serve as mayor of Anaheim and as a moderately notable state senator, known mainly for his centrist views on issues such as abortion, offshore oil drilling, gun control, and gay rights—all areas where he sided more with liberal colleagues even as the Republican Party begun its humorless march to the right. Never a leader in those areas but far from a retrograde, he passed for what remained of the liberal Republican wing. When Wilson named him, the *New York Times* called it a "characteristically pragmatic move."[15] He moved into Wilson's seat in early 1991 but would face a special election to retain it the following year—and another in 1994, when the seat's term expired. Since Democratic US senator Alan Cranston, a lion of the Left, was retiring in 1992 as well, it created the rare situation in which two California Senate seats were to be contested simultaneously.

That set off a scramble for seats and matchups as potential candidates sized up whether they wanted to make a Senate run and, if so, which seat to run for (and whom to run against). Brown encouraged speculation that the Senate scramble would include him, ducking questions about which seat he might pursue but leaving it reasonably obvious that he was in the hunt for one of them.

Key to his calculations was Feinstein. Politics knows few friends beyond expedience, so it would not have been inconceivable that the man who had just attempted to help Feinstein win the governorship would then fight her for a seat in the Senate. But the ties between Brown and Feinstein transcended politics. They were intergenerational—Feinstein owed some of her early success to Pat Brown. And they were genuine. Though Feinstein was more conventionally moderate than Brown—most people were—both were iconoclastic Democrats with occasionally surprising views. Moreover, they liked each other. Brown was not inclined to run against her should Feinstein declare for one of the seats.

That left the other opening, whichever one Feinstein did not contest, but the field took some time to gel. Finally, the rivals and potential rivals fell into position: Feinstein announced plans to take on Seymour for his seat, considered the less desirable of the two because of its quick turnaround into reelection. Her entrance into the race chased off other Democrats, so ambitious politicians gathered around the opening left by Cranston: Lieutenant Governor Leo McCarthy, of liberal San Francisco; Congressman Mel Levine, of moderately liberal Los Angeles; and Congresswoman Barbara Boxer, of very liberal Marin County. Several Republicans announced as well.

Then there was the national context. The Senate races took shape in 1991 under the cloud of an explosive controversy: the confirmation battle over Judge Clarence Thomas, nominated by President Bush to succeed Thurgood Marshall on the United States Supreme Court. Few believed Thomas was genuinely well qualified to sit on the Supreme Court, and the idea of his replacing the iconic Marshall stuck in many a liberal craw. Nevertheless, the complexities of racial politics made it difficult for Democrats to mount a full-bore effort to defeat him. His nomination appeared set for begrudging Senate confirmation until a law professor named Anita Hill was thrust into the spotlight—over her objections—by Senate staff who had reviewed an FBI interview with her and decided to force the issue by making it public.

Hill had worked for Thomas at the federal Department of Education and the Equal Employment Opportunity Commission and, as she told a spellbound Senate committee and millions of viewers on October 1, 1991, Thomas had repeatedly sexually harassed her during their time together. He had boasted of the size of his penis, quoted from pornographic videos, and, weirdly, remarked on a pubic hair on his Coke. Thomas took the stand after Hill's testimony and vehemently disputed her account, though more generally than specifically. The entire episode, Thomas fumed, was a "high-tech lynching for uppity blacks."[16] Senator Joe Biden, then the chair of the Judiciary Committee, shut down the proceedings before witnesses who might have corroborated Hill's version of events could be called, and Thomas won his place on the Court by a close margin—four votes. Both sides went away mad.

Boxer in particular had distinguished herself during that episode, leading a group of Congresswomen who attempted to persuade Biden to probe further. Biden shrugged them off, but their effort tapped anger at the conduct of the proceedings and the willingness of the all-male committee to brush aside Hill's charges. That gave Boxer a leg up in her Senate race, especially in an atmosphere that some commentators described as the political "year of the woman." California's two prominent female Senate candidates were an integral part of that narrative, and Jerry Brown sensed clearly that his bid would be impaired by that focus, not to mention by Boxer's formidable skills as a fund-raiser and her solid liberal base.

So Brown opted for the next best thing, at least in his world: he announced his third campaign for president. This time, he did so with a notably caustic tone. His previous presidential slogan had suggested optimism: "Protect the earth, serve the people, explore the universe." Now he opted for a darker theme: "Take back America." Political leaders, he charged, "fail to do their job." It was the job of people to "strip them of their power." The Gannett news service said Brown "vilified Washington politics" and suggested that his message was "too fuzzy" to win over voters, particularly given the head starts of candidates such as Senators Tom Harkin, Bob Kerrey, and Paul Tsongas, of Iowa, Nebraska, and Massachusetts respectively, as well as the candidacy of the Virginia governor, Douglas Wilder, and the Arkansas governor, Bill Clinton.[17]

To call Brown's campaign structure an organization would have been misleading. Jacques Barzaghi, back in the role of odd sidekick, dismissed questions about who was running the show. "We are not disorganized," he insisted. "Our campaign transcends understanding."[18]

Brown trudged into battle. Fresh from his work as a fund-raiser for the California Democratic Party, he forswore money in politics, capping contributions to his campaign at $100. That limited his ability to reach voters, but even in his third run for the presidency, he was a novelty, and free media followed Brown wherever he went. Moreover, Brown tackled the 1992 race in full high dudgeon, making news at a series of debates between the Democratic candidates with his sharp jabs at Clinton.

Asked in one debate whether he believed Clinton had "an electability problem," Brown jumped at the invitation. "I think he's got a big electability problem," Brown said. "He is funneling money to his wife's law firm for state business. That's number 1. Number 2, his wife's law firm is representing clients before the state of Arkansas agencies, his appointees." Brown waved a copy of the *Chicago Tribune* in front of Clinton and the audience and accused Clinton, through his conflicts of interest, of sanctioning "an environmental disaster" by allowing Arkansas's poultry industry, represented by Hillary Clinton's law firm, to pollute state rivers.

In contrast to Brown's pugnacity, Clinton came off as cool and condescending. "I feel sorry for Jerry Brown," Clinton responded in his slurry drawl. "He reinvents himself every year or two."

Clinton continued until the moderator interjected, urging the candidate to answer the questions about Hillary's work. By then, Clinton's composure was cracking; he had had enough. "Let me tell you something, Jerry," he said. "I don't care what you say about me. I knew when Pat Caddell told me what you were going to say that you were going to reinvent yourself and you were going to be somebody else's mouthpiece; you would say anything. But you ought to be ashamed of yourself for jumping on my wife. You're not worth being on the same platform as my wife." Clinton jabbed a finger at Brown as he delivered that broadside, and Brown pointed right back. "I'll tell you something, Mr. Clinton. Don't try to escape it."[19]

Jerry reacted with the instincts of a sharp middleweight in the moment but later saw the artistry in Clinton's retort. "I didn't criticize Hillary," he said in 2018. "That was a very clever rhetorical pivot...As a debater, I can appreciate it."[20] Barzaghi was less sanguine. Clinton, he said, "looks like he sleeps with a hairnet."[21]

The rancor between Clinton and Brown would never disappear entirely—neither is a man to forget, much less forgive—but a few weeks later, the two holstered their slingshots and came together in what may have been the campaign's most thoughtful discussion, one that aired as a special report on daytime television, of all things. On April 6, 1992, Brown and Clinton shared a table supplied by host Phil Donahue, who remained off-camera and silent. The studio was empty, so the candidates sat before a room of empty chairs, eliminating any temptation to play to the crowd. Donahue introduced the conversation by saying simply: "I'm pleased to present Governor Brown, Governor Clinton." He then sat back in his chair and did not utter another word.

Instead, the two governors spoke to and with each other, mostly in civil tones, on the eve of primary elections in New York and Wisconsin. After an awkward moment of realizing that Donahue did not intend to guide the conversation, Brown began with a gentle statement about his ambitions for the campaign and country. Clinton followed suit. Brown then sketched his biography, admitting his childhood discomfort with his father's "backslapping" politics and acknowledging both his work as a fund-raiser and his conversion against it. "We're bringing the many back into the process," he insisted.[22]

Brown's gentle tone in his opening remarks seemed to take Clinton by surprise, but Clinton followed suit, beginning with a brief sketch of his growing up and emphasizing points in common with Brown. What followed was a searching, genuine discussion of America's place in the international order, the influence of money in the nation's politics, income and wealth inequality, aging and care for the elderly, crime and social justice, and values. They even conducted a prescient discussion of health care: Brown advocated a single-payer system; Clinton argued for overhaul of the current system but something short of a single payer. The two candidates asked each other questions, apologized when they interrupted each other, and sincerely attempted to grapple with serious issues. It was, Donahue said as the event ended and after the camera was off, "the most civil encounter of the campaign." Rarely have two candidates of such intelligence debated issues of such consequence with such consideration. It was a high-water mark in modern American political discourse.

It was also Brown's last memorable moment of the 1992 campaign. The next day, he came tantalizingly close to upending Clinton in Wisconsin, losing by less than three percentage points. But New York was the big prize, and Clinton convincingly won there. For all practical purposes, that ended Jerry Brown's third run for the Democratic nomination. Reflecting on it years later, Brown was resigned. "It was not a successful campaign," he acknowledged. Clinton had momentum going into New York, and an offhand comment by Brown—that he would consider Jesse Jackson as a possible vice president—doomed him at the crucial moment. "You fit the mood of the time," he said more than twenty-five years later. "I didn't that time."[23]

By then, Brown was mostly over the loss and done with the idea of the presidency. But there were hints of regret and bitterness at other moments of reflection on the 1992 campaign, his third and last for the presidency. In later years, Brown ruminated on his unconventional youth and wondered what price he had paid for it. "I didn't have a wife then," he reflected in 2016. "If I had had a governor's mansion and a wife, I might have been president."[24]

Brown returned to California to find his home state crashing hard. On April 29, a jury of Ventura County residents returned verdicts in the case of four Los Angeles police officers accused of using excessive force in the 1991 arrest of Rodney G. King, an African American motorist who was on parole and fled when highway patrol officers attempted to pull him over for speeding.[25] The video of the LAPD officers clubbing and kicking King had shocked the nation but provided some hope in black communities of Los Angeles, where residents had long complained of mistreatment by police and felt the video at last supplied proof. The tape seemed so definitive that conviction of the officers was assumed, so when the verdicts were read—not guilty on all counts but one, on which the jury was deadlocked—the subdued jubilation at LAPD headquarters was matched by unrestrained outrage outside.[26]

As anger spread and darkness fell, the LAPD froze. The department's controversial chief, Daryl F. Gates, was missing in those early hours. Amazingly, he was attending a fund-raiser in a wealthy section of the city to raise money to defeat a ballot measure on police reform. Leaderless and afraid to do anything that might provoke rioters, one group of LAPD officers huddled inside police headquarters while rioters hurled rocks at the building; another massed at a command post in South-Central but stayed there even as a furious gathering of young black men took over a busy intersection, at Florence and Normandie Avenues, and began dragging white, Latino, and Asian drivers and passengers from their cars. One of them, Reginald Denny, was pulled from his truck and pummeled, kicked, and bludgeoned with a block of cement in an eerie mirror image of the King assault—this time, with black assailants and a white victim. Televised live from a hovering news helicopter, the images of Denny being beaten nearly to death convinced viewers that police had surrendered the city. Fires came next, accompanied by looting. Mayor Tom Bradley declared a state of emergency shortly after dark on April 29; Governor Wilson dispatched the National Guard, though troops would not arrive on city streets until the afternoon of April 30—and when they did, many had just one bullet in their guns.[27] Los Angeles fell apart.

The riots that consumed Los Angeles in April and May of 1992 were the sizzling tip of a smoldering fire that had quietly burned for years. Its fuel included the noxious leftovers from Watts in 1965 along with old favorites such as poverty, racism, police brutality, and inequality, which had all churned through Los Angeles for decades. The 1980s had brought two more combustible contributions: the growth of gangs and the introduction of crack cocaine.

Gangs were to Los Angeles at the end of the 1980s what AIDS had been to San Francisco in the early years of the decade: an unsparing killer of mostly young men, infectious and resistant to any solution. AIDS was propelled in part by official indifference—Reagan's long refusal to do so much as utter the word thwarted efforts to alert the public and spur a response. In the case of the overlapping epidemics of crack cocaine and gangs, the official response was not silence but hostility. Gates, the LAPD chief, refused to consider the pathology beneath this epidemic and instead elected to escalate his department's reliance on force. He commissioned a mechanized battering ram to knock down crack houses, dispatched aggressive CRASH units (like so many things in policing, that was an acronym, standing for Community Resources Against Street Hoodlums), and employed sweeps to round up potential gang members, inevitably arresting innocent young men, mostly black and Latino, along with criminals. Those efforts antagonized many in Los Angeles's minority communities while doing nothing to turn back violent crime. By 1991, more than one thousand people a year were being murdered in Los Angeles, a number that would peak in 1992, when the riots added scores to the annual count.[28]

It took three days for the riots to burn out, and even then they did so only after National Guard troops trickled out from Los Angeles Memorial Coliseum into ravaged neighborhoods. The damage was costly and fatal: more than fifty people died as a result of violence connected to the riots, and more than $1 billion worth of property was lost to looting and fire. Most of those killed or injured were black or Latino. Ten people were killed by police.[29] Most lasting was the wound to Los Angeles's sense of self—a metropolis once proud of its diversity and cultural melding smoldered in the ashes of those ideals. Gates declined to shoulder any responsibility for his department's tardy and hesitant response. Asked later what the LAPD might have done differently, he replied: "Clearly that night we should have gone down there and shot a few people. In retrospect, that's exactly what we should have done. We should have blown a few heads off."[30]

In the ruins of 1992 Los Angeles, city leaders resumed the work they had started and then dropped after the Watts riots in 1965. None other than Warren Christopher, who had served on the McCone Commission, which examined the causes of Watts, was summoned back to service by Mayor Bradley after the King beating but before the riots. His commission—it was almost always called the Christopher Commission, though Christopher himself declined that honorific in favor of its formal name, the Independent Commission on the Los Angeles Police Department—generated a far more practical blueprint for reform than the one McCone and his colleagues had produced in 1965.[31] Rather than cite such endemic problems as poverty, racism, and the dashed expectations of remedial aid from Washington, Christopher and his colleagues directed their study at the more contained questions of police brutality and racism within the LAPD. The commission documented those terrible contaminations and uncovered patterns—use of force within the ranks, it found, was concentrated among relatively few "problem officers." Moreover, the department's ancient systems for monitoring police conduct had failed to identify warning signs or highlight trouble cases, and LAPD management, including its chief, had failed the city. The commission recommended a term limit for police chiefs and gently but unmistakably called for Gates to leave.[32]

The commission's reforms required an amendment to the Los Angeles city charter, and it was that ballot measure that Gates was attempting to defeat when the riots erupted on April 29. The riots sapped the police chief of any political strength he had remaining, and voters approved the Christopher reforms in June of 1992. That marked the beginning of a Los Angeles comeback, but it would be a long and arduous one. A year after the riots, *Time* magazine took stock of Los Angeles. Against an abstract backdrop of fires, traffic congestion, and police stops, *Time*'s cover asked: LOS ANGELES: IS THE CITY OF ANGELS GOING TO HELL?[33] It was not entirely a rhetorical question. Richard Riordan, a Republican businessman running for mayor of a heavily liberal and Democratic city, won his campaign a few weeks after the *Time* cover appeared. Riordan's slogan also suited the era. He boasted that he was "Tough enough to turn LA around."

The Los Angeles riots capped a grim decade for California. While Brown had skirted the edges of California politics and government, the state had struggled with crises, some natural and others self-inflicted. AIDS and gangs posed two lethal threats to the state's well-being, but subtler erosions were under way as well. Funding for California's schools, once a source of pride in the state, slipped from ranking among the highest in the nation to among the country's lowest. Governors Deukmejian and Wilson toughened the state's crime-fighting efforts and prison sentences as crime soared. The result: prisons filled to overflowing, and crime continued to rise. The state, long enriched by immigration from within the United States and around the world, saw large numbers of residents leaving for other parts of the country, *out-migration* joining *immigration* in the California vocabulary.

In such an environment, race relations were often strained—and well-meaning people of all colors sometimes were startled to realize what different worlds they inhabited. One such reminder came through the unlikely vehicle of a once outstanding but by then washed-up athlete living out his retirement as a second-rate actor in Brentwood, California.

Late at night on June 12, 1994, a young man working at Mezzaluna restaurant in Brentwood dropped by a condo a few blocks away to return a pair of glasses that a patron had left behind earlier that evening. As he approached the front door, he was attacked, probably by an assailant waiting in the bushes. He was stabbed repeatedly and killed. At about the same time, perhaps alerted by the commotion, the owner of the condo emerged from the front door. She, too, was stabbed, and her throat slashed—so deeply that the knife nicked her spine.

A dog barked. One neighbor marked the time at shortly before midnight. Not until the morning of June 13 were the bodies of Nicole Simpson and Ron Goldman found and identified. Nicole's two children, whom she shared with her ex-husband, O. J. Simpson, were asleep inside the house as their mother was murdered. There were bloody footprints leading away from the carnage; to the left of those footprints were drops of blood that matched neither of the victims.

O. J. Simpson was in Chicago when the discovery of the bodies was announced. He had checked into an airport hotel there around 6:30 a.m., having arrived early that morning on a red-eye from Los Angeles. Police summoned Simpson back to California as the investigation of his ex-wife's murder unfolded. On June 17, four days after the bodies were found, Simpson agreed to turn himself in to police, then failed to show at 11:00 a.m. as scheduled. After a frantic search, he was spotted in the back seat of a white Ford Bronco with his friend Al Cowlings at the wheel. Simpson cradled a gun, a passport, and a picture of his mother. Police engaged the Bronco in pursuit, and Simpson and Cowlings slowly made their way back to Simpson's home. In a spectacle that was odd even by the standards of a strange era, crowds gathered along overpasses, at the freeway exit, and outside Simpson's estate to welcome him back. Shortly after 8:00 p.m., Simpson agreed to give himself up. He was taken, this time by police, to Parker Center, headquarters of the LAPD, where he was booked on suspicion of the murders of his ex-wife and Ron Goldman.

Thus began a fourteen-month trial, much of it broadcast live, that riveted and divided Americans. Simpson's capable defense team argued that jurors should disregard what otherwise seemed like powerful evidence: the blood drops at the scene were consistent with Simpson's DNA, and blood found in his car and on socks recovered from his bedroom was consistent with the DNA of Nicole Simpson and Ron Goldman. The defense argued, however, that samples could have been contaminated by incompetent police or planted by malevolent police. Coming on the heels of the Rodney King case and other indignities committed by the LAPD, those claims seemed plausible in Los Angeles in 1994. Simpson was acquitted of the murders on October 3, 1995. Images of African Americans celebrating a verdict that alarmed many whites were reinforced by a poll a few days later: 88 percent of African Americans believed the jury decision to be correct, compared to 41 percent of whites.[34]

Peter Schrag, a journalist and historian, published a clear-eyed, incisive account of California at this juncture. Released in 1998, it scrupulously documented the state's alarming decline and was aptly titled *Paradise Lost*.

Overarching many of California's new difficulties were the reverberations of Proposition 13. The initiative's delayed effects fundamentally altered the state's solvency once the Brown surpluses were exhausted, and budgeting became an annual crisis. Moreover, the proposition's impact reached beyond the obvious—a persistent shortfall in tax revenue in a state accustomed to funding services and institutions—to influence areas of public life its authors hadn't envisioned. It encouraged local governments, for example, to approve retail construction, especially high-volume stores and auto dealerships, because they generated sales-tax revenue that could make up for lost property taxes. Malls and suburban sprawl were thus encouraged at a time when planners argued for centralization to combat traffic and pollution. Proposition 13 never meant to contribute to sprawl, pollution, and traffic, but it did.

It also, over time, shifted the property tax burden from businesses to homeowners, since homes sold more often than businesses and Proposition 13 dictated that properties were to be reassessed at market value every time they changed hands. The notion that a homeowner-protection initiative would ultimately shift more tax burden to homeowners went largely unremarked as Proposition 13 acquired protected status and became known as the "third rail" of California politics. Touch it, the metaphor implied, and you're dead.

One last perversity: Proposition 13's provision that properties would be reassessed when sold delivered some of the initiative's greatest benefit to country clubs, which often owned valuable land and almost never were sold. Well into the 2000s, country clubs still enjoyed appraisals that were rooted in their 1975 values, with only 2 percent per year of appreciation. To cite just one example, a tony country club in central Los Angeles, complete with a golf course and clubhouse, paid less in taxes than did a condominium complex across the street. Only in California could a populist measure intended to keep middle-income old people from being taxed out of their homes end up benefiting those rich enough to belong to country clubs.[35]

A recession in the early 1990s brought California's precariousness into unmistakable focus. Economic uncertainty joined fiscal and budgetary struggles. Southern California, where the end of the Cold War meant the contraction of the aerospace industry, was particularly hard hit, and the jobs that disappeared were the kind that make societies cohere—well-paid positions in research and manufacturing that had once enriched San Diego, Orange, and Los Angeles Counties. The middle-class enclaves of Los Angeles's Westside hollowed out. Housing prices plummeted. Fortunes and futures were lost. Seeking someone to blame, populist forces settled on the easiest target: immigrants, particularly those in the country illegally. In true California fashion, they circulated petitions and gathered signatures for what became known as Proposition 187.

Not since Proposition 13 had a California initiative so captured a burgeoning national sense of alarm. In this case, Proposition 187 attempted to wrest authority over illegal immigration from Washington, where, proponents thought, there was lackluster interest in the issue. If Washington would not control illegal immigration, the argument went, then California would.

The initiative, which backers called the Save Our State measure, seethed with resentment and identified illegal immigrants as a source of grievance and suffering. The proposition opened with words that expressed those grievances: "The People of California find and declare as follows: That they have suffered and are suffering economic hardship caused by the presence of illegal aliens in this state. That they have suffered and are suffering personal injury and damage caused by the criminal conduct of illegal aliens in this state. That they have a right to the protection of their government from any person or persons entering this country unlawfully."[36]

Since California did not control the border, nor did it have the power to deport, it would command whatever resources it had at its disposal. To that end, Proposition 187 sought to deny illegal immigrants the benefits that California offered to other residents—most notably, public education and public health services. Proposition 187 contained five major provisions. First, it required schools, beginning on January 1, 1995, to check students' immigration status and permit only those who were citizens or legal residents to attend. Second, health-care providers were similarly required to check immigration status before administering any nonemergency services, including prenatal care and immunizations. Third, illegal immigrants were prohibited from receiving any governmental assistance, such as welfare. Fourth, public employees who were charged with checking immigration status also were required to report anyone found to be in the country illegally—this applied to social workers, doctors and nurses, and teachers and school administrators, among others. Finally, Proposition 187 made possessing or using false immigration documents a felony under California law.[37]

Some of the logic of Proposition 187 was surprising. Better, its proponents implicitly argued, to deny illegal immigrants vaccines and thus render them susceptible to contagious diseases than to protect all Californians from the spread of tuberculosis or polio or whooping cough. Effectively, that meant supporters were willing to risk their own health in return for endangering the health of illegal immigrants. But the specifics were less important than the message: passage of Proposition 187 would send the signal that illegal immigrants were unwelcome within California's borders and thus encouraged to stay home or, if they were already in the country, leave.

The resentments and ill will that bubbled beneath Proposition 187 surfaced dramatically when the initiative became embroiled in the 1994 campaign for governor, a rematch of sorts between Wilson and Brown, though the Brown this time was not Jerry but Kathleen.

As the years since 1994 have passed, Wilson has tried to amend the narrative of that year's gubernatorial campaign. Reflecting on the contest, he argued in 2017 that he had been accused of racism and that it was untrue and unfair. "I may have my flaws," he said, "but racism is not, never has been, never will be, one of them."[38]

Fair enough, but that was not precisely the accusation. Rather, it was that Wilson and his campaign, by attaching themselves to Proposition 187 and airing a memorable ad to make the case for it, aligned themselves with a movement that had distinctly racial overtones and that identified immigrants as a threat rather than a source of vitality. Even decades later, the ad has the capacity to startle. "They keep coming," it began, its ominous narration backed by grainy video of immigrants darting through traffic at a border crossing. "Two million illegal immigrants in California. The federal government won't stop them at the border."

The ad then shifted to Wilson himself, who declared that he was suing the federal government to control the border and "working to deny state services to illegal immigrants. Enough is enough."[39]

The ad borrowed from a discredited bit of deep California history. When Upton Sinclair campaigned for the governorship in 1934, the state's powers fought back, in part with a phony newsreel that purported to depict hoboes streaming into California to join Sinclair's promised Socialist utopia. "They keep coming," that newsreel declared, just as

Wilson and his ad did decades later, this time with immigrants at the Mexican border. The 1994 ad was shocking and appalling, and it worked. It helped Wilson defeat Brown, though she did her part by waging a confused campaign and running out of money with weeks left to go, effectively disappearing from television just as voters were making their final choices.[40]

Wilson's was a costly victory. It shattered his reputation as a moderate and alienated a generation of Latinos from the Republican Party, first in California and then beyond. Latinos might feel some connection to the GOP—on some social issues, for example—but, as the old saw goes, it's hard to talk about issues when you're deporting someone's grandmother. Whatever appeal the party had, Wilson helped dash it, and then, in 2016, candidate Donald Trump went even further, demonizing immigrants as rapists and thugs and promising to build a wall to hold them out. Wilson never liked Trump, but he supported the idea of a wall. Wilson's 1994 gubernatorial campaign, at least with respect to immigration, became the playbook for Trump's 2016 presidential bid. Both succeeded in the short run; both did incalculable damage to their party in the long run.

For Brown, it was a disheartening campaign. She had been favored to win but lost. She had wanted to talk about education and rebuilding California but was dragged into destructive debates about crime and illegal immigration. She raised tons of money but spent it poorly, draining her resources in the primary and then turning to the general election without money in the bank. She was disappointed in herself for not running a smarter race and disappointed in Wilson for having deliberately divided voters in order to win.

The experience left her angry. Not until Easter Sunday of the following year did she finally summon the strength to forgive Wilson and put it behind her. In doing so, she took some solace in her unwavering opposition to Proposition 187. "I stood for something," she said more than twenty years later. "My father ingrained [this] in me—not by his words but by his actions, by being booed on the death penalty or booed on Prop[osition] 14, the fair housing bill. That was my north star of what public service was about. You make a lot of compromises, you wheel and deal, you bargain, you get things done, but on the core values, you don't compromise."[41]

# 17

# Climbing Back

P at Brown died on February 16, 1996, at his home on Kip Drive in Beverly Hills, where he had been fading for months, his scope of alertness and interest steadily narrowing. "He was so sleepy," Jerry Brown recalled. "He'd wake up and then immediately want to go back to sleep."[1] Pat Brown still had his moments, though: when Kathleen or Jerry entered the room, he'd perk up. "What are you running for?" he'd call out. Pat tracked Kathleen's 1994 bid for governor, working himself up into a lather when she described her opponents, first those in the primary and then Wilson, in the general election. Pat's focus was intermittent, but when Kathleen told him she'd lost, he took the news seriously and dropped the subject.[2] At the time of Pat's death, no Brown held any office in California, a rarity in the late twentieth century.

When he received word of his father's death, Jerry Brown was at his Oakland headquarters, speaking in the We the People auditorium, and someone took his arm as he left the stage, whispering the news to him. Jerry was braced, if not entirely surprised. He left the venue and made his way to Los Angeles.

As the family gathered to memorialize Pat Brown, Jerry was accompanied by a woman who had gotten to know his parents and sisters, along with his nephews and nieces, in a way no other girlfriend ever had. Anne Gust, soon to become known to Californians at large, was close enough to Jerry Brown in 1996 that they experienced the death of his father together. As the Brown family rallied in memory of its patriarch, it included Anne Gust and enveloped her in the complicated and emotional task of saying farewell to a father, a grandfather, and a governor.

The memorial service for Pat Brown was held five days later in San Francisco. It was a moment of grief for the family and for California, of course, not just for Jerry, but as the attendees gathered, eyes naturally turned to Jerry for his testimonial. He was, after all, not just Pat's son but also his successor, the second Democrat of the twentieth century to be reelected in California and the second in his family as well. Some nine hundred mourners gathered at Saint Cecilia Catholic Church in San Francisco, a few blocks away from the home where Jerry grew up. The California Highway Patrol provided an honor guard for the fallen governor. A line of San Francisco police saluted his casket. Four National Guard helicopters buzzed the service in "missing man" formation. All four Brown children attended, along with ten grandchildren and fourteen great-grandchildren. Bernice Brown attended in a wheelchair, which her son pushed.[3] Kathleen and Jerry Brown both spoke. Their less political sisters, Barbara and Cynthia, did not.

Governor Pete Wilson, the one man who had beaten both Jerry and Kathleen at the polls, attended and would graciously pay tribute to his predecessor after the service, though he was not invited to speak at the memorial itself.

Kathleen remembered her father's good cheer and love of politics. "This is my father's kind of day," she said. "He's in the news. And there's political news after New Hampshire…and the Republicans are in disarray." Her father, Kathleen added, "was a man of pride but never of vanity."

Then it was Jerry Brown's turn. His father, Jerry said, had remarked that his proudest achievement as governor was to restore welfare benefits to noncitizens in California. Political reporters, sniffing for controversy, assumed Brown was drawing a contrast to Wilson's support for Proposition 187 and its denial of such benefits to illegal immigrants. Remembering his father, Brown also mentioned the death penalty and his father's commutation of the sentences of twenty-three men on death row. "Very few since then," Jerry said, "have had the guts to do that."

"There was drama" around Brown's eulogy, the *San Francisco Examiner* reported, which "included pointed comparisons of his father's record on law and order to Wilson's."[4]

Nonsense, Brown said later. "I didn't even think of Pete Wilson," he said in 2019. "He didn't enter my mind. I was just trying to remember my father."[5]

After his modest beginnings and life of public service, Pat Brown had spent his postgovernorship doing lucrative legal work, and he left a significant estate to his children and grandchildren. His assets were equally divided between Brown and his sisters, but Brown believed he had a special claim on the family property in Colusa County, about an hour north of Sacramento. He alone was prepared to fix it up and live there, Brown said, and his sisters all had families and children who had received gifts from Pat and Bernice during Pat's lifetime, while Jerry had been single. Without consulting his sisters, Jerry asked his mother to deed him the shares in the property that she and Pat held.

The property was symbolically significant to the Browns, whose progenitor, August Schuckman, had purchased the land in 1878 and there ran a boarding house, tucked in a modest pass ascending into the range of hills just west of the town of Williams. It had remained in the family ever since, willed in 1959 to twenty-two heirs whose interests were consolidated into a family corporation overseen by Pat Brown and his brother in 1962. At the time of Pat's death, that same corporation remained the owner. Its shareholders owned seven thousand shares, of which Pat and Bernice held two thousand.

Part of Jerry's proposal to his mother was that he was prepared to make improvements to the property, which was beautiful and extensive, some 2,500 acres, but hardly a gold mine. It had neither running water nor electricity and produced only modest income from allowing neighbors to graze their cattle on its gentle hillsides. The Mountain House itself had burned down, twice. Colusa County, said to be home to more rattlesnakes than people, was not a tourist destination.[6]

After hearing Jerry out, his mother agreed, and deeded over to him the shares that she and Pat held in the property, making Jerry the largest single shareholder of the corporation. At first, Jerry Brown's sisters were not pleased. Asked about it years later, Barbara exclaimed: "He took it!" She laughed as she said it and hastened to make clear that she had never wanted the property and was not offended that it ended up with her brother. For his part, Jerry was at first defensive when asked about the property in 2019. Prodded by his wife, Anne, Brown defended his inheritance of the land and noted that his family was happy with the arrangement now. Interviewed separately, his sisters agreed.

By the late 1990s, and not for the first time, Jerry Brown was looking for a way back into the action. He'd been governor for eight years and waged three campaigns for president, falling short each time, though in ways that suggested that inflections of timing or message might have delivered him the big prize. He lost his one grab for a seat in the United States Senate, but he had otherwise won every state and local office he'd pursued. He'd been chairman of the state Democratic Party but hadn't liked it much. In 1998, he would turn sixty years old, and his father was gone. The questions for Jerry Brown were, Where, if ever, to stage a comeback? And when, if not now?

First was the issue of where to live. He'd returned to San Francisco after his ventures abroad and had been living in the city since 1989, when he'd relocated from Los Angeles in order to run for party chairman. But San Francisco was not a perfect launching pad for a return to politics. It was too liberal and too precious to confer credibility on a statewide candidate, and besides, Brown already was solid there, so it would not expand his natural base.

Initially, Los Angeles seemed appealing. It was California's largest city and thus a natural base for a candidate who aspired to greater things. Brown thought seriously enough about a bid for mayor of Los Angeles to meet with a group of potential supporters there. "Boy, was it a mistake," Brown said of the meeting. "They were so disparate in their reactions and opinions." Not one of those present said what he was hoping to hear: "Boy, come on, we need you to run for mayor."[7]

As that meeting suggested, Los Angeles was a tough political market, driven by media more than by a ground game—it's hard for volunteers to fan out across a city as sprawling as LA. It was—and is—an expensive place to practice politics, and it was still reeling from the 1992 riots, which scrambled traditional allegiances by placing a heavy emphasis on public safety and thus creating the opening for Riordan's 1993 election. Brown ruled out LA as a base of operations.

Where else? San Diego was too conservative and San Jose too remote from the political center. Brown wanted something novel, gritty—a place where he could both attract attention and make a difference. His ruminations led him to Oakland. It was California's eighth-largest city, diverse and challenging. Its hills were wealthy, its flats poor. It was among the first cities to have no majority ethnic group, leading a trend that would soon characterize other parts of California and eventually the state as a whole (and presumably, though not as of this writing, the nation).

"Oakland, I thought, would not take much money because I [was] so well known," Brown said.[8] He set his sights on the city and built a 17,000-square-foot complex, including 10 bedrooms and an auditorium, not far from Jack London Square, one of Oakland's few landmarks. He shared the new living space with Barzaghi, who remained at Brown's elbow, and Barzaghi's wife.

Brown created a foundation that combined elements of a food co-op and a law office. He called it We the People and from it spun off a more public aspect: a radio talk show, which he hosted himself. He first placed it at the Talk America network and later moved the show to KPFA, the Pacifica station in Berkeley and an anchor of the Bay Area counterculture. The show, like the foundation, was called *We the People;* it aired five days a week. Brown was a little establishment for KPFA, but he enjoyed the platform and used it to stretch his intellect and politics, in keeping with the station's history. "My hope was to clarify tacit assumptions and test them against common sense and democratic principles," he said in introducing a highly edited collection of some of his radio work.[9] Indeed, the early shows verged on ponderous, opening with Brown speaking over theme music by the iconic Los Angeles band Los Lobos, then segueing into long stretches of Brown philosophizing into a microphone.

The topics were dizzyingly eclectic, including intensive gardening, self-government, home births, cooperative business, responsive government, and "Lies My Teacher Told Me."[10] But the work grew on Brown, who gradually ceded more airtime to his guests and demanded less of it for himself. And guests—some of them, anyway—warmed to his inquisitive, unusual style. Among those who gave Brown interviews were Angela Davis, Tom Hayden, Paolo Soleri, Noam Chomsky, Gary Snyder, Allen Ginsberg, Alfre Woodard, and Thich Nhat Hahn. At his best—as he was with author Jonathan Kozol in 1995, Ivan Illich in 1996, and Alice Walker in 1997—Brown was a high-minded interrogator, asking about current events or ideas set against larger backdrops. "It's not easy being a talk show host," he said later, "but I enjoyed the ideas and the preparation—and sometimes the interviews."[11]

The program ran weekly from 1994 through October 28, 1997, when Brown signed off for the last time. He had decided to return to public office.

Brown announced his candidacy for mayor of Oakland. The city's political culture did not exactly bow down to him. On the contrary, a large field gathered for the 1998 campaign. Brown faced ten opponents, all of them black or Latino, including an Oakland city councilman, an Alameda County supervisor, and a professor of urban planning. Brown might have taken his victory for granted and coasted on his name recognition. He did not. He threw himself into the race. He worked libraries and meeting rooms, engaging with voters at a level that governors, at least of California, do not waste much time with. He favored local hiring, vowed to improve schools, promised to address the city's crime, and offered suggestions for luring new business to the city's ailing downtown. A few locals complained of carpetbagging; Brown grew up in San Francisco and had lived in Los Angeles but hadn't shown much interest in Oakland until moving there. But the flip side of Brown's new interest was that his campaign drew attention to a city long accustomed to being outside the spotlight. Residents seemed to like it. As the *San Francisco Examiner* noted, "It's not every day that the national editors of the [*New York*] *Times* show journalistic interest in Oakland politics."[12]

Brown carried every precinct but two in the June election, and he won the election outright in the first round by tallying more than 50 percent of the votes cast despite the large field of candidates. He had expected to win, and Brown shifted swiftly to governing. Even before the ballot count was completed, he dropped in on Ignacio De La Fuente, the Oakland city council member who had been among the crowd of candidates that Brown beat for mayor. "It looks like I've won," Brown told De La Fuente. "I just wanted to come by and see you and tell you that I want to work with you." A friendship was struck.[13] That same night, Brown looked ahead to the next election, pivoting to his campaign for a charter reform to enhance the powers of his new office.[14]

By most estimates, Brown's tenure as mayor of Oakland was successful, certainly in terms of the goals he set for it. Oakland grew by a few thousand residents. Some of that growth was in the city core, where Brown focused most of his redevelopment energy. Crime fell at first, then slowly rose, overall ending slightly below where it was when Brown took office. He spearheaded revitalization of the city's historic Fox Theater, and a brightly lit nightlife took hold in formerly decrepit blocks around the theater. Schools struggled but showed some progress, and Brown energized that effort by supporting the creation and development of two charter schools—the Oakland School for the Arts and the Oakland Military Institute—work that antagonized some community and labor activists. Overall, the effect was positive. Oakland, once seen as a dangerous and forbidding place, became an edgy and inviting one, enticing to businesses and residents.

Bernice Brown outlived her husband by six years. She stayed in their home, but her health suffered, and she lived with a caregiver. She joined the family's annual vacation to Hawaii for a year or two and reveled in her grandchildren, but it was increasingly hard for her to participate in family activities. She read—mostly newspapers and travel material, but books, too. She especially appreciated Kay Graham's memoir. Published to acclaim in 1997, it told Graham's story of surviving her husband's death (by suicide) and rising to power at the *Washington Post,* her family's proud possession. Bernice Brown admired Graham's tenacity and courage.

Bernice's hearing had long been spotty, and then her eyes began to fail. Within a couple of years of Pat's death, Bernice was blind.[15] Still, she persevered. She enjoyed spending time in a corner of her yard, surrounded by the flowers and scents of Southern California, lush in winter, bright in spring. She retained enough hearing to enjoy being read to.

She entered into a steep decline in early 2002. Jerry was in Oakland when he received word that she had died, on May 9, 2002, and he rushed to Southern California to be with his family. She was described by the *Los Angeles Times* as "charming" and "gregarious," and that was half right. Bernice was charming and warm, frugal and serious, understanding and kind. She was not exactly gregarious, but she adapted herself to politics and thrived within its constraints. Wife of one governor and mother of another, she lived long enough to see her son inherit the office of her husband. Ninety-three at the time of her death, Bernice Brown united California's past and its present and, more than she knew, its future.

Jerry Brown's mayoral tenure, like his time as governor, was largely unmarred by personal or political scandal, but his association with Barzaghi, often at Brown's side since the early 1970s, by then had became a handicap.

In July of 2004, Oakland police received a call about a domestic disturbance at Barzaghi's home. The call came from his wife, Aisha, who said Barzaghi had pushed her during an argument. Their home, at 200 Harrison Street, was the residence that Brown and the couple had once shared, though Brown had since moved out. When police arrived, both husband and wife accused the other of starting the shoving, but both also declined to press charges. No arrests were made.[16] But Barzaghi was at last wearing out his long welcome with Brown. The once gnomic figure had accumulated a string of complaints of sexual harassment, and in one case, the city of Oakland paid $50,000 to a complainant to settle her claims. Police were involved, and Brown's inner circle, most notably his increasingly indispensable adviser, Anne Gust, urged him to break his ties to Barzaghi, particularly if he intended to make another run for state office, as he was considering. One source close to Brown said Gust was emphatic that Barzaghi needed to go. Six days after the incident at his home, Brown's press secretary announced that Barzaghi was no longer working for the city of Oakland. Brown would not discuss the matter, then or later. "I fired him," Brown said curtly in 2017. "That was that. We had a parting of the ways." Barzaghi drifted away, eventually settling in Morocco.[17]

The most significant effect of Brown's mayoral tenure was not on the city of Oakland but rather on Brown himself. Being mayor taught Brown about the role and impact of government that his career to that point had, interestingly, allowed him to avoid. Through his tenure as secretary of state and governor, Brown said years later, he "didn't even know localism existed."[18] The job of the mayor, he added, "is concrete. It's getting people to come to Oakland. Getting Whole Foods to come to Oakland. I tried to get Trader Joe's. They wouldn't come. I drove around myself. 'Look at this site, look at that site.' 'No.' They wouldn't come. I knew the man from Whole Foods. He came."[19]

Politics at this level was not abstract, and much of Brown's life to that point had been lived at the level of abstraction: whether it was the Jesuits or Zen or *Small Is Beautiful,* his experience had been one of remove rather than engagement. He was repelled by his father's retail politics, but then it was his turn. Nathan Gardels, always a smart observer of his friend, viewed the mayoralty as a twinning of the threads of Brown's character. Part of Brown wanted to be president; another part wanted to be a monk. Being mayor was perfect, Gardels said: "Now he was a parish priest."[20]

This was not studies or bills or theories. It was crime and schools and buildings. Environmentalists and labor and farmworkers were allies, movement figures, in Sacramento, but in Oakland they were individual people interacting with their government, and therefore they were not always supportive of a mayor determined to make palpable change rather than merely cross intellectual swords. Peace activists opposed Brown's plan for a military academy charter school and for military exercises: Brown, who might once have sympathized, saw those proposals in terms of education and jobs, not as extensions of the military-industrial complex. He shrugged off the protests and went ahead. "Development has its critics," he said. "But blight is worse."[21]

Environmentalists challenged this project or that. Brown was used to support from the environmental community, but he was also a proponent of downtown revitalization. He surprised himself when he clashed with old friends in the movement, as he occasionally did in this incarnation.

His attempt to populate downtown Oakland with ten thousand new residents in approximately six thousand new units of housing came up slightly short—around four thousand units were complete when he left office, though the recession beginning in 2008 was at least partly to blame, because another 2,100 units had been approved but not yet built. The effort brought Brown closer to developers and construction workers, strange bedfellows for the Brown some thought they knew. De La Fuente, Brown's opponent and then ally, described his colleague's transformation "from the liberal hypothetical philosophical guy to a guy that learned that the only way to get stuff done is pushing the system."[22]

As Brown put it: "When I was governor, it was 'labor' or 'the environment.' In Oakland, it was somebody wanting to build a house on a lake."[23]

Introduction to the real, the concrete, also meant reexamination of some allegiances and a new appreciation for the unreasonableness of mobs. As he sought to build up Oakland, opponents arose reflexively, not always in response to real issues but occasionally by instinct or affiliation. To some, police were always bad, the environment was always good, development was always suspect. "I was encouraging, and they were blocking," he said. "I thought, you need to have units. Yes, there will be more traffic. Yes, there will be more noise. But we need more noise. We need more vitality." Looking back, he said, "I may be more aware of how people line up in their various tribal divisions, and they base their claims on belief rather than evidence. So there's a lot of ungrounded belief on all sides of many issues."[24] Moreover, there were real struggles: Oakland's police department resisted efforts at reform, and crime was a stubborn foe.

Through experience, the abstract Brown became more corporeal, more tangible. He developed a lighter, less biting sense of humor. He acquired a taste for self-deprecation—gentle, to be sure, but a willingness to see himself from outside his own vision. It is no coincidence that it was during this period that Brown made the most agile evolution of all. He found a partner. On June 18, 2005, Brown ended his long and famous life as a bachelor. He married Anne Gust.

Anne Gust was introduced to many Californians when she married Brown, but she already had a place in the Brown family, and she already was a person of stature and accomplishment. Born outside Detroit to a politically active Republican family, Gust was the fourth of five brothers and sisters, joined by two cousins when she was twelve after their parents died and her parents took them in. It was, she told the *California Sunday Magazine,* a "big, boisterous" family. Gust was a standout student in high school and migrated to California to attend Stanford University, where she began her studies during Jerry Brown's first term as governor.

Gust did not pay much attention to Brown when she was a student and he was governor. She left California after graduating from Stanford to attend law school at the University of Michigan. She returned to San Francisco—it's a hard place to leave—and commenced her professional life as a litigator. In 1991, she accepted a job as in-house counsel at the Gap.

Brown was in his improbable stint as chairman of the California Democratic Party at the time. He and Anne traveled in overlapping circles—both lived in San Francisco's Pacific Heights neighborhood—and one of her friends asked Anne to introduce them. Anne agreed, but the handoff failed. It was Anne who took a liking to the former governor, and he responded with a Jerry Brown sign of affection: he asked her to represent him and the Democratic Party in court and offered to pay her nothing. She accepted. And, in Anne Gust fashion, she won.[25]

They began a romance in May of 1990, guarded, then casual, then full. By the following year, they were sufficiently committed to each other for Brown to ask Gust to meet his mother and father, who were planning to be in San Francisco for a visit. Pat and Bernice Brown were coming for dinner, along with a sister or two, and Jerry asked Anne to join them.

Brown was living in a converted firehouse, complete with a pole, and Gust arrived, punctual as usual, snaking her way past the pole and up the elevator to Brown's apartment. The elevator opened directly into the apartment, and as Gust stepped from it into the room, she could see that the Browns already were sitting down at the dinner table. She was flustered at interrupting and worried that she somehow was late.

Jerry Brown did not make matters better. "This is Anne," he announced. "She's my neighbor."

In mild exasperation and bemusement, Gust glanced around. Bernice grasped her confusion and smiled sympathetically. "She knew," Gust remembered. "She had a look in the eye."[26]

Anne Gust and Jerry Brown dated for fifteen years, during which she saw him through his stint as party chair and his campaign for president. Gust made an impression on Brown's family, unaccustomed as they were to seeing their son and brother so at ease. "She brings out the very best in him," Barbara said of Anne, an observation echoed by countless Brown confidants.[27]

Brown proposed to Gust on the evening of March 15, 2005, Gust's birthday. Three months later, while he was still serving as Oakland's mayor but pivoting toward his next campaign, he and Gust were married, a first for both. Gust left her job at the Gap just before the wedding, working into May before marrying Brown in June. Brown vowed to lose some weight before the ceremony and took to jogging.

When the day arrived, Senator Dianne Feinstein officiated at the ceremony, which took place in the rotunda of Oakland's city hall. Gust, forty-seven, wore a white dress, designed by Brown's friend Diane von Furstenberg; Brown, sixty-seven, wore a charcoal suit with a white tie. Six hundred guests, including California's leading Democrats, attended. Among them were Gavin Newsom, the mayor of San Francisco, who later would follow Brown to Sacramento; Willie Brown, the former San Francisco mayor and speaker of the California assembly; and Kamala Harris, then the district attorney of San Francisco and on her way to bigger offices. Brown's sister Kathleen, the former state treasurer, was in attendance, as was Gray Davis, Brown's former chief of staff and at that point, like Brown, a former governor. It is probably safe to say that many of those in attendance had long ago given up the idea that they would attend the wedding of Jerry Brown.[28]

The ceremony was unapologetically traditional. Gregorian chants were performed. A chorale sang "Ave Maria," and program notes briefly sketched the "sacramental history of matrimony," dating back to Saint Augustine. Anne was accompanied by her father and entered to "Filiae Jerusalem." Nieces served as flower girls. Feinstein, delighted to preside over a service involving two people she regarded as close family friends, led a traditional exchange of vows, and then made her pronouncement: "We wish for them wisdom and devotion, that each may be to the other a strength in need, a counselor in perplexity, a comfort in sorrow, and a companion in joy."[29]

"This is more than traditional," Willie Brown exclaimed. "It would have satisfied anything the Kennedy clan would have put together."[30]

Following a smaller, Catholic ceremony across the bay at San Francisco's Saint Agnes Church, where Pat and Bernice Brown were married, the newlyweds hosted a dinner for friends and family in Oakland. They departed the next day for a brief honeymoon in the northern California wine country, then returned to the fight, this time for Jerry Brown's return to statewide office and his determination to lead the most unconventional possible political life. Brown, as he and Gust acknowledged during and around their wedding, was to be a candidate for attorney general, the job his father held on his way to the governorship and a job that Jerry would seek, perhaps, as a way back to it.

As mayor, Brown's focus had narrowed—from national to state to local politics and issues. But the larger beat droned on as California politics entered another bumpy patch. Brown's former chief of staff Gray Davis was elected governor in 1998, then reelected in 2002. Calm and capable, if somewhat colorless, Davis often seemed more a man on a march than one inspired to achieve great things in office. His support was broad but lackluster, as manifested by the exceptionally low turnout for his reelection. Even Brown, his onetime patron, had mixed feelings about Davis—impressed by his tenacity but also repelled by his preoccupation with fund-raising and determination not to overpromise. Longtime friend Stephen Reinhardt recalled Brown once describing Davis to him as "just an ATM," though Brown emphatically denies that.[31]

Turnout became an important measure in the Davis reelection because of what happened afterward. California was plunged into an energy crisis, triggered in part by the maneuvering of energy companies, such as Enron, that manipulated supply in order to boost prices and profits. The result was blackouts up and down the state, and a crisis that began with the state's power supply migrated to politics.

The shallowness of support for Davis became clear when his critics began circulating petitions to recall him from office, a process made easier by the low turnout in 2002, because California law sets the qualifying threshold for such a petition based on a percentage of votes cast in the previous election. Although no governor had ever been recalled, Davis's foes qualified their recall petition in July of 2003, and California voters, who just a year earlier had reelected him, were then given the chance to "dump Davis," as the campaign slogan proposed. As laid out in the curious rules of the recall, Davis's name would appear on the ballot, and voters could signal yes or no to his continued tenure. If they voted no, he would be recalled, and voters could then select the person they preferred to succeed him.

Davis's difficulties were compounded by the state's flagging economy and its effect on the California budget. A dot-com bubble burst in 2003, and California's budget, so dependent on income taxes from affluent residents, took a hit. The budget shortfall that year topped $20 billion, and Davis was desperate to find a fix that avoided a general tax increase, which was both politically unlikely and personally repugnant given Davis' general aversion to risk. Rather than lobby for a tax hike, Davis settled on increasing the state's vehicle license fee—because it was a fee, not a tax, it was not subject to Proposition 13's requirement that two-thirds of the legislature approve it. In fact, Davis was merely restoring the fee, popularly if misleadingly known as the car tax, to its level of five years earlier, before the legislature cut it in 1998. But when Davis raised it this time, nearly tripling the amount that Californians paid to register their vehicles, motorists rebelled.

Robert Greene, an elegant editorial writer for the *Los Angeles Times,* captured the controversy perfectly:

So there California was, in the midst of the dot-com hangover, on June 20, 2003, with a budget precariously out of balance, a gubernatorial recall threatened and a decision by Davis' finance director to make the state's general fund whole by removing the offset against the car tax. Drivers, that year, would have to pay the car tax themselves, just as planned in the original offset legislation. Anyone here have a problem with that?

Well. Yes. There was a problem with that, as any AM radio talk show host would have been happy to explain. A tripling of the car tax! Outrageous Democrats, who spent California into a budget hole![32]

The Davis recall placed leading California Democrats in a quandary. Initially, most felt the strongest strategy was to defend Davis and retain the governorship by fending off what they regarded as a usurpation of Davis's 2002 victory—what Davis called a "right-wing power grab."[33] On the other hand, they recognized Davis's vulnerability and worried that sticking with him risked handing over the governorship to a Republican. Many eyes focused on Senator Feinstein, who almost certainly could have secured the governorship had she entered the race, but doing so would have been at the expense of her fellow Democrat Davis. Feinstein paused while a crazy field took shape. Former Los Angeles mayor Richard Riordan considered a run, as did the lieutenant governor, Cruz Bustamante—the former a Republican, the latter a Democrat. Leon Panetta, the popular Democratic former congressman and chief of staff to Bill Clinton, weighed his options, though vowing only to consider it if Feinstein declined to run. Meanwhile, a grab bag of would-be governors entered the race, many just on a lark, as a California collection of actors, businessmen, a porn star, and a few wack jobs tossed their hats in the ring.

Stranded by a divided Democratic party and a restive electorate, Davis fought but lost. "Tonight the voters have decided it's time for someone else to serve," Davis conceded on election night. "I accept their judgment."[34] The *New York Times* captured the feeling: FOR GRAY DAVIS, GREAT FALL FROM THE HIGHEST HEIGHT.[35]

And just to make the event a perfect crystallization of political up-heaval, voters selected as Davis's successor the most unlikely of governors. Arnold Schwarzenegger, a politically active action hero best known as the Terminator, became the governor of America's largest state. He was quickly and lamentably dubbed the Governator, of course.

Schwarzenegger presented a puzzle: he exceeded the exceptionally low expectations for his intellect and political acumen, but he also came to Sacramento with no real allies or support from either party. The nature of his election—a crowded field overshadowed by the recall itself—allowed Schwarzenegger to bring his moderate Republican politics to the governor's office, but once there he discovered himself to be a party of one. He courted both sides, persuading neither, and failed in a gambit to win voter support for a bevy of ballot measures, including one strongly opposed by labor, while also hiring a prominent Democrat, Susan Kennedy, to serve as his chief of staff. Still, Schwarzenegger could point to some notable achievements. He supported an initiative to place redistricting in the hands of a citizens' commission as well as the creation of the so-called top-two primary, wherein the top finishers in an election's first round proceed to a runoff regardless of their party affiliation—two proposals intended to trim the partisan and ideological excesses of a state drifting toward polarization. Schwarzenegger also signed AB-32, a landmark greenhouse-gas measure that helped place California at the forefront of the effort to recognize and combat climate change. By signing the bill, he invigorated the place of the Republican Party in that conversation: his message failed to reach Washington, however, as the GOP moved away from science and reason just as the climate-change crisis crested around the world.

Schwarzenegger served out Gray Davis's unexpired term and so faced reelection in 2006, on the same ballot where Jerry Brown was plotting his return. Brown was ready to reenter the world of California state politics, where he had long reigned and from which he had been even longer absent.

He faced a new generation of voters, many of whom did not know him from his first time as governor. That was both a blessing and a curse as Brown presented himself freshly to the electorate. His first challenge was to win the Democratic primary for the office of attorney general, which incumbent Bill Lockyer was vacating to plan a run against Schwarzenegger. With the office open, that left Brown with one major opponent, the Los Angeles city attorney, Rocky Delgadillo. On paper, Delgadillo was impressive. More than twenty years younger than Brown, he was born and raised in Los Angeles and went on to great success. He graduated from Harvard and then from Columbia Law School, returning home to join the firm of O'Melveny and Myers, where he ensconced himself as a protégé of Warren Christopher, adviser to two generations of Browns. Delgadillo was a cheerful, likable young man, and he landed a job with Mayor Riordan in Los Angeles, serving as Riordan's deputy mayor for economic development. In that post, he helped woo businesses to Los Angeles and became an upbeat spokesman for the rebounding city. Politically, that made him the rare California politician who had the potential to enjoy prominent bipartisan support. His office, city attorney in the state's largest city, with its teeming cast of lawyers and legal work, gave him a natural fund-raising base, and the prospect of electing a Latino as attorney general created energy and excitement for his campaign.

Given all that, Brown could not afford to take Delgadillo lightly. And so, after he and Anne wrapped up their brief honeymoon, the candidate and his closest adviser sized up the man standing in the way of Brown's return to Sacramento. Brown wanted outside guidance as well and was intrigued by an up-and-coming political operative, Ace Smith, who had just run Antonio Villaraigosa's successful campaign for mayor of Los Angeles. They ran into each other at Villaraigosa's inauguration, and Brown asked Anne what she thought of him. Smith and Gust met at Tommaso's, a classic Italian restaurant in San Francisco's North Beach, and Gust recommended to Brown that he hire Smith, which Brown did.

The biggest challenge, Smith and Gust said later, was finding the right degree of appreciation for Delgadillo. He was a serious challenger, but so was Brown, after all. In fact, as they mulled the matter over, they concluded that they should resist the temptation to take Delgadillo too seriously. For all his surface strengths, Brown and his advisers concluded, he could not match Brown's name recognition or equal the affection voters had for him, particularly in Northern California, where Democratic voters are plentiful and active in a primary. Early polls, both the campaign's internal surveys and those available to the public, confirmed that Brown's name recognition had faded some in Southern California, where he had not had a constituency since 1983, but he remained recognizable and well-liked in the Bay Area, which would deliver the lion's share of the votes in the June 2006 primary. The conclusion: run hard against Delgadillo, but do not break the bank on beating him.

"If we got to the general [election] with a full bank account, we'd be okay," Smith said in 2018.[36]

That calculation proved shrewd. Once the campaign engaged, it became clear that Delgadillo was stronger on paper than in person. A slightly clumsy candidate, he came off as younger than his years, bobbing at Brown without ever really doing much damage. In one debate, he questioned Brown's commitment to abortion rights, an area where Brown was unlikely to be bested. Delgadillo also accused Brown of allowing crime to flourish in Oakland and sneered at his family tree. "I'm not the son of a governor," Delgadillo said. "My name is Delgadillo, not Brown."[37] But that was weak tea, and it was hard for Delgadillo to match his experience against that of a former governor. Brown chose to combat Delgadillo mostly by ignoring him. It worked. Brown won handily, then turned to the general election with a full campaign war chest, exactly as planned. It was, Smith joked later, the first time anyone had "outcheapskated Jerry Brown."[38]

In the general election, state senator Chuck Poochigian, a Sacramento veteran who had worked for both Deukmejian and Wilson, carried the Republican banner, but it was a losing fight from the start. Brown was sensitive to the charge that crime was on the rise in Oakland, but he defended his record aggressively, and Poochigian was left to try stunts. The most memorable was a challenge to Brown's eligibility for the office, as Poochigian's allies alleged that Brown had allowed his bar membership to become inactive. California law requires the attorney general to have been a member of the state bar for five years, and lapsed bar membership would preclude that, Republicans asserted in a lawsuit they filed to block Brown from seeking or holding the office. "Neither Jerry Brown's political pedigree nor his sense of entitlement can help him resolve this problem," Poochigian said. "He is not above the law."[39] Ace Smith mocked the challenge, commandeering the Poochigian dais at the press conference and comparing the attack to the infamous "Swift Boat" attack on Democratic presidential candidate John Kerry.[40] The lawsuit went nowhere—the court found that inactive was not the same as lapsed bar membership—as did Poochigian. Brown beat him by twenty points.

Brown's time as attorney general had its moments, but it felt like a way station. He was in that office when the American economy collapsed, taking California with it. And given the breadth and importance—culturally, economically, politically—of housing in California, the damage to the state's real estate markets was felt especially keenly. Brown was part of the effort to respond, filing a lawsuit against Countrywide Financial for business practices that the attorney general's office claimed misled homeowners into applying for loans they could not afford. The Countrywide case lost some of its sizzle when Bank of America bought Countrywide, but the eventual settlement allowed 125,000 Californians who were dealing with risky mortgages to file for reduced payments and loan modifications, a significant achievement given California's extreme exposure to a crisis that left more homeowners at risk there than in any other state. All told, the settlement was valued at $8.7 billion nationally, $3.5 billion of which was available to Californians.[41]

The case more likely to reverberate in history from Brown's attorney generalship, however, was launched on Election Day of 2008, when Californians overwhelmingly voted to elect Barack Obama president but also more narrowly passed Proposition 8, which outlawed gay marriage in the state (confusingly, a vote in favor of Proposition 8 was thus a vote against gay marriage; California history is littered with the ramifications of confusing ballot measures). Black voters, who overwhelmingly turned out for Obama and harbored reservations about gay marriage, helped explain the odd pairing of those two results. As Obama, who also opposed gay marriage at the time, went on to the White House, California officials were left to pick up the pieces of the marriage debate.

Both Brown and Governor Schwarzenegger had opposed Proposition 8, meaning that both had favored preserving the legality of gay marriage, and both had argued that the proposition was not just wrong but also unconstitutional. Its passage thus posed a legal and ethical question for the state's top officials. Did they have an obligation to defend the will of California voters if it defied their own judgment and that of California's supreme court, which had ruled earlier that year that a law banning same-sex marriage in California was unconstitutional? Brown decided that they did not.

His decision was not universally popular, even among his liberal friends, some of whom suggested that Brown had a duty to the voters that overrode his view of the case. Still, Brown's refusal to support the measure emulated the actions of his father a generation earlier. As governor, Pat Brown had refused to defend Proposition 14, the property-rights initiative that overturned his work on fair housing. In both cases, the two officials argued that their constitutional duties forbade them from defending unconstitutional acts, even those adopted by the voters. An even earlier case, this one from the Earl Warren governorship, raised a similar conflict. That time, the state of California lost its effort to defend school segregation at the appellate level. Rather than appeal to the US Supreme Court, California authorities chose not to contest the ruling, handed down by the United States Court of Appeals for the Ninth Circuit. Not until Warren became chief justice, in 1953, would school segregation squarely present itself to the Court again, and by then, the former California governor would lead his new colleagues on the Court in deciding *Brown v. Board of Education*.

The same-sex marriage case took years to work its way to the United States Supreme Court, which refused to let supporters of Proposition 8 act as its official defenders in court, in a sense vindicating Brown's actions by delivering the result he had hoped for. The Court's refusal to recognize the standing of the initiative's backers left in place an appellate court ruling that overturned Proposition 8, meaning that gay marriages could resume in California. It had taken five years from Proposition

8's original passage to its ultimate dismissal, during which time Brown had moved on from the attorney generalship. But he was in place to welcome it.

"After years of struggle," Governor Brown said at the time, "the U.S. Supreme Court today has made same-sex marriage a reality in California. In light of the decision, I have directed the California Department of Public Health to advise the state's counties that they must begin issuing marriage licenses to same-sex couples in California as soon as the Ninth Circuit confirms the stay is lifted."[42]

# Part Five

Return

# 18

# New Brown

B rown's desire to resume his governorship, his private yearning to surpass his father's two-term tenure, and his commitment to apply the lessons of his wilderness years to governing California again had bubbled within him at least since the early 1990s. Once he was elected attorney general, in 2006, many presumed he was en route back to his old office. The elections of 2010 were tailor-made for that return.

Schwarzenegger had run his course. His administration had not been as bad as some had feared, but it hadn't been nearly as good as some had hoped. He registered a few successes and left a few reminders that he had passed through the office, but his tenure would be remembered more for its novelty than for its achievement. He had weathered the Great Recession of 2008 and 2009, but California's peculiarly vulnerable budget cycle had been battered. His successor would inherit a daunting shortfall.[1] Indeed, the state's problems were so large and mounting so fast that commentators wondered not so much who would follow Schwarzenegger as who would want to. Davis's recall had introduced one element of political chaos, but just one. It was layered on top of term limits and tax constraints, populism and partisanship, and division that made compromise seem laughable. California, it was said, had become ungovernable, something akin to Italy or Greece—consigned to paralysis and doomed to fail, a loser state overwhelmed by the gap between its needs and its willingness to pay.

Viewing this catastrophe from London, the *Guardian* dipped deep into its well of conventional wisdom and summarized the situation:

California has a special place in the American psyche. It is the Golden State: a playground of the rich and famous with perfect weather. It symbolizes a lifestyle of sunshine, swimming pools and the Hollywood dream factory. But the state that once was held up as the epitome of America has collapsed. From its politics to the economy to its environment and way of life, California is like a patient on life support.[2]

Joel Kotkin, a doomsayer closer to home, essentially agreed. Pointing to vacancy rates in Silicon Valley and blaming environmental protection measures for "impoverishing whole regions," Kotkin foresaw that the end was near. "The dream has been evaporating," he wrote in 2010, in an article headlined THE GOLDEN STATE'S WAR ON ITSELF: HOW POLITICIANS TURNED THE CALIFORNIA DREAM INTO A NIGHTMARE.[3]

Who would seek such a prize? In politics, despair can suggest opportunity, and for Republicans, the race in 2010 did just that. Two prominent Republicans, similar in some ways and quite different in others, set out to follow Schwarzenegger. The state's dire circumstances gave each hope that he or she would capture the office at a moment when its challenges might dissuade hard-to-beat office seekers.

Steve Poizner was successful as a student and interested in business. He stood out at the University of Texas and earned an MBA from Stanford. He enjoyed politics, serving as a White House Fellow in the period before and after 9/11. He developed a love for—and an alternative theory of—teaching and founded an organization to advance California charter schools. He liked to apply business principles to public service, championing competition, accountability, and the like. He was sincere and well meaning, cheerfully convinced that he had the skills, temperament, and background to improve the lives of others.

And so, politics. In 2004, he ran for a position in the California state assembly and, to his own surprise, lost a narrow race to an incumbent Democrat in a moderate district. Two years later, he raised his sights and sought a position that appealed to business-minded California Republicans—that of state insurance commissioner. This time, to the surprise of others, he won—a rare Republican statewide victory in a period when the party's decline was making victories increasingly uncommon.

By 2010, then, Poizner was, at least by dint of his résumé, the Republican most suited to seek the governorship of California. He held statewide office, had shown some mettle as a candidate, and brought a background that blended personal decency, ample ambition, and a taste for politics in pursuit of the public good.

Poizner's first problem in translating that into the governorship was another politician of a type not so different from Poizner's. Meg Whitman was the classic chief executive officer who, having shown her capabilities in private enterprise, prepared to teach the public sector the lessons of her experience. Like Poizner, she was a young standout—Princeton and Harvard in her case—and found early success in business. But for Whitman, the success was more than notable. It was spectacular. She spent a decade as chief executive officer of a young company called eBay, during which time the firm turned a simple business idea—an online auction service for everything from fine art to white elephants—into a humming enterprise. She grew eBay from thirty employees to fifteen thousand. Politicians courted her and flattered her. Whitman was rich, with a fortune valued at more than $1 billion, and she dipped into it to dabble in politics in the way rich people do. She had no experience in government—indeed, she had so little interest in it that she didn't bother to vote for decades.[4] But in 2009, she decided to enter politics by running for governor of the largest state in the union. "I love California too much to let it fail," Whitman, a New York native, said upon announcing her candidacy.

Poizner and Whitman vied for the Republican nomination in a manner that came to define GOP politics in California during the 1990s and early 2000s (and that persists as of this writing). With the party shrinking as an influence in the state, what was left was an extreme base. That made statewide primaries a race to the right, which then had the effect of weakening the nominee in the general election, where Democrats and especially independents held sway. The pattern held true in 2010.

Both candidates were, by nature, moderates, but both felt the pressure of politics to demonstrate that they were something else. Both said they would repeal taxes that held back business growth; both said they would repeal AB-32, the greenhouse-gas law signed by Schwarzenegger, which these Republicans labeled a job killer. Both vilified illegal immigrants. In their debates, Poizner accused Whitman of being too liberal for California's Republicans. "I want to stop illegal immigration by cutting off taxpayer-funded benefits," Poizner insisted. "Meg doesn't want to go that far." Icing the cake, Poizner remarked on an interview Whitman had done with National Public Radio. "I don't listen to NPR," he said.[5] Poizner's attacks did little to move the dial, especially as Whitman drew upon her personal fortune to pay for television and direct-mail advertising that established her as the front-runner and never let Poizner fully into the race. Still, Whitman's early instinct to avoid interviews and the press generally established a distance between her and the electorate, and Poizner's questions about her suitability for office—as well as her own lack of experience and involvement in politics—weakened her as a candidate in the general election, after she thoroughly trounced Poizner for the nomination.

Jerry Brown was ready. "Sacramento isn't working today," Brown said in announcing his candidacy. "Our state is in serious trouble…What we need is not some scripted plan cooked up by consultants or mere ambition to be governor. We need someone with insider's knowledge but an outsider's mind."[6] And who would that be? "At this stage in my life," he said, "I'm prepared to focus on nothing else but fixing the state I love."

Brown's campaign strategist from the attorney general race, Ace Smith, was unavailable for this contest, since Smith also had represented Antonio Villaraigosa, and Villaraigosa, then the mayor of Los Angeles, considered a run for governor in 2010. Instead, Brown turned to Steve

Glazer, a longtime adviser, for the campaign that would, if successful, return Brown to his historic seat. Working with the candidate and his wife, Glazer set out to run an unusual campaign—reintroducing Brown to older Californians who had gone a long time without hearing from him and selling that same veteran as a newcomer to younger voters. Moreover, they had to do that against a well-funded opponent who was prepared to outspend them at every turn.

As expected, Whitman spent lavishly on her own candidacy, eventually breaking all records for a nonpresidential effort. Brown was, as usual, careful to the point of parsimony with money. Whitman walled herself off from the press, nervous about misstatements that might damage her campaign; she traveled by private plane, turned down interview requests, relied heavily on paid media. Brown was open, almost to a fault, whirling in Latin, rope-a-doping with Whitman. She polled extensively, spending around $1.7 million on surveys: that was roughly eleven times what Brown, who knew California better and trusted his instincts more thoroughly, invested in learning what voters wanted.[7] She spent $2.6 million on travel and lodging. Brown and his aides flew coach on Southwest Airlines; their total travel and lodging budget was $70,000. But if Brown spent sparingly, he also spent wisely. He rationed his money until the end, when he blitzed California televisions with a burst of advertising.

Tactically, Brown benefited from a strange decision on Whitman's part. She elected to label Brown as a "tax-and-spend liberal," tempting political jargon but singularly ill suited to Brown, whose great mistake, in some minds, was to allow California's surplus to grow so large in the 1970s that it supplied a target for proponents of Proposition 13. As governor, Brown had proved far more stingy than even Reagan, whose tax increase was historic. Brown was a liberal and not averse to taxes, but he was hardly a spender. As Willie Brown, the former speaker and San Francisco mayor, said with a laugh, "Just once, I'd love for that [guy] to pick up a check!"[8]

But the state surpluses and tax cuts of the Brown years, the self-abnegation and the mattress on the floor, the exasperation of Democrats who begged him to spend on this program or that—all that had played out long before, and Brown's team was concerned that Whitman's charge would get traction at a time of economic distress, that some voters might assume that she, as a businesswoman, would be more fiscally conservative than the otherwise liberal Brown. To fend off that line of attack, Brown made a risky commitment. "In this time of recession, when people are financially strapped," Brown said, "there will be no new taxes unless you, the people, vote for them."[9] Brown took some heat for that. Californians were hardly known for raising their own taxes, after all, and many observers, especially on the left, believed the candidate had locked himself in with an undeliverable promise. California, they believed, needed new taxes to preserve services, but Californians could not be trusted to approve any tax increase, so Brown's promise, if he kept it, would stifle the very recovery that California needed. The *Los Angeles Times,* for example, endorsed Brown but fretted over the promise, which it said "would only deepen California's governmental stalemate. His assertion that the Legislature will buckle down and make hard decisions if only he lays out all the information before it sounds naïve."[10]

Brown was uninterested in that critique, especially from the *Times*. Asked about the promise in 2018, he defended it with spirit. "Taxes are not popular. This is Politics 101!" Pointing to his new dog, a mixed-breed border collie and poodle named Cali, Brown added, "Even Cali doesn't like taxes!" It was easy, he added, to stay aloof from real politics in an editorial, but it was not so pretty on the ground, where votes were tallied and policies made. He was running against Whitman in 2010, with all her money and with some uncertainty about where he stood with voters. "Maybe I could have beaten her anyway, but it would have given her an opening," he said.

Substantively, Brown added that the promise was less than it seemed. "There was no way to get a tax without it," he said of allowing a popular vote on the measure. "I couldn't get a two-thirds vote [of the legislature] even to put it on the ballot…There was no way to get a tax. Not possible."[11] Given that he was unlikely to succeed in the legislature, why not try his luck with the voters? Brown gambled and suggested he would consider raising taxes—leaving himself that option while constraining his own ability to do so by insisting that voters would have the last word.

Meanwhile, demographics had their say. The great shift under way in California by 2010 was the emergence of Latinos as a significant—eventually dominant—share of the electorate. That created part of the stress in the Republican primaries, as Poizner pushed Whitman to be as aggressive as Republican Party stalwarts demanded on immigration without going so far as to alienate Latinos in the general election, when she would need their support. Whitman did all she could to navigate the nearly impossible pull of those opposing forces. She argued in the primaries that she, too, opposed illegal immigration and would deny public benefits to those in the country illegally. At the same time, she tried to temper that position by speaking up on behalf of legal immigrants and attempting to dodge questions about such things as whether she would allow those in the country to pursue a path to legal citizenship and whether she would prevent the children of illegal immigrants from gaining legal status by going to college or joining the military. Brown dogged her. Responding to a question from an undocumented student during one of the debates, Whitman bobbed; Brown did not. "She wants to kick you out of this school because you are not documented, and that is wrong, morally and humanly," Brown said to the student.[12]

Still, Whitman led most polls for most of the way. In the campaign's crucial stretch, between Labor Day and Election Day, Brown turned up the pace of his television advertising. He began to make up ground. Then reporters uncovered information that Whitman had fired her longtime housekeeper, Nicandra Diaz Santillan, in 2009, ending the undocumented woman's nine years of work for Whitman's family just as the candidate entered the governor's race. With that, her attempts to depersonalize the immigration debate—to please Republicans with her calls for tough borders and neutralize Democrats with her generic support for immigrants—came tumbling down in accusations of hypocrisy and meanness. Whitman lamely attempted to deflect the issue by blaming Brown for the leak. Brown claimed no involvement—as if that would have mattered—and archly noted that

Whitman had called for employers to be responsible for checking the immigration status of their workers even as she had long failed to do so.[13]

Whitman, who once acknowledged that she could not win without the support of California's Latinos, faced her election with strong reason to believe that she would not get that support. She was right to worry. Among those who stated a preference, Latinos broke 73 percent to 18 percent for Brown, and Whitman lost.

"I understand the political part," he told supporters in Oakland as the returns came in. "But I also understand what it's all about, vision… That's the spirit that I want to take back to Sacramento, twenty-eight years later, full of energy, full of creativity, and ready to serve you, the people of California." Looking back, Brown said he regarded the race as not that hard, just another campaign in a long life of contests.[14]

After the election, Jerry and Anne briefly considered that there might be time for a vacation. There was not. The week was not out before Anne began interviewing candidates for positions in the administration. Even as volunteers packed up the campaign office, near Jack London Square, in Oakland, Anne, whose business background exceeded that of her husband and whose nearly complete confidence she enjoyed, took the lead in staffing the administration, sizing up duties and fitting them to potential staff members.

There was no chance of returning to Brown's original team. His first chief of staff, Gray Davis, had gone on to his own governorship, followed by its abrupt end with his recall. B. T. Collins, who followed Davis as chief of staff, had died of a heart attack in 1993. It would be a new team with new leadership.

Jim Humes had been Brown's top aide in the attorney general's office. Brown liked and trusted him, appreciated his candor and his strong relations with that office's staff. Brown wanted a place for him in the new administration, but he also resisted the idea of a formal chief of staff. He had faith in his own instincts and experience and was loath to entrust responsibility for his success to anyone, even Humes. So even as Jerry and Anne reserved a spot for Humes, they agreed that they should search for another top aide to complement him and round out the administration's upper ranks.

Anne asked around. Maria Shriver, First Lady from the Schwarzenegger years, had recommendations. So did old contacts from Anne's legal career. Top Democrats across the country chimed in. One name came up several times: Nancy McFadden, a lawyer then working as a senior vice president of public affairs for Pacific Gas and Electric. At Anne's request, McFadden joined her for a meeting at the campaign office.

It was not an instant connection. McFadden was a lawyer, a graduate of the University of Virginia, and her career, like those of so many Democratic political figures in late twentieth-century California, had been shaped in part by Warren Christopher, counselor to presidents, governors, and candidates, including three generations of Browns. At Christopher's urging, McFadden had attached herself early to the campaign of Arkansas governor Bill Clinton. With Clinton's election, both Christopher and McFadden went to Washington, Christopher as secretary of state, McFadden to the Justice Department and later the staff of Vice President Al Gore. But Clinton and Brown had never been close—the opposite was closer to the truth—and McFadden did not leap at the chance to work for Brown. Brown and Gust also were noncommittal, though Gust warmed to McFadden as they talked. Convinced that McFadden's skills in politics and legislative affairs would complement Humes's background in legal affairs, Gust recommended McFadden to her husband. He agreed to meet with McFadden, and they enjoyed each other. Brown agreed to extend an offer, then Gust had to persuade McFadden to take it. The return of Jerry Brown, his wife suggested to his potential deputy, would mark an exciting, eventful period in the history of the state and nation. Jerry himself was nothing but interesting. The national political scene was, for the moment, quiet. "What is it that you have to lose?" Gust asked McFadden. McFadden agreed.[15]

The result was, in retrospect, a slightly awkward management arrangement, though one custom-built for the two exceptionally capable officials charged with leading it: McFadden and Humes were named co–executive secretaries, with divided but discrete duties, both reporting to Brown.

Eventually, Humes would leave to pursue his dream of a judgeship, and McFadden would effectively become chief of staff for most of Brown's third and fourth terms, working as a troika with Brown and Gust. It was a team redolent with talent and, most notably, mutual trust.

There was continuity in Brown's return. He took up residence in the office he had vacated twenty-eight years earlier, its windows overlooking the capitol grounds he had wandered a generation before. In terms of formal duties and obligations, the job of the governor had not changed much: he was charged with considering bills passed by the legislature, reviewing petitions for clemency, and responding to crises, which, in California, were alarmingly frequent. There was a fun trick of history: both times Brown assumed the governorship, he inherited it from an actor—first Reagan, then Schwarzenegger.

And there were differences, both in the challenges and in the man who confronted them. Reagan had left a fairly stable government in 1975. California upon Reagan's departure enjoyed a modest surplus, thanks in large measure to his support for the huge tax increase passed in his first term and his rigorous control of spending in the years since. Not so in 2011, when Brown came to office staring at the largest shortfall in California history as well as a deeply polarized legislature and two sets of constraints: the rules established by Proposition 13, which made tax increases impossible without the support of two-thirds of the legislature, and the confines imposed by Brown himself, who had promised not to increase taxes without a vote of the people.

Then there was the governor. Jerry Brown in 1983 was chastened by defeat in his Senate race against Pete Wilson, but he was young and irrepressibly brash. He'd left politics at a time when most people were just getting in. He was single and intellectual and a little weird. He was forty-four years old.

Now he was seventy-two. That alone created different dynamics around his governorship. In his first iteration, Brown had surrounded himself with contemporaries. Tony Kline, Gray Davis, and Rose Bird— even Gary Snyder and Gregory Bateson—these were men and women who were similar to Brown in age and experience, even a bit older. He populated his administration, the state government, and the courts with lawyers and advocates of his generation. Cabinet meetings and other gatherings of his administration were extended explorations—debates and discussions that more resembled late night at a law school than an evening with the Reagan cabinet. It was a life in the inquiry that had deliberations among peers at its center. In relation to the legislature, that had implications, too. California's elected leaders in 1975 almost all were older and more experienced than Jerry Brown. They had known his father and were inclined to see the young governor as more of a whippersnapper than a political or intellectual force.

When Brown returned, his age and experience set him apart, this time in an entirely different way. He was older than his peers and counterparts. Term limits had shortened the lives of legislators, and Brown already had been governor. He liked to joke that he once had little use for experience but that he'd come to appreciate it. Whereas his counterparts in state government had once looked him in the eye or even down at him, they now gazed upward.

"In the second administration, virtually everyone [was] a subordinate," said Diana Dooley, who joined Brown at age twenty-four and was one of a handful of associates to see him through all four terms, ending her tenure as Brown's final chief of staff. "These days, he's the wise man."[16]

Brown's changed relationship with the government extended to a new perspective on its possibilities. Once determined to shrink the range of government activity and responsibility, Brown at this point entertained bigger possibilities for it, akin to those his father once backed. As governor in the 1970s, Brown had supported, unsuccessfully, the construction of a waterway known as the Peripheral Canal, intended to divert water from the Sacramento River and pour it into the aqueduct that carried water from Northern to Southern California. The project made sense from an engineering perspective—drawing water from the Sacramento–San Joaquin Delta, as the system then did, placed it in danger of being damaged by a serious earthquake. That's because a series of earthen levees separated fresh and salt water in the delta, and an earthquake could crumble them, allowing salt water to foul the supply that provided much of Southern California with its lifeblood. But the idea of the canal opened old wounds, resentments in Northern California about the "theft" of its water in order to green Los Angeles lawns. The canal was rejected by voters on Brown's first try; upon his return, he advocated for a pair of tunnels that would accomplish the same objective, and he prepared to wage political battle on their behalf, even at the risk of inflaming old passions between north and south.

At the same time, he lit upon a futuristic project that combined the goals of a builder, an environmental visionary, and a train enthusiast. Jerry Brown did not invent the idea of a bullet train for California. The project actually was launched by his predecessor Schwarzenegger and had been contemplated long before that. In a sense, it was a natural: with San Francisco at one end and Los Angeles on the other—and with a broad expanse of mostly flat agricultural land in between—a train seemed an obvious way to link the two regions.

For the state's environmentally conscious governor, it had the added appeal of taking cars off freeways and perhaps even supplanting air traffic. Air pollution in the Central Valley was a growing concern, and if the train could be routed through the eastern edge of that valley, with stops in Bakersfield, Fresno, and elsewhere, it might alleviate some of that problem as well. The entire project harked back to California's roots, to the days when the Southern Pacific shipped freight and people up and down the state and to and from the rest of the nation. Finally, for Brown, it was a kick: "I love trains!" he exclaimed in amusing bursts of ebullience that seemed so unlike the monkish Brown. Proof of his commitment to the bullet train was that he entrusted much of the research and organization around the idea to Anne Gust.[17]

Both the train and the pair of tunnels would stand as departures from Brown's traditional aversion to big government projects, and each would encounter its share of trouble and dissent. The train in particular seemed peculiar to many Brown observers, to the point where some speculated that he pined for a bit of his father's ability to leave a mark on the land. That was trite—Brown was justifiably annoyed by the suggestion that he was building a monument. In fact, that charge contributed to his dismissal of "legacy" questions in his final term. As his time in office wound down, he would fight to cement progress on both projects in hopes that his work would make it harder for his successor to undo.

One further note is in order, especially as regards the train. This project did not capture Jerry Brown's enthusiasm in the way that public works once attracted his father. In Pat Brown's case, waves of new arrivals to California demanded an education; he responded by investing in the University of California. Farmers and cities worried about water supplies, and he built aqueducts. The train, by contrast, was visionary and, in a sense, top down. Leaders, including Brown, looked into the future and saw the possibilities for rail; Brown jumped on the idea, well ahead of any voter or constituent demand for it. That was testament to the younger Brown's determination to govern for the future, but it also weakened the political case for the project in the present. It's not always easy to be a man of tomorrow.

Jerry Brown in 1975 knew plenty about Saint Ignatius and Zen meditation and raw power politics. But he was somewhat sheltered and very much aloof. He dated, but without lasting personal commitment. He considered government as an intellectual and philosophical exercise but had not experienced its impact at ground level. He had led and pioneered but never really served.

He returned to the governorship with a new bushel of experiences. He was a married man, one who had learned to trust another person deeply and lastingly. He had been a mayor, had worked on issues as they manifested themselves in the lives of people, rather than as they affected interest groups or voting blocs. Jerry Brown in 2011 had dogs. He was no longer an abstraction: he was, at last, a rounded, complete person.

"I'm better at it," Brown said of being governor in 2016. "I know more. My mind is good. My energy level is all right. And I have forty years of experience."[18]

With the resumption of his work in 2011, Brown was given that rarest of opportunities in life, certainly in politics. He was permitted a second chance, the chance to use what he had learned and try again—arrayed against new challenges but armed with similar powers and enhanced experience. Diana Dooley, who had watched Brown closely across that long span, described his change: "He was more concerned about the ideas the first time," she said. "Now, he's more aware of the operational."[19]

Brown agreed. "I knew a lot when I was governor the first time, but I didn't see it in as broad a light as I see things now," he reflected in 2018. "Whether it's the court or labor or business or the environment—decades of experience enrich one's perception by having more elements in mind...I have a broader perspective."[20]

# 19

# Return to Power

H e began with the budget. Brown ran thinking that the shortfall was roughly $16 billion, a staggering sum that required a dramatic response. Commentators predicted that California would face bankruptcy and pondered the economic fallout from the default of the world's eighth-largest economy. Would California's failure bring down the United States? Could international markets, already reeling, handle the collapse of the economic hub of the Pacific Rim?

Those were not idle questions. Brown prepared to make drastic cuts and to propose at least some increased taxes, albeit with awareness of his promise to submit them to voters first. And then the news got worse. By the time he took office, the plummeting American economy had drawn down anticipated revenue from taxes and increased demand for California services. The shortfall was predicted to reach $25.4 billion. Cutting could not possibly be enough.

Brown began with symbolic moves, cutting staff cell phones and hosting a low-key inaugural, adopting the personal austerity that suited him anyway (the mattress on the floor from his first terms still remained part of his image). Then, less than a month after taking office, Brown presented his proposal for addressing California's economic distress. It was, he conceded, "a tough budget for tough times."[1] He recommended cuts of $12.5 billion, most of it from welfare, social services, and higher education. He also advocated a tax hike—or, rather, an extension on existing sales and income taxes as well as an increase in vehicle license fees. That last proposal was particularly worrisome to Democrats, because it was a hike in the vehicle license fee that helped inflame anger against Gray Davis and lent energy to the recall effort. Consistent with his campaign pledge, Brown proposed that the taxes should be presented to voters in a June election. If voters refused, Brown said he would propose yet another round of cuts. The state's legislative analyst reviewed Brown's package and called it a "good starting point for legislative deliberations." It was also, the analyst added, "more straightforward" than the convoluted budget gimmicks advocated by Schwarzenegger.[2]

In its private deliberations, Brown's administration feared the worst. Without new taxes, aides contemplated deep cuts in state fire-protection and health services, including elimination of health programs for the indigent—reductions with potentially far-reaching and extreme implications for California, with its annual fire emergencies and abundant population of poor, mentally ill people. Funding for public schools also would be cut "by a large amount," in the words of one nervous assistant.[3]

The legislature fiddled. There was plenty to dislike in Brown's package—it's hard to like a plan that cuts services many depend on and that raises taxes in tough economic times. Liberals flinched at elimination of California's redevelopment authorities, entities that had sometimes abused their authority but were responsible for transforming blighted areas in some cities. Moreover, the agencies were popular: they had the power to dole out tax breaks and exemptions for businesses locating in redevelopment areas, which gave them built-in constituencies that complained loudly at the prospect of elimination. Conservatives, meanwhile, deplored Brown's determination to increase taxes, with or without public support. The state's representatives thus went to work on their own alternatives, laboring through the spring to come up with a budget that was, for liberals, less painful and, for conservatives, less reliant on new revenue.

One point of contention was the budget for California's university system, Pat Brown's pride and his son's occasional whipping boy. In his proposal, Jerry suggested that extensions of the state's income taxes, sales taxes, and license fees could partially offset the need for tuition increases at the state's universities. Without the extensions, he proposed to slash spending on the universities, and school administrators warned that students could then face tuition hikes of more than 30 percent, from $11,124 to $14,700 (for in-state students, excluding room and board). That had precisely the intended effect: it mobilized students and put them at odds with Republican legislators, who then became identified with tuition hikes. Brown and his allies were pleased.

The legislature, meanwhile, sat on Brown's proposed tax extensions, and though he signed a number of so-called trailer bills that incorporated some of his proposed cuts, including some for education, the legislature rejected the revenue side of his package. Democrats were prepared to go ahead, but Republicans, who commanded just enough votes to prevent Democrats from securing the necessary two-thirds majority on tax hikes, blocked the revenue portions of the main budget bills.[4]

On June 16, Brown did what no other California governor had ever done: he vetoed the budgets produced by the legislature.[5] He made it abundantly clear whom he felt was to blame. "Republicans in the legislature blocked the right of the people to vote on this honest, balanced budget," Brown said in his veto message. "I am, once again, calling on Republicans to allow the people of California to vote on tax extensions for a balanced budget and significant reforms...If they continue to obstruct a vote, we will be forced to pursue deeper and more destructive cuts to schools and public safety—a tragedy for which Republicans will bear full responsibility."[6]

Legislators were stunned. Brown "angered members of both parties" with his veto, the Associated Press reported. One group of Republican lawmakers complained that it was actually Democrats who were obstructing a fair deal by insisting that voters only be allowed to consider tax hikes, not a broader government restructuring. Charles Calderon, the Democratic majority leader in the assembly, said Brown's veto "prolongs the public confusion" over where the state was headed.[7] The senate president, Darrell Steinberg, a Democrat, said he was "deeply dismayed." The assembly speaker, John Perez, another Democrat, blamed Brown for failing to deliver the votes needed for passage. The *Los Angeles Times* said

Brown's action was responsible for "opening wide a rift within his own party and throwing the state's financial future into limbo."[8]

Publicly, Brown promised to keep working with Republicans to find a compromise on taxes and fees. Privately, he was delighted. The legislature's rebuff, he said in 2016, cleared the way for him to run an outsider campaign on behalf of the tax extensions, pitting his popularity against that of the legislature and allowing him to argue more forcefully and naturally to voters. It was, he acknowledged later, a "gift."[9]

First, though, Brown had to have a measure to campaign for, and it took months to hammer out the details of what voters would consider. He led with a three-part proposal: increasing the state income tax on couples earning more than $500,000 a year for five years, increasing the state sales tax by a half cent for four years, and "locking up" most of the revenue from those increases to pay for K–12 and community-college education. The last of those elements was intended to enhance the measure's political viability.

Meanwhile, the California Federation of Teachers, one of the state's most powerful labor groups, moved forward with a tax initiative of its own, one that emphasized taxes on the rich and thus was dubbed the "millionaire's tax." And then a wealthy and influential Los Angeles lawyer and civic activist named Molly Munger advanced yet another tax proposal, this one aimed more squarely at schools. In economic terms, Munger's proposal had merit: schools were popular among California voters dismayed at their decline since the 1980s, and Munger's proposed tax was an across-the-board hike in income taxes of 1 percent. Her plan eliminated the sales tax hike, which would affect the poor dispropor-tionately, and the reliance on very wealthy taxpayers, whose incomes fluctuate more wildly than those of working people and who are more able to leave the state with their assets, both of which contributed to California's boom-and-bust budget. Moreover, unlike Brown's proposal, Munger's locked in rates permanently, providing a reliable stream of revenue into the future, while Brown's tax hikes were temporary. Brown and his camp leaned on Munger to back down, but she would not, arguing that voters were uniquely prepared to accept her proposal and that to withdraw it would be "public policy malpractice."[10]

Those who argued for a tax hike of some sort worried that the three competing proposals would doom one another, as voters, ever temperamental, would throw up their hands and vote against all of them. Anticipating that, Brown and the CFT joined forces in support of a single proposal that contained elements of each, though with a heavier emphasis on Brown's approach. The combined measure reduced the sales tax hike from a half cent to a quarter cent and placed an income tax surcharge on the highest earners. That tilted the burden toward the rich, sweetening its political tastiness while increasing its volatility. Brown saw the political benefits of the package and enthusiastically endorsed it.

That left Munger, and she persisted, refusing entreaties from Brown and Gust that she shelve her idea in favor of unity. "It's awkward for friends of both of them," said Bill Carrick, a leading Democratic political consultant in California.[11] Munger's plan had merits, but it did not have Brown. At first, the governor tended to business in Sacramento as the tax debate played out, but when Proposition 30 began to struggle in the polls, he hit the stump. Some worried that it was too late. An October poll showed support dropping below 50 percent, and legislators began to backpedal.[12] John Perez, speaker of the assembly, praised Brown for campaigning but added, "It would have been great if he had started on Day 1."[13] Dan Schnur, a moderate and popular Republican operative then at USC, warned in early November that Proposition 30's "prospects were waning" and urged Brown to withdraw his support for the high-speed train, which he argued was undermining Brown's contention that the tax hike was urgently needed to patch the state's finances. Dropping his treasured train, Schnur said, would "convince voters he is serious about conserving money."[14]

Privately, Brown's camp was less concerned, and he certainly never considered dropping the train. Despite some slippage in the final weeks, Brown's internal polling showed strong support for the tax hike among young people, especially students, and the campaign, guided again by Ace Smith, targeted those voters in the home stretch. The campaign's polling modeled turnout more cleverly than the public surveys, correctly anticipating that President Obama, running for reelection on the same ballot, would galvanize young people and liberals, boosting turnout in those sections of the electorate and tweaking the overall vote. But Brown was not about to take victory for granted. At the moment that pundits began to lose hope for the initiative, Brown barnstormed the state, charmingly accompanied by his corgi, Sutter, who appeared with the governor and even sometimes on his own. Sutter, a gift from Brown's sister Kathleen, joined his adoptive owner as the two blitzed campuses. The measure's support stabilized.

Results were so close that newspapers published on the morning of November 7, the day after the election, were reluctant to call the race definitively. By the following day, however, Proposition 30's victory was clear, as was Brown's. Seasoned political analysts marveled that California, home of the property tax revolt, happily endorsed raising its own taxes. George Skelton, the veteran political columnist for the *Los Angeles Times,* gave Brown his due: "The wily old pol pulled it off," he wrote on November 8.[15] The measure's success vindicated Brown's budget vision: it secured $6 billion toward eliminating the state's shortfall. It vindicated his faith in voters: he had asked for their support and hooked his fortunes to it, even when others were alarmed. And it ended speculation about California's impending demise. The comparisons to Greece stopped, as did talk of the "failed state" and California's ungovernability.

Brown was pleased, if reserved. "We are cutting, and now we have more revenue, but that revenue will be used prudently and judiciously," he said on November 7.[16] Asked whether the new taxes would embolden Democrats to raise spending, Brown enjoyed himself in response:

Well, I was preparing myself for that question. I reviewed the first book of the Bible, the Genesis. The story of Joseph and the Pharaoh. The Pharaoh had this dream about these lean cows and these fat cows. He didn't understand what it meant, so he summoned Joseph, who happened to be in prison at that time, and Joseph explained to him that there is going to be seven years of plenty and seven years of famine. So when those seven years of plenty come about, you have to save all the crops and put them in your granaries so that when the famine comes you are ready. And seven years later, that's what happened. If you look back, we have periods where money flows in and then we have periods with not enough money. We need the prudence of Joseph going forward in the next seven years, and I intend to make sure that this is the story we look [to] for our guidance.[17]

Finally, did the results suggest a personal mandate? "There are two things I'm very skeptical about," he said, in a case of significant understatement. "One is mandates and the other is legacies. So I'm just going to carry on."[18]

Brown expected performance from his assistants and was not quick with compliments or praise. He came to appreciate and rely on McFadden, but when describing her role to others, he invariably began by saying that she was a strong writer, among the highest of compliments from Brown. McFadden, who organized and supervised Brown's entire staff, felt the praise as mild, though she was inclined to be amused by it more than hurt.

And Brown could be hard to read. Evan Westrup, who would become Brown's principal communications deputy through the third and fourth terms, came away from their first meeting convinced it had not gone well. Brown asked him about his college professors and other aspects of his life that seemed off point, and it took Anne, also present, to bring the conversation back to the job. "I was totally confused," Westrup conceded later.[19]

As that meeting suggested, though, Brown knew enough of his own shortcomings to recognize where he needed help. McFadden and Gust provided much of it. They made sure aides understood that Brown appreciated them, and they pushed Brown himself to reach out. Though Brown instinctively was more driven by ideas than principles of management—"I am not a manager," he said emphatically in 2019[20]—he attended staff functions, happy hours, birthdays, and the like in his third and fourth terms, tending to those details he had ignored in his previous time as governor.

The rewards of working for Brown, those close to him said, were not those of compliments or raises or praise. They came from the realization that he was in pursuit of genuine and lasting change, that he was determined to improve the lives of Californians and address the most pressing needs of his state in this, his last great opportunity. For most, that was enough.

Students helped put Brown's tax increase over the top. There was mischief in that, because Brown's relationship to the education system his father had so enthusiastically built was complicated, sometimes to the point of dark. In the 2000s, so the joke went, Jerry Brown was the worst governor for California's higher education system—since Jerry Brown.

Brown's sins against the university were not all tangible. He was stingy with spending, but that was true beyond higher education. More puzzling was his seeming lack of appreciation for the work of teachers and administrators. He wondered aloud why they needed to make so much money, why they deserved so much time off. Shouldn't the rewards of educating young people be remuneration enough? he asked. Wasn't there "psychic income," as he put it, associated with the good work of teaching? Those were questions asked with a willful indifference to the lives of those he was questioning, callousness Brown never would have demonstrated to, say, farmworkers.

In his first terms, Brown's frugality and rhetoric had revolved around the state's declining resources, especially after Proposition 13 reassembled the state's revenues. The university had survived that crisis—elementary and high school education, which relied directly on property taxes, suffered more acutely. The university held its own through the Schwarzenegger years, too, and the economic collapse of 2008 and 2009. Brown held higher education hostage during the Proposition 30 campaign, galvanizing students by warning that tuition increases would be needed if the tax extensions failed. But the measure passed, and the university was released unharmed.

In 2012, all that was past. The tax increases had been approved. The economy was on the mend. Students, teachers, and administrators naturally assumed that the recovery would mean reinvestment in the university. Brown, as usual, refused to be taken for granted.

Far from bestowing goodies on the university, he renewed his challenge to its mission. The campuses, he argued to the *Los Angeles Times,* needed to "reconfigure themselves so that they are more effective and they're able to do excellent work, but do it in a way that will not keep the costs escalating."[21] Leaders of the university felt slighted, but Brown professed to being puzzled at their reaction. Similarly, he advocated for online education, though privately he would acknowledge that his own education was most influenced by those with whom he had lasting personal contact, including Ivan Illich and Gregory Bateson, to name two.[22]

Brown ended up between two poles on the university. He helped win modest budget increases year after year—3 or 4 percent—but he opposed tuition increases, depriving the university of the money that would have come from those hikes. That was a defensible position in political terms, but it substantially reduced the effect of Brown's nominal support for expanding university programs. He struggled with the balance between the university as a research institution and as a center of teaching, particularly for undergraduates. Frustrated by endless discussions over compensation and efficiency, Brown retreated from closely supervising the university. It continued on its own, largely uninfluenced by his stated views.[23]

In retirement, Brown acknowledged that he had not much changed the university system. "I thought the university could be more integrated in the pursuit of a more coherent framework of learning," Brown said. "That didn't seem to be the multiversity's nature."[24]

California's prisons were overflowing, and the problem had gone from worrisome to urgent. The system was built to house eighty thousand inmates, and by the time Brown returned to the governorship after his long hiatus, it held 156,000. That made it the largest prison system in the United States. In addition, more than one hundred thousand men and women, mostly men, were under state parole supervision—again, the most of any state in the country.[25] Prison overcrowding so taxed the system that it was impossible for inmates to receive the mental and medical care they were entitled to.

In 2009, a panel of three federal judges ruled the system unconstitutional and ordered a reduction in prison population: the state, led by Attorney General Brown, appealed. Two years later and five months after Brown returned to the governorship, the United States Supreme Court upheld the panel, concluding that California was violating the rights of its inmates to be free from cruel and unusual punishment as guaranteed by the Constitution's Eighth Amendment. "Crowding," the Court concluded, "creates unsafe and unsanitary conditions that hamper effective delivery of medical and mental health care. It also promotes unrest and violence and can cause prisoners with latent mental illnesses to worsen and develop overt symptoms."[26]

California's prison crisis dovetailed with Brown's misgivings about the criminal justice reforms he had supported in his first terms as governor, which over time had taken on a new cast. Determinate sentencing appealed to his sense of fairness in the 1970s, but it had become increasingly punitive in the years since, as each legislature—and then the public—found new crimes to be appalled by and dictated long sentences in response. The instinct toward harsh punishment in response to new outrages was most demonstrated in 1994, when California voters, shocked by the kidnapping and murder of a twelve-year-old Petaluma girl named Polly Klaas, approved the state's "three strikes" law, which doubled the mandated sentence for any felon convicted of a second offense. For a third felony, that defendant would be required to serve twenty-five years to life in prison.[27] The system appealed to voters' frustration at repeat offenders being allowed to commit crimes over and over again, and, for reasons never quite explained, it applied the rules of baseball to criminal justice. Three strikes and you're out, the reasoning went. Whether or not that made sense as a matter of crime and punishment, it had decided effects on a crowded prison system.

Confronting Governor Brown, then, was a problem that included elements of justice, constitutional law, fairness, cost—and his own misgivings about his contributions to the problem. To comply with the Court's ruling, he needed to reduce prison crowding; to enforce the will of the public, he had to do so in a way that would not endanger safety; to conform with his own sense of political order, he wanted to place responsibility for criminal justice at the appropriate level of government. Compounding the tension was a personal element: The judge who led the panel that was forcing change in California was Stephen Reinhardt, who had been instrumental in launching Brown's career. Now, decades later, it was Reinhardt who was forcing Brown to act, and Brown who was resisting the demands of his friend and ally.

Another idea came into play. Brown drew upon a Catholic theological principle known as subsidiarity, the concept that problems are best addressed at the level closest to them—that governments, for example, should refrain from taking over problems that individuals or families are best equipped to confront. In the context of social and political organization, subsidiarity suggests that nations should delegate authority to states when a problem is within their ability to handle and that states similarly should defer to local agencies when possible. Applying subsidiarity to the problem of criminal justice in California meant, in Brown's formulation, pushing inmates out of the state system and downward, toward cities and counties. The resulting proposal became known as realignment.[28]

Brown first advanced realignment in early 2011, and the legislature passed a bill adopting it in March. The reforms went into effect in October, just a few months after the Supreme Court had upheld the lower court finding that California's prisons were constitutionally unfit. The fundamental principle of realignment was that local law enforcement—probation departments and sheriffs—was better suited to supervise low-level offenders than were the state prisons and parole boards. That meant pulling offenders without sexual or violent criminal histories out of prison and incarcerating them in local jails. That would alleviate prison overcrowding and would prevent the public safety and political consequences that would result from simply releasing convicted criminals. Upon their release from jails, those inmates were to be turned over to county probation departments rather than state parole officers.

All of which added up to a huge reconsideration of the way California jailed and supervised criminal offenders. When Matt Cate, the director of the state's Department of Corrections, first heard of Brown's plans, he flinched. "I understand why we need to do something big with the prison population," he said at the time. "But this seems too big to me."[29]

Within a year, realignment had taken a significant bite out of the state prison population, which dropped by more than twenty-seven thousand in the twelve months after realignment went into effect, in late 2011.[30] After that initial burst, however, prison populations increased slightly. Two more efforts were needed to bring the state into compliance with the Court-ordered reductions. Both reversed decades of tough-on-crime initiatives that had dominated criminal justice in California during the years when Brown was out of office.

First was a voter-approved amendment to the 1994 three strikes law. In the aftermath of that law's passage, some voters had been surprised at the draconian application of the measure. Iconic was the case of Jerry Dewayne Williams, who was convicted of stealing a slice of pepperoni pizza on July 30, 1994. He had multiple previous felony convictions, so under the rules of three strikes, he was sentenced in early 1995 to twenty-five years to life for the pizza theft. Dan Lungren, then the California attorney general, defended the sentence as being given to "precisely the type of person" three strikes was intended to punish—repeat offenders seemingly unable or unwilling to reform.[31] Perhaps. But the specter of sending away a twenty-seven-year-old man, even a repeat offender, for his entire adult life for the crime of petty theft struck some as beyond the intention of three strikes. Some prosecutors, notably the Los Angeles County district attorney, Steve Cooley, began to draw back from asking for the application of the third strike for nonviolent offenses. On November 6, 2012, California voters reconsidered their earlier vote on three strikes, this time scaling it back and allowing the sentence of twenty-five years to life to be imposed for a third offense only if that offense was "serious or violent." The vote, from the same electorate that had long pioneered tough sentencing, was greeted by policy makers nationally as an indication of a new era in criminal justice reform. It was evidence, said one, "that taxpayers are ready for a new direction in criminal justice."[32]

Trimming three strikes helped curb the flow of permanent inmates into the California system, but other tough-on-crime laws continued to swell the prison ranks. Then, in 2014, voters approved yet another measure that relaxed the strictures adopted during the years when lawmakers attempted to arrest away the scourge of crime. This time, the target was nonviolent drug offenses and low-level property crimes—neither of which was exactly victimless, but the arrests had the effect of incarcerating those guilty of relatively minor offenses alongside much more serious criminals. Spearheaded by the San Francisco district attorney, George Gascón, and presented to voters as Proposition 47 on the November 2014 ballot, the measure sought to reclassify a number of drug and property felonies as misdemeanors. Other prosecutors and law enforcement organizations opposed the measure, to no avail. Voters approved it on November 4, suggesting that commentators who perceived a new direction in the California electorate were right. California, once the vanguard of tough criminal sentencing, was leading the nation down the opposite path.

Brown was the engine behind realignment, and though others took the lead on Proposition 36, Brown backed it, and he later crafted and raised money to pass Proposition 57, which broadened the opportunities for parole for some inmates while extending more protections to juveniles charged with crimes. Voters approved that measure, too, despite a desultory campaign by police unions to defeat it. When all three reforms were in place, California's prison population turned down and eventually dipped below the caps imposed by the federal courts.

There was criticism of Brown and of each of the proposals he helped shepherd through. Crime ticked up modestly in the early 2010s, and some pointed to one or more of the initiatives as being responsible. Nevertheless, California by the time Brown left office was vastly safer than it was when he started (part of a broader national trend during the same period). And that safety came even as its prisons returned to normal levels of occupancy, safety, and constitutionality.

For Brown, it was a valuable corrective in a long trip down the halls of retribution. "What do we do to them?" Brown asked of inmates sentenced to very long prison terms under the old rules. "Locking someone in a cage and having guards who are not allowed to be familiar, very mechanistic, lockdowns and gang members, crazy people yelling and screaming, dope being smuggled in, tobacco being sold, people being prostituted, people being raped. Is that a good thing? It doesn't sound like it, does it?"

That system grew at the expense of reason, and Brown was pleased at his attempts to rein it back in. "You have to at least think: 'How do we make it better?' I've been working on that for a long time."[33]

In July of 2012, the California Energy Commission released a series of reports analyzing the effects of climate change on California from myriad perspectives. It was the third batch of such studies, the first of which was mandated by Governor Schwarzenegger via executive order in 2005, creating a state Climate Action Team and requiring regular reports to the governor and legislature regarding the state's progress toward responding to climate change. The reports delivered in 2012 were the first such updates provided during Jerry Brown's tenure. They were startling in their revelations about California's vulnerability to the greatest looming ecological disaster of modern times.

In one sense, California was lucky. Thanks to early bipartisan appreciation for the dangers of climate change, the state led most of the country in amassing and analyzing data that could help guide responses. In other respects, however, the state was startlingly exposed. California is large and encompasses many climates with varying degrees of vulnerability to climate change. It depends on snowpack for its water supply, and warm winters threaten the amount of snow that might fall and the cool temperatures needed to hold it in place for late spring and summer melting. According to one 2012 report, the state's warm areas are destined to grow warmer, producing "heat waves [that] will be more frequent, hotter and longer."[34] Its forests and their neighboring communities are susceptible to fire, and that danger will grow: "Earlier snowmelt, higher temperatures and longer dry periods over a longer fire season will directly increase wildfire risk." San Diego already thirsted for water; that thirst would deepen. Statewide energy demand would increase. Faster-rising seas, already up seven inches along the coastline in the past century, would increase the damage caused by coastal storms and could flood valuable land and infrastructure, from the Port of Los Angeles to the ring of wetlands, highways, levees, seawalls, and even fire stations spanning the area around San Francisco Bay. Wildlife would suffer, as would agriculture, a major industry of the state, which boasts the largest and most bountiful crop production areas in the nation.

The reports, which represented the collective work of more than 120 researchers, were bracing in their specificity and consensus: this was not a problem for future generations, the studies made clear. It was real and present and called for immediate responses, from relocating fire stations to rethinking crop selections to adopting new predictive methods for analyzing infrastructure investments.

Ken Alex, a policy adviser to the governor, welcomed the findings and underscored the urgent need for policy makers to recognize the science and respond to it. "We accept that cigarette smoking causes cancer and that HIV causes AIDS," he said. "As a state, we make decisions based on those scientific considerations. We are not in the same place with climate change."[35]

Brown's engagement with climate change as governor was hardly a turn for him. He had been touting the merits of environmentalism at least since the early 1970s, after the Santa Barbara oil spill injected the issue into California politics and he began to think beyond conservation in considering the fate of the earth. Water pollution, offshore drilling, smog, noise pollution, acid rain, nuclear power—all these had crossed Brown's desk as governor and occupied his thoughts when he was a candidate for state and national office. Climate change, however, was environmentalism with a new dimension, one that spoke of survival itself—one that possessed the gravity that had always attracted Brown's intellect. And he had the resources of his office, second in America only to that of the president himself when it came to marshaling a response to a growing global threat. In California, he said during a 2016 interview, "we have the vision, we have the precedent, we have the institutions, and we have the support of the public."[36]

Pausing and reaching deeper, he added: "Most of politics is pretty mundane. I try to make it more grand. I try to think of this big flow of history." He digressed to consider Luther and the Catholic Church, nuclear weapons and the history of education, a riff only he would attempt. And then, just as suddenly, he was back: "That's why climate change is the most consequential program in terms of California leading the way. We have the capability. We have the research. We are very well positioned. It reaches broadly, and California is very well positioned to lead."[37]

Brown led at all levels. On the basics, he launched a website in August of 2012 to debunk the growing group of cranks, many emanating from the energy industry, who sought to deny or downplay the significance of climate change. He called the site Climate Change: Just the Facts and targeted it at what he called a "small-but-vocal group" that "has spread misinformation about the science, aiming to cast doubt on well-established findings and conclusions."[38] That was in cyberspace. On the ground, he helped create a regional plan for preserving Lake Tahoe, a liquid jewel of northern California (shared with Nevada) threatened by depleted snowpack and coastline development. He issued one executive order in March of 2012 to accelerate the availability of electric cars in California; a second order, just a month later, called for the state to curb energy purchases and follow guidelines in a new Green Building Action Plan, familiar to veterans of the Office of Appropriate Technology from Brown's first incarnation as governor.[39]

Initially, Brown's efforts in California complemented a growing non-partisan awareness of climate change and its implications for mankind. As such, he attracted attention but not much controversy. That would soon change. As the politics of Washington were upended in the following couple of years, the contours of the debate would adjust, as would Brown's place within it. He would graduate from state leader to international icon. He took office as a young maverick interested in solar energy and space exploration. By the time he finished, he would be recognized around the world as the nation's most prominent defender of the earth itself.

Brown had a knack for suiting California and being well suited to it. In the 1970s, California was a wacky and uncertain place, and Brown seemed carved from it, with his refusal to adapt to political norms, his mattress on the floor, his rock-star girlfriend. By the time he returned, both he and his state had matured. He was married and graying; California had sobered into its role as leader, not just of the kooky but also of the thoughtful. Brown had always been frugal, but that was regarded in the 1970s as just part of his oddity; later, his instincts were those of a seasoned politician, familiar with California's boom and bust and determined to ride that cycle responsibly. As Brown resumed his governorship, his instincts and those of his state merged, this time more constructively than they had in the 1970s.

Even baseball returned to form. Beginning in 2010, the San Francisco Giants, Brown's hometown team, commenced a run that would allow the team's fans, for the first time since the Giants came west, to talk of their franchise as a dynasty. The Giants won the World Series that year, then won it again in 2012 and yet again in 2014. They were the dominant team of the decade, yet underdogs throughout—immigrants to California who made good despite the odds, exemplars in each of those regards.

Brown's budgets for his third term documented California's return from the precipice and his resumption of command. He first warned of a "tough budget for tough times" and urged the legislature to join him in the difficult work of cutting services and raising taxes. The legislature had to be dragged into the debate, and Brown only got his tax increase after elected officials of both parties had largely given up. By the following year, he was looking forward to the ballot measure that would undergird the recovery, and he talked of the economy continuing "to slowly recover."

In 2013, presenting the third budget of his third term, Brown boasted that his spending plan "finally puts California in a path to long-term fiscal stability." There was still risk, he warned. "What must be avoided at all costs is the boom and bust, borrow and spend, of the last decade." But there was hope in sight, within the grasp of a government committed to realizing that "fiscal discipline is not the enemy of democratic governance, but rather its fundamental predicate." In January of 2014, the end of his third term, Brown declared victory. "With a decade of intractable deficits behind us," he wrote, "California is poised to take advantage of the recovering economy and the tens of thousands of jobs now being created each month."

Brown was gracious in victory, but his pride was unmistakable. "Each of you," he wrote to the legislators, "can be rightfully proud of the role you played in helping to make this happen."[40]

# 20

# A Brief History of a New Politics

P at Brown was the first Democratic governor of California in the twentieth century to be reelected. Jerry Brown was the second. California went for Nixon in the presidential election of 1960, when he lost, and in 1968 and 1972, when he won. The state voted for Reagan in the presidential contests of 1980 and 1984, both of which he won easily. The state elected Republican governors Reagan, Wilson, Deukmejian, and Schwarzenegger in the 1960s, 1970s, 1980s, 1990s, and 2000s. California favored every Republican candidate for president from 1952 to 1988 with the exception of Barry Goldwater in 1964, and Goldwater was a washout everywhere. George W. Bush carried the state in 1988.

And then the California Republican Party hit a wall. As of 2011, when Brown returned to the governorship, every single statewide office was held by a Democrat. Party registration overwhelmingly favored Democrats, and the Democratic Party advanced positions that were popular with the electorate on issues from education to housing to immigration to the environment.

Political realignment was accompanied by cultural adjustments. Brown grew up in his father's California. Rivalries split the state horizontally: it was Giants versus Dodgers, San Francisco versus Los Angeles, with San Diego as a major appendage but an afterthought in politics, culture, and sports. San Francisco was labor and liberal, Los Angeles business and conservative. By the 2000s, those lines had been redrawn: San Francisco and Los Angeles anchored a liberal stripe along the coast, and labor had gained influence in Los Angeles—even *Los Angeles Times* workers, first its press operators and later its journalists, unionized. The political lines in California then ran vertically: a liberal Democratic coast contained most of the state's population and political power, while a small but steadfastly conservative Republican stripe ran up the state's Central Valley and Sierra Nevada foothills.

If you lived close enough to see the ocean, the saw went, you were a Democrat. Indeed, when Hillary Clinton faced off against Donald Trump, in 2016, she carried every California county that borders the ocean but one—tiny Del Norte County. Her victories included those in San Diego County and, amazingly, Orange County, the latter an iconic Republican stronghold.

What happened? Two things: demographics and the environment.

California's culture and politics began to change in the 1960s. In the south, Los Angeles drifted steadily away from its conservative moorings. The *Los Angeles Times* both led and reflected the shift. When, in 1972, the paper endorsed Richard Nixon for president, it precipitated a near rebellion within the staff. The paper's loyalty to Nixon reflected its political and family roots; its staff, meanwhile, lacked those connections and was appalled by Nixon, Vietnam, and Watergate. The following year, Otis Chandler decreed that the paper would no longer endorse any candidates for president or governor, an edict that remained in place until the 1994 gubernatorial election, when the *Times* endorsed Pete Wilson, and the 2008 presidential election, when the paper backed Barack Obama.[1]

The paper's shifts were mirrored in Los Angeles itself. Tom Bradley became mayor in 1973, a year before Brown captured the governorship, and held that post until 1993. Bradley was the city's first African American mayor and its longest-serving chief executive. Bradley was hardly a radical. He was a police officer and had grown up in the LAPD. But he brought together African American voters across the southern reaches of the city with liberals, especially Jews, on the city's Westside. Decades of rule by police chiefs and Republican mayors faded in the 1970s, and with them disappeared the *Times*'s support for those forces.

Underlying these changes was the transformation of California itself. Between 1960 and 2010, California's population more than doubled, from fifteen million to thirty-seven million. The fastest-growing segment of that increase was among Latinos, who went from being a significant minority group to, in 2014, the largest ethnic group of all, bypassing whites. Those trends continue, and California, which by the early 2000s lacked an ethnic majority, is on its way at the time of this writing to being a majority Latino state.

The political impact of those changing demographics was, at least at first, less than dramatic. Latinos grew faster as a segment of the population than as a percentage of the electorate. Many were immigrants, some in the country illegally and ineligible to vote. Even in cities such as Los Angeles, where Latinos formed a huge segment of the population, they remained underrepresented in government into the 1990s. That changed.

Politics hit home for many Latino Californians in the 1994 gubernatorial election, the race that pitted Kathleen Brown against Pete Wilson and that became a referendum on immigration once Wilson endorsed and championed Proposition 187, which promised to deny state services to anyone in the country illegally. It was shatteringly significant for California Latinos, who initially seemed untroubled by the proposal but swung against it late in the campaign. Frank del Olmo, the deputy editorial page editor of the *Los Angeles Times,* was allowed the rare opportunity to publicly dissent from the paper's editorial position— on the pages of the *Times* itself—and astutely predicted the political implications of Wilson's support for Proposition 187.

"By aligning himself with the immigration issue in its most nativist form, he has given legitimacy to an ugly streak of bigotry in California. And Latinos everywhere will never forgive him for that," del Olmo wrote. "Wilson's pro-187 campaign will stick in our craws for generations."[2]

Truer words were rarely written. But it needn't have happened that way. Latinos might have fallen into the Republican fold—the party's positions on abortion, for example, might have fit Latinos more comfortably than did those of Democrats. But immigration, especially given the racial language employed by Wilson and then more vehemently by Trump, was a deal breaker. From 1994 on, Latinos in California and elsewhere wheeled against the Republican Party. The fastest-growing demographic group in the United States had been persuaded to align with the Democratic Party: for Republicans, it was a nightmare, one rooted in the history and politics of California.

And then there was the environment.

In the early years of the modern environmental movement, Democrats and Republicans, especially in California, stayed fairly close on environmental protection. That was politically advantageous in California, where voters from both parties ranked the environment at or near the top of their lists of concerns. As noted earlier, Republicans and Democrats responded with comparable fervor to the Santa Barbara oil spill, and Earth Day crossed party lines.

That alliance began to fray around 2000, however, when Al Gore emerged as a leading voice on climate change, or global warming, as it was more commonly referred to in those days. Gore's work was vital. The 2006 documentary *An Inconvenient Truth,* which featured Gore exploring the dire and fast-approaching consequences of a warming planet, introduced the topic into modern politics and helped energize the world to respond. It also had the effect of associating that campaign with Democrats and liberals, polarizing a debate that called for unity of purpose.

Nationally, Republican leaders found themselves in the uncomfortable—if not entirely unfamiliar—position of denying solid, apolitical science. By the 2000s, majorities of Republicans in many parts of the country simply did not believe that climate change was real or that it posed much of a threat. That, of course, was redoubled with the campaign and election of Donald Trump, who famously rejected climate change as a hoax perpetrated by the Chinese government.

Shifting allegiances on climate change had another effect in California. They contributed to the withering of the Republican Party and the disappearance of its credibility with voters. A 2017 survey by the Public Policy

Institute of California found that 72 percent of Californians (including 66 percent of likely voters) agreed with new state laws responding to climate change. Although Democrats were far more likely to support those policies than Republicans, 42 percent of Republicans agreed as well, a sizable chunk of a party whose national leadership denied the existence of the problem and rejected government efforts to respond to it. "There is broad consensus for the state's efforts to address climate change," observed Mark Baldassare, the president of the PPIC.[3]

That had obvious implications for environmental policy in California. It gave Brown and his allies ample room to work, knowing that the public was solidly in favor of those efforts. Less remarked upon were the implications for the GOP generally. Continuing to argue against science and to refuse to respond to a problem that the electorate accepted distanced the party's leadership from its membership, especially in California.

The emergence and energizing of Latinos and the disavowal of environmental protection as a party value combined to have ruinous effects on Republican strength in California. The state that gave rise to Earl Warren, Richard Nixon, and Ronald Reagan became increasingly hostile to Republican candidates and ideas. In 1998, 46 percent of Californians registered as Democrats, 35.8 percent aligned with the Republican Party, and 12.4 percent registered but declined to state a party affiliation. Over the course of the following twenty years, Democratic registration held fairly constant: 44.4 percent registered as Democrats in 2018. Republican registration, meanwhile, dropped to 25.1 percent, and "decline to state" registrations more than doubled, to 25.5 percent. In other words, by 2018, more Californians declined to state their party preference than registered as Republicans.[4]

By 2010, the electorate that put Brown back in office had morphed into one much more comfortable with his politics than the one that had voted him in during the 1970s. Brown had grown up in the twenty-eight years that he was absent from the governorship. So had California.

# Part Six

## Icon

# 21

# Resistance Leader

It was a sunny morning in Sacramento in June of 2017. Jerry Brown was working the phones. President Obama's health-care law, the Affordable Care Act, was under attack in Washington, and Brown was trying to kill the measure that was trying to kill the law. He sat on a sofa in the California governor's mansion, a cup of coffee by his side. Books were strewn across a nearby table, and he carried a pad of paper, though he barely glanced at it. Aides placed the calls. Once the recipient was on the line, Brown joined. He did not take notes, nor did he consult the notes he had made beforehand.

First up was Brian Sandoval, governor of Nevada, where Senator Dean Heller was seen as a potential Republican vote to protect the health-care system. Sandoval had not supported Obamacare, as the act was known, but he was reluctant to see it go, and Brown wanted Sandoval to speak up publicly on behalf of it. Brown stressed how much difference it was making in California. "We have people who rely on that care," he said. The cost of replacing Obamacare in California, Brown said, would roughly equal the amount that the state paid for its vaunted university system. Could a future governor be counted upon to make the kinds of cuts necessary to keep Californians insured if Obamacare disappeared? If not, what would become of those men, women, and children who had acquired their insurance through the federal program and stood to lose it? He hoped for Sandoval's help in fighting off those who would restructure health care at the expense of those who needed it.

Next call: Senator Susan Collins, of Maine. "I know a little bit about Maine," Brown began. "I ran for president there a few years ago." He shifted to the point. Losing Obamacare, he said, would deprive countless Californians of therapeutic drugs, treatment for mental illness, and remedies for other ailments. "It would be devastating for us." Moreover, the consequences of such a vote on American politics were real. Collins liked to dabble with what was left of the political center, occasionally breaking with her party or at least hinting that she might. She valued bipartisanship and cooperation, as Brown well knew. So he pushed that button. This proposal, Brown said, fed on divisiveness, not unity. "I'm very worried about the increasing division in our country," Brown said.

In between calls, Brown conferred with McFadden. Where was the Ohio governor, John Kasich? Could he be counted on to rally Republicans in defense of the act? And "what about our friends in Arizona?" Brown asked. "Any chance of getting McCain?"

The next call was to Senator John McCain, of Arizona. "We gotta lot of veterans here in California who depend on this coverage," Brown said, addressing the Senate's best-known veteran. "I don't know what we would do" if it were repealed. "This is way beyond normal politics." To lose this coverage so abruptly, he said, would cause "havoc" and "poison further our political life."

There was a pause while McCain spoke. Brown responded: "I'm seventy-nine, John. I don't have to bullshit anymore." For McCain to stand by and see the health-care law eviscerated, Brown added, would be "the biggest hit to the greatest number of people in your political life."

Brown hung up. "I guess it's simple," he told a visitor, speaking almost to himself. "If this happens, a lot of people are going to get hurt." Three weeks later, the United States Senate upheld Obamacare by a single vote. John McCain cast the deciding ballot.[1]

Jerry Brown was serving his fourth term as California governor when he was called upon to defend Obamacare. Every campaign had presented challenges, and the fourth race unfolded under a new set of rules. The partisan primaries had been eliminated, replaced with a top-two system. Still, party loyalties affected the precampaign sifting that settled the field. Once Brown announced his intention to seek a fourth term, his overwhelming popularity chased off any Democratic challengers as well as most ambitious Republicans. Democrats Gavin Newsom, Antonio Villaraigosa, and Kamala Harris all thought about a run but decided against it; Meg Whitman turned down the chance for a rematch. Ultimately, the leading opponent to Brown was Neel Kashkari, a Republican and a former assistant treasury secretary who had played an instrumental role in the nation's economic recovery but who had never held elected office. Kashkari was intense, with piercing eyes and a demanding speaking style. He was articulate, politically moderate, and vastly overmatched.

Brown and Kashkari debated just once, and Kashkari did his best. He criticized Brown's plans for a high-speed rail line, which Kashkari called the "crazy train"; he charged that criminal justice realignment was releasing "dangerous people onto our streets"; he blamed Brown for chasing off business investment—Tesla had just announced its plans to build a battery factory in Nevada, not California—and he bemoaned the prevalence of poverty amid California's general prosperity.

Brown was unfazed. Debating in a tiny Sacramento television studio on a Thursday night for an election that he was almost certain to win, he nonetheless tangled roughly with Kashkari. "What a salesman," Brown said to Kashkari at one point. "I guess you learned that on Wall Street, where you sold all that stock." Kashkari looked puzzled, amused, and a little desperate.

On its merits, Brown defended realignment, which he said was largely a success in its first two years. He argued that Tesla was demanding too much in tax relief and defended his overall record. "California's not perfect," he said. "We've got our problems. But boy, what momentum do we now have."[2]

Brown won. "He who perseveres," he said, "shall be saved."[3]

Jerry Brown was old enough to have lived, briefly, without the threat of nuclear weapons. He was seven years old when Hiroshima burned.

In his first tour as governor, Brown had challenged the propriety of the University of California's place in the development and testing of nuclear weapons. He had called for the university to separate itself from the nuclear weapons research being conducted at the Lawrence Livermore Laboratory. He framed the question in grandiose, even apocalyptic terms, describing himself as a "prophet against the tide, for life and against death."[4]

The regents rejected that call, but Brown continued to fulminate about nuclear weapons and their implications for society. He supported arms control and a freeze on nuclear weapons development. In 1982, campaigning against Pete Wilson for the United States Senate, he aggressively challenged Wilson over the nuclear freeze. Brown taped an ad featuring well-known personalities doing what they did best—Dodgers third baseman Ron Cey, conductor Leonard Bernstein, actress Candice Bergen—and proclaiming that they wanted to keep on doing it. The ad then segued to the image of a mushroom cloud billowing behind a group of children, with one child saying: "I want to go on living." "Pete Wilson opposes the nuclear freeze," the announcer said. "Jerry Brown supports it. Vote for your life."[5]

Wilson howled that the ad was "character assassination," but it reflected two things: the growing popularity of arms control as a political issue and Brown's continued preoccupation with the nuclear threat.

Nor was Brown's concern limited to nuclear weapons. He had reservations about nuclear power as well. After first hesitating—proponents argued, correctly, that it could provide a significant alternative to oil and gas—Brown generally opposed the technology. He had fought licensing of the Diablo Canyon nuclear power plant, near San Luis Obispo, and announced at the No Nukes concert, in 1979, that he "personally intend[ed] to pursue every avenue of appeal" if the federal government green-lighted the project. Brown also headlined a 1979 antinuke rally in Washington, DC, where he joined Tom Hayden, Jane Fonda, Ralph Nader, and other activist friends and leaders to denounce the risks of nuclear power, freshly highlighted by the Three Mile Island accident. Nuclear power, Brown told the crowd, was a "psychological addiction" that was "storing up for generations to come evils and risks that the human mind can barely grasp." Protesters marched and carried signs. They chanted, "Hell, no, we won't glow."[6]

Though Brown's denunciations of nuclear power were sometimes cabined by his duties as governor, he was generally associated with the no-nukes movement of the 1970s and 1980s. Working behind the scenes, he produced more subtle but lasting change. It was under his leadership that the California Public Employee Retirement System, known as CalPERS, drafted guidelines that effectively prohibited its investment in any utility that derived 20 percent or more of its electricity from nuclear power. Given the enormous power of California's investment portfolio, the restriction had far-reaching effects. "That, more than anything, killed the financing of nuclear power," said Nathan Gardels, who participated in that effort.[7]

Brown's immersion in the policy and politics of nuclear weapons and energy, then, was thorough by the time he entered his second round of gubernatorial terms. Nevertheless, a 2015 book by William Perry, American secretary of defense from 1994 to 1997, riveted Brown's attention. "I know of no person who understands the science and politics of modern weaponry better than William J. Perry," Brown wrote of Perry's memoir in the *New York Review of Books*. "We should take heed."[8]

Perry's memoir, which Brown first read in manuscript form, described his long journey through the world of nuclear weapons development and containment, a journey that led the scientist and policy maker through the Cuban Missile Crisis and across the Cold War. His story was full of successes, but even those victories often seemed attributable to luck as much as to design. And Perry, writing at a moment when many policy makers imagined the threat of annihilation being in retreat, sounded the opposite alarm.

During the Cold War, Perry wrote, the United States faced almost incalculable danger. The Soviet Union was an aggressive adversary, committed to an ideology of world domination and in possession of a nuclear armory that included thousands of warheads, mounted on land and at sea, some fixed, some mobile, some on aircraft. Once launched, the missile-based systems were difficult, sometimes impossible, to recall. Annihilation stood at civilization's door across continents and generations. Time and again, sometimes without the public knowing it, the end of humanity loomed just moments away.

Then, after creaking and wobbling for a bit, the Soviet Union suddenly gave way.

America's most heavily armed and devoutly hostile adversary, almost overnight, disappeared from the face of the earth. One day the Berlin Wall held back masses; the next it was rubble to be swept away. To the West, it was almost too much to have hoped for. Policy makers imagined a grand "peace dividend," the reallocation of resources so long squandered in holding back a foe. Men and women across the world breathed easier, confident that the threat of a mushroom cloud enveloping still another city had at last receded.

Perry argued that such relief was powerfully misguided. The Cold War's threat, he wrote, had been matched by sophisticated and highly tuned systems for detecting danger. Both sides were dangerously armed but also on hair-trigger alert, conscious that mistakes could be as catastrophic as an intentional attack. With the fall of the Soviet Union, however, the systems and trust required to communicate during emergencies fell into disuse, and while the danger of all-out war between nations diminished, the threat of a nuclear explosion did not disappear but actually grew. "The likelihood today of a nuclear catastrophe," he said, "is *greater* than during the Cold War."[9]

Moreover, that danger was so intense, so immediate, that it undermined other evidence of human progress—the decline in violence, the freeing of societies by market forces. "This upward progress is indeed hopeful," Perry wrote, "but nuclear conflict could in a blink of history be the ultimate reversal of all such outcomes.

"Our chief peril," Perry added, "is that the poised nuclear doom, much of it hidden beneath the seas and in remote badlands, is too far out of the global public consciousness. Passivity shows broadly."[10]

It was the paradox of Perry's warning that captured Brown's intellect— its challenge to conventional wisdom spoke directly to Brown's skepticism. He read it and reached out to Perry directly. They were unlikely allies in some ways: Perry was a mathematician steeped in nuclear science and politics, a man of science to Brown's background in spirituality, a veteran of Washington and the type of wise man that Brown once cut his teeth challenging. Brown had run against both Jimmy Carter and Bill Clinton; Perry had served in each of their administrations. And yet Brown and Perry hit it off. Brown visited Perry in Palo Alto; the two spoke for hours, then regularly after that. When Perry's book attracted little attention, Brown reached out to reviewers urging them to take note. When they didn't, he contacted the *New York Review of Books*, where editor Robert Silvers suggested that Brown write something himself. Brown did, and produced his own review.[11] Brown appeared at a nuclear weapons forum in 2016; he opened by saying, "I am here because, basically, I talked to Bill Perry, and he scared the hell out of me."[12]

He checked his reaction with others. "I called Colin Powell and asked, 'What do you think?'" Brown said. "Colin Powell is not worried…Deterrence is holding."[13] He called members of Congress, scientists, academics. Most told him they were concerned but not preoccupied.

That only bothered Brown more. Sanguinity may be the characteristic Brown most deplores, and in this case he argued that it led to the opposite of what was needed: intense vigilance and action. He saw evidence of neither. On the contrary, leaders insufficiently worried about the threat of war were instead building for it, he observed during two long ruminations on this topic, one in 2016 and another in 2018. "Complacency and routine," he said, spitting out the words. "A lot of what we do is to block off the awareness of danger…Why aren't people worried about nuclear weapons? Why aren't people worried about another war?"

As he spoke—partly to an interviewer, partly to himself—Brown reviewed devastating moments of historical obliviousness. There was the firm conviction that alliances would prevent a world war in the early twentieth century. Until they didn't. The disbelief that Hitler would actually pursue his promised campaigns of Jewish annihilation and world domination. Until he did. In each case, false optimism led to profound despair and tragedy on a scale that the earth had not known. Those, Brown observed, were failures caused by exaggerated confidence, unwillingness to face up to real threats, and reliance on hope over analysis. And then he was back to the present.

326 • JIM NEWTON

"The problem with deterrence," he said, "is that it works until it doesn't. One of the ways you achieve deterrence is by constantly ratcheting up, which we've been doing for over fifty years. So when it fails, it'll be a big failure."[14]

He paused. "These are big issues," he said, "bigger than the mundane governor issues."[15]

Brown's thinking on nuclear weapons, his immersion in climate change, his public statements on immigration and health care—all were accelerated by the 2016 American presidential elections.

Brown tiptoed through the early months of that contest, refusing to run without quite saying so. Interviewed by journalist Wolf Blitzer in September of 2015, he pointedly did not endorse a candidate—this at a time when Hillary Clinton was the party's presumptive nominee, Vice President Joe Biden was debating a run, and Vermont senator Bernie Sanders was making his case. "I haven't endorsed anybody," Brown said on CNN. "I will say though, about the Clintons, with some experience, they are very formidable. And I would not underestimate Hillary Clinton."[16]

Brown's playful, slightly coy responses to Blitzer kicked off a brief moment of "Why not?" speculation as analysts considered whether the recently reelected governor might make a fourth try for the White House. Writing in *Vanity Fair,* Michael Kinsley took a long look at Brown and wondered at how history seemed to have bent his way: "All that New Age stuff that seemed so weird when Brown ran for president the first time (in 1976) is still part of his repertoire. But he'd be helped if he ran by the extent to which yoga and brown rice and so on have become part of American culture. Jerry Brown hasn't gone mainstream (or at least not much), but mainstream has gone Jerry Brown."[17]

Not this time. Having dangled the possibility of a run, Brown then edged back out, hinting that he was too old. If he had a time machine, Brown intimated, maybe he'd try again. But he didn't.

Instead he joined the rest of the country in amazement at what developed. The Democratic field largely shaped itself around Clinton, with Sanders emerging as her principal opponent. Sanders peppered

Clinton with a populist potpourri of proposals—breaking up big banks, increasing taxes on capital gains, offering free college to young people, increasing the minimum wage. Clinton dodged any sustained combat with Sanders, convinced that patience would prevail. She was right, mostly. Sanders never posed a realistic threat to Clinton, but he prevented her from sealing her nomination until the eve of the Democratic convention, and their fractious struggle reinforced questions about Clinton's electability.

It was the Republican contest, however, that went off the rails. More than a dozen Republican contenders—the Florida governor, Jeb Bush; Florida senator Marco Rubio; Texas senator Ted Cruz; the New Jersey governor, Chris Christie; Dr. Ben Carson; and the Ohio governor, John Kasich, generally were considered the first tier, with a trailing pack of wannabes—waged a series of bizarre debates, gradually knocking each other off while one of the race's dark horses, flamboyant executive Donald Trump, survived round after round. Trump's crude, combative, and sometimes racist appeals flummoxed fellow Republicans and enraged his opponents but found purchase with a small but solid section of the Republican base, enough to let him outpoll his rivals in the crowded field. By the time the GOP leadership understood the gravity of his candidacy, Trump was far ahead and, it seemed, beyond the reach of normal politics and accountability

In a season of mind-boggling remarks, three seemed to spell Trump's doom. On June 2, closing in on the Republican nomination, he questioned the ability of a federal judge, Gonzalo Curiel, to fairly consider a pair of cases alleging fraud by Trump University. Curiel, born in the United States and raised in Indiana, is the son of two naturalized American citizens from Mexico, which Trump had sharply criticized for "sending" illegal immigrants to the United States. ("When Mexico sends its people, they're not sending their best," he had said in announcing his candidacy, in June of 2015. "They're bringing drugs. They're bringing crime. They're rapists.") Trump also famously advocated building a "wall" to halt future illegal immigration and promised that he would make Mexico pay for it. Given these comments, Trump declared that Curiel could not be fair to him because Curiel is "of Mexican heritage." It was,

Trump said, "an inherent conflict of interest" based solely on the judge's ethnicity.

A month later, in July, at the Democratic National Convention, a Muslim couple, Khizr and Ghazala Khan, honored their son, an American soldier who died in action in Iraq. Mr. Kahn spoke for the couple. He brandished a copy of the Constitution and questioned whether Trump had ever read it. Responding, Trump implied that Ghazala Khan, a Muslim woman, had been muzzled, that her faith required her subjugation. "Maybe she wasn't allowed to have anything to say," Trump ventured.[18] Trump had attacked the parents of a fallen soldier and questioned the role of their faith in the expression of their grief. Democrats sputtered. Trump continued.

And then, once the nomination was secure, reporters obtained a tape of Trump speaking with an *Access Hollywood* reporter, Billy Bush, both unaware that they were being recorded. On the tape, Trump boasted of making a sexual advance on a married woman. In the wave of controversies that would envelop Trump, it was easy to forget the last one as the next one crested. For posterity, then, this is what Trump said on the *Access Hollywood* tape: "I did try and fuck her," he said. "She was married." Trump described taking the woman furniture shopping—go figure—and weirdly added: "I moved on her like a bitch." As their bus pulled up to its destination, Trump and his trailing interviewer ogled a publicist who was meeting them. Over Bush's delighted giggles, Trump popped in a breath freshener "just in case I start kissing her." He was confident he could do so, he said, because "when you're a star, they let you do it. You can do anything." What did mean by "anything"? "Grab 'em by the pussy," he said.[19]

Presidential historians will long read those words and wince. They would have sunk any other candidate for the nation's highest office—history's ash heap is filled with the remains of candidates who committed far less egregious sins—but by then the country had entered a bewildering political phase. Trump bumbled and swaggered through the general election, and the common consensus was that Clinton would win on Election Day. That was partly right: Clinton did win the popular vote, including a gigantic victory in California, but Trump edged her out in the Electoral College. He was inaugurated as president on January 20, 2017. It was, Trump said, the biggest crowd ever to witness a presidential inauguration. Except, of course, that it was not.[20]

Trump's victory created a welter of conflicting implications for Jerry Brown. On matters of substance—notably, immigration and climate change—it denied Brown and California the support of the White House, potentially limiting Brown's ability to complete the balance of his agenda in his final two years in office. His plans for a high-speed train and tunnels to complete the state water system, for example, both depended on support from the federal government. Trump had campaigned in favor of federal infrastructure improvements, but would he follow through? California had just thumbed its nose at Trump, and Trump was not known for forgiveness.

Politically, the results demonstrated the degree to which California's identity was entirely its own: Hillary Clinton won the national popular tally by just under three million votes. She carried California by more than four million, though, meaning that her entire margin of victory— and then some—came from California. Put another way, without California, Clinton not only would have lost the Electoral College, she would have lost the popular vote as well. For Brown, that reinforced a fundamental message from his electorate: it detested Trump, and Brown need have no political reservations about challenging the new president.

Finally, the results presented him with a platform, though not one he had sought. With the presidency in Republican hands, Brown was the nation's senior Democrat and leading chief executive. He commanded America's largest state and was the longest-serving governor in the nation. He moved on an international stage, as recognized in Paris and Beijing as he was in San Francisco and Fresno. Brown did not see himself as a rebel leader, but Trump's victory ensured that his final years in office would take on that cast, as California happily announced itself as the center of the resistance to Washington. T-shirts were printed, fists clenched, crowds activated. Like it or not, Brown, at age seventy-eight, became the leader of that resistance, the intellectual and spiritual head of a government in exile, one that was accepting of immigrants, generous with health care, admiring of science, awed by nature, respectful of God. California could not be ignored, as it continued to grow in size and influence. By 2016, it had become the fifth-largest economy in the world, and Brown, once destined for the priesthood, stood atop it. He did not ask to champion resistance to a nation whose presidency he had sought three times; indeed Brown resisted the mantle. But it suited him.

One out of every eight of Donald Trump's constituents lived in California. No matter. The new president wrote off the state almost from the beginning. "In many places, like California, the same person votes many times; you've probably heard about that," he said. "They always like to say, 'Oh, that's a conspiracy theory.' Not a conspiracy theory, folks. Millions and millions of people."[21]

All of that was false. There was no evidence of anyone, much less "millions and millions of people," voting in California "many times." But Trump not only imagined widespread fraud escaping the notice of California's authorities, he also dreamed up the idea that people in the country illegally were behind the supposed fraud. Illegal immigrants, in fact, were at the heart of Trump's California critique. In Trump's view, California's approach to illegal immigration amounted to "deadly and unconstitutional sanctuary state laws," which provided "safe harbor to some of the most vicious and violent offenders on earth."[22]

Those two themes—California as a haven for dangerous illegal immigrants and as a repository of illegal voting—overlapped in Trump's vision of California, and the intersection was manifested in his response. In early 2018, Trump complained that California was allowing "animals" to stay in the country by offering immigration sanctuary rather than cooperating with officers of the Immigration and Customs Enforcement (ICE) agency. "We're getting no help from the state of California," he said. "They have the highest taxes in the nation. And they don't know what's happening out there. Frankly, it's a disgrace...If we ever pulled our ICE out, if we said, 'Hey, let California alone. Let them figure it out for themselves,' in two months, they'd be begging for us to come back. They'd be begging. And you know what? I'm thinking about doing it."[23]

As if to prove it, the attorney general, Jefferson Sessions, popped up in Sacramento a few weeks later. Without consulting Brown or California's attorney general, he announced that the Justice Department was filing suit against California to challenge its laws protecting immigrants who were in the country illegally. "Federal law is the supreme law of the land," said Sessions, once a strident advocate of states' rights. "I would invite any doubters to go to Gettysburg... This matter has been settled."[24]

Given the federal supremacy to which Sessions was a new convert, he went on, California's refusal to enforce deportation statutes represented a violation of federal law. The result, he added, was an "open border," a "radical idea" that Sessions and Trump rejected. After ticking off actions by local officials who resisted cooperating with federal deportation efforts, Sessions then accused the California state legislature of passing laws deliberately intended to thwart those same efforts. "This is a great state. I don't want to be in this position of having to challenge these laws," he said. "But I can't sit by idly while the lawful authority of federal officers [is] being blocked by legislative acts and politicians."[25]

Brown was incensed. "It's not what you'd expect from an attorney general of the United States," he privately said the next day. "It's more political games. He is a politician, a questionable politician on civil rights. He has polluted his office with politics."[26] Sessions's motives were clear, Brown said. They were to politicize immigration and demonize California. What was worse was that Sessions had misrepresented California's position. "He also lied," Brown said. "I'm not for open borders...I amended the bill substantially to allow criminals to be deported."

As for Trump's threat to withdraw ICE from California, Brown had withheld public comment because he wanted to avoid a tit for tat with the president. Privately, however, he was contemptuous. "I didn't react to it because I don't think it's serious," he said. "What's he going to do? Pull in the army? I'm sure we would find a remedy if he did that. But it's inconceivable. It would be a dereliction of duty...The fact that he would say that is more like a barroom conversation than White House discourse."[27]

*     *     *

The legitimacy of Trump's presidency was questioned almost as soon as he took office. During the summer presidential primaries, Rob Goldstone, a business associate of Trump, emailed Donald Trump Jr. to say he had been contacted by a Russian government official offering to provide damaging material about Hillary Clinton. The information "would incriminate Hillary and her dealings with Russia and would be very useful to your father," Goldstone wrote. "This is obviously very high level and sensitive information but is part of Russia and its government's support for Mr. Trump." Trump's son could, of course, have rejected that information on the grounds that it was inappropriate—not to mention illegal—for a campaign to accept something of value from a foreign power attempting to influence an American election. That was not Donald Trump Jr.'s response. "If it's what you say," he answered three minutes after receiving the email, "I love it especially later in the summer."[28]

That was clear evidence of the campaign's desire to work with Russia, and Trump's ties to Russia and its leader, Vladimir Putin, became increasingly clear as investigations occupied the Trump administration's first two years. Among other things, it was revealed that even as he was seeking the presidency during the summer of 2016, Trump was pursuing a deal to build a skyscraper in Moscow. Those negotiations included offering Putin a suite in the skyscraper, presumably in return for his favorable consideration of the project. Trump repeatedly lied about those connections, suggesting that he was hiding culpability, if not necessarily illegality.

That gave ample ammunition to Democrats, who seized upon Trump's relations with Putin and questioned his odd docility in the face of Putin's authoritarianism. That scrambled certain assumptions about domestic and international relations: for generations, it was Republicans who most aggressively challenged Russian—then Soviet—trustworthiness. Now it was Democrats who emphasized Russian meddling and ill intent. Some Republicans, meanwhile, downplayed Putin's misdeeds in an effort to excuse Trump's apparent affection for the Russian leader.

Brown was a Democrat. He lobbied to save Obamacare. He led his party on climate change. But he rejected his party's pivot on Putin, regardless of the implications it had for Trump. Brown's concern for the threat of nuclear weapons overrode political considerations and caused him to continue to view Russia and Putin as essential partners in a common campaign to protect the world from annihilation. With that as his polestar, he resisted his party's move and staked out his own, typically iconoclastic, terrain. Whatever his faults, Brown said of Putin, it was the obligation of an American president to court working relations with him in order to minimize the threat of war between great powers and to join forces in opposing the proliferation and possible misuse of nuclear weapons. The odd effect of all that was to have Brown, who loathed Trump and was despised by the president, standing up for him in connection with the notion of maintaining relations with Russia. Not for the first time, Democrats puzzled over Brown's actions.

He was not naive. Brown understood that Putin had intervened in Syria, where Russian forces helped prop up the vile regime of Bashar al-Assad, and Brown recognized that Russia was illegally occupying Crimea, politically a part of Ukraine. But those were matters for debate, he argued, not grounds for alienating Putin and threatening Russia with an ever-encroaching NATO, which Brown viewed as provocative and destabilizing in a world already dangerously unstable.

"Deal with the issues in Syria and killing diplomats and Ukraine and Crimea and all the rest of that," he fumed in 2019. "But that doesn't warrant a nuclear blunder that kills billions of people, or millions."[29] Brown recognized that his endorsement of engagement with Russia put him uncomfortably closer to Trump than to his fellow Democrats on that issue, but he refused to bow down to party orthodoxy or even basic party strategy. Asked what he thought of the Democratic approach to Putin, Brown responded: "I think it is stupid for Democrats to be attacking Putin on all issues and not holding open the channel of nuclear dialogue."[30]

Brown was not to be moved from this position. In mid-2019, he was at home one morning and considering the question of how to evaluate leaders and their responsibility. Was Putin more evil than, say, George W. Bush? he asked. Bush was responsible for thousands, perhaps hundreds of thousands, of deaths in the Iraq War, yet Bush, at least at that moment, was seen as a somewhat benign elder statesman, a nostalgic counterpart to Trump. Brown's point? Leaders of major powers need to talk to one another in order to protect their nations and civilization. Moral judgments, he insisted, must take second place to global responsibility.[31]

For Brown, the big picture—an existential threat—would always prevail over the smaller demands of party loyalty and partisan advantage. He could be shrewd and transactional, but he would not alter his fundamentals. He would not criticize Trump for seeking a relationship with Putin. He would, however, challenge Trump on almost every other aspect of his character and presidency.

Over the course of sixteen years as governor of California, Jerry Brown appointed eleven justices to the state's supreme court and hundreds of judges to the state's trial and appellate benches. Just as he sometimes confounded and angered university officials for his unorthodox management of and appointments to that system, so, too, did his reshaping of the judiciary follow unconventional lines.

Three of Brown's appointees from his terms in the 1970s—Rose Bird, Cruz Reynoso, and Joseph Grodin—were wiped out in the retention election aimed at Bird. Further events subsequently eroded Brown's remaining influence on the court. Wiley Manuel, the court's first African American justice, whom Brown appointed with Bird in 1977, was stricken with colon cancer and died in 1981 at the age of fifty-three. In his place, Brown named Otto Kaus, who stayed just four years before getting cold feet after narrowly beating back a retention challenge. Kaus retired in 1985. Frank Newman, another Brown appointee, came to the court from UC Berkeley and returned to human rights work in 1982, when Brown replaced him with Grodin, who left after the fateful anti-Bird campaign. Brown's final appointee during his first terms, Allen Broussard, the rare jurist appointed by both Pat and Jerry Brown (Pat put Broussard on the superior court in Alameda County, and Brown elevated him to the state supreme court in 1981), survived the same retention challenge that spooked Kaus in 1982 and served until 1991, when he retired and was replaced by Ronald George, a Wilson appointee.

Together, that meant that the bench Brown helped create in the 1970s and early 1980s was gone by the time he returned, and the court was once again stacked with Republican appointees. Brown started over. In his third and fourth terms, he remained committed to diversity on the bench—in terms of gender, ethnicity, and legal background.

Over the course of his final terms in office, Brown named four justices to the California Supreme Court: Goodwin Liu, Mariano-Florentino Cuellar, Leondra Kruger, and, just as his final term was concluding, Joshua Groban. Liu is an Asian American man, Kruger an African American woman, Cuellar a Latino man, and Groban a white man. They joined a bench whose chief, Tani Cantil-Sakauye, is an Asian American woman appointed by a Republican, Schwarzenegger. As a result, the court that Brown shaped during the 2000s was among the most ethnically diverse and gender balanced of any in the world.

It had its commonalities, however: three of Brown's four appointments in his final terms graduated from Yale Law School.[32] The exception, Groban, graduated from Harvard. And of the four, not one had ever served as a trial judge before joining the supreme court. That irritated some California judges who aspired to a position on the state supreme court and felt their experience was ignored by a governor who had little regard for their work. Brown was unfazed. "I was appointing a lot of women and minorities who hadn't been appointed before," he explained. "Where do you find them?"

Brown came to office both times after long runs of Republican and conservative governorships, periods during which appointees were generally white men drawn largely from the ranks of prosecutors, a pattern followed not only by governors Reagan, Deukmejian, Wilson, and Schwarzenegger—all Republicans—but also by Davis, a Democrat. "There wasn't a lot of material to work with" at the trial-court level, Brown said. "You're not going to find a Liu or a Cuellar toiling on the superior-court level."[33] So Brown looked to other sources—the academy, the federal bench, his own circle—to find justices who generally upheld liberal principles (no Brown justice, for example, was likely to oppose gay marriage or abortion rights in California) and whose defining characteristics were intellectual acumen and independence.

He was also strategic: Brown waited until after the final elections of his tenure to name Groban, his legal affairs secretary, to the bench. That delayed Groban's first date with a retention election, proving that Brown had learned from the Bird episode of previous decades. Brown bought Groban time to make his own record in the event that some future movement sought to clear Brown's appointees in a Rose Bird reprise.

Brown's supreme court justices ensured that his influence would continue to be felt in the law of the nation's most populous state for years after he was gone, but his most fundamental contribution to California's judiciary was likely felt in its more modest ranks. By the time he had wrapped up his governorship in 2019, Brown had appointed more than a third of all the sitting judges in California, and he had transformed the character of that sprawling legal network.

More than 50 percent of Brown's appointees were women. Roughly 40 percent were nonwhite. That, as Chief Justice Cantil-Sakauye said near the end of Brown's tenure, was "a huge step" in a state whose judicial ranks once were overwhelmingly white and male.[34] Brown also insisted on diversity of backgrounds in his trial and appellate court appointments. Whereas the overwhelming majority of judicial appointments under his Republican predecessors went to prosecutors and former prosecutors, Brown reached out to public-interest lawyers, defense attorneys, and public defenders. The San Francisco public defender, Jeff Adachi, emphasized what a difference that made. Before Brown, he said in 2018, there was a saying: "Unless you're a prosecutor, don't even put your application in."[35]

The bench that Brown formed in the 2000s was the nation's largest. It was 36.3 percent female, and around one-third of its judges were men and women of color.[36] More than 10 percent identified as Hispanic, the largest percentage in the history of the California judiciary. Because of Brown, California's judges were younger, more female, more ethnically diverse, and more populated by men and women of varied backgrounds. It wasn't always comfortable, but Brown could point to the California bench as proof of his legacy—if he were willing to discuss legacies.

# 22

# Humility

Donald Trump denied the importance and even the fact of climate change. During the campaign, he called global warming a hoax and suggested it was concocted by the Chinese government—arguments so ludicrous that many experts puzzled over how to reply. Trump's views in this area seemed so outlandish, in fact, that some commentators imagined they were a put-on. They hoped for a new, more "presidential" Trump once the election was over and assumed that among the positions he would jettison would be his scientifically unsound rejection of climate change. It was not to be. Trump continued his harangue after November, and his postelection moves included naming climate change skeptics to head the Environmental Protection Agency and Department of Energy. In California, Brown took note.

As he rose to speak to the American Geophysical Union at the group's fall meeting in San Francisco, he was given a warm standing ovation, startling even Brown, who was adjusting to becoming the leader of a nation-state in rebellion. As he warmed to the role, Brown seemed to enjoy himself. California, he noted, was well equipped and eager to lead on climate change, no matter what the message was from Washington. "We got the scientists," he said. "We got the lawyers. We're ready to fight."

He continued in that vein. "We will persevere," he said. "Have no doubt about that." Later: "We'll set the example. Whatever Washington thinks they're doing, California is the future." And then, memorably, in response to the incoming administration's threat to turn off the satellites used to monitor climate change, Brown recalled that in the 1970s, he'd argued for California to explore space. "They called me Governor Moonbeam for that," he said, as the crowd tittered appreciatively. "I didn't get that moniker for nothing.

"Well," he added, "if Trump turns off the satellites, California will launch its own damn satellite. We're going to collect that data."[1] The resulting applause may have been the most fulsome expression of appreciation ever uttered by a group of geophysicists.

Six months later, Trump withdrew the United States from the international agreement on climate change drafted in Paris in 2015. "I was elected to represent the citizens of Pittsburgh, not Paris," he said.[2] His base cheered. The rest of the world shook its head in disbelief.[3] Among those who were obviously disappointed was Jerry Brown. Trump's move, Brown replied, was "wrong on the science. Totally wrong."[4]

But Trump's decision had other ramifications for Brown. Washington's reversal of course—from the practical embrace of solutions advanced by the Obama administration to the rejection of science and international cooperation—left Brown as America's most prominent advocate for the most significant issue facing humanity. The day after Trump's announcement, Brown traveled to China, where he signed agreements with leaders of Chinese provinces and was ushered in to meet with President Xi himself. Brown, who had welcomed Xi's father to California decades earlier, was greeted with the pomp normally accorded heads of state. The joint memorandum released by the governments of China and California on June 6 referred to the "long history of successful collaboration" between the two parties. It made no mention of Trump or Washington.[5]

To Brown, Trump's denial of climate change was something worse than cynical politics or special-interest pandering—though it was both those things, too. It felt to Brown like hubris, a willful refusal to accept that there are powers greater than the presidency or the president. Few ideas mattered more to Brown than that of humanity's relationship to greater powers, whether God or the environment. In this instance, a so-called conservative thumbed his nose at those ideas, leaving the liberal, Brown, to speak up for them.

Trump's character failing, said Brown, was a lack of humility, a disconnect from faith. "I don't think President Trump has a fear of the Lord," Brown told *60 Minutes* in 2017. The president, he added, lacked "the fear of the wrath of God."[6]

Brown was required to be more than a high priest of climate change. His position as governor demanded that he fight for change in the political realm as well. In a life long lived in the gyration between the monastery and the smoke-filled room, he ultimately was called to both. In Brown's fourth term, that meant fulminating over the president's belief in God while also securing a future for California's cap-and-trade program, which allows polluters to trade credits with other polluters in an effort to reduce emissions overall. Brown launched his proposal to extend that program in January of 2017, the same month that Trump was inaugurated president.

California's cap-and-trade system was first authorized under Governor Schwarzenegger and intended to cap emissions while allowing the market to determine efficient ways to achieve those caps. In essence, some four hundred polluters were ordered to limit their cumulative emissions to a cap established by the state. They could then trade credits with each other within that limit. High polluters could buy credits from those who had them to spare, establishing an effective pollution price point. Annually, the state would reduce the cap, making credits more expensive and creating incentives for the polluters to reduce their emissions. In 2017, the program required reauthorization.

It had both friends and enemies. Some conservatives were bothered by the government imposition of a cap and argued that it chased off certain kinds of businesses, including job-rich manufacturing, by adding to the cost of doing business in California. Some environmentalists complained that the caps were too high and allowed for too many emissions. Some of them argued instead for a carbon tax, a direct way of making pollution more expensive and thus creating an incentive for its reduction. Also, by giving companies flexibility, the system allowed polluters to concentrate their emissions in some geographical areas while cutting back elsewhere, with sometimes ruinous consequences for poor neighborhoods. Brown's position was that cap and trade was imperfect but effective, far better than direct regulation in terms of efficiency and far better than an unencumbered market for addressing climate change. He supported the extension passionately.

His political problem was obvious: the extension required a two-thirds vote of both houses of the legislature, and Democrats were short of that mark.[7] Even if Brown could get every legislative Democrat on board, at least a few more votes were required. Moreover, he telegraphed his commitment to the bill, so every legislator understood that it was something he badly wanted, giving wavering legislators the power to extract other concessions from the governor. That said, Brown also had advantages: he was popular with voters, as was environmental protection. And cap and trade spun off benefits, too. Auctions held every three months by the Air Resources Board for emissions credits generated revenue that Brown could help direct toward the needs identified by legislators. In other words, he had popularity, principle, and money at his disposal.

As the legislature debated the extension bill, AB-398, Brown attempted to fend off critics from both his left and his right. He enlisted Schwarzenegger for help with Republicans, reminding them that partisanship had not historically divided Californians when it came to the environment. More important, Brown reminded conservatives that he had already signed legislation committing the state to cutting emissions to 40 percent below 1990 levels by 2030. Without the cap-and-trade system, he warned business leaders, the state would be forced to impose regulations to achieve that goal. And those regulations would be dictated by Sacramento without the flexibility of cap and trade. Realizing that the alternative would be worse, some business groups lined up behind Brown and urged their allies, most of them Republicans, to join.

That scrambled typical politics in Sacramento, where Democrats held sway and could generally govern without Republicans. This time, Brown wrangled interests, sometimes meeting with various groups in separate rooms of the capitol, generally with McFadden running the show and Brown making appearances and closing deals as needed. The energy industry wanted flexibility in addressing caps, and the environmentalist community, somewhat split, for the most part wanted low and rigid caps. The trick," said Dana Williamson, an adviser who worked on the issue with McFadden, was "finding the sweet spot"—a limit industry could live with that would still achieve the environmental goal of greenhouse-gas reduction.

Money helped. A portion of the revenue generated by the state emissions-credit auctions helped fund Brown's high-speed rail project, a bone thrown to Republicans in the Central Valley along the train route, because the project already was creating jobs there. Without the trading system, that revenue would disappear, endangering the project and the jobs that went with it. Money helped with liberals, too. To those who complained that the cap-and-trade program left the poor exposed to pollution, Brown agreed to a companion bill that would invest a portion of the money toward environmental protections for poor communities. That brought assemblywoman Cristina Garcia and others on board. Brown even agreed to spend some of the revenue on forest-fire fighting, always popular and necessary in California.

The two bills were scheduled for a vote in July of 2017. On the eve of those votes, Brown made a rare appearance at a legislative committee hearing, coming in person to make the final push for the bill most central to his mission. He was introduced by state senator Kevin de Leon, who described the bills as a product of negotiation and compromise and urged his colleagues to approve them. De Leon's remarks were business-like and political, about what one would expect on such an occasion.

Brown's were not. He arrived with notes but barely looked at them— a reminder of the challenge that Westrup and Brown's communications staff had in managing him. He came to talk about two bills but veered into the fate of America and humanity itself. "Things are not well in the Republic," he began. "America is facing not just a climate crisis with the rest of the world. We are facing a political crisis. Can democracy actually work? Is there a sufficient consensus that we can govern ourselves? That, I submit to you, is an open question."[8]

Brown had bigger questions on his mind, but he dutifully touted the strengths of the measure, emphasizing the compromise nature of cap and trade—the cap attempting to achieve environmental goals and the trade allowing businesses to respond with flexibility. Brown emphasized that the system was not of his making but called it efficient and elegant, contrasting it with the command-and-control system of regulation, which would be required in its absence. As he spoke, Brown became more impassioned, and his voice rose as his exhortations drew upon a lifetime of environmental advocacy and the sharp realization of what was at stake. "Climate change is real," he shouted. "It is a threat to organized human existence. Maybe not in my lifetime. I'll be dead. What am I? Seventy-nine? Do I have five years more? Do I have ten years more? Fifteen? I don't know. Twenty? I don't know if I even want that long."

Brown faced the committee as he spoke, with the audience behind him. But when he joked about his mortality, the audience laughed, and Brown turned to face it. "When I look out here, a lot of you people are going to be alive," he said. "And you'll be alive in a horrible situation. You're going to see mass migrations, vector diseases, forest fires, Southern California burning up. That's real, guys. That's what the scientists of the world are saying. I'm not here about some cockamamie legacy that people talk about. This isn't for me. I'm going to be dead. It's for you. It's for you, and it's damn real."

He turned again, back to the committee. "So I just ask you: take it seriously," he said, "and give us that vote."[9]

And he wasn't done. Brown touted the importance of the accompanying bill, with its focus on poor communities. Nor was he above politics. "Whatever I gotta do, I'm going to do it," he said, alluding to the wavering members of the committee and legislature. "The people who join with us, I'll do whatever I can to help you…We're not going to leave you alone here. I know it's tough."

"This," he stressed, "is the most important vote of your life…Unless you think I'm lying. And I was in the seminary for three years, studying to be a good searcher of truth. And I'm telling you: this is the truth as I understand it. The only way I can be wrong is if I don't get it, if I'm stupid and ignorant. And I'm not."[10]

Three days later, the California legislature took up AB-398. It required fifty-four votes to pass in the assembly; it got fifty-five. It needed twenty-seven votes in the senate; it received twenty-eight. Eight Republicans voted yes in the assembly, and one voted yes in the senate. Brown signed the bills the following week, extending California's cap-and-trade system until 2030.

When Brown expounded on nuclear weapons and climate change, he sometimes contrasted those existential questions with "mundane governor issues." But he did not neglect those matters. Roads and taxes, for example, may lack the moral urgency of nuclear weapons and the grinding threat of climate change, but they touch people where they live. They are not abstract, and politicians fighting for them often go down swinging. As Jerry Brown approached the final years of his very, very long time in office, he once more faced the question of whether to ask Californians to increase the amount they pay for something they value, following closely on the heels of his successful campaign for hikes in income and sales taxes to restore California's financial health in 2011 and 2012.

There were two divergent analyses of the personal implications of a tax increase for road repairs in Brown's final years. On the one hand, Brown could duck the issue and leave office without another bruising battle, playing defense with his reputation in the late innings. Conversely, the opposite argument went, he alone had the stature in Sacramento to lead others who were afraid to be out in front but might be willing to follow. Brown had the credibility with Republicans to call for more spending and with Democrats to channel the money toward road repairs rather than social programs. Brown opted to fight one more time.

Gas taxes had a certain appeal. Building trades liked them, since they created construction jobs. Californians drive and have historically shown a willingness to invest in road and highway infrastructure. In addition, and somewhat at odds with that fact, raising gas taxes would increase the cost of driving and using those roads, building in a gentle incentive to move from gas-powered to electric vehicles and thereby advancing Brown's urgent insistence on addressing climate change. Finally, there was the historical context for gas taxes. As the price of gas rose, state and federal taxes based on a per-gallon levy actually fell as a percentage of overall gas purchases. In the first few years of the twenty-first century, combined state and federal excise taxes on gasoline and diesel fuel hovered at around seventy cents per gallon; by 2016, they had fallen to around sixty cents per gallon, though computing the precise tax is complicated by overlapping fees and taxes that contribute to the overall state charge—a "bewildering array of frequently changing explicit and implicit taxes," as one think tank dubbed the system.[11]

Brown and legislative leaders concluded that gas taxes filled a substantive need and presented a political opportunity. Together, they crafted a ten-year package estimated to raise $52.4 billion. Money would be earmarked for roads and bridges, as well as transit, though spending in those areas would in part relieve the general fund of those obligations, so in some respects the gas tax represented a general tax. Money is money. The cost to taxpayers came to around twelve cents a gallon, along with a hike in vehicle registration fees. Diesel users also faced an uptick, of twenty cents a gallon. Republicans focused on the cost, Democrats on the benefit. State senator Kevin de Leon called it "the largest investment in the state's history."

The politics of a tax hike in early 2017 were favorable, but only if Brown was willing to lead. The campaign to succeed him already had begun, and candidates in that race—notably, the lieutenant governor, Gavin Newsom—were unlikely to champion a tax increase at the same time as they were currying favor with voters. No member of the legislature, meanwhile, had the stature to persuade others to follow a path toward higher taxes.

Brown stepped up. He announced his support for a tax hike early in the negotiations, then backed up his support with promises to help legislators who supported him and to oppose those who did not. Needing a two-thirds majority to win approval for the hike, Brown traveled to Concord, California, where one legislator, state senator Steve Glazer, was wavering. Backed by union leaders, Brown emphasized the local impact of increasing gas taxes: $30 million worth of construction in Concord, another $238 million in nearby San Jose, and another $97 million in nearby Oakland. In return, Brown said, residents would see improved roads and bridges.

"It's pay now or pay later, pay a lot more," Brown said. "That's the price of civilization. We've got to fix stuff and pay attention so things don't get worse."[12]

That was the carrot. Then there was the stick. Supporters of the tax hike posted on social media a huge picture of a pothole in Orinda, Glazer's home. The caption read: "Senator Glazer, fix this now—Vote Yes on SB 1." After deliberating for weeks, Glazer opted to vote against the tax hike; he was stripped of his committee chairmanship, a lesson to others who might stray.[13]

As the debate crested, many inside Brown's administration believed it was simply too much. "We're done," one aide exclaimed near the end. "We can't lift the votes."[14]

McFadden stepped in. "Nope," she replied, and she proceeded to make a last push on three wavering legislators.

On April 6, both houses of the legislature approved the tax increase. Brown indicated his support immediately and formally signed the bill on April 28. "Using a mix of public pressure, private arm-twisting, a late-night meeting at the governor's mansion and nearly $1 billion of pork, Brown showed the political acumen that's made him California's longest-serving chief executive," the Associated Press reported.

At first, it appeared that Brown and the Democrats had handed Republicans a gift. HIGHER GAS TAX IS A RIPE TARGET FOR STATE GOP, a headline in the *Los Angeles Times* read. Republicans saw it that way, too: Democrats were now on the hook for taxes, precisely what Republicans had predicted when Democrats moved into solid control of the legislature and state offices. Hoping to capitalize, Republican operatives circulated petitions to put the matter before voters in the form of a repeal of the tax hike—and then, with luck, ride a wave of voter discontent back into power in Sacramento.

The trouble with that strategy was that voter discontent failed to materialize. The tax hike went into effect in November of 2017, amid wild gyrations in the price of gas and diesel fuel. Many motorists probably could not tell how much of the price at the pump was the result of taxes compared to other factors. Republicans qualified a measure for the ballot, but it never caught fire. Brown raised money to defeat it—proponents marshaled some $40 million to defend the tax—while

Democrats were aided by ballot language that described the repeal in terms of its effect on road construction and repairs. In one ad, Brown appeared at a desk, United States and California flags behind him in soft focus. He touted the virtues of road repairs and earthquake safety, then warned: "Proposition 6 would stop these critical repairs. Prop. 6 eliminates $5 billion every year for transportation projects. Bridges and road repairs will grind to a halt. So please, vote no on Proposition 6. It's dangerous and bad for California."[15]

And then there was Trump. Although Donald Trump did not appear on the 2018 ballot, the midterm elections that November—the same ballot upon which the gas-tax repeal appeared—were widely framed as a referendum on his leadership. In California, that spelled trouble for Republicans. Indeed, it brought historic setbacks in Republican representation, including a wipeout of the GOP in what had historically been one of its most sturdy redoubts. Every single Republican congressional representative in Orange County lost his or her seat. Once the counting was over, Democrats held those and other seats across the state, tightening their hold on California politics. And Brown's gas tax withstood the challenge, winning easily and vindicating Brown's willingness to stake his reputation on it.

Brown and his staff were thrilled by the victories in cap and trade and the gas tax. Some had worried about both fights, and then both were won. Nancy McFadden, who had worked the legislature as well as the legislation, was palpably relieved and proud of the achievement. It was McFadden, more than anyone, who had the job of confronting legislators—asking for their help and threatening those who balked. She was the one, Anne Gust said, who "cracked the knuckles."[16]

McFadden loved it. "That time," she said of cap and trade, "we saved the world."[17]

What no one, least of all McFadden, knew in the summer of 2017 was that it would be her last opportunity to save the world. Years earlier, she had been treated for ovarian cancer. It was frighteningly serious but under control during her time as Brown's top deputy. Then, in the fall of 2017, it worsened. She underwent chemotherapy and lost her hair; she put on a wig and continued to work. It worsened still. She worked more often from home. She was on the phone continually and brightly predicted her imminent return. "I'll be back next week," she would say. Then it was the week after that. Then a month.

McFadden's friends worried about her and reported to Jerry and Anne that her energy was dropping, that she was fading. For weeks, the governor and First Lady hesitated, respecting McFadden's privacy and allowing her to set her own schedule.

"She had lost so much weight, and there wasn't really any discussion of her treatment," Anne said. "The doctors were saying, 'Let's get your weight back, and then we'll talk about treatment.'"

In early 2018, Anne prevailed on some of McFadden's friends to allow the Browns to visit her at home. They did in February.

By then, McFadden was weak and depleted, plainly near death. At first, they discussed other things. Jerry Brown and Nancy McFadden talked about their Catholic faith, then she asked unexpectedly, whether he thought she should see a priest. He stood quietly for a moment, until Anne interjected. "Whether you like it or not, Jerry is going to have a whole mass for you," she said. "Jerry will take care of everything."

McFadden, so nervous up to that point, suddenly relaxed. "She let it go," Anne said. The three spoke for a while more. Brown asked her what she would miss. "Everything," McFadden answered.[18]

A month later, McFadden died. It was March 22. She was fifty-nine, and she died at home. Tributes came from Clinton and Gore, from friends and former colleagues. At her funeral, Brown began by observing that she was a "great writer," touching an old nerve among her friends. But he went on to speak movingly of her passing and her importance to him and to California. Many cried quietly. Steve Maviglio, an old friend who had worked alongside her, paid especially moving tribute by recalling a commencement address that McFadden delivered to her undergraduate alma mater, San Jose State, in 2014.

"Try being kinder," McFadden advised the graduates on that occasion. "Be grateful. Live consciously and aware and not on the default setting of self-centeredness. Show courage and faith. Have purpose and passion. Trust in something."[19]

Do what you are doing.

\* \* \*

Do what you are doing. Live in the inquiry.

No two ideas were more associated with Jerry Brown, save perhaps for "small is beautiful." He spent decades mulling them over, in public and in private. He relied upon them as commands, as guides to life and governance, to focusing work and seeking out perspective.

It's worth noting, then, that the two notions are to some degree in conflict. The first suggests serenity, humility, acceptance of one's mission, and concentration of moral energy toward its achievement. To genuinely do what one is doing argues for the infusion of work with principle and objective, whether one is crushing grapes as a young seminarian or fighting for the planet as a candidate for president. It is a serious command that binds Zen and Saint Ignatius, and it forms a moral and practical foundation for a life of purpose.

The latter tacks in a different direction. To live in the inquiry is not necessarily a mission of humility. It is a call to pose questions, to challenge accepted wisdom, and to dig at presumptions that seem to pass as fact. Brown refused to accept the idea that governors have legacies, for example, when everyone around him assumed it. He bristled at liberals who believe that hierarchy thwarts creativity and who reflexively respond to suffering with laws. He wrestled with the demands of punishment and mercy, questioning both. And, as anyone close to Brown knows all too well, he can argue about anything. Even in the most casual encounters, Brown will challenge. Once, when a visitor opened a conversation by asking, "How are you doing?" Brown launched into a critique of the question. How could he be doing anything but well? he demanded. He was alive and healthy and governor and in the thick of life. It was, he insisted, a ridiculous question. Of course he was doing well.[20]

Brown's sparring on that occasion was lighthearted, indulged in for fun and for stimulation, yet it revealed something: he lived in the inquiry, or tried to. To really live in such a place is to question even the most basic assumptions. It is to wonder and to doubt, which are not the same as accepting one's place and finding peace within it. To do what one is doing, to truly do it, requires suspension of inquiry; to inquire is, or can be, to question what one is doing.

Can one be accepting and skeptical, humble and demanding? Brown is not the only person to have wrestled with those competing impulses. Consider, for example, Reinhold Niebuhr's Serenity Prayer, written around the time of Brown's birth and shared with millions through the work of Alcoholics Anonymous. "God," it begins, "grant me the serenity to accept the things I cannot change, the courage to change the things I can, and the wisdom to know the difference." When Brown was doing what he was doing, he was accepting. When he was campaigning and leading, he was practicing the courage of his convictions. He was often seeking wisdom.

To put all this another way, Nathan Gardels's observation about his friend seems fitting as well. Brown, he said, seemed torn between wanting to be a monk and wanting to be president. That's why Gardels saw the Oakland mayoralty as such a good fit for Brown. It positioned him as a parish priest, with both spiritual and earthly obligations.

Gardels's observation captured Brown at a particularly pivotal moment of his life, and it has resonance in the context of this continuing spiritual and intellectual tension. Monks seek serenity, while presidents must demonstrate the courage to change. Monks do what they are doing. Politicians—good ones—live in the inquiry. Brown spent much of his life moving between those ideas, and in that quest, he searched for the wisdom to know the difference and to apply it at the right time, toward the right result.

For those who wondered about Jerry Brown's contradictions, the answers were brilliantly on display. He made no effort to hide them. On the contrary, he had been sharing them all along.

Brown's legislative and electoral victories in 2017 and 2018 upgraded his standing in the environmental movement and established him as something approaching a wizard in California politics. With not a single vote to spare, he secured California's place at the head of a movement to which he had devoted much of his life. He defied naysayers and persuaded Californians, yet again, to raise their own taxes. Brown's reputation soared, both in California and among environmentalists worldwide.

Brown's time in office was to end in January of 2019. Before that, leaders of and contributors to the global campaign to combat climate change would gather one last time during his governorship. This time, the setting was San Francisco, and Brown was to host the event.

San Francisco warmed to the Global Climate Action Summit as only San Francisco could. This was more than a conference. It was the gathering of a tribe, a convergence of a movement, and thus it spoke directly to San Francisco's sense of itself. The San Francisco Ballet staged a special performance—*Glacier: A Climate Change Ballet*. The Fort Mason Center for Arts and Culture featured a photography and video exhibition entitled *Coal + Ice*. The ClimateMusic Project put on a six-hour event called Play for the Planet. Nearly every hotel room in the city was booked.

At Grace Cathedral, a multiethnic group of people prepared the 3:30 p.m. service, hoping that Brown and his lieutenant governor, Gavin Newsom, the city's former mayor, would attend. The group formed a line, with one small knot of men in sombreros, another of women in traditional attire from Latin America and Asia. Five women with green painted faces dangled branches and leaves; they stood on stilts, towering above the procession. "I'm a little-bit-of-everything tree," one said. "We're a non-species-specific type of tree," countered another. On the cathedral's front steps, a group of protesters objected to Brown's anticipated appearance. The governor had opposed efforts to ban fracking, arguing that as long as California required some fossil fuels for its economy, it was better off extracting it within the state than importing it from elsewhere. The protesters didn't buy it and hinted darkly that Kathleen Brown stood to be enriched by continued exploration in California. Michael Bloomberg, the former New York mayor allied with Brown on climate change, was amused. "Only in San Francisco do environmental protesters protest an environmental conference," he said.[21]

The business of the conference was to promote and grow the alliance that Brown and Bloomberg were putting together—one of state, provincial, and regional governments committed to meeting the emissions goals set by the Paris accords. One initiative begun by Brown was called the "Under2 Coalition," and set out to keep the earth's temperature from rising more than two degrees centigrade. A related effort, launched by

Bloomberg, brought together universities and businesses, also seeking to respond to climate change.

Although Trump was withdrawing the United States government from the Paris agreement, his action did not prevent states and other entities from acting on their own, and Brown's group, an "alliance of the willing," as he and others called it, aimed to fill that void. The Under2 Coalition included two hundred states, countries, and provinces, enough to qualify as the third-largest economy in the world. "We said, 'If you're out, we're in,'" the Los Angeles mayor, Eric Garcetti, said. "We are doing it for ourselves."[22]

Brown had vowed not to turn the conference into an attack on Trump—aides said he was resolved not even to mention the president's name. But when the question was put to him, he could not resist. Asked at a morning press conference how he thought historians would regard Trump's position on climate change, Brown began by saying, "It all depends on how long he's around and how much damage he can do." He mentioned three Trump initiatives: subsidizing coal production, curbing California's encouragement of electric cars, and relaxing restrictions on the use of methane. "Together, that's a major assault on the well-being of the people of California and America and the world," he said. "It borders on not only insanity but criminality." How will Trump be remembered? "I don't know," Brown concluded. "Liar, criminal, fool. Take your choice." Mary Nichols, Brown's longtime ally in the fight for clean air and one of his first appointees to the Air Resources Board—and now its chair—stood next to him as he spoke. She grimaced a little, then smiled.[23]

That evening, Brown joined supporters and legislators aboard a ferry on San Francisco Bay. It was a cool afternoon but bright and sunny, reminiscent of the afternoon in 1960 when he stood by his father's side for the opening of Candlestick Park; the ferry was electric and departed from just outside the gate of the Giants' new stadium. On board, Brown signed a host of bills, fighting off the breeze. He was accompanied by Anne and enjoyed a glass of wine. Smiling broadly, he resisted proclaiming the conference a success—it was still under way, and the battle was far too big and complicated to savor any one event, he insisted, always the combatant. Still, he conceded, it was a powerful demonstration of the world's commitment to fighting climate change, even in the face of Washington's recalcitrance.

The next day, Brown announced that California was working with a San Francisco–based earth-imaging company. Together, he said, the public and private sectors would monitor heat-trapping pollutants and trace their sources. Forty years after Brown first floated the idea, California at last would get its own satellite.

For sixteen years, California legislators had done what legislators do. They had introduced and debated bills, passing some of them and sending them to the capitol's corner office for their governor, Jerry Brown, to consider. He had sifted through the legislature's achievement pile sixteen times, first in 1975 and then, for the final time, in 2018. During those years, more than twenty thousand bills had crossed his desk.

To a remarkable degree, he was guided in considering those bills by the same principles that he had brought with him to office the first time: he studied them in detail, looking for flaws, challenging assumptions. It was not enough to convince Brown that the legislature had discovered a problem. He needed to be convinced that the problem was real, that the state of California was the best entity to address it, and that the solution created by the bill was the best way to do so.

Many bills failed one or more of those tests. Over the years, he had rejected dozens of bills that would have criminalized dumb behavior when he thought the bills were unnecessary or frivolous. In 2015, he rejected nine such bills at once, writing: "Each of these bills creates a new crime—usually by finding a novel way to characterize and criminalize conduct that already is proscribed." Rather than pass more such bills, he suggested, "I think we should pause and reflect on how our system of criminal justice could be made more humane, more just and more cost-effective."[24] He vetoed a bill to require signature gatherers to wear badges, rejecting the temptation to have the state decide "what citizens must wear when petitioning the government."[25] He vetoed a bill passed in the outrage over Donald Trump's refusal to release his income tax returns that would have required such disclosure of any candidate who sought a place on California's ballot. "I hesitate to start down a road that might well lead to an ever-escalating set of differing state requirements for presidential candidates," Brown wrote, his reason overwhelming his impulses.[26] He even vetoed a bill that would have required children to wear ski helmets on the slopes. "Not every human problem," he said, "deserves a law."[27]

Brown equivocated over some bills. In 2018, he weighed the merits of hiking California's minimum wage and found compelling arguments on both sides. Economically, he fretted, "minimum wages may not make sense." They may displace some workers, as companies pay higher wages to fewer employees. That gave Brown pause. But he recognized another dimension, less quantifiable but deeper. "Work is not just an economic equation," he noted. "Work is part of living in a moral community. And a worker is worthy of his or her hire, and to be worthy is to be able to support a family." That tipped the scales for Brown. He signed the bill raising California's minimum wage and allowing for it to increase annually going forward.[28]

Brown signed other bills, too, of course. In 2015, he shared his careful review of a proposal to establish a right to die in California. "I have considered the theological and religious perspectives that any deliberate shortening of one's life is sinful," he wrote. "I have also read the letters of those who support the bill, including heartfelt pleas from Brittany Maynard's family and Archbishop Desmond Tutu. In addition, I have discussed this matter with a Catholic Bishop, two of my own doctors and former classmates and friends who take varied, contradictory and nuanced positions." Brown elected to sign the legislation, despite his lingering reservations. "I do not know what I would do if I were dying in prolonged and excruciating pain. I am certain, however, that it would be a comfort to be able to consider the options afforded by this bill. And I wouldn't deny that right to others."[29]

His last batch of bills came in a deluge that frustrated Brown. "Motorized legislation," he complained privately as he and his staff sifted through hundreds of approved proposals at the end of the legislature's 2018 session.[30] That large stack—in Brown's final year, he would sign 1,016 bills and veto 201[31]—included many that he was expected to sign, including one that few paid much attention to but that seemed unlikely to attract any objection from the governor. The beverage, hospitality, and restaurant industries, for example, all liked a small bill that would allow large California cities to authorize businesses in their jurisdictions to extend serving hours for alcohol from 2:00 a.m. to 4:00 a.m. It did not require cities to approve that change, merely allowed them to do so. And it was natural that different locales would have different rules: what constitutes responsible drinking in San Francisco is unlikely to be identical to what defines it in El Centro. Given that evident localism, subsidiarity, which Brown had applied to problems from prison overcrowding to school management, suggested that this was a matter best handled by cities and counties, not mandated by the state.

But Brown was always a blend of principle and instinct, and this one offended his gut. "I believe we have enough mischief from midnight to 2:00 without adding two more hours of mayhem," he said in his veto message. Privately, he was more vehement.

One supporter, Brown said, had argued, "We have to support our nightlife industry." "Why?" Brown asked rhetorically. "That's the market *über alles*. We used to have Sunday closing laws. When I was in law school, Earl Warren struck them down [on the grounds that they were religiously based]. What else is there? Only the market— unfettered buying and selling by distant corporate aggregates [operating in a] multibillion-dollar dimension. That trumps thousands of years of custom and tradition and religious sentiment. Those things are unprivileged, unlike anything that deals with exchange, with buying and selling...Did this enhance our freedom? Did this enhance what it is to be a citizen or a person? That wasn't the question. The only question was the economics, the market, the profit, the loss of the situation."

The problem bothered Brown, placed his faith in tradition against the wishes of his constituents and the interests who purport to represent them. "Can the community propound a value separate and apart from markets?" he asked. Yes, he answered implicitly; it could, and he did. There would be no more early morning drinking because of Jerry Brown. He would not be bowled over by the market, would not yield tradition to fun. And as for subsidiarity, "I believe it except when I don't," he said.[32]

Brown vetoed that bill, then turned to the last piece of legislation that would require his signature during his long time in office. It wasn't much of a bill, and he didn't think much of it—it sought to raise the maximum loan amount in a pilot program being run by the state to help increase access to small loans. He signed it, "reluctantly," he said, but chose the moment to put a period on his tenure. "From the time of Moses, usury has been condemned," he wrote. "The Legislature should heed the words of Exodus 22:25, where it is written: 'If thou lend money to any of my people that is poor by thee, thou shalt not be to him as an usurer, neither shalt thou lay upon him usury.'"

And then Brown added a footnote: "And now onto the Promised Land—Colusa County!"[33]

Trump and Brown talked past each other for two years. Trump fulminated about climate change and immigration. He lambasted Brown, characterized him as a nut, and framed California politics as kooky and out of touch, drawing up old stereotypes that were out of date during Brown's first administration, painfully so by his fourth. Still, the two men never spoke directly.

Then, in the final months of Brown's term, a series of wildfires swept through two separate regions of California. One area, northwest of Sacramento, was laid waste, with hundreds of homes destroyed and, at one point, thousands of people unaccounted for. Such devastation normally would warrant a presidential visit, but both sides were wary of Trump wandering into such inhospitable terrain—and with such a potentially hostile host.

Trump's people pressed for a visit anyway. Gavin Newsom had just been elected governor, and at first his aides agreed that he would host the president. Brown, however, was still in office and unwilling to let the moment go without being present himself. Plans were shuffled: both Brown and Newsom would greet Trump, take him to the fire area, and then see him off.[34]

Trump arrived in California on November 17, landing at Beale Air Force Base, north of Sacramento. Smoke from the fires cloaked the field, making Brown, Newsom, and Trump almost invisible from a distance.

The three men, accompanied by White House chief of staff John Kelly, Jared Kushner, and two members of the military, boarded a helicopter to take them from the airport to the ravaged community named, of all things, Paradise, California. Brown sat opposite Trump while Newsom and Kushner were nearby and Kelly was off to the side. Trump did most of the talking during the forty-five-minute flight, declaiming but not asking questions. He spoke about his "good friendship" with Brown and Newsom, a remark that prompted the governor and governor-elect to exchange a brief, amused glance. "He used the word *friendship* in a way more loosely than was warranted," Brown said later. But he did not interject. As Brown noted, Trump "expressed his opinions in a way that did not invite difference or disagreement."

So while Brown and Newsom bit their tongues, Trump lectured the governor and governor-elect. "All the environmentalists support us now," Trump told Brown and Newsom. Two Democrats with lifelong support from the environmental community representing one of the most environmentally conscious areas of the world were being informed about what environmentalists wanted by a man who built golf courses and skyscrapers for a living. "They don't like to see all that water go out to sea."

Brown stewed. "The notion that the river flow is important, the way environmentalists or scientists would see it—that was not a thought that had any room," he said. "There was no space for that thought."

At the scene in Paradise, the men stiffly kept up appearances. When Trump announced that he was saddened by what he had seen in "Pleasure," as he called it, the camera caught Brown off to the side muttering "Paradise," fighting the urge to publicly correct the president's odd, even Freudian, slip. Asked by a reporter whether his visit caused him to reconsider his dismissal of climate change, the president was even more flatfooted. "No," he said. "I have a strong opinion. I want great climate, and we're going to have a forest that is very safe. We can't go through this every year."[35]

And as for forest management, Trump said more was needed. "We've got to take care of the floors, you know, the floors of the forest," he said, adding that he had recently met with the president of Finland, who had spoken of Finland's successful efforts to control fires in that country. "They spend a lot of time raking and cleaning and doing things, and they don't have any problem."[36] Finland's president later denied saying any such thing.

If anything, Newsom, whose ex-wife was then dating Trump's son Donald Jr., had been even more sharply critical of Trump than had Brown, a position that had only helped Newsom in the gubernatorial campaign. But Brown and Newsom had vowed to maintain decorum. They were appealing for federal help and resisted the urge to debate Trump at such a moment. They watched in silence as Trump dominated the stage. Trump at one point invited Newsom to join him in addressing the press corps. Newsom declined.

The governor and governor-elect's resolve to remain silent was tested at another point that day when Trump explained to them the proximate cause of the fires. "He talked about, 'You just gotta sweep up the leaves,' and management more generally," Brown said. "The idea of a prolonged drought, lack of humidity—that was very remote from the conversation."

Newsom did push back a bit, Brown said. But to no obvious effect. Trump continued to offer his observations and insights, never asking his hosts for their opinions or thoughts. "I have this phrase that you may have heard: 'Living in the inquiry,'" Brown said later. "That was not my helicopter experience."[37]

A few months after his tour of the fire area, the president erupted at California again. "Billions of dollars are sent to the State of California for Forest fires that, with proper Forest Management, would never happen," Trump tweeted on January 9, 2019, two days after Brown left office. "Unless they get their act together, which is unlikely, I have ordered FEMA to send no more money. It is disgraceful situation in lives & money!"[38] That was a lie. Trump did not, in fact, order the Federal Emergency Management Agency to cut off California, nor could he legally. Brown and Newsom ignored him.

Brown thought for himself. He believed strongly in the competing demands of order—of society's right to safety along with its obligations of compassion and mercy—and rejected the simple solutions of ideologues.

Brown as a young politician had sided most often with safety, some-times at the expense of mercy. As he grew older, he thought about forgiveness more deeply. The tension between safety and compassion occupied Brown every Friday for most of sixteen years as he weighed the applications he received for pardons and commutations of sentences as well as the actions of the state parole board that called for his review.

One intellectual guide in this deeply personal aspect of his work was Michel Foucault, the brilliant and notoriously difficult French philosophical historian. Foucault was a natural discovery for Brown. Just twelve years older than the governor, he shared with Brown a lifelong unwillingness to accept convention. He was a critical historian, deter-mined to challenge assumptions and accepted truths, and his principal intellectual preoccupation was with state power. His writing was dense and eclectic: he ranged across subjects, applying his voracious intellect and passionate politics to his historical analysis. Even Brown, who stud-ied and enjoyed classics and forced himself through the works of Ludwig Wittgenstein, found Foucault hard to follow. Brown persevered.

Foucault's grand project—cut short by his death, at age fifty-seven, from AIDS—was the quest to create an overarching history of thought. In the course of that work, he wrote histories often dismissed by historians but rich in argument and reinterpretation. He examined and produced treatises on madness, medicine, sexuality, and incarceration, the last subject being the one that had the greatest influence on Brown. Foucault's *Discipline and Punish,* among his most respected and debated works, was published in 1975, the year that Brown became governor of California for the first time.

There is nothing in Foucault's work that is intended to inform, at least directly, the decision of a governor weighing the clemency petition of an inmate. But Foucault's focus on the power of the state turns clemency upside down: from his perspective, it is the system that is suspect, not the petitioner. Neither Foucault nor, certainly, Brown denied the presence of evil or the need to punish. But Brown was informed by Foucault—and, later, by his experience with determinate sentencing—in such a way as to open his conscience to the pleas of those who had served time and who believed they had learned from it.

Those instincts were reinforced by his faith and religious training, with their emphasis on mercy and redemption. Brown believed that even those who had committed crimes could change, that age mattered, and that a man or woman who broke the law, even with violence, could learn to be peaceful again and could be trusted with freedom. These were the lessons upon which Brown had drawn in 1960, when he emerged from three years in the seminary, freshly full of the wisdom and compassion of the Jesuits, and fiercely argued from a pay phone in Berkeley with his father, the governor of California, about commuting the sentence of Caryl Chessman.

In 1960 he asked whether Catholic teaching could tolerate the death penalty—whether his father, as a good Catholic, could administer such a punishment, be party to such an offense. In 2018, older than his father had been at the time, Jerry Brown questioned the efficacy, morality, and rationality of sentences that incarcerated men and women for their entire lives to punish them for acts committed in moments of immature stupidity. "Is it right for all of them to be locked up in cages because they did something once?" he asked plaintively, weeks after his governorship had concluded.[39]

Brown granted clemency, in the form of pardons or commutations, to drug dealers and forgers and even murderers. Most did not simply go free. The majority of pardon applications came from inmates who had served their sentences and were free but hoping to clear their records. Even those who sought release from prison or supervision almost never were freed immediately upon receiving it, but Brown's grants of those petitions gave those who received them the chance to make their cases at hearings that otherwise would have been denied them.

Politically, it would have been safer to deny those petitions, as his predecessors overwhelmingly did. But Brown resolutely believed, as he said, that "there's wisdom in having the possibility of hope."[40]

And so, week after week, Brown met with the members of his clemency team. They presented him with files containing details about the original offenses—how old were the perpetrators when the crimes were committed? What were their roles in the offenses? Were the sentences just by modern standards? Or were they aberrations, imposed during a period when determinate sentencing mandated punishments that later struck Brown and others as beyond historical norms? Did the prosecutors object? What were the views of family members, those closest to the victims of serious or deadly crimes? And how about the inmates' records in custody? Did they show signs of rehabilitation? Had they obeyed prison rules, demonstrated a determination to reform? On top of those questions, asked in every case, were layers of abstractions. Was a sentence grounded in something real or was it merely reflective of society's shifting, sometimes arbitrary need to punish? How, Brown asked, could it have been appropriate for a defendant to receive a sentence of seven years to life during the decades leading up to the 1970s and later, charged with and convicted of the same crime, face a minimum of twenty-five years in prison? The crime had not changed, merely society's evaluation of it. If justice is something more than the superficial application of shifting societal norms, surely that sentence bears scrutiny.

Most petitions were denied, and most prisoners remained in custody. But some, because of Brown, had their records cleared. And some went free altogether.

Walter "Earlonne" Woods was an inmate at San Quentin with twenty-one years behind bars for attempted second-degree robbery in 1997. He admitted that during an attempted robbery, he pointed a gun at the victim. One of Woods's associates sprayed the victim with pepper spray. Woods was convicted and sentenced to thirty-one years to life. He was twenty-seven years old.

Twenty years later, Woods had served much but far from all of his sentence. He earned his GED behind bars, joined Narcotics Anonymous, and worked in the prison media program, founding a popular and often moving podcast about life in prison called *Ear Hustle*. Woods reached out to Brown to ask for clemency. "I have made profound changes in the way I think and behave," he said. Should he be released, Woods said he would dedicate his life "to working with young people to ensure that they do not pursue a criminal lifestyle as I did."[41]

Brown reviewed his petition, listened to the podcast, talked to family members and others, and concluded that Woods was no longer the man he was when he was locked up for a crime he committed in his twenties. "He has set a positive example for his peers and, through his podcast, has shared meaningful stories from those inside prison," Brown wrote. Woods, Brown was convinced, was "a sweet man" determined to make the most of freedom; prison no longer served any purpose in his case.[42] He signed the commutation on November 21. Brown's legal team contacted Woods at San Quentin, and he was released the following week, home in time for Christmas.

From then on, Woods said, "every day is going to be Thanksgiving."[43]

Woods's release got a little attention, but not much. It was one of thirty-eight pardons and seventy commutations that Brown released that day. The *San Francisco Chronicle* ran a modest story; the *Los Angeles Times* mentioned Woods in two paragraphs of a longer story. National Public Radio followed up with a short piece. No editorial pages weighed in.

This was not the typical work of a high-profile governor. His review of petitions for mercy was done far away from fire scenes and press events. It was quiet labor, performed in the sanctum of the mansion that once was his father's. There, Brown questioned as a Jesuit, meditated as a monk, read through the admonitions of Foucault. On average, he reviewed around twenty petitions every week.[44] In his later terms, he would often consult his wife and occasionally reach out to a friend or an adviser. He was charged with the opportunity to grant mercy, and he did not take it lightly.

His predecessors had considered these questions and made their decisions. Governor Deukmejian served for eight years and granted 325 pardons. Pete Wilson served for eight as well. He authorized thirteen pardons and commuted another four sentences. Gray Davis, Brown's former chief of staff and governor for an abbreviated five years, did not reduce the sentence of a single inmate.

Jerry Brown granted 404 pardons in his first two terms, along with one commutation. In his second set of terms, he issued 1,332 pardons and 283 commutations. All told, that meant he had pardoned 1,736 inmates and commuted the sentences of 284—more than all his immediate predecessors combined.

Brown finished the last of those in his final days as governor. Mercy dispensed, business done, he patted Cali, gathered up his things, and went home to the Promised Land—Colusa County.

# 23

# The Legacy, with Apologies

T ry as Brown did to squelch questions about his legacy, his final days in office and those immediately thereafter were dominated by such talk. Yes, it was often posed as an idle question, but there was merit, too, in taking stock, not so much of whether one project or another constitutes Brown's "legacy" but rather how history will regard his influence.

Brown's accomplishments were far-flung and significant, and they ranged from the subtle and long-term to the striking and immediate. Most visible was his work restoring California's economic and budgetary health. Brown inherited a state at the brink of ruin and left his successor, Gavin Newsom, a surplus and a healthy economy, the fifth largest in the world, behind only those of the United States, China, Japan, and Germany. (California's economy is roughly the size of Great Britain's.) In his final two terms, Brown twice persuaded voters to raise or maintain taxes—on income, sales, and gas. Those allowed for significant investments, mostly in technology and systems to slow global warming and respond to its effects in California.

More broadly and historically, those tax measures and their endorsements by the public marked votes of confidence in the fundamental agreement between a government and its people: the people entrust the government with their resources, and the government delivers services that the people cannot supply themselves. The people of California wanted roads and environmental protection and police and schools, and they agreed, at Brown's request, to pay for those and other services. The economy recovered, then boomed.

"Our state has been on a journey together since the worst of the Great Recession," Newsom said in his inaugural address, with Brown impatiently looking on. "Back then, we were $27 billion in debt. Unemployment above 12 percent. The worst credit rating of any state in our nation. Today, our economy is larger than all but four nations in the world. We've created nearly three million jobs and put away billions for a rainy day."[1]

Stability in the budget was important, but what allowed it was a broader achievement in the Brown years. When he took office for the second time, in January of 2011, just 38 percent of Californians believed the state was on the right track, compared to 54 percent who believed it was not. When Brown left in 2019, those numbers were reversed: 55 percent said California was headed in the right direction, compared to 40 percent who thought otherwise.[2] California was governable again.

In his early terms, the balance of accomplishment and disappointment was more complicated: for example, Brown gave California coastal protection but saddled it with a cumbersome and difficult architecture for enforcing it. The California Coastal Commission has achieved great things—and stumbled badly—in the years since. Brown also championed political reform, overseeing the creation of the Political Reform Act and the commission that enforces it today: there, too, the results are mixed. Contribution limits and other reforms have blunted some of the worst excesses of influence peddling, but not all of them. And Brown himself has alternately stuck to those limits and expressed disdain for their rigidity. In criminal justice, he helped reduce caprice and bias with his support for determinate sentencing, but he left a system that his successors used to make sentencing more punitive, less constructive and merciful. Brown used the governorship to infuse that system with mercy, but other governors have shown less willingness to do so. Finally, Brown pressed for diversity—in terms of gender, race, and background. Sometimes, he pushed so hard that the backlash overwhelmed the effort, but he vastly diversified the state workforce in America's most dynamic state, and he set a standard that future governors must at least acknowledge.

To those who followed Brown across the long, interrupted arc of his four gubernatorial terms, the first two times out seemed more brash and boundary-breaking, whereas the last two felt more coherent and productive. Connecting them across the decades were strong threads: environmental protection, fiscal responsibility, commitments to diversity, and fresh thinking. At the end of the Brown years, California stood apart from and ahead of much of the nation that contained it. California in 2019 was more prosperous and more protective of the environment, more welcoming of immigrants, and more generous with its protections and benefits than most parts of the United States. It demonstrated that a place—a very big and diverse place—could be all those things at once. Jerry Brown was instrumental in that.

To Brown's justifiable frustration, talk of his legacy often focused more on projects than on intellectual and cultural change. There, Brown was late to the endeavor and halfhearted about it: a governor who emphasizes limits is not a likely standard-bearer for big infrastructure.

As Brown left office, his signature late-governorship projects—the water tunnels and the high-speed rail—faced an uncertain future. Immediately after succeeding Brown, in January of 2019, Gavin Newsom announced plans to cut the tunnel project from two tunnels to one, but he accepted the need for and the premise of the undertaking, and a water-conveyance system to address the issue of the Sacramento–San Joaquin Delta appeared a nearly settled matter. On high-speed rail, Newsom tried to split the baby and was left with a mess. In his first State of the State address, delivered on February 1, he sent mixed messages on the train. The project, "as currently planned, would cost too much and take too long," he said. "Right now, there simply isn't a path to get from Sacramento to San Diego, let alone from San Francisco to L.A. I wish there were."[3] That seemed to signal that Newsom was dumping the rail line, but he instead pivoted, arguing to complete the first link, from Modesto to Bakersfield, and leaving open the possibility for more construction after that.

It was a baffling proposal. It is hard imagine great demand for rail service between Modesto and Bakersfield. And the proposal's reception was worsened by lazy reporting that concluded that Newsom had given up on high-speed rail altogether. No less than President Trump responded that if California was abandoning the train, the federal government wanted its money back (the federal government, as of early 2019, had invested $3.5 billion in the project). Newsom backpedaled, insisting with some justification that he had been misunderstood and that the project would continue, albeit in truncated form. Brown, reading reports of the controversy, took it in stride. "The train is a good public work," he said in March. "We have to get off of fossil fuels, and this is part of that."[4]

Will it ever connect California's great cities? "It remains to be seen," Brown replied.

Brown left some problems unsolved. He made some improvements to the state's pension systems for teachers and other public employees and was aided in that by the booming economy of his final two terms. Nevertheless, the retirement systems remained precarious when he left office. They were built at a time when retirees did not live as long as they do now, and they were burdened by overly optimistic investment predictions and provisions for generous benefits. Longer lives and shakier markets left them vulnerable. Politics intervened as well: public officials like to give generously to workers whose unions help elect those officials, and they often prefer pensions, which future generations have to pay, to salaries, which cost money in the present. California was not the only state that created pension problems for itself, but it had the biggest of those systems, and it had some of the biggest problems. Brown nibbled, but only at the edges, of this possible crisis. California's labor unions and public agencies will fight that out another day: the courts were already beginning to weigh in as Brown left Sacramento.

The tax system was similarly riddled with unresolved issues, and Brown knew it. A more stable structure for California would have balanced income, property, and sales taxes. Relying on all three in roughly equal measure would have helped protect California against the wild gyrations of its budget, which have plagued state leaders ever since the full effects of Proposition 13 began to be felt, in the 1980s. Brown arguably had the political stature to tackle Proposition 13 in his final terms—others proposed a so-called split roll, which would treat business and personal property differently, addressing the increasing and unpredicted effect that Proposition 13 had in shifting more of the tax burden to homeowners, since houses change hands more often than business properties. Just as Brown had successfully stumped for extending income and sales taxes in his third term—and had won legislative approval and voter affirmation of gas-tax hikes in his fourth—he could have turned to property taxes as well.

But Brown had been lastingly shaken by Proposition 13, and his pragmatism outweighed his reformism—the courage to change is moderated by the wisdom to recognize what is possible. Nathan Gardels observed that Brown took away from the Proposition 13 battle a lifelong aversion to tinkering with middle-class taxes. "For Jerry, pragmatism sometimes equals limits," Gardels said. "That has roots in his experience."[5] Brown let that battle go. It, too, will almost certainly have to be reckoned with in the future, beyond Brown's watch.

So will the persistent demands of human suffering. California in the early twenty-first century saw homelessness increase as housing prices soared. It is a side effect of affluence—rising home prices are, for many, a good thing, not a bad one—but there is no denying the pain of those who struggle to earn enough to live safely and comfortably or just to have a home at all. Alongside the wealth that grew in California—from its farms to the movie business to Silicon Valley to tourism and trade—inequality rose, too. It matters little to a minimum-wage worker in Long Beach that the nearby port booms or that Facebook executives are bumping up the price of real estate in Palo Alto. Late in his final term, Brown signed the legislation to raise California's minimum wage and later pointed to that as evidence of trying to address inequality. That was true, but in a very limited way. No one earning even the increased minimum wage could hope to live in one of California's tonier communities. As Brown left office, he left a California of great wealth but of shocking poverty and glaring inequality as well.

And yet the standard of successful leadership is not the elimination of all problems but rather proof of progress. By that measure, Brown was undeniably successful. He left the governorship on January 7, 2019, to wide and almost universal acclaim. *Governing* magazine reported that no other American governor "has accomplished as dramatic a turnaround [in state finances] as Brown, who is leaving plenty of money in the bank for his successor."[6] California newspapers agreed. "Jerry Brown was the right leader for a precarious time in the state's history," the *San Francisco Chronicle* concluded. Brown, the paper's editorial board argued, deserved credit for correcting the state's finances, leading on climate change and prison reform, and returning California to rationality, proving that it was governable.[7] That same day and in similar language, the *Los Angeles Times* thanked Brown for his service, calling him "the idiosyncratic but sagacious senior statesman whose deep understanding of the state's unique political landscape and shrewd tactical skills made him the governor California needed at this crucial point in history."[8]

Seasoned reporters echoed the sentiments of editorial boards. Writing in the *Atlantic*, savvy political journalist Todd Purdum called Brown "perhaps the most successful politician in contemporary America."[9] Adam Nagourney, whose work for the *New York Times* adroitly captured Brown in his later terms, observed of the soon-to-depart governor: "He has been such a fixture…that it seems impossible to imagine California without him."[10] And George Skelton, the veteran Sacramento columnist for the *Los Angeles Times* who dogged Brown for decades and was more than willing to call out his mistakes, was generous in the end. "It's time to grade Gov. Jerry Brown," Skelton wrote. Skelton identified Brown's most important achievements as balancing the budget, leading on climate change, hiking taxes to pay for highway repairs, investing in schools, and reducing the state's prison population. All in all, the gently cantankerous Skelton acknowledged, it was quite a record. "No need to think twice," Skelton said of Brown. "He earned an A for his final two terms as governor."[11]

Brown's success as governor was secure. His legacy, no matter how much he would argue against it, was sound and solid, built on an ideologically broad foundation. He made California better.

In the very end, Brown's great contribution to his state and nation was not found in any budget or bill or bridge or program. It was not captured by any statistic or metric. Jerry Brown brought his searching, restless intellect to the questions of human existence. He governed less by polls than by the conviction that great questions—prudence, humility, justice, mercy—demand rigorous exploration. He was not satisfied to be a liberal, though that would have been the easiest path for him in California. He believed that government should observe limits, a deeply conservative principle, and that it should help where it could, a defining liberal notion. He did not believe that every human problem deserved a bill, but he signed more bills than any person in the history of California. And he vetoed more of them, too. He was, as even his critics would grant, thoroughly and completely his own person. He proved that one can be those things and still succeed. That may not be a legacy in traditional terms, but it is an achievement worthy of study and emulation. It is a gift to history.

# Epilogue

The way to the Mountain House winds north from Sacramento along Interstate 5. It cuts west at the second Williams exit, heading straight through town and then up into the foothills. The hills, which are unnamed, rise gently above almond orchards, their blossoms thick and white as snow in the spring, their branches bulging with crops in summer and fall. Below, in the long valley running north from Sacramento, are rice paddies and olive groves, fields of hay and alfalfa, ranches of walnuts and farms of tomatoes, truck stops and diners, a taqueria or two and a hardware store. As the road cuts off the highway and into a crevice in the hills, it veers upward, the view back to the east and the little town square of Williams. Then the road turns into a notch of the hills, and there, in a little valley by a stream, is the Mountain House. A California flag flies out front.

Jerry Brown and Anne Gust Brown live in the Mountain House, but it's not the one that the venerable August Schuckman, Jerry's ancestor, built in the waning years of the California gold rush. That house burned down, a couple of times. The governor and First Lady built a new one on the property. The iron gate across the front of the drive reads: MOUNTAIN HOUSE III. This home is distinctly that of Anne and Jerry Brown.

There's no electrical power or running water in these hills, so the Browns installed solar panels for power and dug a well for water. They planted a grove of olive trees and are pressing olive oil from the fruit. The house itself is rustic and modern—fitting for a man whose shelves include the latest poetry by Gary Snyder and sixteenth-century reflections on the obligations of a Jesuit. There's a basement full of files—"the good stuff," Brown calls it—recording his service across decades, along with the awards, photographs, and other ephemera that collect around a man in public life since birth.

A few weeks after leaving office, Brown was settling in at the Mountain House. He wore a plaid wool shirt and hiking boots lightly caked in mud. Colusa—the corgi—and Cali romped on the green hillside beyond the home's north-facing floor-to-ceiling window. Jerry gripped a cup of coffee—he takes it black—and reheated it in the microwave when it cooled. Anne worked nearby, building a small composter that the couple intends to use to build up a garden. Cows grazed on the facing hillside. A light rain fell intermittently.

On that Thursday morning, Brown was playfully argumentative, not for the first time. He bristled at being called a skeptic. Granted, he said, "I was always interested in having a fresher view of things. That took a little more time. It took a little more inquiry."

But that did not mean, he insisted, that he was a skeptic. "I don't like the idea of being a skeptic. *Skeptic* has a negative connotation. A skeptic is an unhappy person."

Wondering out loud, Brown questioned: "Was H. L. Mencken a skeptic or a cynic?" Offered the suggestion that Mencken was a cynic based on his conviction that man's lesser instincts generally prevail, Brown agreed that the word *cynic* applied to Mencken, then suggested that he, Brown, could perhaps be described as a "humanitarian skeptic." Or maybe a "believing, enthusiastic skeptic."

"I tend to be an enthusiast," he ventured. Anne, working in the background, then joined. "You are a skeptic, Jerry," she called from the kitchen.

"Aren't I also an enthusiast?" he asked.

Yes, she responded. "You are an enthusiast, and you are also a skeptic."

Brown fought on for another few moments, then settled on a description for himself: a "Catholic skeptic enthusiast…and a romantic." Anne agreed with that. Brown was satisfied, too.

For Californians who grew up with Brown as governor twice, his departure felt both familiar and odd. He'd left before, but he'd returned. He was leaving again, but there still was plenty to do. The defining issues of Brown's public life—environmental stewardship, criminal justice reform, the control and safety of nuclear weapons—hardly were resolved at the end of his governorship and, in any case, cried out for leadership well beyond the governor's office. Would he depart altogether? That seemed unlikely. Brown could guide policy makers on climate change and criminal justice as effectively from Colusa as from Sacramento, and he was determined to do so. Not conventionally, perhaps, but by traveling and speaking and writing, sounding an urgent call that will only grow more urgent as climate change accelerates and nuclear weapons tempt the trigger fingers of despots and idiots. Similarly, Brown resolved to remain engaged on issues of criminal justice, where his own intellectual evolution had been long and sometimes tortuous.

Brown's convictions were not selfish. As he memorably told that legislative committee in 2017, the most devastating effects of climate change might not be felt for a decade or two. "Maybe not in my lifetime," he piercingly observed then. "I'll be dead."

Instead, Brown was fighting for those who come after him—not his own children, since he has none, but for his nieces and nephews, all ten of them, and for those beyond his vision or reach. He had spent his life understanding humility: service to God, deference to nature, observance of limits. He would spend the rest of his days propounding those understandings. Jerry Brown would not go quietly.

There's a desktop computer just outside Jerry and Anne's bedroom. Brown pauses at it occasionally. On the screen one breezy afternoon in March was displayed a pair of graphs showing, hour by hour, how much solar energy the cells outside the Mountain House were generating and, also by the hour, how much power the house was using. On this day, the power generated far exceeded the usage.

"That's good," Brown said, showing off his little contribution to a healthier planet that day. "It will be harder in the summer, when we're running the air-conditioning."

Then again, he noted, the power generated will peak on those days, too. Long, sunny days mean lots of light for the cells to absorb and convert. "We'll have a lot to work with," he concluded, exhibiting a bit of the zeal of a skeptically Catholic enthusiastic romantic. There was balance in that chart and his appreciation of it—drawing from the sun, living within limits, respecting the earth, taking nothing for granted, questioning conventional wisdom and enjoying it. Life in the inquiry.

# Acknowledgments

Governor Jerry Brown and First Lady Anne Gust Brown made this book possible by making themselves vulnerable. They agreed to reveal their lives to me, at the cost of time and sometimes discomfort. Even as he governed through his final two terms, Governor Brown repeatedly set aside long stretches for us to meet—in the governor's mansion, in his office, in his Oakland offices, at the Colusa ranch, even on a San Francisco ferry. Those were sacrifices, and they were compounded by risk—that I would misunderstand or misinterpret or simply disagree. He stuck with it. Neither the governor nor the First Lady read this book prior to its publication and neither insisted on doing so, In short, any credit due this work for its comprehensiveness is owed to the governor and Anne. Any mistakes, of course, are mine, as are all matters of interpretation.

The title page carries my name, but that's misleading. My brilliant and caring editor, Vanessa Mobley, shaped these words into a narrative and was not shy about pointing to spots that needed something more (or, in several cases, something less). I'm an editor, too, and I appreciate a good one. I know of no greater compliment than to acknowledge that this book is a story because of Vanessa. Meanwhile, the book exists at all because of Tina Bennett, whose taste, energy, and insight know no bounds. As I finished this manuscript, our fourth project together, I realized that Tina and I have been at this for nearly twenty years. Tina is the reason that I am able to enjoy the life of a book writer.

At Little, Brown, I also am indebted to a team of editors and others who labored to bring this book across the finish line. I enjoyed the expert copyediting and fact-checking of Barbara Clark, the cheerful direction of Michael Noon, and the publicity energy and guidance from Elizabeth Garriga. Ruth Mandel supervised the selection and display of photographs, lending her expert eye and exquisite taste to that job. Thanks to all.

I don't have the space here to acknowledge all the many generous men and women who opened up their lives to my inquiries. A list of interviews appears in this volume, and even it is partial, including only those who sat for formal or repeated conversations, not the many others who offered suggestions or hints, often off the record. I am indebted to all those who agreed to speak with me, and I offer special thanks to Kathleen Brown and Barbara Casey, my subject's sisters and important sources for insight into him and the rest of the Brown family.

Beyond those who agreed to interviews are those whose knowledge of Brown or California or music or protest or counterculture or any number of other topics enriched these pages. They include current and former colleagues, friends from the *Los Angeles Times* and UCLA, and some of the many wise men and women I've had the chance to meet over a lifetime of living in and writing about California. At the top of that list is my cherished friend of many years Henry Weinstein. It would not be quite right to say that I interviewed him repeatedly for this book: it's more accurate to say that I relied on him continuously—for memory, wisdom, and, most especially, friendship. Other long-standing and reliably shrewd advisers who enriched this project include Zev Yaroslavsky, Gary Segura, Tim Rutten, Robin Kramer, Nick Goldberg, Sue Horton, Robert Greene, the late Tom Hayden, Ace Smith, Bill Wardlaw, and Joanne Heyler—all of whom I admire and am pleased to regard as friends.

Five generous souls read drafts of the manuscript, and I am especially appreciative of their time and discernment. Bill Parent, my UCLA friend and neighbor, was the first, catching errors and making valuable suggestions about storytelling. Four others lent their intelligence. Evan Westrup and Justice Tony Kline, both of whom know Brown well—and from different eras and vantage points—read a nearly complete version of the manuscript, as did Christine Wiley, who diligently fact-checked the pile of pages that became this book. Finally, Zev Yaroslavsky, a student of California history as well as a fulsome contributor to it, gave the manuscript a final and characteristically thorough review. Again, I thank those readers profusely for their help and absolve them of responsibility for any errors, even while acknowledging that we may have different opinions about some of the events and characters described in these pages.

A word about my debt to those who have plowed these fields before me: Brown has been the subject of countless profiles and several books, though by definition none has been able to take the full measure of his career, given its longevity. Early and influential takes include Orville Schell's *Brown* and Robert Pack's *Jerry Brown: The Philosopher Prince*, both of which capture Brown in his first iteration as governor, when the presidency seemed still to beckon. More critical was J. D. Lorenz's *Jerry Brown: The Man on the White Horse*, which also is rooted in Brown's early tenure. Ethan Rarick's superb biography of Pat Brown includes insight into the relationship between father and son and sets much of the context for Jerry Brown's emergence, while Miriam Pawel's longer look at the Brown family and the surrounding history of California offers a broader perspective. I'm happy to count Ethan and Miriam as friends and to attempt to build here on their important work. Finally, a nod to California's most important historian and a friend whom we lost two years ago: the late Kevin Starr encouraged me to take on this project, which I did only after confirming with him that he had no plans to round out his grand California history with a book addressing the period covered here, which is to say, roughly 1960 to the present. Kevin did look at a sliver of that period, 1990–2003, but assured me he did not plan to cover the 1960s and 1970s. "Counterculture," he told me years ago, "doesn't do much for me. It's all yours." With his blessing, then, this project commenced. I only wish I could share it with him now.

As Kevin Starr's death, in 2017, sadly served to remind me, books take time, and so does life. As a result, I have another deep well of gratitude: to those friends and family who nursed me across the difficulties that threatened to intrude upon, even upend, this long and complicated project. Merrick Bobb has graced me with his inspiring friendship and intelligence for many years, especially of late, as has Marshall Goldberg. One of life's great outings is a night at the ballpark with Marshall. Carol Stogsdill and Steve Stroud have always supplied love and warmth; so have Beth Shuster and Michael Healy, long and dearly appreciated sources of respite and encouragement; Paul and Victoria Barrosse, whose stimulating cordiality I have enjoyed for decades but never more than in the past couple of years; and Fran Schwartzkopff and Eric Guthey, now thriving in beautiful Denmark, our bonds strengthened by time and unhindered by distance. Finally, a deep thank-you to two warm souls brought to me by marriage and sealed by life: Brad and Julia Hall are cheer and wisdom combined, individually and together. Brad brings his relentless decency to all things, and Julia is a fountain of intelligent kindness.

Brad was there in 2018 (along with Marshall and Steve and Carol and Beth and Michael and Julia and Henry and Paul and, memorably, Victoria) when I most needed a friend. My life turned on their friendship that summer. From those months, I also owe a special thanks to my trusted colleague Jon Thurber, who supplied badly needed guidance at a crucial moment. Among other gifts, Jon introduced me to Tom Holler, a new friend and one for life.

Two other good men, both friends of many years, deserve special note. Bill McIntyre is my oldest and most trusted confidant; we have seen each other through a time or two. Indeed, his overwhelming kindness has shaped my life—more than once, but most certainly in the home stretch of this undertaking. Rick Meyer is another great soul, a colleague across our time together at the *Los Angeles Times* and now *Blueprint* magazine. Our esteemed friend in common, the late John Carroll, once told me that some editors edit stories, others edit people. Rick does both, and I'm the better for it. Bill and Rick are very dear to me, and I am pleased to be able to thank them here.

This is a book about many things, but central to its understanding is the complicated question of fathers and sons. I am both, and I am grateful for it. I thank my parents, Jim and Barbara Newton, for their steadfast love, and my son, Jack Newton, for all that he is and is becoming. I am proud of Jack's resilience, I admire his heart, and I love him dearly. I also love and appreciate John Newton, my adventurous and ever-growing little brother. As this book comes to completion, John and his husband, Marc Perrotta, are embarking on an exciting new chapter of their lives in Mexico, happily at arm's length from some of the political clamor that darkens this country today. Debts to family are deep and complicated, and I am happily aware of them. My thanks to my family.

Above all is my gratitude to my wife, Karlene Goller. Karlene has let me share her life, and I cannot imagine mine without her. Everything I write is, at some level, a letter to Karlene. That's certainly the case with these pages, which are dedicated to her. Thank you, my love.

Thank you all.

# A Note on Sources

Endnotes throughout the text identify specific sources for quotations and other facts. In addition, this work was informed by many books, archival materials (some in personal collections), and interviews. On the following pages is a list of material that influenced my research and enhanced my understanding of Jerry Brown and his times.

### ARCHIVAL RESOURCES

Personal collection of Anne Gust and Jerry Brown
> These files were being processed while I was working on this book. They consist of 234 boxes of personal papers, photographs, and ephemera maintained by the Browns at their home in Williams, California

Personal files and collections of Larry Pryor, Robert Stern, and others

Bancroft Library, University of California, Berkeley
> Records, correspondence, and other papers from Pat Brown's governorship
> Oral History Center: http://www.lib.berkeley.edu/libraries/bancroft-library/oral-history-center

*Blueprint* magazine, UCLA, Los Angeles, 2015–present

California Department of Finance, Sacramento
Budgets and supporting budget material

California Governor's Office, Sacramento
Speeches, memos, correspondence, biographical material

*California Journal: The Monthly Analysis of State Government and Politics*, Sacramento, 1970–2005

*California Legal History*, California Supreme Court Historical Society, Fresno, CA

California Secretary of State, Sacramento
Voting records, registration statistics, and material related to California demographics

California State Archives, Sacramento
Material on Earl Warren governorship and general history

Museum of the City of San Francisco
Online archives and materials: http://www.sfmuseum.org

Newspapers
I have relied on newspapers from across the country and over many decades. Particularly helpful were the library and online archives of the *Los Angeles Times,* the *San Francisco Chronicle,* the *New York Times,* the *Balitmore Sun,* and the *Washington Post.*

Special Collections, Charles E. Young Research Library, University of California, Los Angeles
Political and natural history of California

Special Collections, University of Southern California Libraries
Records, correspondence, and other papers from Brown's first two terms as governor

United Nations climate change reports
https://www.un.org/en/sections/issues-depth/climate-change/

## INTERVIEWS

The core of this book is Brown himself, as the governor agreed to more than a dozen interviews—some lasting more than five hours—over the course of four years. They took place at his offices in Oakland, in the governor's office in Sacramento, at the governor's mansion, and, following the conclusion of his governorship, at his home near Williams, California. Anne Gust Brown joined a number of those conversations and also was interviewed separately.

### *Conversations with Jerry Brown*

July 14, 2015
November 13, 2015
January 29, 2016 (two interviews)
May 6, 2016
August 15, 2016
December 19, 2016
July 26, 2017
March 8, 2018
September 13, 2018 (aboard the ferry)
October 5, 2018
December 12, 2018
February 8, 2019 (Williams)
March 8, 2019 (Williams)
June 26, 2019 (Williams)
February 2–4, 2020

### *Conversations with Anne Gust Brown*

October 5, 2018
February 8, 2019 (Williams)
March 8, 2019 (Williams)
March 18, 2019 (telephone)
June 26, 2019 (Williams)

## Other interviews

Listed below are formal interviews or running conversations with people close to Brown or otherwise familiar with his life and work. Most were conducted specifically for the book, though a few draw upon my time as a reporter and columnist for the *Los Angeles Times* or as the editor of *Blueprint*. Not included are dozens of shorter, more specific conversations, follow-up interviews to check facts, and off-the-record discussions.

David Axelrod, January 24, 2019
Xavier Becerra, April 24, 2017
Howard Berman, June 2, 2016, and December 28, 2018
Michael Bloomberg, September 12, 2018
Bill Boyarsky, various
Eli Broad, July 6, 2017 (and various)
Kathleen Brown, August 28, 2015; December 12, 2018; May 1, 2019
Willie Brown, September 15, 2015
John Burton, September 15, 2015
Bill Carrick, March 2012
Barbara Casey, March 15, 2019
Eli and Arlene Chernow, November 2, 2018
Warren Christopher (various, 1993–2010)
Mariano-Florentino Cuellar, various
Gray Davis, April 8, 2019
Diana Dooley, October 5, 2018
Maria Elena Durazo, January 20, 2017
Jodie Evans, March 30, 2017
Dianne Feinstein, April 2, 2019
Raymond C. Fisher, October 5, 2015
Eric Garcetti, July 14, 2016
Nathan Gardels, January 30, 2019
Kamala Harris, March 11, 2015
Tom Hayden, various
Bob Hertzberg, March 8, 2018

Joanne Heyler, May 14, 2016
Mickey Kantor, July 11, 2016
George Kieffer, December 17, 2018
Tony Kline, December 4, 2015
Quentin Kopp, December 29, 2017
Norman Lear, October 19, 2017
Bill McKibben, August 19, 2019
Molly Munger, March 2012
Mary Nichols, January 5, 2016
Leon Panetta, February 2, 2017 (and various)
Larry Pryor, July 12, 2016
Tom Quinn, August 29, 2018
Stephen Reinhardt, May 10, 2016
Ace Smith, September 15, 2105; March 9, 2018 (and various)
Robert M. Stern, January 25, 2018
Antonio Villaraigosa, July 31, 2018
Henry Weinstein, various
Kathryn Werdeger, October 1, 2018, and November 7, 2018
Evan Westrup, October 4, 2018 (and various)
Dana Williamson, April 11, 2019
Zev Yaroslavsky, various

# Notes

## PROLOGUE

1   National Baseball Hall of Fame, "Jocko Conlan," at https://baseballhall.org/hall-of
    -famers/conlan-jocko.
2   Frances Moffat, "By Boat, by Bus to the Ball Game…They Went by Cable Car, Too!," *San
    Francisco Examiner,* April 13, 1960.
3   "Finds Skeleton of Skin Diver," *Eureka Humboldt Standard,* April 12, 1960.
4   Rose Marie Turk, "The Heiress to an Acting Legacy," *San Francisco Examiner,* April 10,
    1960.
5   Dennis McDougal, *Privileged Son: Otis Chandler and the Rise and Fall of the L.A. Times
    Dynasty* (Boston: Da Capo, 2001), 224–25.
6   David Shaw and Mitchell Landsberg, "Otis Chandler: A Lion of Journalism," *Los Angeles
    Times,* Feb. 28, 2008.
7   Curly Grieve, "Cepeda and Jones Win Opener, 3–1," *San Francisco Examiner,* April 13,
    1960.
8   Robert Reinhold, "Edmund G. Brown Is Dead at 90," *New York Times,* Feb. 18, 1996.
9   Edmund G. (Pat) Brown with Dick Adler, *Public Justice, Private Mercy: A Governor's Edu-
    cation on Death Row* (New York: Weidenfeld & Nicolson, 1989).
10  Peter Hartlaub, "Mays Meets Nixon: The Weirdest Giants Home Opener in History," *San
    Francisco Chronicle,* Jan. 31, 2018.
11  Jerry Brown interview with the author, Jan. 29, 2016; also see Clint Mosher, "Nixon Stars
    on Sidelines, Praises Giants Play," *San Francisco Examiner,* April 13, 1960.
12  Jerry Brown interview with the author, Jan. 29, 2016.
13  Jerry Brown interview with the author, Jan. 29, 2016.

# CHAPTER ONE

1 See coverage, generally, from *San Francisco Examiner* and *San Francisco Call-Bulletin,* April 7, 1938.

2 Charles A. Fracchia, *Fire and Gold: The San Francisco Story,* 2nd ed. (Dallas, TX: Heritage Media, 1997), 154.

3 Fracchia, *Fire and Gold,* 156.

4 "LaGuardia Discusses Needs of Bay Counties Defense Work," *Oakland Tribune,* Dec. 10, 1941.

5 "Grim Reality of War Grips Pacific Coast," *Press Democrat* (Santa Rosa), Dec. 8, 1941.

6 "F.B.I. Seizes 2030 German, Italian, Japanese Nationals in U.S.," *Oakland Tribune,* Dec. 10, 1941.

7 "Japan Holds 1270 U.S., British Nationals," *Oakland Tribune,* Dec. 10, 1941.

8 "America Is United," editorial, *Oakland Tribune,* Dec. 8, 1941.

9 Kevin Starr, *Embattled Dreams: California in War and Peace,* 1940–1950, Americans and the California Dream 6 (Oxford, UK: Oxford University Press, 2002), 74.

10 United States Marines, "Marine Corps Base Camp Pendleton," at http://www.pendleton.marines.mil/About/History-and-Museums/.

11 *National Defense Migration: Hearings Before the Select Committee Investigating National Defense Migration,* part 29, San Francisco hearings, Feb. 21 and 23, 1942 (Washington, DC: Government Printing Office, 1942), 10974, at https://ia800209.us.archive.org/29/items/nationaldefensem29unit/nationaldefensem29unit.pdf.

12 Barbara Casey interview with the author, March 15, 2019.

13 They later formalized their marriage in the Church and were wed at Saint Agnes Church in San Francisco in May of 1940. Bernice did not convert to Catholicism.

14 Kathleen Brown interview with the author, Aug. 28, 2015.

15 Casey interview.

16 Casey interview.

17 Jerry Brown interview with the author, Jan. 29, 2016.

18 Casey interview.

19 Casey interview.

20 Jerry Brown interview with the author, July 14, 2015.

21 Attributed to Dorothy Parker.

22 Starr, *Embattled Dreams,* 55.

23 *Reynolds v. Sims,* 377 U.S. 533 (1964), at http://cdn.loc.gov/service/ll/usrep/usrep377/usrep377533/usrep377533.pdf.

24 Upton Sinclair, "End Poverty in California: The EPIC Movement," *Literary Digest,* Oct. 13, 1934, available from the Virtual Museum of San Francisco at http://www.sfmuseum.org/hist1/sinclair.html.

25 OurCampaigns.com, at http://www.ourcampaigns.com/RaceDetail.html?RaceID=103765.

26 "Merriam or Sinclair?," editorial, *Los Angeles Times,* Aug. 29, 1934.

27 Madalyn O'Hair, "The Hon. Atheist Governor: Culbert L. Olson," *American Atheist* 32, no. 4 (April 1990), 20–28.

28 Jim Newton, *Justice for All: Earl Warren and the Nation He Made* (New York: Riverhead, 2007), 1–11.

## CHAPTER TWO

1   Jerry Brown interviews with the author, July 14, 2015, and Dec. 12, 2018.

2   Jerry Brown interview with the author, Feb. 8, 2019.

3   Jerry Brown interview with the author, Dec. 11, 2018.

4   Jerry Brown interview with the author, Jan. 29, 2016.

5   Ethan Rarick, *California Rising: The Life and Times of Pat Brown* (Berkeley: University of California Press, 2005), 82.

6   Robert Pack, *Jerry Brown: The Philosopher Prince* (New York: Stein and Day, 1978), 12–13.

7   Rarick, *California Rising,* 82.

8   Jerry Brown interview with the author, July 14, 2015.

9   Jerry Brown interview with the author, July 14, 2015.

10  "Bill Clinton, Jerry Brown Trade Jabs at 1992 Democratic Primary Debate," broadcast in March of 1992 by CBS and posted to YouTube on Nov. 10, 2015, at: https://www .youtube.com/watch?v=K5kUITklALQ.

11  Orville Schell, *Brown* (New York: Random House, 1978), 73.

12  "*Bulletin of the Atomic Scientists* 2019 Doomsday Clock Announcement," National Press Club, Washington, DC, Jan. 24, 2019, at https://clock.thebulletin.org/.

13  Thomas Maloney, "Governor Brown and Rules 11 and 12 of the Summary," February 26, 1975, carton 2, Pat Brown papers, Bancroft Library, University of California, Berkeley.

14  Jerry Brown interview with the author, Aug. 15, 2016.

15  Jerry Brown interview with the author, Aug. 15, 2016.

16  Jerry Brown interview with the author, Aug. 15, 2016.

17  "Bill Clinton, Jerry Brown Trade Jabs at 1992 Democratic Primary Debate," broadcast in March of 1992 by CBS and posted to YouTube on November 10, 2015, at: https://www .youtube.com/watch?v=K5kUITklALQ.

18  Jerry Brown interview with the author, Dec. 11, 2018.

19  *U.S. News and World Report,* Jan. 18, 1957.

20  Morrie Landsberg, "Shock Waves Reverberating from Knowland's Decision," *Daily Independent Journal,* Jan. 8, 1957.

21  Don Shannon, "California Congressmen Regret Knowland Action," *Los Angeles Times,* Jan. 8, 1957.

22  James C. Anderson, "State Republicans Suffer Disaster," *The Press Democrat,* Nov. 5, 1958.

23  Morrie Landsberg, "Brown Wins; Engle's Lead Widens Steadily," *The San Bernardino Sun,* Nov. 5, 1958.

24  This period has been captured by historian Kevin Starr. The life of Pat Brown himself is expertly documented in Ethan Rarick's *California Rising: The Life and Times of Pat Brown.*

25  Pat Brown, Inaugural Address, Jan. 7, 1959, https://governors.library.ca.gov/addresses /s_34-JBrown1.html

26  Diary, entry for June 16, 1959. Pat Brown papers, Volume 25.

27  https://www.dfeh.ca.gov/wp-content/uploads/sites/32/2017/06/InitialStmtReasons _ConsiderCriminalHistory.pdf?la=en.

28  "State's First FEPC Takes Up Duties," *Los Angeles Times,* Oct. 3, 1959.

29  Oral history with John Anson Ford, UCLA Oral History Program, 1967, p. 193.

30  "State's First FEPC Takes Up Duties," *Los Angeles Times,* Oct. 3, 1959.

31  Diary entry for Dec. 20, 1959, Pat Brown papers, Volume 25.

32  Jerry Brown interview with the author, Dec. 11, 2018.

33    Jerry Brown interview with the author, July 14, 2015.

34    http://www.extracrispy.com/culture/638/the-beat-generation-bagel-shop-that-didnt-sell
      -bagels.

35    Jerry Brown interview with the author, July 14, 2015.

36    Jerry Brown, interviews with the author, July 14 and Nov. 13, 2015.

37    Pat Brown, *Public Justice, Private Mercy*, p. 33.

38    Brown Personal Papers, Williams, CA.

39    Pat Brown, *Public Justice, Private Mercy*, p. 22.

40    David Ulin, "Caryl Chessman's Infamous Death," *Los Angeles Times*, Sep. 19, 2006.

41    Diary entry for October 15, 1959, Pat Brown papers, Volume 25.

42    Pat Brown, *Public Justice, Private Mercy*, p. 36.

43    "Brown Bars Chessman Clemency," *Los Angeles Times*, Oct. 20, 1959.

44    Some of the details and language here come from Brown's copies of the rough draft of his
      interview with *Playboy* magazine. The draft is dated Dec. 27, 1975, and is included in his
      personal papers, Brown Personal Papers, Williams, CA.

45    Pat Brown, *Public Justice, Private Mercy*, p. 40.

46    Pat Brown, *Public Justice, Private Mercy*, p. 40.

47    Brad Williams, "Reprieve! Gov. Brown Gives Chessman Stay, Will Put Matter Before Legislature,"
      *Los Angeles Times*, Extra, Feb. 19, 1960.

48    Tom Cameron, "Red Influence Hit," *Los Angeles Times*. Feb. 20, 1960.

49    Walter Ames, "Chessman Denies Guilt as He Dies," *Los Angeles Times*, May 3, 1960.

50    Ethan Rarick, *California Rising*, p. 180.

51    Ethan Rarick, *California Rising*, pp. 171–172.

52    Pat Brown, *Public Justice, Private Mercy*, p. 52.

53    Diary entry for March 8, 1960, Pat Brown papers, UC Berkeley, Volume 26.

## CHAPTER THREE

1     Jerry Brown interviews with the author. We discussed this on several occasions, including
      Dec. 12, 2018, and Feb. 8, 2019.

2     Jerry Brown interview with the author, Dec. 12, 2018.

3     Jerry Brown interview with the author, Dec. 12, 2018.

4     Jerry Brown interview with the author, Dec. 12, 2018.

5     John Jacobs, *A Rage for Justice*, p. 66.

6     Willie Brown interview with the author, Sept. 15, 2015.

7     SF Weekly Staff, "The Last Seduction," *SF Weekly*, Oct. 18, 1995.

8     SF Weekly Staff, "The Last Seduction," *SF Weekly*, Oct. 18, 1995.

9     Willie Brown interview with the author, Sept. 15, 2015.

10    "Brown Disclaims Any Support Commitment," *Los Angeles Times*, Jan. 24, 1960.

11    "Brown to Choose Sunday," *Pasadena Independent*, July 8, 1960.

12    Howard Kennedy, "State Gives Kennedy 33½ Votes, 31½ to Stevenson, Governor Re-
      ceives Only ½," *Los Angeles Times*, July 14, 1960.

13    "Brown Foes Lose 'Halt-Kennedy' Suit," *San Francisco Examiner*, July 13, 1960.

14    New York Times News Service, "Democrats Puzzled by Rebuff to Gov. Brown, His In-
      ability to Control Own Delegation Causes Serious Blow to His Prestige," *Los Angeles
      Times*, July 14, 1960.

15    New York Times News Service, "Democrats Puzzled by Rebuff to Gov. Brown, His In-

ability to Control Own Delegation Causes Serious Blow to His Prestige," *Los Angeles Times*, July 14, 1960.

16 "Louis Lurie, 84, Dies on Coast; Realty Man and Theater Angel," *New York Times*, Sept. 8, 1972. (A side note: *The New York Times* reference to California as "on coast" says much about the paper's regard for California during this period.)

17 Lurie's son, Bob Lurie, bought the San Francisco Giants in 1976, heading off a group of investors that wanted to move the team to Toronto. The Lurie family thus occupies a special place in the hearts of San Franciscans to this day.

18 Greer would go on to become a controversial figure. He was accused of raping a student in 2005–2006 and was ordered to pay a $21.7 million judgment (see: https://www .newhavenindependent.org/index.php/archives/entry/judge_shea_greer_verdict/.

19 Jose A. Del Real, "California Today: Jerry Brown Warns of Recession and Reveals His Final Budget," *New York Times*, Jan. 11, 2018.

20 Nor, incidentally, have I ever heard Brown challenge Earl Warren's claim to a California legacy, undoubtedly in part because my biography of Warren is part of what drew us together.

21 Richard Riordan interview with the author, Aug. 20, 1997.

22 Pat Brown, Oral History, p. 16: https://www.documentcloud.org/documents/3718228 -Oral-History-California-Water-Issues.html.

23 "Brown Pledges Fish, Wildlife Preservation," *Feather River Bulletin*, April 21, 1960.

24 "Basic Questions on State's Water Problems Answered," *Los Angeles Times*, April 10, 1960.

25 "Brown Assails All Foes of Water Bond Issue," *Los Angeles Times*, Aug. 31, 1960.

26 Kenneth Umbach, "Pat Brown's Building Boom," p. 28.

27 Ethan Rarick, p. 228.

28 Grace Hechinger, "Clark Kerr, Leading Public Educator and Former Head of California's Universities, Dies at 92," *New York Times*, Dec. 2, 2003.

29 Clark Kerr, "The Great Transformation in Higher Education," p. 210.

30 *Times* Sacramento Bureau, "Brown Has Wary Eye on Nixon," *Los Angeles Times*, Jan. 14, 1961.

31 James Bassett, "California Democrats Gird Against Nixon," *Los Angeles Times*, Feb. 21, 1961.

32 James Bassett, "Nixon Announces He's in Governor Contest," *Los Angeles Times*, Sept. 28, 1961.

33 James Bassett, "Nixon Announces He's in Governor Contest," *Los Angeles Times*, Sept. 28, 1961.

34 James Bassett, "Nixon Announces He's in Governor Contest," *Los Angeles Times*, Sept. 28, 1961.

35 Evan Thomas, *Being Nixon*, p. 134.

36 "Losing Like a Mosquito Bite—Nixon," *Los Angeles Times*, Nov. 8, 1962.

37 November 7, 1962, partial video is available through the Miller Center, University of Virginia archives. Transcripts of the full address are widely available.

## CHAPTER FOUR

1 "House Red Probe Meeting Draws Protest, Support," *Oakland Tribune*, May 11, 1960.

2 Seth Rosenfeld, *Subversives*, pp. 77–78.

3 "General Riot Breaks Out at Red Quiz," *Oakland Tribune*, May 13, 1960.

4 "1,500 Gather Outside Probe at S.F. City Hall," *Oakland Tribune*, May 14, 1960.

5 Jerry Brown interview with author, July 14, 2015.

6    Jerry Brown interview with author, Jan. 29, 2016.

7    Jerry Brown interview with author, Feb. 8, 2019.

8    The bill carved out exceptions for owner-occupied dwellings of fewer than five units (heaven forbid that owners might be compelled to live alongside those of different races) and also exempted some fraternal and religious organizations.

9    Wolfinger and Greenstein, "The Repeal of Fair Housing in California: An Analysis of Referendum Voting," American Political Science Review, Sept. 1968.

10   Rosenfeld, Subversives, pp. 159–167.

11   Rosenfeld, Subversives, p. 174.

12   "Visual History: Free Speech Movement, 1964," University of California, Berkeley, http://fsm.berkeley.edu/free-speech-movement-timeline/.

13   Mario Savio, "On the operation of the machine," posted on YouTube on March 18, 2016, https://www.youtube.com/watch?v=Yew51uYHYV4.

14   Jerry Brown interview with author, July 14, 2015.

15   Jack McCurdy and Art Berman, "New Rioting, Stores Looted, Cars Destroyed," Los Angeles Times, Aug. 13, 1965.

16   "1,000 Riot in L.A.," Los Angeles Times, Aug. 12, 1965.

17   Jack McCurdy and Art Berman, "New Rioting, Stores Looted, Cars Destroyed," Los Angeles Times, Aug. 13, 1965.

18   Joe Alex Morris Jr., "Brown Flying Home, Pledges Aid to Parker," Los Angeles Times, Aug. 14, 1965.

19   Jerry Brown interview with author, May 6, 2016.

20   Lyndon Johnson, "Remarks at the White House Conference on Equal Employment Opportunities," Aug. 20, 1965 (courtesy of the American Presidency Project).

21   "Violence in the City: An End or a Beginning" (Report of the McCone Commission), p. 1.

22   "Violence in the City—An End or a Beginning," pp. 5–6.

23   Leonard Koppett, "Marichal Hits Roseboro With Bar and Starts Brawl as Giants Top Dodgers; Catcher Suffers 2-inch Head Cut," New York Times, Aug. 23, 1965.

## CHAPTER FIVE

1    Joan Didion, Where I Was From, p. 157.

2    Ken Kesey, Conversations with Ken Kesey, p. 148.

3    Conversations with Ken Kesey, p. xi.

4    Hillary Reder, "Serial & Singular: Andy Warhol's Campbell's Soup Cans," Inside/Out, MOMA, April 29, 2015: https://www.moma.org/explore/inside_out/2015/04/29/serial-singular-andy-warhols-campbells-soup-cans/.

5    Ferus, pp. 24–27.

6    http://diebenkorn.org/the-artist/biography/.

7    Michael Kimmelman, "Richard Diebenkorn, Lyrical Painter, Dies at 71," New York Times, March 31, 1993.

8    Gerald Norland, Richard Diebenkorn, p. 187.

9    Gerald Norland, Richard Diebenkorn, p. 188.

10   John Patterson, "California dreamers: The story of art in the 1950s and 60s," The Guardian, Oct. 7, 2009: https://www.theguardian.com/artanddesign/2009/oct/08/california-1960s-art.

11    Adrian Glick Kudler, "The Case Study house that made Los Angeles a modernist mecca," *Curbed Los Angeles*, June 4, 2008: https://la.curbed.com/maps/los-angeles-case-study-house-map-modern-architecture.

12    The image is of Koenig's Case Study House #22, included in the National Register of Historic Places.

13    Images of the Case Study House #22, also known as the Stahl House, can be found here: https://www.laconservancy.org/locations/stahl-house-case-study-house-22.

14    Susan Clark, "The History of The Sea Ranch from the Pomo Indians to Present," available at: https://www.tsra.org/news.php?viewStory=138.

15    Susan Clark, "The History of The Sea Ranch from the Pomo Indians to Present," available at: https://www.tsra.org/news.php?viewStory=138.

16    *Conversations with Ken Kesey*, p. 65.

17    Emily Witt, "The Science of the Psychedelic Renaissance," *The New Yorker*, May 29, 2018: https://www.newyorker.com/books/under-review/the-science-of-the-psychedelic-renaissance.

18    *Subversives*, p. 322.

## CHAPTER SIX

1     Lou Cannon, *Governor Reagan*, pp. 11–52.

2     Ronald Reagan, "A Time for Choosing," posted on YouTube on April 2, 2009: https://www.youtube.com/watch?v=qXBswFfh6AY.

3     Ronald Reagan, "A Time for Choosing," posted on YouTube on April 2, 2009: https://www.youtube.com/watch?v=qXBswFfh6AY.

4     DeGroot, *History*, Vol. 82, No. 267, pp. 429–448.

5     "Demos Assail Reagan's Speech," *Oakland Tribune*, Jan. 5, 1966.

6     Jack S. McDowell, "Brown Taunts Reagan," *San Francisco Examiner*, Sept. 22, 1966. See also: *San Francisco Chronicle*, March 13, 1966.

7     Dave Hope, "Reagan Tosses Hat in Ring, Urges a 'Creative Society,'" *Oakland Tribune*, Jan. 5, 1966.

8     Dave Hope, "Reagan Tosses Hat in Ring, Urges a 'Creative Society,'" *Oakland Tribune*, Jan. 5, 1966.

9     Andersen and Lee, *Western Political Quarterly*, 1967, p. 536.

10    Lou Cannon, *Reagan as Governor*.

11    Degroot, *History*, Vol. 82, No. 267, pp. 429–448.

12    Accessed via YouTube: https://www.youtube.com/watch?v=442rW8QaRtA.

13    ABC News, Election Preview, Nov. 6, 1966.

14    This description of the tax debate draws on the works of Lou Cannon and Bill Boyarsky.

15    Bobby Seale, *Seize the Time*, p. 85.

16    Adam Winkler, *Gunfight*, p. 234.

17    Winkler, *Gunfight*, p. 237.

18    Winkler, *Gunfight*, p. 240.

19    Jerry Gilliam, "Security Tightened at Capitol; Reagan Death Threats Told," *Los Angeles Times*, May 4, 1967.

20    This quote appears in many places. I found it here: https://www.history.com/news/black-panthers-gun-control-nra-support-mulford-act.

21    Jerry Gilliam, "Governor Signs Law on Abortion," *Los Angeles Times*, June 16, 1987.

22 "Summer of Love," Chapter 1, *The American Experience*, PBS.

23 Jerry Garcia, *Jerry on Jerry*, p. 118.

24 Timothy Leary, Leary's creepy, spoken-word album from that period bore the title of his famous slogan: https://www.youtube.com/watch?v=78WvMFKc4hM.


CHAPTER SEVEN


1 Raymond Fisher interview with the author, Oct. 5, 2015.

2 Fisher interview with the author, Oct. 5, 2015.

3 Eli and Arlene Chernow interview with the author, Nov. 2, 2018.

4 Eli and Arlene Chernow interview with the author, Nov. 2, 2018.

5 McFadden, *Trailblazer*, p. 38.

6 Tom Quinn interview with the author, Aug. 29, 2018.

7 "Election Results," *Los Angeles Times*, April 3, 1969. Those totals reflect the election results with 3,479 out of 3,501 precincts reporting, so the exact totals may have changed slightly after recounting.

8 Jerry Brown interview with the author, Aug. 15, 2016.

9 Board minutes, obtained by author via California Public Records Act.

10 "English Teacher Reinstated After Dismissal Over Poem," *Los Angeles Times*, Dec. 5, 1970; also: Howard Kennedy, "Trustees to Appeal Hoag Reinstatement," *Los Angeles Times*, Dec. 9, 1970.

11 Jerry Cohen, "Savage Mystic Cult Blamed for 5 Tate Murders, 6 Others," *Los Angeles Times*, Dec. 2, 1969.

12 Dave Smith, "Zodiac Kills 5th Victim, Again Taunts Police," *Los Angeles Times*, Oct. 16, 1969.

13 Jerry Cohen, "Savage Mystic Cult Blamed for 5 Tate Murders, 6 Others," *Los Angeles Times*, Dec. 2, 1969.

14 Carl Greenberg, "Edmund G. Brown, Jr. Enters Race for Secretary of State," *Los Angeles Times*, March 3, 1970.

15 Carl Greenberg, "Pat Brown Declines to Back Yorty or Unruh in Primary," *Los Angeles Times*, April 15, 1970.

16 "Secretary of State Jordan, 81, Dies at Home," *Los Angeles Times*, March 31, 1970.

17 Jon Thurber, "James Flournoy, 1915–2009: 1st African American nominated for a partisan state office," *Los Angeles Times*, March 5, 2009.

18 A photograph of the swearing-in ceremony is contained within the Brown Personal Papers, Williams, CA. Brown discovered it to his delight one afternoon as we rummaged through the papers in March of 2019.

19 Jerry Brown interview with the author, March 8, 2019.

20 McFadden, *Trailblazer*, p. 56.

21 National Law Journal: https://www.law.com/nationallawjournal/almID/900005464984/Jerry-Brown-Version-30-Hits-the-Trail/?slreturn=20190611124619.

22 Valenti to "Dear Gerry Brown," March 20, 1972, Brown Personal Papers, Williams, CA.

23 Robert Stern and Howard Berman interviews with the author, Jan. 25, 2018, and June 2, 2016.

24 Jerry Gilliam, "Proposition 9 Battle to Erupt on Radio, TV," *Los Angeles Times*, May 27, 1974.

25 Editorial, "Political Reform: Yes on Prop. 9," *Los Angeles Times*, May 24, 1974.

26   Author interview with Quinn, Aug. 29, 2018.

27   Richard Bergholz, "Goals Outlined by Brown as He Formally Enters Governor Race," *Los Angeles Times*, Jan. 29, 1974.

28   Jeffrey Toobin, *American Heiress*, p. 68.

29   Toobin, *American Heiress*, p. 87.

30   Toobin, *American Heiress,* pp. 178–79.

31   Al Martinez and Robert Kistler, "SLA Hideout Stormed, 5 Die," *Los Angeles Times*, May 18, 1974.

32   Toobin, *American Heiress*, p. 310.

33   Moretti letters to Brown, April 4 and April 25, 1974, Brown Personal Papers, Williams, CA.

34   Contemporary sources set the amount of this contribution at $25,000, but Brown said the full amount that unions gave and raised came to $100,000.

35   Robert Pack, *The Philosopher Prince*, p. 58.

36   Joseph Ball, "A Century in the Life of a Lawyer: Reflections by Joseph A. Ball," *California Western Law Review*, Vol. 36, No. 1, 1999, p. 88.

37   Ball, "A Century in the Life of a Lawyer: Reflections by Joseph A. Ball," *California Western Law Review*, Vol. 36, No. 1, 1999, p. 90.

38   Ball, "A Century in the Life of a Lawyer: Reflections by Joseph A. Ball," *California Western Law Review*, Vol. 36, No. 1, 1999, p. 92.

39   "A Feisty 82, Joe Ball Speaks His Mind," *Long Beach News*, June 27, 1985: http://www.californiascapitol.com/2013/05/a-feisty-82-joe-ball-speaks-his-mind/.

40   This story was widely covered in its day, but the lion's share of credit for revealing it and pursuing it belongs to Dan Walters, the veteran Sacramento columnist. One iteration of his long-running coverage appears here: https://www.sacbee.com/news/politics-government/politics-columns-blogs/dan-walters/article44656767.html.

41   George Skelton, "Brown Not Folding in Stretch Run," *Los Angeles Times*, May 15, 1974.

42   Dennis J. Opatray, "Brown Rejects Oil Pledges," *San Francisco Examiner*, May 21, 1974.

43   Brown family birthday card, Pat Brown Papers, Bancroft Library, Carton 2.

44   Tom Hayden, "Jerry Brown: The Mystic and the Machine," *Rolling Stone*, Dec. 19, 1974.

## CHAPTER EIGHT

1    Jim Newton, *Eisenhower: The White House Years,* pp. 158–59.

2    https://www.americanwarlibrary.com/vietnam/vwatl.htm.

3    https://www.americanwarlibrary.com/vietnam/vwatl.htm. The originating source for this material is the Department of Defense Manpower Data Center.

4    George Murphy, "The 'Camp' Meeting at Cal," *San Francisco Examiner*, May 22, 1965.

5    https://www.sfchronicle.com/thetake/article/1967-Vietnam-War-protest-photos-show-savagery-by-12338190.php.

6    "Draft Protest Halted, Police Wield Clubs—New UC Rally," *San Francisco Examiner*, Oct. 17, 1967.

7    Hubert J. Bernhard, "Police Smash Draft Riot—Rout 10,000," *San Francisco Examiner*, Oct. 20, 1967.

8    Sim Van der Ryn, *Design for an Empathic World*, p. 80.

9    Sim Van der Ryn, *Design for an Empathic World*, p. 81.

10   Tom Dalzell, *Berkeleyside*, Jan. 2, 2019.

11 Alan Copeland and Nikki Arai, editors, *People's Park*, pp. 114–115.

12 "Downtown Berkeley Jammed," *San Francisco Examiner*, May 16, 1969.

13 "Downtown Berkeley Jammed," *San Francisco Examiner*, May 16, 1969.

14 Copeland, *People's Park*, p. 115.

15 Copeland, *People's Park*, p. 116.

16 Copeland, *People's Park*, p. 109.

17 "Riots, Civil and Criminal Disorders," Hearings Before the Permanent Subcommittee on Investigations of the Committee on Government Operations, United States Senate, Aug. 4–6, 1970, pp. 5758–5792. Available online at: https://www.ncjrs.gov/pdffiles1/Digitization/82211NCJRS.pdf.

18 "Riots, Civil and Criminal Disorders," Hearings Before the Permanent Subcommittee on Investigations of the Committee on Government Operations, United States Senate, Aug. 4–6, 1970, p. 5574.

19 National Archives, Vietnam War U.S. Military Fatal Casualty Statistics, as of April 29, 2008.

20 Leonard Kleinrock, UCLA lecture, Jan. 13, 2009: https://www.youtube.com/watch?v=vuiBTJZfeo8

21 Leslie Berlin, *Troublemakers*, p. 103.

22 Jerry Brown interview with the author, Feb. 8, 2019.

## CHAPTER NINE

1 Tom Quinn interview with the author, Aug. 29, 2018.

2 Lisa Robinson, "An Oral History of Laurel Canyon, the 60s and 70s Music Mecca," *Vanity Fair*, Feb. 8, 2015.

3 Tony Kline interview with the author, Dec. 4, 2015.

4 Jerry Brown interview with the author, Aug. 15, 2016.

5 Jerry Brown interview with the author, Feb. 8, 2019.

6 Jim Lorenz, *Jerry Brown: The Man on the White Horse*, p. 24.

7 Alessandra Stanley, "On the Road With: Jacques Barzaghi; What's That Glimmering Behind Jerry Brown?" *New York Times*, April 2, 1992.

8 Raymond Fisher interview with the author, Oct. 5, 2005.

9 Jerry Brown interview with the author, Aug. 15, 2016.

10 Bill Boyarsky, "Brown Says Voters Did Not Give Him a Blank Check," *Los Angeles Times*, Nov. 7, 1974.

11 Jerry Brown interview with the author, Jan. 29, 2016.

12 Mary Nichols interview with the author, Jan. 5, 2016. See also: *Blueprint* magazine, Spring 2016.

13 Mary Nichols interview with the author, Jan. 5, 2016. See also: *Blueprint* magazine, Spring 2016.

14 Robert Pack, *Brown: The Philosopher Prince*, pp. 65–66.

15 Edmund G. "Jerry" Brown, Jr., First Inaugural Address, Jan. 6, 1975: https://governors.library.ca.gov/addresses/34-Jbrown01.html.

16 Edmund G. "Jerry" Brown, Jr., First Inaugural Address, Jan. 6, 1975: https://governors.library.ca.gov/addresses/34-Jbrown01.html.

17 Editorial, "The New Governor Sets the Tone," *Los Angeles Times*, Jan. 7, 1975.

18 Guy Wright, "One Brownie Point," *San Francisco Examiner*, Jan. 7, 1975.

19 Jim Lorenz, *Jerry Brown: The Man on the White Horse*, p. 201.

20 Jim Lorenz, *Jerry Brown: The Man on the White Horse*, p. 246.

21 Steven Greenhut, "The Conventional Jerry Brown," *City Journal*, Sept. 16, 2011.

22 Sim Van der Ryn, *Design for an Emphatic World*, p. xiii.

23 Phil Smith, "If small is beautiful, why does OAT keep growing"? April 1981 (copy from personal collection of Bill Parent).

24 Bill Parent, "OAT in California: Appropriate Technology in the Mainstream," 1982 (copy from Parent's personal collection).

25 Andrew Holzman, "Sacramento's Worst State Buildings: Number 4," *Sacramento Bee*, Aug. 14, 2015.

26 Jim Lorenz, *Jerry Brown: The Man on the White Horse*, p. 33.

27 Jerry Brown, *Dialogues*, p. 52.

28 Jerry Brown interview with the author, Aug. 15, 2016. Brown was not entirely consistent on this point, sometimes embracing the word and other times questioning whether it suited him. It did.

29 Ivan Illich, *Deschooling Society*, p. 10.

30 Ivan Illich, *Limits to Medicine*, p. 3.

31 Nathan Gardels, interview with the author, Jan. 30, 2019.

32 " 'These are hard times'—Brown," *Bakersfield Californian*, Feb. 11, 1976.

33 Jerry Brown interview with the author, Feb. 8, 2019.

34 Jerry Brown interview with the author, Feb. 8, 2019.

35 Mary Catherine Bateson, "Six days of dying": http://www.oikos.org/batdeath.htm.

36 Jerry Brown interview with the author, March 8, 2019.

37 Joan Didion, "Many Mansions," 1977 (included in *The White Album*, p. 67).

38 Pack, *The Philosopher Prince*, p. 90.

49 Well into Brown's third term as governor, in 2014, he attended a funeral in Los Angeles. I watched as various city and county officials arrived, each surrounded by aides, sheriff's deputies, and police officers. As the service was about to begin, Brown came to the door of the cathedral, asked directions of an usher, and made his way to his seat alone.

40 Jerry Brown interview with the author, Oct. 5, 2018.

41 George Skelton and William Endicott, "Jerry Brown—Friends, Relatives Appraise the New Governor," Jan. 6, 1975.

42 These recollections come from Brown associates who asked to remain anonymous.

43 Governor's correspondence, USC files, Feb. 18, 1975, Mrs. Richard Buchanan, Jr.

44 Jerry Brown interview with the author, Dec. 19, 2016.

45 Craig Brown, *Ninety-Nine Glimpses of Princess Margaret*, p. 346.

46 "Prince Charles Ends U.S. Visit on West Coast," *New York Times*, Oct. 30, 1977.

47 Linda Ronstadt, public appearance at the Ace Hotel, Los Angeles, Oct. 2018.

48 "The Pop Politics of Jerry Brown," (cover) *Newsweek*, April 23, 1979.

## CHAPTER TEN

1 Ethan Rarick, *California Rising*, p. 352.

2 Patrick K. Brown, *The Rise and Fall of Rose Bird*, p. 3.

3 Paul Durham, "The Public Record of Jerry Brown," 1976, contained in Brown Personal Papers, Williams, CA.

4 Howard Berman interview with the author, Dec. 28, 2016.

5   Willie Brown interview with the author, Sept. 15, 2015.

6   George Skelton, "Brown Offers Bill on Farm Workers," *Los Angeles Times*, April 11, 1975.

7   Miriam Pawel, *The Union of Their Dreams*, pp. 153–155.

8   "Bishop, Farmer, Unionists on New Farm Labor Unit," *Los Angeles Times*, Aug. 17, 1975.

9   *Times* staff writer, "Growers Unit Opposes Brown's Nominees to Farm Labor Board," *Los Angeles Times*, Aug. 10, 1975.

10   Editorial, "Down on the Farm: Chaos…," *Los Angeles Times*, Oct. 3, 1975.

11   Tony Kline interview with the author, Dec. 4, 2015.

12   Greer J. Oppenheimer, "The Governor's Son as Governor," *Family Weekly*, Jan. 11, 1976, Pat Brown papers, Carton 2.

13   *Family Weekly*, Jan. 11, 1976, Pat Brown papers, Carton 2.

14   Gray Davis interview with the author, April 8, 2019.

15   Robert Scheer, "*Playboy* Interview: Jerry Brown," draft, Dec. 27, 1975, Brown Personal Papers, Williams, CA. See also: *Playboy* magazine, April 1976.

16   *Playboy* interview draft, Dec. 27, 1975, Brown Personal Papers, Williams, CA.

17   Pat Brown papers, Carton 2, Jerry Brown correspondence. See letters dated Feb. 11 and Feb. 23, 1972.

18   Pat Brown papers, Carton 2, Jerry Brown correspondence, Dec. 5, 1975.

19   *Firing Line*, William F. Buckley: "The Practical Limits of Liberalism," Oct. 3, 1975. The telecast, still available on YouTube, is dated Oct. 11, but the program notes indicate it was filmed the week before. Here is a link to the program on YouTube: https://archive.org/details/csth_00001.

20   Edmund G. Brown, Jr., State of the State Address, Jan. 7, 1976: https://governors.library.ca.gov/addresses/s_34-JBrown1.html.

21   Jack Weber, "The Brown '76 Response: 'It'll do…No so hot,'" *San Francisco Examiner*, Jan. 8, 1976.

22   Bob Schmidt, "Governor came late, spoke briefly, left fast," *Long Beach Independent*, Jan. 8, 1976.

23   Editorial, "Brown's New Expectations," *Los Angeles Times*, Jan. 9, 1976.

24   Bob Schmidt, "Governor came late, spoke briefly, left fast," *Long Beach Independent*, Jan. 8, 1976.

25   Jack Weber, "The Brown '76 Response: 'It'll do…No so hot,'" *San Francisco Examiner*, Jan. 8, 1976.

26   Raymond Fisher interview with the author, Oct. 5, 2015.

27   Tom Quinn interview with the author, Aug. 29, 2018.

28   Raymond Fisher interview with the author, Oct. 5, 2015.

29   "Huge Tax Hikes Seen As Result of Public Worker Strike Bill," *Daily Independent Journal*, March 19, 1975.

30   Raymond Fisher interview with the author, Oct. 5, 2015. Also, author interview with Howard Berman.

31   "Bargaining rights granted," *The Times Standard*, Oct. 1, 1977.

32   Jordan Diamond, et al., "The Past, Present, and Future of California's Coastal Act: Overcoming Division to Comprehensively Manage the Coast," University of California, Berkeley, 2016: https://www.law.berkeley.edu/wp-content/uploads/2017/08/Coastal-Act-Issue-Brief.pdf.

33   "Beilenson Introduces 'Save the Coast' Bill," *Hanford Sentinel*, Feb. 11, 1976.

34   Edmund G. Brown, Jr., State of the State Address, Jan. 7, 1976: http://governors.library.ca.gov/addresses/s_34-JBrown1.html.

35   Hill Gladwin, New York Times News Service, "California's Coastal Plan," *Honolulu Star-Bulletin*, June 24, 1976.

36    "Coastal Bill Amendment Sparks No Big Outcries," *Santa Cruz Sentinel*, Aug. 25, 1976.

37    "Brown signs landmark coastal bill," *The Times Standard*, Sept. 30, 1976.

38    "Brown Says He'll Run for President," *The San Mateo Times*, March 13, 1976.

39    Orville Schell, *Brown*, p. 2.

40    Mickey Kantor interview with the author, July 11, 2016.

41    William E. Hawkins and Robert Timberg, "Area Officials Greet Gov. Brown," *The Evening Sun*, April 29, 1976.

42    Tom Quinn interview with the author, Aug. 29, 2018.

43    New York Times News Service, "The platform, point-by-point," *San Bernardino County Sun*, July 14, 1976.

44    "Brown Sr. disappointed by son's surrender," *The Press Democrat*, July 15, 1976.

45    "Brown Sr. disappointed by son's surrender," *The Press Democrat*, July 15, 1976.

46    "Brown Sr. disappointed by son's surrender," *The Press Democrat*, July 15, 1976.

## CHAPTER ELEVEN

1    K.C. Clarke and Jeffrey J. Hemphill, "The Santa Barbara Oil Spill, A Retrospective," University of California, Santa Barbara, 2002: http://www.geog.ucsb.edu/~kclarke/Papers/SBOilSpill1969.pdf.

2    Predictably, the low estimate came from Union Oil, while the high end was supplied by the Coast Guard.

3    "Oil Well Break off Coast Spreads 10-Mile-Long Slick," *Long Beach Independent*, Jan. 30, 1969.

4    Photo caption, "Beaches Threatened by Oil." Story by Harry Trimborn, "Battle Shaping Up Over Offshore Oil." Both from *Los Angeles Times*, Feb. 2, 1969.

5    K.C. Clarke and Jeffrey J. Hemphill, "The Santa Barbara Oil Spill, A Retrospective," University of California, Santa Barbara, 2002: http://www.geog.ucsb.edu/~kclarke/Papers/SBOilSpill1969.pdf.

6    Nixon Foundation, "RN's Response to the Santa Barbara Oil Spill": https://www.nixonfoundation.org/2010/07/rns-response-to-the-santa-barbara-oil-spill/.

7    Mike Rinde, "Richard Nixon and the Rise of American Environmentalism," Science History Institute, 2017: https://www.sciencehistory.org/distillations/magazine/richard-nixon-and-the-rise-of-american-environmentalism.

8    Richard Nixon, State of the Union Address, Jan. 22, 1970. Transcript courtesy of the American Presidency Project.

9    Mike Rinde, "Richard Nixon and the Rise of American Environmentalism," Science History Institute, 2017: https://www.sciencehistory.org/distillations/magazine/richard-nixon-and-the-rise-of-american-environmentalism.

10   Jerry Brown, interview with the author, Nov. 13, 2015, excerpts of which were published in *Blueprint* magazine, Spring 2016.

11   E. F. Schumacher, *Small Is Beautiful*, pp. 108–109.

12   Mark 8:17–18, King James Version.

13   Declaration of the United Nations Conference on the Human Environment, paragraph 3.

14   Declaration of the United Nations Conference on the Human Environment, paragraph 6.

15   Richard Nixon, State of the Union Address, Jan. 22, 1970. American Presidency Project.

16    Brown did, briefly, introduce a prescient note into the Secretary of State race with respect to the environment. Speaking to a San Francisco Junior Chamber of Commerce lunch in October of 1970, he suggested that the state could commit to purchasing only "smog-free" cars for its many fleets. That, he offered, could wipe out smog in just five years. His remarks were barely noted. (*Redlands Daily Facts*, Oct. 23, 1970)

17    "Offshore drilling," *Pomona Progress-Bulletin*, Sept. 8, 1974.

18    Jerry Brown interview with the author, Nov. 13, 2015.

19    Galatians 6:7, King James Version.

20    See Earthday.org: https://www.earthday.org/about/the-history-of-earth-day/.

21    Joseph Lelyveld, "Millions Join Earth Day Observances Across the Nation," *New York Times*, April 23, 1970.

22    "And, in the Kingdom of Smog, Multitudes Hail Earth Day," *San Bernardino County Sun*, April 23, 1970.

23    "Earth Day is Success," *San Mateo Times and Daily News Leader*, April 22, 1970.

24    Gaye Le Baron, Untitled column, *The Press Democrat*, April 24, 1970.

25    Editorial, "Every Day an 'Earth Day,'" *Los Angeles Times*, April 24, 1970.

26    Jack Lewis, *EPA Journal*, 1990. Environmental Protection Agency archives: https://archive.epa.gov/epa/aboutepa/spirit-first-earth-day.html.

27    Mike Rinde, "Richard Nixon and the Rise of American Environmentalism," Science History Institute, 2017: https://www.sciencehistory.org/distillations/magazine/richard-nixon-and-the-rise-of-american-environmentalism.

28    Leon Panetta, *Worthy Fights*, p. 94.

## CHAPTER TWELVE

1    Chuck McFadden, *Trailblazer: A Biography of Jerry Brown* (Berkeley: University of California Press, 2013), 72.

2    Tony Kline interview with the author, Dec. 4, 2015.

3    Kline, interview.

4    Rose Bird memorandum to Jerry Brown, "Jurisdictional Resolution of Farm Labor Issue," May 19, 1976, Brown personal papers.

5    Jacqueline R. Braitman and Gerald F. Uelmen, *Justice Stanley Mosk: A Life at the Center of California Politics and Justice* (Jefferson, NC: McFarland and Co., 2012), 185.

6    Braitman and Uelman, *Justice Stanley Mosk*, 186.

7    Jerry Brown interview with the author, Dec. 19, 2016.

8    Diana Dooley interview with the author, Oct. 5, 2018.

9    Tom Quinn interview with the author, Aug. 29, 2018.

10    "Local, School Aid Proposed," *Petaluma Argus Courier*, June 8, 1978.

11    Jerry Brown to Evelle Younger, July 4, 1978, Brown personal papers.

12    Evelle Younger to Jerry Brown, July 18, 1978, Brown personal papers.

13    Ballot text, November 7, 1978, Office of the California Secretary of State.

14    "Prop. 6 Is Gay Rights' Milestone," *The Sun* (San Bernardino, CA), October 25, 1978.

15    Jeff Guinn, *The Road to Jonestown: Jim Jones and Peoples Temple* (New York: Simon and Schuster, 2017), p. 420.

16    Tim Reiterman with John Jacobs, *Raven: The Untold Story of the Reverend Jim Jones and His People* (New York: Jeremy P. Tarcher / Penguin, 2008), pp. 491–495.

17    Guinn, *Road to Jonestown*, p. 424.

18    "Rep. Ryan Slain: Ambush at Guyana Airport," *San Francisco Examiner,* Nov. 19, 1978.

19    Jim Willser, "How They Died: Corpses Covered Ground in Jonestown," *San Francisco Examiner,* Nov. 21, 1978.

20    Reiterman, *Raven,* p. 591.

21    San Francisco is both a city and a county, so it is governed by a board of supervisors (the structure of county governments in California), one of whom is elected mayor (the structure of city government in the state).

22    Dianne Feinstein interview with the author, April 2, 2019.

23    James A. Finefrock, "Aide: White 'a Wild Man,'" *San Francisco Examiner,* Nov. 27, 1978.

24    David Talbot, *Season of the Witch: Enchantment, Terror, and Deliverance in the City of Love* (New York: Free Press, 2012), pp. 322–26.

25    Sydney Kossen, "Feinstein Vows to Put City Back on Course," *San Francisco Examiner,* Nov. 28, 1978.

26    CNN, "The Day That Shaped Dianne Feinstein," *Badass Women of Washington with Dana Bash,* https://www.youtube.com/watch?v=M4-vjp6crKk.

27    Feinstein interview.

28    "No Bail as D.A. Cites New Law," *San Francisco Examiner,* Nov. 28, 1978.

29    Talbot, *Season of the Witch,* p. 328.

30    Finefrock, "Aide: White 'a Wild Man.'"

31    I was a high school student in Palo Alto, California, on the day of the Moscone and Milk assassinations. Feinstein's handling of those events remains one of the most indelible moments of my young life.

32    "Dianne Feinstein Announces Harvey Milk's Death," video posted to YouTube by Max Robins on January 3, 2015, at https://www.youtube.com/watch?v=5NikqzmwbgU.

## CHAPTER THIRTEEN

1    Evan Westrup interview with the author, Oct. 4, 2018.

2    Jose A. Del Real, "California Today: Jerry Brown Warns of Recession and Reveals His Final Budget," *New York Times,* Jan. 11, 2018.

3    Tony Kline interview with the author, Dec. 4, 2015.

4    Governor's budget, Jan. 10, 1975 (courtesy of the California Department of Finance).

5    Governor's budget, Jan. 10, 1976 (courtesy of the California Department of Finance).

6    Governor's budget, Jan. 10, 1979 (courtesy of the California Department of Finance).

7    Undated memo reviewing the relationship between the University of California and the United States Department of Energy, Brown personal papers.

8    "Brown and the UC Weapons Issue," editorial, *San Francisco Examiner,* May 22, 1979.

9    Sharon Rosenhause, "UC Regents Snub Brown, OK Ties to Nuclear Labs," *Los Angeles Times,* July 21, 1979.

10    George Kieffer interview with the author, Dec. 17, 2018.

11    Victoria Brittain, "The African Jaunt," *Washington Post,* April 16, 1979.

12    Brittain, "The African Jaunt."

13    "A Conversation with Jerry Brown," *Bill Moyers Journal,* May 7, 1979. Transcript from personal files of Larry Pryor.

14    "A Conversation with Jerry Brown."

15    Jerry Brown to Jimmy Carter, Jan. 6, 1980, personal files of Larry Pryor.

16   "Brown, Connally Blast Carter Debate Pullout," *Pittsburgh Press,* Dec. 30, 1979.

17   The decision on the case, 26 Cal. 3d 111, is available on the Justia website at https://law.justia.com/cases/california/supreme-court/3d/26/110.html.

18   The arguments in this case included two advocates who would become major figures in American legal circles. Tony Kline, Brown's law school classmate and later a member of the California Courts of Appeal, argued for Brown. Theodore Olson, who would become a go-to advocate for the conservative movement and then, unexpectedly, an important proponent of gay marriage, represented Mike Curb.

19   "Linda Ronstadt Sings My Boyfriend's Back to Jerry Brown," video posted to YouTube on Jan. 31, 2011, by jpspanishfan3, at https://www.youtube.com/watch?v=U -QmdzBYDWA.

20   Tom Quinn interview with the author, Aug. 29, 2018.

21   Eleanor Clift, "Kennedy Enters 1980 Presidential Race," *Newsweek,* Sept. 23, 1979.

22   Jesse Walker, "Friday A/V Club: Jerry Brown and Francis Ford Coppola's 'Transmission from Some Clandestine Place on Mars,'" *Reason,* June 6, 2014, at https://reason.com /blog/2014/06/06/friday-av-club-jerry-brown-and-francis-f.

23   Mike Royko, "Should America Fence Off California?," *Los Angeles Times,* April 23, 1979.

24   Royko, "Should America Fence Off California?"

25   Mike Royko, "Time to Eclipse 'Moonbeam' Label," *Chicago Tribune,* Sept. 4, 1991.

26   Mike Royko, "Gov. Moonbeam Needs a Brain Lift," *Arizona Daily Star,* Dec. 20, 1979.

## CHAPTER FOURTEEN

1   Jerry Brown interview with the author, Oct. 5, 2018.

2   Phillip E. Johnson and Sheldon L. Messinger, "California's Determinate Sentencing Statute: History and Issues," in *Determinate Sentencing: Reform or Regression,* Proceedings of the Special Conference on Determinate Sentencing, June 2–3, 1977, Boalt Hall School of Law, University of California, Berkeley (Washington, DC: National Institute of Law Enforcement and Criminal Justice, 1978), p. 13.

3   "Brown Backs End to Indeterminate Jail Terms," *Press Democrat* (Santa Rosa, CA), March 25, 1976.

4   "Indeterminate Jail Terms Ended," *Press Democrat* (Santa Rosa, CA), Sept. 1, 1976.

5   Jerry Brown interview with the author, Oct. 5, 2018.

6   Jerry Brown interview with the author, Oct. 5, 2018. On other occasions, Brown was less measured in his reflections regarding the bill and its impact. "It's a treadmill; it's a merry-go-round," he said in 2003. "It's an outrage." (Jenifer Warren, "Jerry Brown Calls Sentence Law a Failure," *Los Angeles Times,* Feb. 28, 2003)

7   Governor's budget, Jan. 10, 1981 (courtesy of the California Department of Finance).

8   California State Library, "Governors' Gallery: Edmund G. Brown Jr.," State of the State Address delivered Jan. 8, 1981, at http://governors.library.ca.gov/addresses/s_34-JBrown6.html.

9   California State Library, "Governors' Gallery."

10   Richard Bergholz, "Roberti Hits Brown Speech for Lack of Specifics," *Los Angeles Times,* Jan. 10, 1981.

11   Douglas Shuit, "Legislature Passes Rival Budget Bills," *Los Angeles Times,* June 5, 1981.

12   California State Legislature, Legislative Analyst's Office, "Analysis of the Budget Bill of the State of California for the Fiscal Year July 1, 1981, to June 30, 1982," A-11.

13    California State Legislature, "Analysis of the Budget Bill," A-7.

14    W. B. Rood and George Reasons, "State Funds Being Used by Brown for Politics," *Los Angeles Times,* Dec. 6, 1980.

15    News conference of Governor Edmund G. Brown Jr., July 13, 1981 (transcript from the personal files of Bob Stern).

16    Harry Nelson, "Outbreaks of Pneumonia Among Gay Males Studied," *Los Angeles Times,* June 5, 1981.

17    "A Huge Anti-Nuke Rally," *San Francisco Examiner,* May 13, 1979.

18    Frederick Mielke to Jerry Brown, July 29, 1979, Brown personal papers.

19    Mielke to Brown, July 29, 1979.

20    *Wall Street Journal,* Aug. 24, 1981 (clip contained in Brown personal papers).

21    California Highway Patrol commissioner to Lynn Schenk, June 30, 1981, Brown personal papers.

22    Jerry Brown interview with the author, March 8, 2019.

23    USDA Animal and Plant Health Inspection Service, "Mediterranean Fruit Fly," at https://www.aphis.usda.gov/aphis/resources/pests-diseases/hungry-pests/the-threat/med-fruit-fly/med-fruit-fly.

24    James R. Carey, "The Mediterranean Fruit Fly in California: Taking Stock," *California Agriculture* 46, no. 1 (January 1992): 12–17, at http://calag.ucanr.edu/Archive/?article=ca.v046n01p12.

25    Don West, "Multi-Million-Dollar Crop Crisis Precipitated by a Bug," *San Francisco Examiner,* July 31, 1980.

26    "U.S. Joins Fruit Fly Quarantine," *San Francisco Examiner,* July 29, 1980.

27    "War on fruit flies becomes official," *The Press Democrat,* Dec. 25, 1980.

28    Steve Capps and John Flinn, "Aerial sprays start Monday in key area," *San Francisco Examiner,* July 10, 1981.

29    "A shot of malathion—hold the ice," *San Francisco Examiner,* July 15, 1981.

30    Tracy Wood, "Fight Medfly and Be Quiet, Brown Told," *Los Angeles Times,* July 17, 1981.

31    I witnessed these events firsthand. I graduated from Palo Alto High School in June of 1981 and spent that summer tracking the cordon tightening around my community as I prepared to leave for college. When the helicopters finally flew, my friends and I watched from a rooftop. Our neighborhood helicopter looked like a flying bug and dumped malathion on the three of us. It was sticky and pungent, but it came off easily in the shower.

32    Jerry Brown interview with the author, Oct. 5, 2018.

33    Kenneth Reich, "Wilson Courts GOP Establishment," *Los Angeles Times,* Aug. 11, 1981.

34    Katharine Macdonald, "The 1982 Elections: The California Senate Race," *Washington Post,* Nov. 1, 1982.

35    Jerry Brown interview with the author, March 8, 2018.

36    Keith Love and Larry Stammer, " 'I Shall Return,' Governor Says, " 'but Not for a While,' " *Los Angeles Times,* Nov. 4, 1982.

37    Love and Stammer, " 'I Shall Return.' "

## CHAPTER FIFTEEN

1    Centers for Disease Control and Prevention, Morbidity and Mortality Weekly Report, "*Pneumocystis* Pneumonia—Los Angeles," June 5, 1981, at https://www.cdc.gov/mmwr/preview/mmwrhtml/june_5.htm.

2   The definitive history of AIDS is Randy Shilts's haunting *And the Band Played On: Politics, People, and the AIDS Epidemic* (New York: St. Martin's, 1987). I have relied on it here for many details of the early AIDS epidemic.

3   Shilts, *And the Band Played On,* p. 71.

4   Timothy F. Murphy, "Is AIDS a Just Punishment?," *Journal of Medical Ethics* 14, no. 3 (September 1988): 154–60.

5   AIDS.gov, "A Timeline of HIV/AIDS," at https://www.hiv.gov/sites/default/files/aidsgov-timeline.pdf.

6   David Kaufman, "Doris Day's Vanishing Act," *Vanity Fair,* May 1, 2008.

7   Chris Geidner, "Nancy Reagan Turned Down Rock Hudson's Plea for Help Nine Weeks Before He Died," *BuzzFeed News,* Feb. 2, 2015, at https://www.buzzfeednews.com/article/chrisgeidner/nancy-reagan-turned-down-rock-hudsons-plea-for-help-seven-we.

8   "Rock in L.A. Hosp," *Daily News* (New York), July 31, 1985; see also: Shilts, *And the Band Played On,* p. 582.

9   Susan Ager, "Curtain Closes on Most Crucial Role," *Detroit Free Press,* Oct. 3, 1985.

10  AmfAR, "Thirty Years of HIV/AIDS: Snapshots of an Epidemic," at https://www.amfar.org/thirty-years-of-hiv/aids-snapshots-of-an-epidemic/.

11  "Gov. Deukmejian Critical of Brown 'Era of Neglect,'" *The Sun* (San Bernardino), Sept. 10, 1983.

12  Nathan Gardels interview with the author, Jan. 30, 2019.

13  Gardels interview.

14  Jerry Brown interview with the author, Feb. 2, 2020

15  William Endicott, "Brown's Image Remains Low," *Los Angeles Times,* March 9, 1983.

16  "Demo critic," *The Billings Gazette,* April 7, 1984.

17  Gardels interview.

18  Jerry Brown interview with the author, March 8, 2019.

19  Ivan Illich, "Posthumous Longevity: An Open Letter to a Cloistered Community of Benedictine Nuns," addressed in 1989 to Mother Jerome, O.S.B., of the Abbey of Regina Laudis, in Bethlehem, Connecticut, and copied to Brown on May 3, 2000, Brown personal papers.

20  Nathan Gardels to unknown recipient, 1983, Gardels personal papers. Brown recalls these events differently. I have relied on Gardels's material, since it was recorded at the time.

21  Celestine Bohlen, "Ex-Gov. Brown and His Group of 10 Interact with Muscovites," *Washington Post,* Sept. 29, 1984.

22  Bohlen, "Ex-Gov. Brown."

23  Gardels interview.

24  *New Perspectives Quarterly,* "Interview: Nicaraguan President Daniel Orgeta," *San Francisco Chronicle,* March 6, 1985.

25  Gardels interview.

26  Gerald F. Uelmen, "California Judicial Retention Elections," *Santa Clara Law Review* 28, no. 2 (1988).

27  Edmund G. Brown Jr., "Court Critics," *San Francisco Examiner,* March 2, 1986.

28  George Skelton, "Deukmejian to Oppose Grodin and Reynoso," *Los Angeles Times,* Aug. 26, 1986.

29  Jerry Brown interview with the author, Dec. 19, 2016.

30  Jerry Brown interview with the author, Jan. 29, 2016.

31  Kenneth Reich and Sam Jameson, "Brown in Japan to Write and Reflect," *Los Angeles Times,* Jan. 20, 1987.

32  Reich and Jameson, "Brown in Japan."

33  Brown personal papers.

34  "Brown May Help Mother Teresa," *The Sun* (San Bernardino), Jan. 26, 1987.

35  Fred Branfman, "The *Salon* Interview: Jerry Brown," *Salon,* June 3, 1996, at https://www.salon.com/1996/06/03/interview960603/.

36  Jerry Brown interview with the author, Feb. 8, 2019.

37  John Balzar, "Jerry Brown Seeks a Small Job but He's Thinking Big," *Los Angeles Times,* Dec. 18, 1988.

38  Bob Schwartz, "Brown Makes Appearance for State Senate Candidate," *Los Angeles Times,* March 18, 1990.

39  Schwartz, "Brown Makes Appearance."

40  James W. Sweeney, "Popularity of Brown down at end of reign," *San Bernardino County Sun*, March 2, 1991.

## CHAPTER SIXTEEN

1  Kathleen Brown interview with the author, Dec. 12, 2018.

2  Diary entry for May 25, 1959, volume 25 of Pat Brown papers, Bancroft Library, University of California, Berkeley.

3  Diary entry for May 27, 1959, volume 25 of Pat Brown papers.

4  Kathleen Brown interview with the author, Aug. 28, 2015.

5  Brown interview, 2018.

6  Jack McCurdy, "Rice Spells Out Plans for Schools," *Los Angeles Times,* June 2, 1975.

7  Brown interview, 2018.

8  Brown interview, 2018.

9  Brown interview, 2018.

10  Douglas P. Shuit, "Kathleen Brown's Victory Revives a California Dynasty," *Los Angeles Times,* Nov. 8, 1990.

11  Cathleen Decker and Bill Stall, "Jerry Brown Quits as Party Chairman," *Los Angeles Times,* Feb. 5, 1991.

12  James W. Sweeney, "Popularity of Brown down at end of reign," *San Bernardino County Sun*, March 2, 1991.

13  Jerry Brown interview with the author, March 8, 2018.

14  This observation has been widely repeated. Among many sources is Bob Stern, coauthor of the state's Political Reform Act. Stern's op-ed for the *San Francisco Chronicle* on Oct. 9, 2014, expresses his views well.

15  Jane Gross, "New Senator from California Is Named," *New York Times,* Jan. 3, 1991. Seymour may well endure in the history books as a political footnote: he was the last California Republican to hold a United States Senate seat in the twentieth century, a drought that persists well into the twenty-first and shows, at the time of this writing, no immediate signs of breaking.

16  "Flashback: Clarence Thomas Responds to Anita Hill," Senate Judiciary Committee hearings, Oct. 11, 1991, posted to YouTube by CNN on April 23, 2016, at https://www.youtube.com/watch?v=ZURHD5BU1o8.

17  "Brown Launches Run 'Against the System,'" *The Journal News,* White Plains, NY, Oct. 22, 1991. (This wire service report was carried in many newspapers.)

18  Alessandra Stanley, "What's That Glimmering Behind Jerry Brown?," *New York Times,* April 2, 1992.

19  "Bill Clinton, Jerry Brown Trade Jabs at 1992 Democratic Primary Debate," broadcast in

March of 1992 by CBS and posted to YouTube by *Face the Nation* on Nov. 10, 2015, at: https://www.youtube.com/watch?v=K5kUITklALQ.

20  Jerry Brown interview with the author, Dec. 12, 2018.

21  Stanley, "What's That Glimmering?"

22  Jerry Brown and Bill Clinton, *Donahue* taping, New York, April 6, 1992, available at: https://www.c-span.org/video/?25463-1/donahue-debate-taping.

23  Jerry Brown interview with the author, Dec. 12, 2018.

24  Jerry Brown interview with the author, Aug. 15, 2016.

25  Reports and even historians have sometimes described the panel as a "Simi Valley jury," after the largely white town where the trial was held and which was home to many police officers. That is misleading. The case was tried in Simi Valley, but jurors were drawn from the entire county, not just the town.

26  I witnessed these events firsthand as a reporter for the *Los Angeles Times*. I was at police headquarters when the verdicts were read and in the streets that night and in the days that followed.

27  I was present for the National Guard's tentative deployment, which occurred just after noon on April 30 outside the Los Angeles Memorial Coliseum.

28  FBI, Uniform Crime Reporting Statistics. The number of homicides committed annually in Los Angeles dropped precipitously in the late 1990s, after Gates was gone and the city moved to a community-policing model, supervised under a federal consent decree. It dropped below three hundred for the first time in 2010 and has remained below that mark in the years since, despite the city's growth. Other violent crimes declined comparably over those years, making Los Angeles a profoundly safer place in 2010 than it had been twenty years earlier.

29  "L. A. Riots by the Numbers," *Los Angeles Times*, April 26, 2017, at https://www.latimes.com/local/1992riots/la-me-riots-25-years-20170420-htmlstory.html. The precise number of riot-related deaths is more difficult to discern than it seems at first. A certain number of people in Los Angeles die violently over any given period, and this was especially the case in those days, so isolating the riots as the cause is a blunt exercise. Some estimates cite fifty-three as the definitive number; others refer to "more than sixty."

30  Rich Connell and Richard A. Serrano, "L.A. Is Warned of New Unrest, Vows Emergency Plans," *Los Angeles Times*, Oct. 22, 1992.

31  Warren Christopher interviews with the author, 1993–2011.

32  "Report of the Independent Commission on the Los Angeles Police Department" (the Christopher Commission), at https://archive.org/details/ChristopherCommissionLAPD.

33  *Time* magazine, April 19, 1993.

34  "Races Disagree on Impact of Simpson Trial," CNN-*Time* magazine poll, Oct. 6, 1995, at http://www.cnn.com/US/OJ/daily/9510/10-06/poll_race/oj_poll_txt.html.

35  Jim Newton, "Know What Else Prop. 13 Does? It Gives Tax Breaks to Country Clubs," *Los Angeles Times*, June 30, 2014.

36  Rick Oltman, "'Save Our State': Rick Mountjoy and California's Proposition 187," *The Social Contract* 22, no. 2 (Winter 2011–12), at https://www.thesocialcontract.com/artman2/publish/tsc_22_2/tsc_22_2_oltman_printer.shtml.

37  Philip Martin, "Proposition 187 in California," *International Migration Review* 29, no. 1 (Spring 1995): 255–56.

38  Mark Z. Barabak, "On Politics: Pete Wilson Looks Back on Proposition 187 and Says, Heck Yeah, He'd Support It All Over Again," *Los Angeles Times*, March 23, 2017. Wilson made similar remarks on other occasions, including during an appearance at the Ronald Reagan Presidential Library, March 19, 2015.

39  "Pete Wilson 1994 Campaign Ad on Illegal Immigration," posted to YouTube by Pete-WilsonCA on Feb. 15, 2010, at https://www.youtube.com/watch?v=lLIzzs2HHgY.

40    Cathleen Decker, "Analysis of a Doomed Campaign," *Los Angeles Times*, Nov. 14, 1994. The headline of the *Times*'s look back at Brown's campaign spoke volumes.

41    Kathleen Brown interview with the author, Dec. 12, 2018.


## CHAPTER SEVENTEEN

1     Jerry Brown interview with the author, Feb. 8, 2019.

2     Kathleen Brown interview with the author, Aug. 28, 2015.

3     Bill Stall, "Eulogies Recall Brown's Humor, Love of Family," *Los Angeles Times*, Feb. 22, 1996.

4     Carla Marinucci, "Politics, Humor Mix at Funeral for Pat Brown," *San Francisco Examiner*, Feb. 22, 1996.

5     Jerry Brown interview with the author, Feb. 8, 2018.

6     Jerry Brown interview with the author, Feb. 8, 2018.

7     Jerry Brown interview with the author, Aug. 15, 2016.

8     Jerry Brown interview with the author, Aug. 15, 2016.

9     Jerry Brown, *Dialogues* (Berkeley, CA: Berkeley Hills Books, 1998), p. 13.

10    Brown personal papers.

11    Jerry Brown interview with the author, Aug. 15, 2016.

12    "The Other Mayor Brown," editorial, *San Francisco Examiner*, June 8, 1998.

13    Chuck McFadden, *Trailblazer: A Biography of Jerry Brown* (Berkeley: University of California Press, 2013), p. 121.

14    Maria L. La Ganga, "Brown Eclipses Challengers in Oakland Mayor's Race," *Los Angeles Times*, May 27, 1998.

15    Kathleen Brown interview with the author, May 1, 2019.

16    Steve Rubenstein and Janine DeFao, "Oakland: Barzaghi Leaves Jerry Brown's Staff," *San Francisco Chronicle*, July 20, 2004.

17    Brown's personal papers include a number of notes, many undated, referring to Barzaghi and suggesting difficulties.

18    Jerry Brown interview with the author, Oct. 5, 2018.

19    Jerry Brown interview with the author, Aug. 15, 2016.

20    Nathan Gardels interview with the author, Jan. 30, 2019.

21    John Balzar, "Running Mate," *Los Angeles Times*, May 18, 2005.

22    Zusha Elinson, "As Mayor, Brown Remade Oakland's Downtown and Himself," *New York Times*, Sept. 2, 2010.

23    Jerry Brown interview with the author, Oct. 5, 2018.

24    Jerry Brown interview with the author, March 8, 2019.

25    Jerry Brown interview with the author, March 8, 2018.

26    Anne Gust interview with the author, March 15, 2019.

27    Barbara Casey interview with the author, March 15, 2019.

28    Gray Davis interview with the author, April 8, 2019.

29    Dianne Feinstein interview with the author, April 2, 2019; wedding program, "Anne Gust–Jerry Brown, June 18, 2005," Brown personal papers.

30    Tim Reiterman, "In a Rare Nod to Tradition, Jerry Brown Ties the Knot," Los Angeles Times, June 19, 2005.

31    Stephen Reinhardt interview with the author, May 10, 2016.

32    Robert Greene, "The Great Car-Tax Swindle," *Los Angeles Times*, Aug. 31, 2007.

33    Miguel Bustillo and James Rainey, "Davis Concedes Mistakes but Fights 'Power Grab,'" *Los Angeles Times*, Aug. 20, 2003.

34    Katharine Q. Seelye, "For Gray Davis, Great Fall from the Highest Height," *New York Times*, Oct. 8, 2003.

35    Seelye, "For Gray Davis."

36    Ace Smith interview with the author, March 9, 2018.

37    Lee Romney, "Delgadillo Rips into Rival Brown," *Los Angeles Times*, March 25, 2006.

38    Smith interview.

39    Eric Bailey and Robert Salladay, "Suit Challenges Brown's Eligibility for Top Law Job," *Los Angeles Times*, Oct. 20, 2006.

40    Smith interview.

41    E. Scott Reckard, "Countrywide Clients to Get Mortgage Aid," *Los Angeles Times*, Oct. 6, 2008.

42    Office of Governor Edmund G. Brown Jr. Copies of the governor's statement are included in the California State Archives. An excerpt is available here: https://patch .com/california/culvercity/gov-brown-says-counties-must-issue-marriage-licenses-to -samesex-couples.

## CHAPTER EIGHTEEN

1    Commentators unfamiliar with California often refer to the state's "deficit," but that's not quite correct. Unlike the federal government, California is required to balance its budget every year and thus does not technically run a deficit. It does, however, borrow in years when its revenues are exceeded by its obligations, using that borrowing to cover its short-fall. The correct term, then, is shortfall, not deficit.

2    Paul Harris, "Will California Become America's First Failed State?," *Guardian*, Oct. 3, 2009.

3    Joel Kotkin, "The Golden State's War on Itself," *City Journal*, Summer 2010, at https://www.city-journal.org/html/golden-state%E2%80%99s-war-itself-13304.html.

4    This story was first broken by the *Sacramento Bee* on Sept. 24, 2009, and though the orig-inal report proved to have some flaws, the allegations dogged Whitman through the campaign. She responded many times to the implication that she was politically indiffer-ent as a young adult, sometimes acknowledging that it was "unacceptable" to have voted sporadically and other times blaming her various obligations—including her own career, that of her husband, and the stresses of raising a family—as if such distractions would justify failing to vote for decades.

5    Cathleen Decker and Seema Mehta, "Velvet Gloves in Debate by California's GOP Can-didates in Governor's Race," *Los Angeles Times*, March 16, 2010.

6    "Jerry Brown Announcement Video," posted to YouTube by Brown for Governor on March 1, 2010, at https://www.youtube.com/watch?v=EKl8XzIFHQc&feature=youtu.be.

7    Seema Mehta and Maeve Reston, "Governor Rivals Spent Big in Late TV Blitz," *Los Angeles Times*, Feb. 1, 2011.

8    Willie Brown interview with the author, Sept. 15, 2015. Brown did not say "guy."

9    "Jerry Brown Announcement Video."

10   "Brown for Governor," editorial, *Los Angeles Times*, Oct. 3, 2010. I was a member of the *Times*'s editorial board at the time of that endorsement, and I was among those who ar-

gued that Brown's promise was ill-advised. As it turns out, and much to my amazement, I was wrong.

11 Jerry Brown interview with the author, Dec. 12, 2018.

12 Seema Mehta and Michael J. Mishak, "Sparks Fly at Debate," *Los Angeles Times*, Oct. 3, 2010.

13 Mehta and Mishak, "Sparks Fly."

14 Jerry Brown interview with the author, Nov. 13, 2015.

15 Anne Gust interview with the author, March 18, 2019.

16 Diana Dooley interview with the author, Oct. 5, 2018.

17 Brown's personal papers include many folders of material generated by Anne Gust about the train.

18 Jerry Brown interview with the author, Jan. 29, 2016.

19 Dooley interview.

20 Jerry Brown interview with the author, Oct. 5, 2018.

## CHAPTER NINETEEN

1 California Department of Finance, governor's proposed budget 2011–12, governor's message, Jan. 10, 2011, at http://www.ebudget.ca.gov/2011-12-EN/pdf/BudgetSummary /GovernorsMessage.pdf.

2 Judy Lin, "State analyst: Brown budget a 'good starting point,'" *The Desert Sun*, Jan. 13, 2011.

3 Undated memo, 2011, "How to Solve the Budget Gap," Brown personal papers.

4 The legislative history of AB-98 may be found in a July 25, 2011, letter from Tom Torlakson, the state superintendent of public instruction at the California Department of Education, to superintendents, administrators, and other officials; see https:// www.cde.ca.gov/nr/el/le/yr11ltr072511rvsd.asp

5 Records for gubernatorial vetoes extend back as far as 1901, and no governor other than Brown had ever vetoed a budget during that time. It is possible that a governor in the early years of California's history vetoed a budget. If so, no record of it exists.

6 Jerry Brown veto message, June 16, 2011, in Journal of the Assembly, California State Legislature, 2011–12 Regular Session, December 6, 2010, to November 30, 2012, vol. 2: 1984; see https://clerk.assembly.ca.gov/sites/clerk.assembly.ca.gov/files/archive /DailyJournal/2011/AFJ_2011-12_Vol_2_Final_DC.pdf#page=5.

7 Carrie Kahn, "California Governor Vetoes Latest Budget Proposal," National Public Radio, June 17, 2011.

8 Shane Goldmacher and Anthony York, "Brown Veto Dismays Democrats," *Los Angeles Times*, June 17, 2011.

9 Jerry Brown interview with the author, Dec. 12, 2018.

10 Molly Munger interview with the author, March 2012. See: Jim Newton, "A Tale of Two Tax Plans," *Los Angeles Times*, April 2, 2012

11 Bill Carrick interview with the author, March 2012. See: Jim Newton, "A Tale of Two Tax Plans," *Los Angeles Times*, April 2, 2012

12 "Background: The Changing California Electorate," Field poll conducted October 17–30, 2012, at http://reappropriate.co/wp-content/uploads/2012/11/Field-Poll.pdf.

13 Adam Nagourney, "California's Governor Is in High Gear over a Tax Initiative," *New York Times*, Nov. 3, 2012.

14 Dan Schnur, "How Gov. Brown Can Save Prop. 30," *Los Angeles Times*, Nov. 2, 2012.

15 George Skelton, "Big Win, Big Responsibility," *Los Angeles Times*, Nov. 8, 2012.

16 Jerry Brown press conference, Nov. 7, 2012 (transcript supplied by governor's office).

17 Brown press conference.

18 Brown press conference.

19 Evan Westrup interview with the author, March 21, 2019.

20 Jerry Brown interview with the author, June 26, 2019.

21 Anthony York, "Brown Prods UC, Cal State to Streamline," *Los Angeles Times*, January 16, 2013.

22 Jerry Brown interview with the author, Feb. 8, 2019.

23 George Kieffer interview with the author, Dec. 17, 2018.

24 Jerry Brown interview with the author, Feb. 8, 2019.

25 Judicial Council of California, Administrative Office of the Courts, "A Preliminary Look at California Parolee Reentry Courts," June 2012, at https://www.courts.ca.gov /documents/AOCBriefParolee0612.pdf.

26 *Brown v. Plata*, 563 U.S. 493 (2011), at https://www.supremecourt.gov/opinions/10pdf /09-1233.pdf.

27 California Courts, "California's Three Strikes Sentencing Law," at http://www.courts.ca .gov/20142.htm.

28 Brown personal papers.

29 Marisa Lagos, "Five Years Later, Many See Criminal Justice Realignment as Success," KQED News, Sept. 29, 2016, at https://www.kqed.org/news/11108031/five-years-later -many-see-criminal-justice-realignment-as-success.

30 Magnus Lofstrom and Brandon Martin, "Public Safety Realignment: Impacts So Far," Public Policy Institute of California (September 2015), at https://www.ppic.org /publication/public-safety-realignment-impacts-so-far/.

31 "25 Years for a Slice of Pizza," *New York Times*, March 5, 1995.

32 Tracey Kaplan, "Proposition 36: Voters Overwhelmingly Ease Three Strikes Law," *San Jose Mercury News*, Nov. 6, 2012, quoting Adam Gelb, director of the Pew Center on the States' Public Safety Performance Project.

33 Jerry Brown interview with the author, March 8, 2019.

34 California Energy Commission, "Our Changing Climate 2012," p. 3.

35 Tracie Cone, "A Guide for Climate Change Decisions," *Visalia Times-Delta*, Aug. 1, 2012.

36 Jerry Brown interview with the author, Aug. 15, 2016.

37 Jerry Brown interview with the author, Aug. 15, 2016.

38 Craig Miller, "Jerry Brown's Anti-Anti-Climate Science Site," *KQED News*, Aug. 13, 2012, at https://ww2.kqed.org/climatewatch/2012/08/13/jerry-browns-anti-anti -climate-science-site/.

39 Climate Change Unit, California Environmental Protection Agency, "Green Building Action Plan," appended to Executive Order B-18-12, at https://www.climatechange.ca.gov /climate_action_team/documents/Green_Building_Action_Plan.pdf.

40 California Department of Finance, governor's proposed budgets 2011–2014, at http://www.ebudget.ca.gov/.

CHAPTER TWENTY

1 I was the paper's editorial page editor in 2008, when we endorsed Obama. It was the first time in the history of the *Times* that the paper had endorsed a Democrat for president.

2  Frank del Olmo, "A Dissenting Vote on the Endorsement of Pete Wilson," *Los Angeles Times*, Oct. 31, 1994.

3  Mark Baldassare, Dean Bonner, David Kordus, and Lunna Lopes, "Californians and the Environment," Public Policy Institute of California (July 2017), at https://www.ppic.org/wp-content/uploads/s_717mbs.pdf.

4  California secretary of state voter registration historical statistics.

## CHAPTER TWENTY-ONE

1  I witnessed this scene on the morning of June 26, 2017. Brown placed the calls from the governor's mansion in Sacramento. I was not privy to the comments of those on the other end of his calls.

2  Real Clear Politics, "Full CA-Gov Debate: Gov. Jerry Brown vs. GOP Challenger Neel Kashkari," Sept. 4, 2014, at https://www.realclearpolitics.com/video/2014/09/05/full_ca-gov_debate_gov_jerry_brown_vs_gop_challenger_neel_kashkari.html. I was one of the three journalists who posed questions to the candidates in that debate.

3  *CBS Sunday Morning*, "The Zeal of Gov. Jerry Brown," Jan. 11, 2015, at https://www.youtube.com/watch?v=Bv6miQDBrRY.

4  "Brown Makes Weapons Plea," *Washington Post*, May 19, 1979.

5  Doug Willis, "TV Ads On Nuclear Freeze Become Issue in California Race," Associated Press, September 28, 1982. See also: Steven A. Capps, "Brown, Wilson Make One Last Campaign Swing, Await Results," *San Francisco Examiner*, Nov. 2, 1982.

6  Paul W. Valentine and Karlyn Barker, "The Protesters," *Washington Post*, May 7, 1979.

7  Nathan Gardels interview with the author, Jan. 30, 2019.

8  Jerry Brown, "A Stark Nuclear Warning," *New York Review of Books*, July 14, 2016.

9  James Carden, "Former Defense Secretary William Perry Sounds the Alarm over the Present Nuclear Danger," *The Nation*, Nov. 30, 2017.

10  William J. Perry, My Journey at the Nuclear Brink (Stanford, CA: Stanford University Press, 2015), p. 192.

11  Jerry Brown interview with the author, Feb. 8, 2019.

12  Global Zero Forum, March 31, 2016, transcript supplied by governor's office.

13  Jerry Brown interview with the author, March 8, 2018.

14  Jerry Brown interview with the author, March 8, 2018.

15  Jerry Brown interview with the author, March 8, 2018.

16  CNN, *The Situation Room with Wolf Blitzer*, Sept. 15, 2015; transcript at http://edition.cnn.com/TRANSCRIPTS/1509/16/sitroom.01.html.

17  Michael Kinsley, "Why Aren't the Democrats Trying to Draft Jerry Brown?," *Vanity Fair*, Sept. 17, 2015.

18  Maggie Haberman and Richard A. Oppel Jr., "Donald Trump Criticizes Muslim Family of Slain U.S. Soldier, Drawing Ire," *New York Times*, July 30, 2016.

19  "Transcript: Donald Trump's Taped Comments About Women," *New York Times*, Oct. 8, 2016.

20  Lori Robertson and Robert Farley, "The Facts on Crowd Size," FactCheck.org, Jan. 23, 2017, at https://www.factcheck.org/2017/01/the-facts-on-crowd-size/.

21  Miles Parks, "Fact Check: Trump Repeats Voter Fraud Claim About California," National Public Radio, April 5, 2018, at https://www.npr.org/2018/04/05/599868312/fact-check-trump-repeats-voter-fraud-claim-about-california.

22  WhiteHouse.gov, "Remarks by President Trump at a California Sanctuary State Round-table," May 16, 2018.

23  "Trump Considers Pulling ICE Agents to Punish California," posted to YouTube by CNN on Feb. 22, 2018, at https://www.youtube.com/watch?v=1C3coXw2AI0.

24  "Full Video: Attorney General Jeff Sessions Speaks in Sacramento," ABC7News.com, March 8, 2018, at https://abc7news.com/politics/full-video-attorney-general-jeff-sessions-speaks-in-sacramento/3186705/.

25  "Full Video: Attorney General Jeff Sessions."

26  Jerry Brown interview with the author, March 8, 2018.

27  Jerry Brown interview with the author, March 8, 2018.

28  "Read the Emails on Donald Trump Jr.'s Russia Meeting," *New York Times*, July 11, 2017, at https://www.nytimes.com/interactive/2017/07/11/us/politics/donald-trump-jr-email-text.html.

29  "Bulletin of the Atomic Scientists 2019 Doomsday Clock Announcement," National Press Club, Washington, DC, Jan. 24, 2019, at https://clock.thebulletin.org/.

30  "Bulletin of the Atomic Scientists 2019 Doomsday Clock Announcement."

31  Jerry Brown interview with the author, June 26, 2019.

32  Cuellar also has a PhD in political science from Stanford.

33  Jerry Brown interview with the author, March 8, 2019.

34  Scott Shafer, "Brown's Longest-Lasting Legacy: Judges," *KQED News*, Dec. 28, 2018, at https://www.kqed.org/news/11714131/browns-longest-lasting-legacy-judges.

35  Shafer, "Brown's Longest-Lasting Legacy."

36  California Courts, "Demographic Data Provided by Justices and Judges…as of December 31, 2018," at https://www.courts.ca.gov/documents/lr-2019-JC-demographic-data-justices-judges-gender-gov-12011_5_n.pdf.

## CHAPTER TWENTY-TWO

1  John Zipperer, "San Francisco in the Age of Trump," *Marina Times*, Feb. 2017; Brown was speaking at the American Geophysical Union Fall Meeting on December 15, 2016.

2  Michael D. Shear, "Trump Will Withdraw U.S. from Paris Climate Agreement," *New York Times*, June 1, 2017.

3  Shear, "Trump Will Withdraw."

4  Office of Governor Edmund G. Brown Jr., "Governor Issues Statement on White House Paris Climate Agreement Announcement," June 1, 2017.

5  Office of Governor Edmund G. Brown Jr., "Governor Brown Meets with President Xi of the People's Republic of China, Signs Agreement with National Government to Boost Green Technology," June 6, 2017; this agreement was called the "Memorandum of Understanding on Research, Innovation, and Investment to Advance Cooperation on Low-Carbon Development and Clean Energy Resources" and was signed by the government of California and the Ministry of Science and Technology of the People's Republic of China.

6  Brent D. Griffiths, "Brown: Trump Doesn't Fear 'Wrath of God,'" Politico, Dec. 10, 2017, at https://www.politico.com/story/2017/12/10/brown-trump-wrath-god-288863.

7  This point actually was a matter of some dispute. Schwarzenegger had argued that the imposition of the cap and the forced purchase of emissions credits represented a fee, not a

tax, and therefore required only a simple majority of the legislature. The courts upheld that interpretation. But Brown, eager to avoid another lawsuit on that argument, set out to get a two-thirds majority.

8    Liam Dillon and Melanie Mason, "'Not Just a Climate Crisis,'" *Los Angeles Times*, July 14, 2017; Brown was testifying before the California State Senate Environmental Quality Committee.

9    Dillon and Mason, "'Not Just a Climate Crisis.'"

10   "Governor Brown and Sen. De León Comments on AB398," posted to YouTube by California Senate Democrats on July 14, 2017, at https://www.youtube.com/watch?v=nya3U4UmmC4&feature=youtu.be.

11   Robert McClelland, "The Ups and Downs of California's Gas Tax," Urban-Brookings Tax Policy Center, Nov. 1, 2018, at https://www.taxpolicycenter.org/taxvox/ups-and-downs-californias-gas-tax.

12   Sam Richards, "Gov. Brown, Legislators Hit Concord to Tout $52.4 Billion Roads Bill," *East Bay Times*, March 30, 2017.

13   Katy Murphy, "Gas-Tax Payback: Steve Glazer Loses Chairmanship of Senate Committee," *San Jose Mercury News*, May 12, 2017.

14   Dana Williamson interview with the author, April 9, 2019.

15   "Governor Jerry Brown | NO Prop 6, Stop the Attack on Bridge & Road Safety," posted to YouTube by No Prop 6 on Oct. 30, 2018, at https://www.youtube.com/watch?time_continue=30&v=S4W5gHQLkMk.

16   Anne Gust interview with the author, March 18, 2019.

17   Steven Maviglio, "Nancy McFadden Got the Job Done with Confidence & Poise," *Fox and Hounds Daily*, March 26, 2018.

18   Williamson interview.

19   Maviglio, "Nancy McFadden."

20   Jerry Brown interview with the author, Dec. 12, 2018.

21   I attended this conference, so the accounts presented here were gathered firsthand.

22   Kurtis Alexander, "S.F. Firm's Satellite to Monitor Climate," *San Francisco Chronicle*, Sept. 15, 2018. The Under2 Coalition's website can be found here: https://www.under2coalition.org/.

23   "Climate Change Summit in San Francisco Draws Crowds of Protesters," CBS Sacramento, Sept. 13, 2018.

24   Veto message to nine crime bills, Oct. 2, 2015, provided to the author by Governor Brown's office. See also: Patrick McGreevy, "With strong message against creating new crimes, Gov. Brown vetoes drone bills," *Los Angeles Times*, Oct. 3, 2015.

25   Veto message to SB-449, 2011 legislative session, provided to the author by Governor Brown's office.

26   Veto message to SB-149, Oct. 15, 2017, provided to the author by Governor Brown's office .

27   Veto message to SB-105, 2011 legislative session, provided to the author by Governor Brown's office .

28   David Siders, "Jerry Brown: Raising Minimum Wage Moral, Though It 'May Not Make Sense," *Sacramento Bee*, Feb. 6, 2018.

29   Signing message to ABx2 15, Oct. 5, 2015, provided to the author by Governor Brown's office.

30   Jerry Brown interview with the author, Oct. 5, 2018.

31   Dan Walters, "For His Final Bill Decisions, Jerry Brown Paddles Down the Middle," *Sacramento Bee*, Oct. 3, 2018.

32   Jerry Brown interview with the author, Oct. 5, 2018.

33 Signing message to AB-237, Sept. 30, 2018, provided to the author by Governor Brown's office.

34 Planning details for the meeting were provided to the author on a not-for-attribution basis.

35 Kalhan Rosenblatt and Phil Helsel, "Trump Visits Site of California's Most Deadly Fire, Pledges Federal Help," NBC News, Nov. 17, 2018, at https://www.nbcnews .com/politics/donald-trump/trump-visit-california-wildfire-zones-after-criticizing-forest -management-n937546.

36 Kurtis Alexander, "Trump Views Paradise Fire Devastation, Promises to 'Take Care of the People,'" *San Francisco Chronicle*, Nov. 17, 2018.

37 Jerry Brown interview with the author, Dec. 12, 2018.

38 Donald J. Trump, Twitter, Jan. 9, 2019, 7:25 a.m.

39 Jerry Brown interview with the author, Feb. 8, 2019.

40 Rob Kuznia, "In Commuting 20 Murder Convicts' Sentences, California Governor Draws Praise, Condemnation," *Washington Post*, Sept. 9, 2018.

41 Walter Woods, Petition for Commutation of Sentence, included in Brown's grant of commutation, Nov. 21, 2018, provided to the author by Governor Brown's office.

42 Jerry Brown interview with the author, Feb. 8, 2019.

43 Ear Hustle, Nov. 24, 2018, at https://www.earhustlesq.com/episodes/2018/11/24/big -news-its-time.

44 Jerry Brown interview with the author, Dec. 12, 2018, and Evan Westrup interview with the author, Dec. 12, 2018.

## CHAPTER TWENTY-THREE

1 "Transcript: Hear Gov. Gavin Newsom's Inauguration Speech," Capital Public Radio, Jan. 7, 2019.

2 Mark Baldassare, Dean Bonner, Alyssa Dykman, and Lunna Lopes, "Californians and Their Government," Public Policy Institute of California (January 2019), at https://www .ppic.org/wp-content/uploads/ppic-statewide-survey-californians-and-their-government -january-2019.pdf.

3 California State Library, "Governors' Gallery: Gavin Newsom," State of the State Address delivered Feb. 12, 2019, at https://governors.library.ca.gov/addresses /s_40-Newsom1.html.

4 Jerry Brown interview with the author, March 8, 2019.

5 Nathan Gardels interview with the author, Jan. 30, 2019.

6 Alan Greenblatt, "Man of Tomorrow," *Governing*, November 2018.

7 "How Jerry Brown Rewrote the California Story," editorial, *San Francisco Chronicle*, Jan. 5, 2019.

8 "Goodbye, and Thanks, to Jerry Brown," editorial, *Los Angeles Times*, Jan. 5, 2019.

9 Todd S. Purdum, "Jerry Brown's Greatest Legacy Is Proving California Is Governable," *The Atlantic*, Dec. 26, 2018.

10 Adam Nagourney, "For Jerry Brown, the Face of California's Old Order, the Ranch Is Calling," *New York Times*, Jan. 24, 2018.

11 George Skelton, "It's an Easy A for Jerry Brown in His Final Two Terms as Governor of California," *Los Angeles Times*, Dec. 24, 2018.

# Bibliography

Bar-Lev, Amir, dir. *Long Strange Trip: The Untold Story of the Grateful Dead.* New York: Double E Pictures, 2017.

Bateson, Gregory. *Steps to an Ecology of Mind.* Chicago: University of Chicago Press, 1972.

Bateson, Gregory, and Mary Catherine Bateson. *Angels Fear: Towards an Epistemology of the Sacred.* Cresskill, NJ: Hampton Press, 2005.

Benson, Michael. *Why the Grateful Dead Matter.* Lebanon, NH: ForeEdge / University Press of New England, 2016.

Berlin, Leslie. *Troublemakers: Silicon Valley's Coming of Age.* New York: Simon and Schuster, 2017.

Berry, Wendell. *The Country of Marriage.* Berkeley, CA: Counterpoint, 1973.

———. *The Selected Poems of Wendell Berry.* Berkeley, CA: Counterpoint, 1999.

Biemann, Asher D., ed. *The Martin Buber Reader: Essential Writings.* New York: Palgrave Macmillan, 2002.

Bloom, Joshua, and Waldo E. Martin Jr. *Black Against Empire: The History and Politics of the Black Panther Party.* Berkeley: University of California Press, 2013.

Boyarsky, Bill. *Big Daddy: Jesse Unruh and the Art of Power Politics.* Berkeley: University of California Press, 2007.

———. *The Rise of Ronald Reagan.* New York: Random House, 1968.

Braitman, Jacqueline R., and Gerald F. Uelmen. *Justice Stanley Mosk: A Life at the Center of California Politics and Justice.* Jefferson, NC: McFarland and Co., 2012.

Brands, H. W. *Reagan: The Life.* New York: Doubleday, 2015.

Bronson, William. *How to Kill a Golden State.* New York: Doubleday, 1968.

Brown, Craig. *Ninety-Nine Glimpses of Princess Margaret.* New York: Farrar, Straus and Giroux, 2018.

Brown, Edmund G. (Pat), with Dick Adler. *Public Justice, Private Mercy: A Governor's Education on Death Row.* New York: Weidenfeld & Nicolson, 1989.

Brown, Jerry. *Dialogues.* Berkeley, CA: Berkeley Hills Books, 1998.

Buber, Martin. *I and Thou.* Translated by Walter Kaufmann. New York: Touchstone, 1996.

Bugliosi, Vincent, with Curt Gentry. *Helter Skelter.* New York: W. W. Norton, 1974.

Cairns, Kathleen A. *The Case of Rose Bird: Gender, Politics, and the California Courts.* Lincoln: University of Nebraska Press, 2016.

Cannon, Lou. *Governor Reagan: His Rise to Power.* New York: PublicAffairs, 2003.

———. *President Reagan: The Role of a Lifetime.* New York: Public-Affairs, 2000.

Carlsson, Chris. *Ten Years That Shook the City: San Francisco 1968–1978.* San Francisco: City Lights Foundation, 2011.

Carson, Rachel. *Silent Spring.* Boston: Houghton Mifflin, 1962.

Chan, Sucheng, and Spencer Olin, eds. *Major Problems in California History.* Boston: Houghton Mifflin, 1997.

Chessman, Caryl. *Cell 2455, Death Row: A Condemned Man's Own Story.* New York: Prentice Hall, 1954.

Citrin, Jack, and Isaac William Martin, eds. *After the Tax Revolt: California's Proposition 13 Turns 30.* Berkeley, CA: Berkeley Public Policy Press, 2009.

Cleaver, Eldridge. *Soul on Ice.* New York: Ramparts / McGraw-Hill, 1968.

Copeland, Alan, ed. *People's Park.* New York: Ballantine, 1969.

Davis, Mike. *City of Quartz: Excavating the Future in Los Angeles.* London: Verso, 1990.

Didion, Joan. *Run River.* New York: Vintage International, 1994.

———. *Slouching Towards Bethlehem.* New York: Farrar, Straus and Giroux, 1968.

———. *Where I Was From.* New York: Knopf, 2003.

———. *The White Album.* New York: Simon and Schuster, 1979.

Douzet, Frederick, Thad Kousser, and Kenneth P. Miller, eds. *The New Political Geography of California.* Berkeley, CA: Berkeley Public Policy Press, 2008.

Drohojowska-Philp, Hunter. *Rebels in Paradise: The Los Angeles Art Scene and the 1960s.* New York: Henry Holt, 2011.

Drury, Aubrey. *California: An Intimate Guide.* New York: Harper & Brothers, 1947.

Ehrlich, Paul R. *The Population Bomb.* New York: Ballantine, 1968.

Faragher, John Mack. *Eternity Street: Violence and Justice in Frontier Los Angeles.* New York: W. W. Norton, 2016.

Ferlinghetti, Lawrence. *Writing Across the Landscape: Travel Journals 1960–2010.* Edited by Giada Diano and Matthew Gleeson. New York: Liveright, 2015.

Finnegan, William. *Barbarian Days: A Surfing Life.* New York: Penguin Press, 2015.

Foucault, Michel. *Discipline and Punish: The Birth of the Prison.* Translated by Alan Sheridan. New York: Vintage, 1995. First American edition published 1977 by Pantheon.

Fox, Joel. *The Legend of Proposition 13: The Great California Tax Revolt.* Self-published, Xlibris, 2003.

Fracchia, Charles A. *Fire and Gold: The San Francisco Story*, Encinitas, CA: Heritage Media Corporation, 1998.

Fradkin, Philip L. *The Seven States of California: A Human and Natural History.* New York: Henry Holt, 1995.

Gagosian Gallery. *Ferus.* New York: Rizzoli International Publications, 2009.

Gaines, Steven. *Heroes and Villains: The True Story of the Beach Boys.* Boston: Da Capo, 1995.

Gudde, Erwin G. *Bigler's Chronicle of the West: The Conquest of California, Discovery of Gold, and Mormon Settlement as Reflected in Henry William Bigler's Diaries.* Berkeley: University of California Press, 1962.

Guggenheim, Davis, dir. *An Inconvenient Truth.* Los Angeles: Lawrence Bender Productions, 2006.

Guinn, Jeff. *The Road to Jonestown: Jim Jones and Peoples Temple.* New York: Simon and Schuster, 2017.

Hanh, Thich Nhat. *Living Buddha, Living Christ.* New York: Riverhead, 1995.

Hanh, Thich Nhat, and Daniel Berrigan. *The Raft Is Not the Shore: Conversations Toward a Buddhist-Christian Awareness.* Ossining, NY: Orbis Books, 2001.

Harries-Jones, Peter. *A Recursive Vision: Ecological Understanding and Gregory Bateson.* Toronto: University of Toronto Press, 1995.

Harris, Joseph P. *California Politics.* 4th ed. Chandler Publications in Political Science. San Francisco: Chandler Publishing Company, 1967.

Hayden, Tom. *The Lost Gospel of the Earth: A Call for Renewing Nature, Spirit, and Politics.* San Francisco: Sierra Club Books, 1996.

Hearst, Patricia Campbell, with Alvin Moscow. *Patty Hearst: Her Own Story.* New York: Avon, 1988. Originally published by Doubleday in 1981 as *Every Secret Thing.*

Heine, Steven, and Dale S. Wright. *Zen Classics: Formative Texts in the History of Zen Buddhism.* New York: Oxford University Press, 2005.

Hennessy, Kate. *Dorothy Day: The World Will Be Saved by Beauty.* New York: Scribner, 2017.

Hill, Gladwin. *Dancing Bear: An Inside Look at California Politics.* Cleveland, OH: World Publishing Company, 1968.

Illich, Ivan. *Deschooling Society.* London: Calder & Boyars, 1970.

———. *Limits to Medicine: Medical Nemesis; The Expropriation of Health.* London: Calder & Boyars, 1975.

Jacobs, John. *A Rage for Justice: The Passion and Politics of Phillip Burton.* Berkeley: University of California Press, 1995.

Jarvis, Howard, with Robert Pack. *I'm Mad as Hell.* New York: Times Books, 1979.

Kerr, Clark. *The Gold and the Blue: A Personal Memoir of the University of California, 1949–1967.* Vol. 1, *Academic Triumphs.* Berkeley: University of California Press, 2001.

Kesey, Ken. *One Flew over the Cuckoo's Nest.* New York: Viking Press, 1962.

Lorenz, J. D. *Jerry Brown: The Man on the White Horse.* Boston: Houghton Mifflin, 1978.

Marginson, Simon. *The Dream Is Over: The Crisis of Clark Kerr's California Idea of Higher Education.* Clark Kerr Lectures on the Role of Higher Education in Society 4. Berkeley: University of California Press, 2016.

McDougal, Dennis. *Privileged Son: Otis Chandler and the Rise and Fall of the L.A. Times Dynasty.* Boston: Da Capo, 2001.

McFadden, Chuck. *Trailblazer: A Biography of Jerry Brown.* Berkeley: University of California Press, 2013.

McKibben, Bill. *The End of Nature.* New York: Random House, 1989.

———. *Falter: Has the Human Game Begun to Play Itself Out?* New York: Henry Holt, 2019.

McNeill, J. R. *Something New Under the Sun: An Environmental History of the Twentieth-Century World.* New York: W. W. Norton, 2000.

McPhee, John. *Encounters with the Archdruid: Narratives About a Conservationist and Three of His Natural Enemies.* New York: Farrar, Straus and Giroux, 1971.

McWilliams, Carey. *Southern California Country: An Island on the Land.* New York: Duell, Sloan & Pierce, 1946.

Meadows, Donella H., Dennis L. Meadows, Jørgen Randers, and William W. Behrens III. *The Limits to Growth.* New York: Universe Books, 1972.

Miller, Henry. *Big Sur and the Oranges of Hieronymus Bosch.* New York: New Directions, 1957.

Nadeau, Remi. *California: The New Society*. New York: David McKay, 1963.

Newton, Jim. *Justice for All: Earl Warren and the Nation He Made*. New York: Riverhead, 2007.

Nordland, Gerald. *Richard Diebenkorn*. New York: Rizzoli International Publications, 1987.

Norman, Gurney. *Divine Right's Trip: A Novel of the Counterculture*. Frankfort, KY: Gnomon Press, 1971.

Norris, William A. *Liberal Opinions: My Life in the Stream of History*. New Orleans: Quid Pro Books, 2016.

Pack, Robert. *Jerry Brown: The Philosopher Prince*. New York: Stein and Day, 1978.

Parker, Scott F. *Conversations with Ken Kesey*. Jackson: University Press of Mississippi, 2014.

Pastor, Manuel. *State of Resistance: What California's Dizzying Descent and Remarkable Resurgence Mean for America's Future*. New York: New Press, 2018.

Pawel, Miriam. *The Browns of California: The Family Dynasty That Transformed a State and Shaped a Nation*. New York: Bloomsbury, 2018.

———. *The Crusades of Cesar Chavez: A Biography*. New York: Bloomsbury, 2014.

———. *The Union of Their Dreams: Power, Hope, and Struggle in Cesar Chavez's Farm Worker Movement*. New York: Bloomsbury, 2009.

Perry, William J. *My Journey at the Nuclear Brink*. Stanford, CA: Stanford University Press, 2015.

Pincetl, Stephanie S. *Transforming California: A Political History of Land Use and Development*. Baltimore: Johns Hopkins University Press, 1999.

Platt, Rutherford. *The Great American Forest*. Englewood Cliffs, NJ: Prentice Hall, 1965.

Rao, Arun, and Piero Scaruffi. *A History of Silicon Valley: The Greatest Creation of Wealth in the History of the Planet*. Palo Alto, CA: Omniware Group, 2011.

Rarick, Ethan. *California Rising: The Life and Times of Pat Brown.* Berkeley: University of California Press, 2005.

Reich, Charles A. *The Greening of America: How the Youth Revolution Is Trying to Make America Livable.* New York: Random House, 1970.

Reiterman, Tim, with John Jacobs. *Raven: The Untold Story of the Rev. Jim Jones and His People.* New York: Jeremy P. Tarcher / Penguin, 2008.

Reps, Paul, and Nyogen Senzaki, comps. *Zen Flesh, Zen Bones: A Collection of Zen and Pre-Zen Writings.* Tokyo: Tuttle Publishing, 1957.

Rice, Sascha, dir. *California State of Mind: The Legacy of Pat Brown.* Los Angeles: Fire of Life Films, 2011.

Roberts, Jerry. *Dianne Feinstein: Never Let Them See You Cry.* New York: HarperCollins, 1994.

Ronstadt, Linda. *A Conversation with Linda.* October 6, 2018, the Theatre at Ace Hotel, Los Angeles.

———. *Simple Dreams: A Musical Memoir.* New York: Simon and Schuster, 2013.

Rorabaugh, W. J. *Berkeley at War: The 1960s.* New York: Oxford University Press, 1989.

Rosenfeld, Seth. *Subversives: The FBI's War on Student Radicals, and Reagan's Rise to Power.* New York: Farrar, Straus and Giroux, 2012.

Russo, Gus. *Supermob: How Sidney Korshak and His Criminal Associates Became America's Hidden Power Brokers.* New York: Bloomsbury, 2007.

Salzman, Ed. *Jerry Brown: High Priest and Low Politician.* Sacramento: California Journal Press, 1976.

Schell, Orville. *Brown.* New York: Random House, 1978.

Schrag, Peter. *Paradise Lost: California's Experience, America's Future.* New York: New Press, 1998.

Schumacher, E. F. *Small Is Beautiful: A Study of Economics As If People Mattered.* London: Blond & Briggs, 1973.

Selvin, Joel. *Altamont: The Rolling Stones, the Hells Angels, and the Inside Story of Rock's Darkest Day.* New York: Dey Street, 2016.

———. *Summer of Love: The Inside Story of LSD, Rock & Roll, Free Love and High Times in the Wild West*. New York: Dutton, 1994.

Shih, Bryan, and Yohuru Williams, eds. *The Black Panthers: Portraits from an Unfinished Revolution*. New York: Nation Books, 2016.

Shilts, Randy. *And the Band Played On: Politics, People, and the AIDS Epidemic*. New York: St. Martin's, 1987.

———. *The Mayor of Castro Street: The Life and Times of Harvey Milk*. New York: St. Martin's, 1982.

Sluga, Hans, and David G. Stern, eds. *The Cambridge Companion to Wittgenstein*. Cambridge, UK: Cambridge University Press, 1996.

Smith, Richard Candida. *Utopia and Dissent: Art, Poetry, and Politics in California*. Berkeley: University of California Press, 1995.

Snyder, Gary. *Riprap and Cold Mountain Poems*. 50th anniversary ed. Berkeley, CA: Counterpoint, 2009.

———. *The Real Work: Interviews and Talks 1964–1979*. Edited and with an introduction by William Scott McLean. New York: New Directions, 1980.

———. *Turtle Island*. New York: New Directions, 1974.

Speier, Jackie. *Undaunted: Surviving Jonestown, Summoning Courage, and Fighting Back*. New York: Little A, 2018.

Starr, Kevin. *California: A History*. Modern Library Chronicles 23. New York: Modern Library, 2005.

———. *Coast of Dreams: California on the Edge, 1990–2003*. New York: Vintage, 2006.

———. *Embattled Dreams: California in War and Peace, 1940–1950*. Americans and the California Dream 6. Oxford, UK: Oxford University Press, 2002.

———. *Golden Dreams: California in an Age of Abundance, 1950–1963*. Americans and the California Dream 7. Oxford, UK: Oxford University Press, 2009.

Talbot, David. *Season of the Witch: Enchantment, Terror, and Deliverance in the City of Love*. New York: Free Press, 2012.

Thomas, Evan. *Being Nixon: A Man Divided*. New York: Random House, 2015.

Thompson, Gabriel. *America's Social Arsonist: Fred Ross and Grassroots Organizing in the Twentieth Century*. Berkeley: University of California Press, 2016.

Toobin, Jeffrey. *American Heiress: The Wild Saga of the Kidnapping, Crimes, and Trial of Patty Hearst*. New York: Doubleday, 2016.

Travers, Steven. *A Tale of Three Cities: The 1962 Baseball Season in New York, Los Angeles, and San Francisco*. Washington, DC: Potomac Books, 2009.

Turner, Fred. *From Counterculture to Cyberculture: Stewart Brand, the Whole Earth Network, and the Rise of Digital Utopianism*. Chicago: University of Chicago Press, 2006.

Turner, Tom. *David Brower: The Making of the Environmental Movement*. Berkeley: University of California Press, 2015.

Ulrich, Jennifer. *The Timothy Leary Project: Inside the Great Counterculture Experiment*. New York: Abrams, 2018.

Umbach, Kenneth. *Pat Brown's Building Boom: Water, Highways and Higher Education*. Self-published, 2007.

Van der Ryn, Sim, with Francine Allen. *Design for an Empathic World: Reconnecting to People, Nature, and Self*. Washington, DC: Island Press, 2013.

Watts, Alan. *The Way of Zen*. New York: Pantheon, 1957.

Welch, Robert W. Jr. *The Blue Book of the John Birch Society*. Belmont, MA: Western Islands, 1959.

Whitman, Meg, with Joan O'C. Hamilton. *The Power of Many: Values for Success in Business and in Life*. New York: Crown Business, 2010.

*Whole Earth Catalog: Access to Tools*. Fall 1968. Menlo Park CA: Portola Institute. Available at: https://monoskop.org/images/0/09/Brand_Stewart_Whole_Earth_Catalog_Fall_1968.pdf.

Wilson, Brian, with Ben Greenman. *I Am Brian Wilson: A Memoir*. Boston: Da Capo, 2016.

Winkler, Adam. *Gunfight: The Battle over the Right to Bear Arms in America*. New York: W. W. Norton, 2011.

Wittgenstein, Ludwig. *Major Works: Selected Philosophical Writings*. New York: Harper Perennial, 2009.

Wolfe, Tom. *The Electric Kool-Aid Acid Test*. New York: Farrar, Straus and Giroux, 1968.

Zacchino, Narda, with Christopher Scheer. *California Comeback: How a "Failed State" Became a Model for the Nation*. New York: Thomas Dunne Books, 2016.

# Index

**Jim Newton** spent twenty-five years at the *Los Angeles Times* as a reporter, editor, bureau chief, columnist and editor of the editorial pages. He was part of the *Los Angeles Times*'s coverage of the Los Angeles riots in 1992 and the earthquake of 1994, both of which won Pulitzer Prizes for the staff. Newton is also the author of two critically acclaimed bestselling biographies, *Justice for All: Earl Warren and the Nation He Made* and *Eisenhower: The White House Years,* and he collaborated with Leon Panetta on his *New York Times* bestselling autobiography, *Worthy Fights*. In 2015, Newton moved to UCLA, where he teaches and where he founded and now edits *Blueprint* magazine.